Peckinpah's Tragic Westerns

Peckinpah's Tragic Westerns

A Critical Study

John L. Simons
and Robert Merrill

McFarland & Company, Inc., Publishers
Jefferson, North Carolina, and London

LIBRARY OF CONGRESS CATALOGUING-IN-PUBLICATION DATA

Simons, John L., 1944–
Peckinpah's tragic westerns : a critical study /
John L. Simons and Robert Merrill.
p. cm.
Includes bibliographical references and index.

ISBN 978-0-7864-6133-2
softcover : 50# alkaline paper ♾

1. Peckinpah, Sam, 1925–1984 — Criticism and interpretation.
2. Western films— History and criticism.
3. Tragedy — History and criticism.
I. Merrill, Robert, 1944– II. Title.
PN1998.3.P43S57 2011 791.4302'33092 — dc22 2010046631

British Library cataloguing data are available

Front cover: *from left* Ben Johnson as Tector Gorch, Warren Oates as Lyle Gorch, William Holden as Pike Bishop and Ernest Borgnine as Dutch Engstrom in *The Wild Bunch* (1969); background © 2011 Shutterstock

Manufactured in the United States of America

McFarland & Company, Inc., Publishers
Box 611, Jefferson, North Carolina 28640
www.mcfarlandpub.com

For Frear, Daisy, Jack, and Lark

For Dotty

Contents

Acknowledgments

Portions of Chapter One are revised from Robert Merrill's "Ford, Peckinpah, and the Advantages of Making (Many) Westerns," in Leonard Engel, ed., *Sam Peckinpah's West: New Perspectives* (Salt Lake City: University of Utah Press, 2003), 231–47. Permission to reprint comes from the University of Utah Press.

Portions of Chapter Two are revised from John L. Simons' "The Double Vision of Tragedy in *Ride the High Country*," in Leonard Engel, ed., *Sam Peckinpah's West: New Perspectives* (Salt Lake City: University of Utah Press, 2003), 63–86. Permission to reprint comes from the University of Utah Press.

Portions of Chapter Four are revised from John L. Simons' "The Tragedy of Love in *The Wild Bunch*," *Western Humanities Review* 39 (Spring 1985), 1–19. Permission to reprint comes from *Western Humanities Review.*

Colorado College supported John L. Simons' work on Peckinpah through several research travel grants.

David Weddle and Paul Seydor were unfailingly willing to discuss several topics crucial to our study. Without their critical studies as well as their personal knowledge of Peckinpah and his works, this book would be much diminished. We especially acknowledge Paul Seydor's extensive assistance, which has saved us from factual errors (those Garner Simmons did not already note) and a number of undefended assertions. We have also benefited from conversations (electronic or otherwise) with a number of generous folks: the late Sheldon Sacks, Garner Simmons, Barry W. Sarchett, Len Engel, Owen Cramer, Regula Evitt, Rebecca Tucker, Dave Armstrong, Carl Reed, Jim Malcolm, and a number of librarians who made it possible to make our way through the Peckinpah manuscript collection and film stills at the Margaret Herrick Library, the Academy of Motion Picture Arts and Sciences, Beverly Hills, California. We also thank Derrick at Photofest for helping us select film stills from the Photofest Peckinpah collection.

Special thanks go to former Colorado College student Sarah Hoyenck, and current student Ashleigh Willis, who enabled us to put the manuscript together, and extra-special thanks to Colorado College English Department staff assistant Paula Payne, without whose help this project quite simply would never have been completed. With the skill of an Odysseus, the patience of a Penelope, Paula was always there to assist us with whatever problems arose along the sometimes rocky road to completion of this book.

Finally, we would offer heartfelt thanks and condolences to our wives, Frear Simons and Dotty Merrill, who no doubt feared this book would never end. Their assistance was literally indispensable to making sure there was indeed a conclusion to our work. They watched films with us over and over, listened to us argue long into many nights, paid thousands of dollars to cover our telephone bills, and helped sustain us through the years that we have worked together to bring this book to completion.

"We gotta start thinkin' beyond our guns. Those days are closin' fast."

—Pike Bishop, in *The Wild Bunch*

Preface

So far as either of us can remember, we first encountered Sam Peckinpah's films in 1969 when we caught *The Wild Bunch* in a magnificent Edward Hopperesque downtown Chicago theater, the same long day's afternoon-stretching-into-night we watched Sergio Leone's *The Good, the Bad, and the Ugly*. We were roommates at the time, graduate students in the University of Chicago English Department, and whatever impression Peckinpah's great film made on us was more or less laid aside in the arduous routine of completing a doctoral program. Nonetheless, an important seed had been planted.

In 1971 we moved on to our first teaching positions, John at Colorado College, Bob at the University of Nevada, Reno, and we both immersed ourselves in teaching and writing about literature, mostly modern American literature. Over the years, however, our interests in film emerged in a series of film courses and publications on film we produced independently at our respective institutions.

Once, in 1988, we collaborated on an essay on Mike Nichols' *Catch-22*, and several years later we expanded this piece when it was reprinted in a collection of essays on film adaptations of contemporary novels. Later, in 1992, we each contributed essays on Sam Peckinpah for Len Engel's *Sam Peckinpah's West: New Perspectives* (University of Utah Press, 2003). This was Bob's first essay on Peckinpah, but John had written earlier on *The Wild Bunch* and for some time had done extensive research on Peckinpah's films.

At this time John proposed that we work together on a book-length treatment of Peckinpah's tragic films, as Bob's previous studies of tragic form in Faulkner, Hemingway, and Fitzgerald suggested his interests might blend well with John's longtime project on Peckinpah's tragedies. This book is the product of what has become a deeply enriching engagement with the best films of one of America's great directors.

Early on we spent a good deal of time thinking through this project. At first we thought our title would be *Peckinpah's Tragic Films*, as we were going to include chapters on *Straw Dogs* (1971) and *Bring Me the Head of Alfredo Garcia* (1974), as well as the famous Westerns, *Ride the High Country* (1962), *The Wild Bunch*, and *Pat Garrett and Billy the Kid* (1973). Over time, however, we added Peckinpah's superb television adaptation, *Noon Wine* (1966), decided *Straw Dogs* was one of Peckinpah's best films but not a tragedy, and concluded that *Bring Me the Head of Alfredo Garcia* is a modern Western, perhaps the best film in this category.

Thus we arrived at our present title, *Peckinpah's Tragic Westerns*, as we came to feel that all of Peckinpah's tragic films are Westerns of one kind or another, and all are obsessed with the tragically irreversible nature of time. These films differ significantly from each other, and it became one of our tasks to honor and explain these differences even as we pursued the features which make our five tragic Westerns tragic. Peckinpah did other Westerns, of course, and *Junior Bonner* (1972) is one of his better films, but we came to feel that Peckinpah's very best films were the tragic Westerns treated here in individual chapters. We hope you will agree that even the most written-on of these films yield important new insights when studied as tragic actions.

As we explored our subject we came to believe that Peckinpah is the only tragedian among the major Western directors. There are other great Western directors, of course, as Peckinpah acknowledged in his many interviews, but the best of these filmmakers— John Ford, Anthony Mann, George Stevens, Fred Zinnemann, Budd Boetticher, Howard Hawks, Sergio Leone, and Clint Eastwood — almost invariably developed potentially tragic materials in ways which permitted the protagonist to survive physically and morally intact. As we remark at one point in our study, it is as if Peckinpah set out to develop the situations and characters he encountered in the best films of his predecessors but to take them to the disastrous, indeed tragic conclusions implicit in these materials. Certainly he did so in *Ride the High Country, Noon Wine, The Wild Bunch, Pat Garrett and Billy the Kid,* and *Bring Me the Head of Alfredo Garcia*— the most impressive body of tragic works by any American director other than Orson Welles, whose obvious debt to Shakespearean tragedy is rivaled only by that of Sam Peckinpah. Or so we argue in the following chapters.

Our relationship with Peckinpah's previous critics is not unlike Peckinpah's connections with the major Western filmmakers. We have come to appreciate the excellent work done on Peckinpah and his films, a body of criticism more substantial than on any Western director except perhaps John Ford. The most obvious instances are books by Paul Seydor, David Weddle, Garner Simmons, Michael Bliss, and Gabrielle Murray, but excellent essays have been done by Mark Crispin Miller, Kathleen Murphy, Barry W. Sarchett, Len Engel, and many others. A number of these critics, especially Seydor and Weddle, have remarked on the tragic nature of Peckinpah's best films and offered readings which occasionally explore their tragic elements. It has been our intention to expand on such insights as well as offer our own in a book-length treatment. We hope that our own predecessors will appreciate the value of this enterprise even if they inevitably disagree with many of the conclusions we reach.

Chapter One

Peckinpah's Tragic Vision

Almost all serious stories in the world are stories of a failure with a death in it. But there is more lost paradise in them than defeat. To me that's the central theme in Western culture, the lost paradise.

— Orson Welles as quoted in Giannetti [268]

All the tragedies which we can imagine return in the end to the one and only tragedy: the passage of time.

— Simone Weil as quoted in Dienstag [1]

STRANGER: You know, this could be the right place. The time's running out.
WYATT: Yeah — I'm — I'm hip about time. But I just gotta go.

—*Easy Rider* [1969]

I

In the second edition of his *Horizons West* (2004), perhaps the best critical study of Western films, Jim Kitses speaks of Sam Peckinpah's "critical deification" (166) and suggests that the major books on Peckinpah constitute "a collective idolatry" (241, n.15). These judgments may seem a bit odd in a 47-page chapter on Peckinpah which effusively praises his least-admired Westerns, *The Deadly Companions* (1961) and *Major Dundee* (1965), as well as the films typically seen as the core of his achievement, *Ride the High Country* (1962), *The Wild Bunch* (1969), and *Pat Garrett and Billy the Kid* (1973). In any case, they suggest Kitses would be profoundly skeptical about our own project, for we want to argue that Peckinpah's major Westerns are formal tragedies and that Peckinpah is in fact the only tragedian among the major Western filmmakers. Far from critical deification or idolatry, these claims seem to us the best way to account for the widely-acknowledged power of Peckinpah's better films.

Peckinpah's films from *Ride the High Country* to *Bring Me the Head of Alfredo Garcia* (1974) have often been characterized as tragic. In the first edition of *Horizons West* (1969), Kitses refers to Peckinpah's works as tragic on three occasions (166, 168, 169), and in his second edition (2004) he describes *The Wild Bunch* as a "dark tragedy" (202). In 1970, a few months after *The Wild Bunch* first appeared, Robert Culp wrote that "Mr. Peckinpah has created a tragedy" (6). Over the years most of Peckinpah's more prominent critics have described one or more of his films as tragic. Michael Bliss suggests that "the overwhelming emotion of *Ride the High Country* is classically tragic" (1993, 57); Garner Simmons refers to *Noon Wine* (1966) as "a tragic story" (76)[1]; Bliss celebrates *The Wild Bunch* as "Peckinpah's great tragic film" (1993, 78); Paul Seydor cites *The Wild Bunch* and *Pat Garrett and Billy the Kid* as films in which "the effect of tragedy is felt and sustained" (1997, 306); David Weddle argues that

Ride the High Country, *The Wild Bunch*, and *Pat Garrett and Billy the Kid* are "intricately constructed tragedies" (1997, xiv); Bliss proposes (improbably enough) that *The Ballad of Cable Hogue* (1970) is a tragedy (1993, 128); Seydor (1997, 35) and Mark Crispin Miller (13) identify *Bring Me the Head of Alfredo Garcia* as a revenge tragedy; and Neil Fulwood reminds us that no fewer than eight of Peckinpah's 14 films end with the death of a major character (nine of 15 if one counts *Noon Wine*) (50). Given the apparent unanimity about the tragic nature of Peckinpah's better-known films, one might wonder why we propose to write a book on the subject.

We think this study is needed for two reasons. The first is that Peckinpah's distinction among the major Western directors is often overlooked or misrepresented, typically because other directors are seen as having made tragic films themselves. As we shall see later in this chapter, major films by John Ford, Anthony Mann, Fred Zinnemann, and George Stevens have been read (or misread) as tragedies, and major critics of the Western such as Robert Warshow and John G. Cawelti have encouraged the misleading notion that the Western is characteristically tragic in form, at least in its "classic" periods. In this critical context, it has been hard to see that Peckinpah's better films are among the very few formal tragedies attempted in the genre and much the most successful of these films. The second reason justifying this study is even more important, however. Peckinpah's best critics often refer to his films as tragic, but with the exception of Seydor's remarkable chapter on *Pat Garrett and Billy the Kid* (1997, 255–306), they do not analyze the films as formal tragedies. We hope to establish that *Ride the High Country*, *Noon Wine*, *The Wild Bunch*, *Pat Garrett and Billy the Kid*, and *Bring Me the Head of Alfredo Garcia* are best read as tragic actions of one kind or another, and that to approach the films in this way allows us to appreciate Peckinpah's intentions and the extent to which they have been realized.

To speak of tragic actions and Peckinpah's intentions is to reveal (or betray) that our critical sympathies are Aristotelian in nature. We are of course aware that there are innumerable definitions of tragedy, that, as Stephen Booth once wrote, "The search for a definition of tragedy has been the most persistent and widespread of all nonreligious quests for definition" (81). Nonetheless, it seems true to Peckinpah's own understanding of tragedy (as we will see shortly) to begin with Aristotle's *Poetics* and his famous definition of tragedy and the tragic plot (*mythos*):

> Tragedy, then, is a process of imitating an action which has serious implications, is complete, and possesses magnitude; by means of language which has been made sensuously attractive, with each of its varieties found separately in the parts; enacted by the persons themselves and not presented through narrative; through a course of pity and fear completing the purification of tragic acts which have those emotional characteristics [Else 1967, 25].

One can see why Peckinpah was drawn to Aristotle's *Poetics* as a guide to tragedy. The emphasis here is on emotional effects, more specifically what Aristotle calls *pathos*, the unbearable "suffering" (Bushnell 53) which derives from "destructive or painful act[s]" (Else 1967, 37). Aristotle's references to pity and fear and the purging of these emotions (*catharsis*) must have seemed attractive to a director whose first goal was to make us *feel* what his characters are experiencing. As a film director, Peckinpah would also have identified with the stipulation that the story be "enacted" by the characters and not presented through narrative, though this Aristotelian "requirement" has come to seem more and more arbitrary in the presence of modern novels such as *Moby-Dick*, *Anna Karenina*, and *The Sound and the Fury*. Indeed, many critics and scholars have assumed that Aristotle would have altered his theory to accommodate such narratives if he had lived to read them, even though he denies that epics such as Homer's *Iliad* are tragedies (Else 1967, 51, 63–64). In general, Peckinpah was no doubt drawn to a critical approach which focuses on the *actions* of the central characters rather than on more abstract considerations such as tragic themes, tragic visions, or even tragic philosophies. Moreover, Peckinpah's understanding of how these actions function in the tragic work is akin to Aristotle's as summarized by Adrian Poole: "Tragedy is concerned with what people *do* rather than with who they *are*, [Aristotle] says. Success and failure, happiness and misery, good fortune and bad: this is what tragedies show us, not whether the people who enjoy or endure them are 'good' or 'bad.' Tragedy does not simply support our ideas of 'poetic justice'" (2005, 46).

An Aristotelian approach to tragedy is also desirable because it is essentially descriptive rather than evaluative. As Clayton Koelb has shown, critics after Aristotle have come more and more to see "tragedy" as virtually synonymous with "masterpiece" (69), thus using the term in an honorific sense we would never adopt for comedy, say. One consequence is that the tragic canon has inevitably shrunk to a handful of revered plays, several Greek, several Shakespearean, and the range of tragic actions has been all but lost. By contrast, Aristotle speaks about "good and bad tragedy" (Else 1967, 25), and proceeds to analyze how different tragedies range from "worst" to "best" depending on what kind of man undergoes what kind of change of fortune (Else 1967, 38–39) or the extent to which the tragic protagonist is aware of the tragic act before he commits it (Else 1967, 41–42). Some of Aristotle's preferences may seem to us rather strange, as when he argues that the "best" tragic strategy is to depict a protagonist who is about to commit a fatal mistake but is allowed to recognize the error before committing it (Else 1967, 42); but his approach allows us to distinguish between *Macbeth*, a play in which the hero commits an evil deed quite knowingly, and *Oedipus Rex* (central to Aristotle's analysis of tragedy in the *Poetics*) or *Othello*, plays in which the hero acts in ignorance of the truth and only later understands what he has done. Peckinpah's tragic films differ even more profoundly, and the flexibility of Aristotle's approach allows us to get at both similarities and differences among the films to be found along the tragic spectrum.

Aristotle's *Poetics* is not the last word on its subject, however. The *Poetics* deals only with Greek tragedy, primarily Athenian, and may not be entirely adequate for analysis of Elizabethan, Romantic, or modern tragedies, as Raymond Williams pointed out many years ago (29–30) and Terry Eagleton confirms in his more sustained attack on Aristotle's entire theory (152–77). As a major example, Shakespearean tragedy seems to require certain features (e.g., the tragic hero's death) not always present in Greek tragedies. An Aristotelian approach to Shakespeare's tragedies is extremely revealing, but other approaches may help us to understand what is distinctive about a particular work or period. A useful example is Robert Heilman's definition of tragedy, derived in part from Aristotle but rather more precise in defining what should be expected from tragic works:

> To sum up: *tragedy* should be used only to describe the situation in which the divided human being faces basic conflicts, perhaps rationally insoluble, of obligations and passions; makes choices, for good or for evil; errs knowingly or involuntarily; accepts consequences; comes into a new, larger awareness; suffers or dies, yet with a larger wisdom [248].

Heilman speaks here of "the divided human being," whereas elsewhere he accepts the (supposedly) Aristotelian concept of a good man with a "flaw" (248). This is a common view of what Aristotle means by *hamartia* and what subsequent critics have required of tragedies and their heroes. Heilman also requires that the tragic hero achieve "a larger wisdom," by which Heilman means self-knowledge (251), even as the hero suffers or dies because of his "error." Here, too, Heilman speaks for a large majority of post–Renaissance critics, who have denied tragic status to works in which the hero suffers through no moral fault of his own and/or achieves no heightened self-knowledge because of his mistakes.

Heilman sees himself as elaborating Aristotle's classic definition, but in key ways he offers an alternative view. Aristotle does not require "a larger wisdom" on the hero's part, although he does see the hero as coming to understand the nature of his "mistake." Nor does Aristotle necessarily invoke the hero's "tragic flaw," for Gerald Else believes that *hamartia* refers to a "mistake of great weight and consequence" (1967, 38), not a moral flaw, and other critics agree that "mistake" or "missing the mark" (Liebler 43) is the more literal meaning of the Greek word *hamartia.* Heilman and Aristotle agree that the tragic protagonist must achieve a form of what Aristotle calls Recognition (*anagnorisis*), "a shift from ignorance to awareness" (Else 1967, 36), but Heilman insists that the protagonist must recognize his moral culpability, while Aristotle requires only that he come to understand the disastrous consequences of his actions. Heilman also agrees with Aristotle that the tragic protagonist's Recognition must be followed by a Reversal (*peripeteia*), "a shift of what is being undertaken to the opposite in the way previously stated" (Else 1967, 35–36), though this new course of action will always be a moral "shift" for Heilman and may or may not be such for Aristotle. One might well see Aristotle and Heilman as competitors in the endless search for *the* definition of tragedy described by Stephen Booth.

Heilman's understanding of *hamartia* as a moral flaw may square with the common view since at least Shakespeare's time, but recent classicists and critics have tended to interpret Aristotle's *hamartia* as a more flexible concept subsuming "errors" which range from those committed in genuine ignorance to those deriving from moral turpitude. For example, Amelie Oksenberg Rorty offers the intriguing view that *hamartia* points to a mysterious "waywardness that arises from [the tragic protagonist's] character" (10), resulting in actions which lead to catastrophe (11). Presumably this "waywardness" may or may not derive from a moral flaw. Similarly, Adrian Poole de-emphasizes the moral element in tragic acts, arguing that "however much of a character's *propensity* to error we read into the concept [of *hamartia*], the primary emphasis seems to be on the error itself, the fault committed" (2005, 46). Gerald Else agrees that *hamartia* is not so much "a part of the hero's character" as "a technical device, a part of the plot" (1957, 385). And Stephen Halliwell, in his authoritative book-length study of the *Poetics*, renders the meaning of *hamartia* even more problematic when he argues for its untranslatability into English. Expanding on Else, Halliwell interprets the "indefiniteness" of *hamartia*'s meaning as the "consequence of a tension within the theory of tragedy itself" (222). This tension, built on the dynamic relationship between the tragic plot's formal "intelligibility" and the tragic protagonist's personal "instability," turns on the crucial connection between some form of fate, or "tragic misfortune," and the human agent's "implication in the configuration of events" (229). Like Rorty's, Halliwell's view of *hamartia* seems to allow for tragic "mistakes" which either do or do not derive from the protagonist's moral weakness or flaw.

What all of these recent critics share is the belief that the tragic mistake (*hamartia*) is crucial to the structure of a particular tragic plot, and that different tragic plots may or may not turn on the protagonist's "tragic flaw." Peckinpah's understanding of this crucial Aristotelian concept seems consistent with this more recent view, for his films range broadly from those in which the tragic protagonist is not "flawed" and makes no real mistake (*Ride the High Country*), to a more traditional emphasis on the protagonist's errors in judgment leading to a morally redemptive but fatal rejection of his flawed past (*The Wild Bunch*, *Bring Me the Head of Alfredo Garcia*), to the depiction of a protagonist so immersed in the consequences of bad judgment as to be only barely distinguishable from the traditional villain (*Pat Garrett and Billy the Kid*). After *Ride the High Country*, all of Peckinpah's tragic films depict protagonists whose flaws and mistakes are central to the tragic action, but the moral failures presented range from the almost involuntary (*Noon Wine*) to those the protagonist himself recognizes as altogether of his own making (*The Wild Bunch*, *Pat Garrett and Billy the Kid*, *Bring Me the Head of Alfredo Garcia*). Whatever their differences, these films place the protagonist within a tragic action which culminates in disaster, usually including his own death. Other major Western directors have depicted protagonists much like Peckinpah's, men whose faults and mistakes are no less grievous, but virtually without exception they have declined to set these characters within tragic actions from which they cannot emerge triumphant or at least whole. Peckinpah alone seems committed to the notion that *hamartia* is indeed a *tragic* mistake, one which leads inevitably to the cataclysmic resolutions of the films under review in this study.

We have no illusions that we are going to resolve this famous debate about the tragic hero's character. In fact, we think that tragedies great and not so great respond to different approaches and that it makes sense to see Aristotle and Heilman as variously relevant to individual tragic works, including Peckinpah's several tragic films. Indeed, many other tragic theorists offer insights we should not reject simply because their theories do not explain all tragic works. Richard B. Sewall, for example, writes eloquently about "the mystery of undeserved suffering" which informs many modern forms of tragedy despite Heilman's influential rejection of the tragic label for such works as *The Duchess of Malfi* and *Romeo and Juliet* because tragedy cannot depict "undeserved suffering" (252, 254). Similarly, Arthur Miller provides a major insight into many tragic works when he writes, "I think the tragic feeling is evoked in us when we are in the presence of a character who is ready to lay down his life, if need be, to secure one thing — his sense of personal dignity" (148). As it happens, Miller's claim provides an essential clue to the tragic dynamic of Peckinpah's *Ride the High Country* and *The Wild Bunch*, even as it suggests what is missing — or redefined — in *Pat Garrett and Billy the Kid.* Reliance on a variety of tragic guides should lead us to see that it is almost impossible to define even one artist's tragic formula, as in the much-explored topic of Shakespearean tragedy, which should probably be redefined as Shakespearean tragedies.[2] Though we embrace the category of Peckinpavean tragedy, which we hope to illuminate incrementally in the chapters to follow and to define somewhat more precisely in our conclusion, it is perhaps better to speak of Peckinpavean tragedies, plural, so as to do justice to the differences as well as the similarities which mark films as distinctive as *Ride the High Country* and *Bring Me the Head of Alfredo Garcia.* It was in this spirit that we spoke earlier of Peckinpah's tragic actions of one kind or another, some better than others, but in any case significantly different.

We therefore hope to apply our Aristotelianism with something less than rigid adherence to the faith. Nonetheless, we believe this method will allow us to identify a film's principal effects and to explain how they have been achieved. Wayne Booth has noted his difficulty in discussing a work without reference to its overall purpose or form (400). Like Booth, we believe the principal advantage of an Aristotelian approach is that it provides the focus and perhaps even the rigor any serious formal analysis requires. Properly qualified, this method should help us justify our first claim in this study, that to approach the relevant Peckinpah films as tragic actions will produce critical readings which best account for the films as artistic wholes. First, however, we would like to pursue our second claim, that Peckinpah is the only tragedian among the major Western directors. Others may offer flawed and suffering protagonists, but only Peckinpah situates such characters in plots essential to the form we know as tragedy.

II

As we remarked earlier, Robert Warshow and John G. Cawelti, the Western's principal theorists, define the genre as not only marked by violence and death but as tragic in nature. For Warshow, the Western's autumnal character goes back to its beginnings in silent films and runs through the 1940s and early 1950s (Warshow's famous essay, "Movie Chronicle: The

Westerner," was first published in 1954). Warshow thinks the form is all but defined by its singular hero, "a figure of repose" (107) and "unshakable control" (110) who often defends the representatives of civilization against their enemies (Indians, ranchers, outlaws) but whose real motive is rather different: "What he defends, at bottom, is the purity of his own image—in fact his honor ... he fights not for advantage and not for the right, but to state what he is" (110, 111). Thus, rather like Arthur Miller's tragic hero, he is ready to lay down his life for his sense of personal dignity, and in the end "he is killed or goes away when his position becomes problematical" (111). His position becomes problematical when, usually through his own efforts, a new social order is about to emerge, one in which his own unique talents are no longer required and may in fact seem dangerous or even criminal. Warshow therefore believes that "the true theme of the Western movie is not the freedom and expansiveness of frontier life, but its limitations" (114). Even if the hero survives at the end, his story is essentially tragic, for "what we finally respond to is not his victory but his defeat" (113), by which Warshow seems to mean that the hero can no longer assert his personal value in the new order he has helped create. Warshow goes so far as to say of the film version of *The Virginian* (1929), "the movie is still a tragedy, for though the hero escapes with his life, he has been forced to confront the ultimate limits of his moral ideas" (113). Oddly enough, Warshow does not have in mind such apparently relevant examples as Ford's *My Darling Clementine* (1946), Zinnemann's *High Noon* (1952), and Stevens' *Shane* (1953), for he argues that these "later" Westerns unhappily revise the Western paradigm described so passionately (though with no real examples except *The Virginian* and Henry King's *The Gunfighter* [1950]) in the body of his essay.

For Cawelti, on the other hand, the tragic or "classic" Western is precisely the 1940s and 1950s version represented by *The Gunfighter* but also *High Noon* and *Shane*, which for Cawelti are the essential tragic films: "Thus, in contrast to the sense of moral triumph and regeneration through violence that characterize the western of the 1910s and 1920s, the new 'classic' western was typically more muted, elegiac, and even sometimes tragic in its pattern of action" (1976, 245). "In the classic western," Cawelti argues, "the hero increasingly moves toward isolation, separation, and alienation," and the film conveys "a subtle feeling of melancholy for a more heroic life that is passing" (1976, 247). Cawelti suggests that "classic westerns often end in the hero's death" (1976, 248), whereas earlier—and more formulaic—versions typically conclude with the hero's integration into the new social order, often through marriage.

Historically speaking, Cawelti's review of the Western seems far more accurate than Warshow's. We would wonder which pre–1940 Westerns Warshow has in mind in stressing the Western's depiction of its hero's "defeat," for anyone who works through the genre's literally thousands of incarnations will encounter hundreds of social success stories for every alienated hero, let alone a dead hero. In a very interesting letter to the author of *The Virginian* (1902), Owen Wister, Henry James suggests that in his version of the story the Virginian would have died (Perez 236). We take it that James felt about Wister's novel much as Warshow felt about the Western film in its earlier stages and Cawelti felt about the classic Western, and in order to achieve the appropriately tragic effect James would have killed off his hero. James saw the tragic potential in Wister's material but realized that Wister had not taken his novel in this direction; thus James' revision of what he found on the page before him. By contrast, Warshow's argument that Victor Fleming's 1929 film version of *The Virginian* is tragic despite its (hard-earned) happy ending seems critical wishful thinking. It is possible to depict isolation, separation, and alienation without killing off one's hero, but how many viewers of *The Virginian* have seen Gary Cooper's Virginian, holding his soon-to-be-wife Molly (Mary Brian) in his arms at film's end, as so afflicted? The traumatic events he has survived—the hanging death of his best friend Steve (Richard Arlen), killing his enemy Trampas (Walter Huston) on his wedding day—have shaken but not shattered him. In this respect, as we shall see, he closely resembles Cooper's Will Kane in *High Noon*.

Cawelti may be more accurate than Warshow, but his account of the Western's drift toward tragedy is also questionable. Many reviewers have identified with Gary Cooper's isolation, separation, and alienation in *High Noon*, but this is not to say they experience *High Noon* as a tragedy. In a moment we will return to the effects, tragic or otherwise, of *High Noon* and *Shane*, Cawelti's principal examples. First, however, we want to question the assumption shared by Warshow and Cawelti (and many more recent critics), that the Western hero often dies at the end of classic Westerns. One can search a comprehensive review of Western films such as Brian Garfield's *Western Films: A Complete Guide* (1982) and come up with very few Westerns of any period in which the hero dies. Our own no doubt fallible review came up with the following instances: Henry King's *Jesse James* (1939), Raoul Walsh's *They Died with Their Boots On* (1942), King Vidor's *Duel in the Sun* (1946), John Huston's *The Treasure of the Sierra Madre* (1947) (if indeed this film is a Western, as Garfield assumes), King's *The Gunfighter*, Mann's *Devil's Doorway* (1950), Frank Lloyd's *The Last Command* (1955), Arthur Penn's *The Left-Handed Gun* (1958), John Wayne's *The Alamo* (1960), David Miller's *Lonely Are the Brave* (1962), Martin Ritt's *Hombre* (1967), George Roy Hill's *Butch Cassidy and the Sundance Kid* (1969), Robert Altman's *McCabe and Mrs. Miller* (1973), and Don Siegel's *The Shootist* (1976).

It is perhaps no accident that both Warshow and Cawelti cite *The Gunfighter*, for both critics were drawing from a rather short list of films. Even these few examples derive as much from historical necessity—the stories of the Alamo, Custer, Billy the Kid, Jesse James, Butch Cassidy and the Sundance Kid—as an apparent desire to make filmic tragedy. The list would be longer if we included Peckinpah's tragic Westerns, but it would still be well short of persuasively documenting Warshow's or Cawelti's generalizations when we consider the common estimate that some 8,000 Westerns have been made (everything from Saturday serials and TV series to a few three-hour feature films). The truth is that both major and minor Western filmmakers have avoided the death of their heroes as much as humanly possible, as we can see in the major names not included in the list above: John Ford, Anthony Mann (save for *Devil's Doorway*), Fred Zinnemann, and George Stevens. If these Western luminaries have provided formal tragedies, these works have not ended with the death of their heroes. In this as in other crucial respects, Peckinpah should be seen as a major innovator and ultimately the one creator of a body of tragic works.

Of the directors for whom tragic claims have been advanced, John Ford is the most formidable whether we focus on his Westerns or his total output of over 130 films. More so than even Howard Hawks or George Stevens, Ford seems to be the principal exception to Cawelti's unsentimental characterization of the standard Western: "The circumstances in which a Western is produced and consumed do not encourage the creation of unique individual works of art but lead to the production of particular realizations of a conventional formula" (1984, 52). In the same spirit, Cawelti describes films such as *The Godfather* and *Taxi Driver* as "very unlike Westerns in their moral ambiguity and tragic complexity" (1984, 13). As we have seen, Cawelti believes the classic Westerns of the 1940s and 1950s achieved the status of unique individual works of art by incorporating just such features as moral ambiguity and tragic complexity. For Cawelti, Kitses, and many other critics, it is John Ford whose Westerns first tend toward "the tragic and elegiac" (Cawelti 1976, 249), thus transforming the history of the genre. We propose to review Ford's principal Westerns to determine whether he is rightly seen as a tragic filmmaker.

Ford's many silent films complicate any account of his career, but his first talking Western, *Stagecoach* (1939), clearly represents the kind of film Ford felt he could make as he again took up his work with Western conventions, now in the new medium generated by speech. *Stagecoach* is in many ways a wonderful film, a classic Western magnificently filmed in Ford's signature setting, Monument Valley, but Ford's handling of his hero, the Ringo Kid (John Wayne), is almost painfully conventional. Like many Western protagonists, the Kid traffics with those outside the law, but in his case imprisonment is unjust and at no time has he really violated the laws or moral standards of a just society. Indeed, the film seems based on a somewhat tidy inversion of conventional expectations, as our thoroughly well-meaning and good-hearted hero and heroine (Claire Trevor) are cast as outsiders, escaped outlaw and socially ostracized prostitute, respectively. Ringo is too good to be true, just as he is miraculously efficient when he confronts and kills his three antagonists with only three seemingly magic bullets. Ringo is so young we cannot reasonably ask that he be more self-reflective, and the film as a whole does not fail to achieve moral complexity so much as it declines to try for such effects.

Interestingly, Ford's first great Western film, *My Darling Clementine* (1946), offers a protagonist closer in spirit to the Ringo Kid than to the later Ethan Edwards of *The Searchers* (1956). Wyatt Earp (Henry Fonda) is older than the Kid, but his rather similar pursuit of revenge for the deaths of two brothers, the subject of much contemporary criticism (Gallagher 227, Pye 114), seems unambiguously presented as the only thing to do. The film's richest moments, such as the famous "wedding march" of Wyatt Earp and Clementine Carter (Cathy Downs) to the dedication of the new church, all concern the coming of civilized society to the once anarchic streets of Tombstone, not the moral character or cause of Ford's hero. It would be truly ungrateful to lament Ford's "failure" to discover the story of Wyatt Earp's tragic complexity amidst the legendary materials on which he drew, but his uncritical treatment of Earp does help to explain why the later and in some ways less artful *The Searchers* is the greater film. Indeed, *My Darling Clementine* is so far from being a tragedy that Ford apparently wanted to end the film with Earp's betrothal to Clementine and their joint decision to stay in Tombstone (Kitses 2004, 73).[3]

If there is a tragic character in this film, it is not Wyatt Earp but the secondary figure of Doc Holliday (Victor Mature), who is genuinely torn between his past allegiance to an eastern, more repressively civilized way of life, and his equally compelling attraction to the sensuality, violence, and lawlessness of his new home in the wild west of Tombstone. Holliday's consumption is Ford's metaphor for his sick and divided soul. But despite Ford's depiction of Holliday as a kind of Hamlet of the desert (he "performs" his own truncated "To be, or not to be" speech when a Shakespearean actor comes to town), he is neither the film's central character nor the chief focus of its (non-tragic) plot. Like the evil Clanton family, Holliday must die so that Tombstone will one day become a civilized town, opening the way for the future marriage of Wyatt Earp and Clementine Carter.

Ten years separate *My Darling Clementine* from *The Searchers*. The most significant step toward the later film came only two years after *My Darling Clementine* when Ford made the first of his so-called Cavalry films, *Fort Apache* (1948). He was not yet prepared to focus entirely on a morally ambiguous hero, so the John Wayne character in this film, Captain York, remains an almost conventionally virtuous figure, albeit much older than the Ringo Kid. Captain York is a much more interesting study, however, for he is depicted as ultimately embracing the character with whom he is in conflict throughout the action, the notorious Colonel Owen Thursday (Henry Fonda), who leads his troops to a Custer-like disaster sometime before York assumes Thursday's command. For many viewers, Thursday is nothing but the "pompous egomaniac" Max Westbrook takes him to be in an essay which assaults *Fort Apache* as jingoistic blather, Ford's most lamentable venture into militaristic ideology (157). For York, Thursday is a fallen leader who offers the Regiment, as York thinks of it, a model devoutly to be wished — whatever the man's flaws prior to his fatal battle with Cochise. For Ford, we would suggest,

Thursday is a complicated figure whose parts include both those Westbrook excoriates and those York memorializes.

The ambiguous nature of Colonel Thursday is the most striking thing about *Fort Apache* even though York remains the technical protagonist. That York ends up endorsing a man like Thursday, even if he does so for strategic reasons, suggests that Ford's typical hero is moving much closer to the realm of tragic complexity than in the earlier Westerns. Thursday is, as Westbrook and others have argued, a careerist who comes west only because he is ordered to do so and who sees his engagement with the Indians as an opportunity to win reassignment in the more civilized East once he has conquered the ignorant heathen. The contrast between York and Thursday could not be greater, as York is a valued friend to Cochise and extremely sensitive to the Apaches' customs and values. Thursday's insistence on his own superiority (in essence, the white man's superiority) clearly gets his men and himself killed unnecessarily. In this sense, it seems incredible that York should later praise Thursday to reporters and offer up Thursday as a model to the cavalry now charged with reining in Geronimo. But the paradox here is more apparent than real. Thursday was wrong about Indians such as Cochise, but he was not wrong about Indians such as Geronimo, who presents the threat to civilized life Thursday mistakenly saw in all Indians and the younger York failed to see in Cochise's followers such as Geronimo.[4] Nor was Thursday wrong about the Regiment's need for greater discipline and professionalism, even if York is the better man to advance these values humanely. Ford presents in *Fort Apache* a first version of that complex world he would later create in *The Searchers*, a world in which the simple human decencies are not denied by the presence of malign human behavior but instead are seen as fated to co-exist with such evil. If *Fort Apache* had focused more on York's education into this vision it would be a greater film than it is. This education — both York's and our own — is nonetheless crucial to an adequate appreciation of this key film in Ford's evolution as a Western filmmaker.

By the time he made *The Searchers*, Ford had done seven Western features, the many earlier silent films, and other pictures such as *Drums Along the Mohawk* (1939) that share a "Western" concern with the frontier. He was accordingly well-positioned to make the crucial change which transformed his source novel, Alan LeMay's *The Searchers* (1954), into one of our great films. This change is one of narrative focus, for LeMay's novel tells the story of Martin Pauley and Amos Edwards' search for Debbie Edwards from Marty's point of view, and indeed the novel is essentially about Marty's wrenching five-year experience in seeking the safe return of his kidnapped "cousin." In LeMay's novel, the gruff, inarticulate Amos Edwards is seen only at some distance until he dies at the end trying to retrieve Debbie, whether to kill her or to save her we cannot say. It was Ford's genius to see that embedded in this undistinguished novel was a profound story about one of the least John Wayne–like characters Wayne was ever to play, a man all but defined by moral ambiguity and tragic complexity. (Curiously, Peckinpah thought *The Searchers* was "one of [Ford's] worst films [Seydor 1997, 355], but he "loved" LeMay's novel [Simmons 194]. Peckinpah's judgments about major Western films tend to be shrewd and generous, but his take on *The Searchers*, novel and film, seems a major exception.)

Ford's protagonist (rechristened Ethan Edwards) is a man of what seems to be commanding contradictions. At the beginning of the film, we see Ethan return to his brother Aaron's (Walter Coy's) home in a very dusty, very isolated section of Texas a few years after the end of the Civil War. His extremely courteous treatment of Aaron's wife Martha (Dorothy Jordan), his playful exchanges with the young girls, Lucy (Pippa Scott) and Debbie (Lana Wood), and his status as a returning war hero accord with his imposing physical stature to suggest that Ethan is yet another version of the traditional Western hero. From the beginning, however, we see the darker side(s) to Ethan Edwards, a man who returns from Mexico with newly minted gold coins presumably won through theft and perhaps worse. This is the Ethan who taunts the adopted Martin Pauley (Jeffrey Hunter) because of his trace of Cherokee blood, the first sign of Ethan's virulent racism everywhere on display throughout the film; who rejects at once the legal and moral authority of the Rev./Capt. Samuel Johnson Clayton (Ward Bond), who heads the local Texas Rangers; who shoots out the eyes of a dead Comanche so that the warrior will, according to his own beliefs, "wander between the winds," homeless and alone throughout eternity; who will fire randomly at buffalo so as to limit their use by Indians; and who scalps the Indian Chief Scar (Henry Brandon), who kidnapped Lucy and Debbie after murdering Aaron and the rest of his family. This is the Ethan Edwards who interrupts the funeral service for his family members, even as the congregation sings Ford's beloved "Shall We Gather at the River," in order to get a quicker start in pursuit of revenge. Indeed, this is the man who continues to search for Scar and Debbie for almost seven years rather than return to his home to rebuild the family ranch.

Who, then, is Ethan Edwards? The director/critic Lindsay Anderson sees Ethan not as tragically split but impossibly divided, two distinct characters Ford would force us to see as one: "the Ethan who jovially bustles Mrs. Jorgensen back into the house as her daughter's suitors prepare to do battle ... is not the same Ethan we have seen implacable to rescue Debbie from her shame by death" (158–59). In truth, however, the engaging, humane Ethan who bustles Mrs. Jorgensen has been with us throughout: when he suffers so palpably after finding Martha's ravaged body (thus confirming the film's hints that he has always loved Martha); when he covers Lucy's dead body with the Confederate war uniform he values so highly; when he thinks to send the Jorgensens (John Qualen, Olive Carey) a letter reporting the death of their son Brad (Harry Carey, Jr.); when he jokes with Marty about Marty's new "wife" (an Indian maid attached to Marty by mistake); when he comes over time to call Martin "Marty" and to will him the Edwards property. The business with Look, Marty's "wife" (Beulah Archuleta), is unmistakably racist as well as farcically humorous, and Look's cruel death at the hands of the U.S. Cavalry is treated sympathetically but all too briefly by Marty and Ethan. But Ford's schizoid Texas community is everywhere depicted as humane *and* racist; indeed, the film's most racist character is Laurie Jorgensen (Vera Miles), who is also one of its most appealing figures, a contradiction Ford has brilliantly woven into virtually every aspect of the film. Meanwhile, Laurie's "true nature" has been questioned by critics determined to demonize racist Laurie and deny her any kind of humanity (see especially Pippin 119–20, 139–40), which is clearly not John Ford's purpose. In this world, more realistically imagined than any of Ford's other communities, Ethan Edwards is exemplary *both* in his brutality and his ultimate grasp of life's contradictions.

As we read *The Searchers*, Ethan's divided but not irreconcilable features are essential to Ford's primary purpose: to chart Ethan's gradual acceptance of his role within the (flawed) human community. In this light, the film's real climax is Ethan's turning his gun over to Captain Clayton and agreeing to go to Austin for an inquiry concerning three men Ethan has been forced to kill. In the aftermath of this late moment, richly suggestive of his moral evolution, Ethan is able to joke with a Yankee soldier (Patrick Wayne) and to allow Marty to enter Scar's camp before the other men so as to give Debbie a chance to survive the rangers' attack. It is this Ethan, of course, who lifts Debbie (Natalie Wood) from the ground, as he lifted her in the film's first moments seven years earlier, and brings her home to the Jorgensens rather than rescuing her from shame by killing her. He is still a man of strong feelings and a profound sense of alienation; thus his readiness to scalp Scar, who has been killed by Marty, and his famous refusal to enter the Jorgensen home in the final scene, as Debbie is enfolded within the community from which she was taken so many years before. Nonetheless, Ford emphasizes Ethan's morally ambiguous nature and develops his tragic complexity beyond anything in his other films, Western or non–Western, in order to affirm in the end Ethan's severely tested decency even as he begins to walk out toward the desert while the Jorgensen door suddenly and startlingly closes behind him.

Formally speaking, Ford averts a tragic conclusion much as his character does, for both the director and his protagonist struggle with genuinely tragic situations and emotions before assimilating these materials into a mature, non-tragic resolution. Ford wisely acknowledges that this conclusion can come about only after many years of internal as well as external "searching" and that even then it does not entirely integrate a man such as Ethan Edwards within the human community. Ford once said of *The Searchers*, "It's the tragedy of a loner ... [who] could never really be a part of the family" (Bogdanovich 92), but the film itself depicts this loner's incomplete but heroic transformation to prepare for a conclusion far from "happy" but far from tragic as well. Ethan may be excluded from the family reunion, but as always he *chooses* to exclude himself, and Ford, "cinema's great poet of civilization" (Robin Wood as quoted in Pippin 165), seems to want it this way as well. An American isolato, a wilderness figure and Western archetype, Ethan prefers the stark grandeur of the desert and soaring buttes of the desert valley to the family home. He has not been banished to the desert, rather the desert is his true "home," and he chooses to "ride away" into it as the film's theme song intones in the background and the words "THE END" flash upon the screen.[5]

The truth is that none of Ford's Westerns is a tragedy even though the later films include many potentially tragic elements. In this regard, *The Man Who Shot Liberty Valance* (1962) is perhaps the most "tragic" of Ford's Westerns. The film begins and ends with the death of Tom Doniphon (John Wayne), the most traditionally heroic of its characters; the final scenes seem to indicate that the film's heroine, Hallie Stoddard (Vera Miles), loved Doniphon, or rather the old West Doniphon so toweringly stood for, more than her husband of many years, Ransom Stoddard (James Stewart); and the conclusion emphasizes not only the shaky foundations of Stoddard's marriage but the hollowness of his reputation as the man who shot the much-feared outlaw Liberty Valance (Lee Marvin). These somber revelations are not countered by the personal growth we see in Ethan Edwards, for Doniphon dies a drunkard and a defeated man, virtually occluded by history, and Hallie is revealed as someone who may have married the wrong man, while Stoddard's political career is shown to be founded on the false "legend" of having killed the notorious Liberty Valance.

Yet *The Man Who Shot Liberty Valance* resists tragic effects even as it insists on painful ironies involving all of the major characters. Tom Doniphon's decision to assist Ranse Stoddard by shooting Liberty Valance is the stuff of tragedy, for Doniphon violates all codes of Western honor to protect the man he thinks Hallie prefers to him, then declines severely after losing his beloved Hallie as well as his enemy and dark double, Valance, whose death destroys Doniphon's own *raison d'etre* and renders him obsolete in a progressively changing society. But like Ford's Doc Holliday, a character he closely resembles, Doniphon is not the protagonist, his personal collapse occurs off-stage, so to speak, and the tragic content of his story is absorbed into the multiple ironies of the more central action involving Stoddard's marriage and career. The Stoddards could have been depicted as tragic figures, somewhat in the manner of Henry James' later protagonists who have failed to "live" their lives as deeply as they might have, but Ford offers a more mixed portrait, less positive than the ending of *The Searchers* but still respectful of Stoddard's marriage with Hallie and his career. Perhaps things would have turned out better for Doniphon and Hallie if she had chosen Doniphon, but the choice of Stoddard, coupled with Doniphon's decision to kill Liberty Valance, has contributed to nothing less than the development of the West. Ford almost always depicts this social evolution positively, and even here, in his most ironic treatment of the subject, the values of Stoddard's marriage and career are qualified but not rejected. Ford acknowledges the very high price individuals must pay to make civilized "progress" possible, in this instance turning a "wilderness" into a "garden," as Hallie somewhat ruefully reminds Ranse, but Ford was never to deny the necessity or the ultimate value of this process. Quite simply, Ford never embraced a tragic view of life and never made a film structured by such a vision.

Anthony Mann is far less famous than John Ford, but his Western films have generated more specific claims that he should be seen as a tragedian. In the one book-length study of Mann, Jeanine Basinger notes that Mann's second Western, *The Furies* (1950), strongly recalls the trials of the House of Atreus (93) and his seventh Western, *The Man from Laramie* (1955), conveys a "sense of Greek tragedy" (125). Basinger also agrees with Kitses, Mann's other major critic, that all the Westerns portray "Mann's ambivalent and nearly psychotic hero of the old West" (83). In her discussions of Mann's 10 Westerns, however, Basinger makes no claims for any of the films as formal tragedies. Indeed, Basinger sees Mann's "core" films—*Bend of the River* (1952), *The Naked Spur* (1953), *The Man from Laramie* [lamentably she omits the superb *Winchester '73* (1950)]—as all ending with the hero very much alive and "clearly integrated into society, which is seen as a positive and necessary thing" (107). For Basinger, it would seem, Mann's Westerns sometimes draw upon the materials and conventions of Greek tragedy and depict unusually intense protagonists, but they are not structured as tragedies and in fact feature resolutions which are hopeful if not comic in nature. We would add to Basinger's sound conclusions that Mann's choice of James Stewart to play the hero in five of these films—Mann's best work in the Western—hardly seems accidental. Jimmy Stewart is one of Hollywood's all-time "good guys." Even when Stewart's films have an intensely neurotic edge to them—as in Mann—that "edge" is viewed as an aberration, something correctible. For example, suicidal George Bailey in *It's a Wonderful Life* (1948) is rescued by those *he* has rescued, the citizens of Bedford Falls. James Stewart is almost never—an exception would be Hitchcock's *Vertigo* (1958)—depicted as a darkly tragic character.

In Kitses' view, as opposed to Basinger's, Mann is first of all a tragic filmmaker, more consistently so than Ford, Peckinpah, or any other Western director. In a 33-page chapter on Mann's Westerns (204, 139–71), Kitses invokes the concept of tragedy at least 17 times. According to Kitses, Mann was always fascinated by a form of "tragic paradox" (2004, 139); in his films the use of force is both necessary and "tragic" (2004, 148); Mann's hero "restores order, paradoxically and tragically, by descending into the world of the villain" (2004, 151); Mann's *Man of the West* (1958) is built around "the tragic implications of the growth of civilization" (2004, 154), and its antagonist, Dock Tobin (Lee J. Cobb), is "a figure of tragic force" whose de facto son, Link Jones (Gary Cooper), is "caught in an equally tragic situation" (2004, 155); throughout *Man of the West* "Mann creates a sense of tragic inevitability" (2004, 158); while making *The Tin Star* (1957), Mann "must have responded to the tragic potential" of his material (2004, 157); films such as *The Man from Laramie* develop themes which are "at the centre of classical tragedy" (2004, 157); such films depict the hero's "tragic struggles to rise above himself" (2004, 158); even Mann's typical villain, such as Emerson Cole (Arthur Kennedy) in *Bend of the River*, is "a tragic figure" (2004, 161); Mann's films attempt to dramatize above all else "the dialectics of tragedy" (2004, 163); and the most revealing thing to be said about Mann is that he "self-consciously edged the revenge Western towards tragedy" (2004, 175). For Kitses, the Western as a form has been well-defined by Warshow—Kitses refers to "the genre's tragic hero as defined by Robert Warshow" (2004, 34)—and Anthony Mann understood better than anyone else how such a form could be realized.

We think the relevant question is whether Mann "edged" the revenge Western toward tragedy or in fact got there in achieved tragic forms. Ironically, the one Mann film which meets conventional standards for a tragedy is his first Western, *Devil's Doorway*, which is the only film Kitses does not describe as tragic. *Devil's Doorway* tells the story of a Shoshone

Indian named Lance Poole (Robert Taylor) who returns to his home in Wyoming after winning the Congressional Medal of Honor during the Civil War. Once home, Lance discovers that a new law prohibits Indians from owning land and that he must either abandon his tribal home or fight against hopeless odds to defend his tribe's land. His options illustrate the Hobson's Choice so often depicted in tragic works, for Lance must either turn his back on the tribe he leads after the death of his father or face all but certain death in resisting Wyoming's new law. Lance elects to fight, which leads first to his brutalization when he savagely kills the lawyer (Louis Calhern) who has organized the scheme to deprive the Indians of their land and sell it to newly arrived settlers, then to his own dramatic death as the film ends. *Devil's Doorway* is a crude film in some ways, but its uncompromising conclusion reflects its tough-minded commitment to the tragic situation in which its hero finds himself. Ironically, as Mann's reputation and budgets grew during the 1950s, he was never again to work through his violent materials to a tragic conclusion.[6]

Devil's Doorway also differs from the later films because it is not the kind of revenge Western Kitses rightly sees as Mann's typical form. Five of Mann's Westerns (*Winchester '73, Bend of the River, The Naked Spur, The Far Country* [1955], *The Man from Laramie*) focus on the protagonist's obsessive efforts to avenge a major injustice suffered before the film begins or later in the action, while three others (*The Last Frontier* [1955], *The Tin Star, Man of the West*) depict the hero's comparable efforts to protect himself and others against savage forms of violence. All of these films deserve Kitses' favorite epithet, "tragic," insofar as the term refers to violent, irrational materials and the hero's "nearly psychotic" efforts to deal with his unstable world. Kitses acutely analyzes Mann's heroes, who behave "as if driven by a vengeance they must inflict upon themselves for having once been human, trusting, and, therefore, vulnerable" (2004, 142). These heroes end up "ostensibly a part of the community," but for Kitses as for Warshow entry into the typical human community is a "defeat" in which the hero's passion is "exhausted" rather than transformed or purified: "McAdam exhausted in the streets of Abilene [*Winchester '73*], Jones driving quietly away from his family's corpses [*Man of the West*], Glyn McLyntock emerging from a rushing stream that carries his friend's body [*Bend of the River*]—these men seem nothing more than empty shells" (2004, 145). Indeed, Mann's hero is seen as losing what makes him most unique, "enter[ing] the world of ordinary mortals only through a kind of metaphysical suicide, destroying the mirror of his magic" (2004, 156).

It should be clear that Kitses does not accept the apparent implications of the endings to all Mann's Westerns except *Devil's Doorway*. In Kitses' view, the Mann hero reveals his defining "magic" in his nearly psychotic struggle with the evil forces aligned against him, forces which often derive from his own family (*Winchester '73, The Naked Spur, Man of the West*), or from men who have saved his life (*Bend of the River, The Man from Laramie*). These intense and moving "tragedies" involve characters united by blood, a common Greek motif in plays dealing with the ruling dynasties (Else 1967, 40–41). Thus, in *Winchester '73*, Lin McAdam (James Stewart) must track down and kill Dutch Henry Brown (Stephen McNally), the brother who has murdered their father, and in *Man of the West*, Link Jones must kill all the men with whom he has grown up and ridden with in a criminal gang, including his cousin Claude (John Dehner) and his surrogate father (Lee J. Cobb), in order to protect himself and the people with whom he travels. Similarly, in *Bend of the River*, Glyn McLyntock (James Stewart) must literally drown Emerson Cole, a man who has twice saved his life, in order to liberate the wagon train Cole has highjacked. Kitses argues that Mann's heroes are most themselves in the midst of these battles which require remarkable physical powers simply to survive and which suggest that the hero is not isolated and alienated by circumstance alone but also by his essential character.

For Kitses, then, Mann's endings seem unconvincing or deliberately unpersuasive, as each of the heroes is revealed in turn to be a "shell" of his heroic self in returning to or restoring the human community with which he was involved before he was called to battle in order to realize his true character. Kitses takes this character to be genuinely heroic, whereas Jane Tompkins no doubt speaks for many viewers in rejecting this view of Western heroes in general and Mann's Link Jones in particular: "Repeatedly this character finds himself in situations where, we are supposed to believe, he has no choice but to kill or hurt another person, though in doing so he must quell his humanitarian instincts. In the last scene, when the female lead tells him that she loves him and he meets her declaration with stony silence, he has become incapable of any relationship at all" (218). Tompkins goes on to say that Jones does apparently carry a "bruised and bleeding heart ... into the wilderness at the end" (219). Viewers who have seen this film more recently than Tompkins will recall that Jones is not heading into the wilderness at the end but back to the wife, two children, and town he left at the beginning of the film, which explains why Jones does not respond to Billie Ellis' (Julie London's) declaration of love. To be fair, we never see the family and town Jones has left behind, so their "presence" in the film is more as a concept than a physical reality. Nonetheless, it is telling that Kitses ignores the conclusion as much as Tompkins misreads it, for neither critic can reconcile the violent protagonist who kills what amounts to his former family with the man who has lived peacefully for years with his family and their neighbors and who is planning to return to this domestic situation at the end of his ordeal. In their different ways, both Kitses and Tompkins reject Mann's ending as untrue to the story they have experienced in the body of his film.

Some of Mann's endings are more persuasive than others, but the better films are structured to prepare us for the conclusions Kitses and Tompkins all but dismiss. This is to suggest, of course, that they are not structured as tragedies. *Winchester '73*'s Lin McAdam, *The Naked Spur*'s Howie Kemp (James Stewart), and *The Man from Laramie*'s Will Lockhart (James Stewart) are all presented as relatively normal, caring men who suffer grievous injustices which they try mightily, even obsessively, to rectify or avenge, and once this mission is accomplished (or, in *The Naked Spur*, recognized as futile) they are able to turn toward new lives and new loves.[7] This final transition seems especially believable in *The Naked Spur*, perhaps Mann's best film, for the bounty hunting of Howie Kemp, undertaken to amass the money necessary to buy back the farm Kemp's fiancée has sold without his knowledge while he was off fighting in the Civil War, hardly exhibits the hero's "magic" but rather his fall from grace, an understandable fall, perhaps, but one to be regretted rather than admired. The savagery Kemp displays in dealing with his roguish companions, so like the similarly unsettling moments in *Winchester '73*, *Bend of the River*, *The Last Frontier*, and especially *Man of the West*, is depicted in the middle of the action; well before the conclusion, Kemp has begun to turn toward Lina Patch (Janet Leigh) and away from the violence he was capable of earlier. Indeed, as things unravel, Kemp does not kill anyone in the film's grim events leading up to his "exhausted" release from his obsession with recapturing the past and his subsequent plea to Lina to accompany him to California, a conclusion which signals the reemergence of his former and better self. The films which portray men with violent pasts who are trying to make a new, more civil life (*Bend of the River*) or survive challenges to this new life (*Man of the West*) offer conclusions which are somewhat harder to credit, for the violence on display has much deeper roots than in *Winchester '73*, *The Naked Spur*, and *The Man from Laramie*. Even in these films, however, Mann tries throughout the action and not just in the final scene to justify the hero's movement from violence to the kind of social integration Basinger rightly sees as the ultimate goal of all Mann's Westerns after *Devil's Doorway*.

Another way to explain Mann's non-tragic conclusions is to see the director as the victim of studio interference. Kitses says that Mann "bemoaned the lack of courage in producers who would not allow him to make Lockhart still another son to Waggoman [Donald Crisp], Billie the wife of Link" (2004, 158). Kitses also notes that Mann "suffered some interference on the production" of *The Tin Star* (2004, 148), and that the ending of *The Last Frontier* "seems to have been imposed on Mann" (2004, 147). Basinger identifies the source for this last claim, Mann's statement in an interview with *Cahiers du Cinema in English*: "That ending was forced on me" (128). We do not know much about the constraints imposed on Mann, but the examples cited above allow us to speculate about the subject. It is unclear what aspect of *The Tin Star* is at issue, so we cannot say what Mann might have done differently if allowed more creative freedom. To make Will Lockhart the son of Alec Waggoman in *The Man from Laramie* would have advanced the parallel with Greek legend mentioned earlier, but it is not clear that the film would have been better or more tragic with this change. Of the two men who have sold Indians the guns which figure in the death of Lockhart's younger brother, Dave Waggoman (Alex Nichol) is not killed by Lockhart but by Vic Hansbro (Arthur Kennedy) and Hansbro himself is exposed but not killed by Lockhart, who leaves Hansbro to be killed by the Indians whose latest gun shipment has been destroyed. In *Winchester '73* Mann does dramatize the killing of brother by brother, but without changing much more than Lockhart's parentage he would not have introduced fratricide into this later film except as an unrealized possibility. To make Billie the wife of Link Jones would, of course, materially alter *Man of the West*, perhaps for the better insofar as it would eliminate the awkward absence of those to whom Link has committed himself. Presumably, Link would be reunited with Billie at the end, however, so it remains unclear how this change would make the film more tragic.

The Last Frontier is the most interesting example here because the film's conclusion is in question and therefore its form as a whole. Kitses sees the protagonist, Jed Cooper (Victor Mature), as the community's victim as Cooper aspires to join the cavalry, which is protecting a fort from hostile Indians, and to acquire the wife (Anne Bancroft) of the fort's commanding officer, Colonel Marston (Robert Preston). Kitses presents Cooper as a noble savage whose "purity ... must be destroyed before he can enter the community" (204, 157), as he does at the end when he is accepted into the cavalry and the good graces of the now-widowed Mrs. Marston. This reading is vintage Warshow, even more so than Kitses' other interpretations, for we are given to believe that the hero's victory in saving the troops from the Indians is really his defeat because it leads to his assimilation into "an irrational, suicidal world" (2004, 157), that is, the modern social order.

Given this reading, it is unclear why Kitses would change the ending, which seems of a piece with the other deliberately "weak" conclusions to Mann's Westerns. Basinger reflects a similar confusion by agreeing with Kitses that the film "reinforces and demonstrates" that "civilization is a restrictive force" (128) and that Cooper "accepts the limits of civilization into his personal life" (84), while arguing that "the audience has been prepared for Mature's acceptance into the forces of civilization by the entire film" (135). Basinger's final point is crucial, for one of the more important changes made in adapting the source novel, Richard Emery Roberts' *The Gilded Rooster* (1947), was to convert Cooper from a man who is implacably opposed to joining the cavalry (until the extremely implausible ending) and who stays in the fort only to pursue another officer's wife into a man who asks Captain Riordan (Guy Madison) to let him enlist before he even sees Mrs. Marston. Mann may have disliked the ending's implication that Cooper and Mrs. Marston are destined to be together, for this union is far less plausible than those which conclude his other films. If Mann did not want to end with Cooper's enlistment, however, he wanted to make an entirely different film. It seems to us that the film as we have it amply justifies Cooper's enlistment, his adaptation to the social world of the fort, with all its limitations and restrictions.

Indeed, the real problem with seeing Mann as somehow censored by his studio masters is that all of his Westerns except *Devil's Doorway* are structured throughout to justify their non-tragic conclusions. Perhaps Mann did aspire to a different kind of film and was "forced" to make the films he made to continue to work in the industry. It is hard to believe these unmade pictures would have been superior to *Winchester '73*, *The Naked Spur*, and *The Man from Laramie*, but of course there is no way to say what might have been. We can say that Mann did not make these uncensored films, and so his career differs from that of Sam Peckinpah, whose films were constantly reworked by his studios and producers in ways we can evaluate because in most cases the director's intentions have survived in actual footage which can be reassembled into something like "final" form.

Ford and Mann stand out as Western directors who made a number of films which have been read as tragedies. Among the individual films proposed as tragic, Fred Zinnemann's *High Noon* and George Stevens' *Shane* are much the most famous candidates. These films come out of a unique period in Western filmmaking, the early 1950s, for the film industry's cultivation of the Western was unsurpassed at this time. In 1952, for example, *High Noon* was one of 108 Western features released (Drummond 28). Even at the time Zinnemann's film was perceived to be an early version of what we have come to call the anti-Western, sufficiently revisionist to strike John Wayne as "the most un-American thing I've ever seen in my whole life" (Lewis 90). *High Noon* provoked John Wayne and inspired Howard Hawks to "respond" by making *Rio Bravo* (1959) because Zinnemann's film casts a very cold eye on the western community of Hadleyville, which effectively abandons its marshal, Will Kane (Gary Cooper), to the revengeful Frank Miller (Ian MacDonald) and his three compatriots. The film has been unfairly treated as "an anti-McCarthyite tract," an "indictment of civic complacency" (Mitchell 191, 192), as if its controlling features were those of social allegory, and rather crude allegory at that. It seems to us that Zinnemann's handling of his Western materials is much shrewder than such readings imply. He is especially good at characterizing the people of Hadleyville, whether they attend church or the saloon this fateful Sunday, and he elicits from Gary Cooper one of the most intense and powerful performances by an American actor. The film's harsh black and white realism — Zinnemann used unfiltered lenses throughout the filming of *High Noon*— is especially useful in rendering the extremely dramatic, even melodramatic, events of this 90-minute test of a town's moral character. The people of Hadleyville are all too believable, as opposed to the caricatures in more recent Westerns such as Philip Kaufman's *The Great Northfield Minnesota Raid* (1972) and Lawrence Kasdan's *Silverado* (1985). Its memorable but perhaps excessive music aside, *High Noon* is a brilliant first venture into the Western by one of the better directors of the 1950s.[8]

Nonetheless, *High Noon* illustrates the limitations of even the best first-time Westerns. As an experienced European director, Zinnemann did not bring to his task the ideological commitments, pro or con, of a Kaufman or a Kasdan (the former a determined anti-Westernist, the latter a celebrant of the traditional Western), but he did harbor views about the Western which effectively restricted what he could do in the form. "The characters have to be rather primitive types, not subtle or complex personalities," Zinnemann once said about the Western. "Once you grasp the form, it is fairly easy to fit the whole thing together" (Phillips 154). This comment from the film's director perhaps suggests why Cooper's Will Kane is not an even greater or more compelling character. The film hints at but does not develop Kane as a man of tragic complexity. The fact that Kane has had an extended affair with Helen Ramirez (Katy Jurado), the ex-mistress of Frank Miller, the man Kane sent to prison five years before the events depicted in the film, is handled very cautiously. So far as we can tell, Zinnemann's hero organized the town's efforts to rid itself of Frank Miller and his gang for the most honorable reasons, then later became involved with the admirable Mrs. Ramirez, perhaps the film's most sympathetic character. How Helen Ramirez allowed herself to become involved with Frank Miller is not explored in a film which focuses on Kane, and in any case we are naturally much more interested in Kane's motives and complexities. Cooper admirably conveys Kane's mounting frustrations as he is rejected by one after another of his "friends," the very people who had helped him in the past, and even the woman (Grace Kelly) he has married that very morning (she later comes to his rescue). Kane's very human fatigue is captured in a series of agonized closeups— uncharacteristic for Westerns— which reveal his personal rather than his traditionally heroic qualities. Ultimately, however, Kane is not particularly subtle or complex, his moral worth is never in question, and while this is apparently what Zinnemann desired, it perhaps accounts for the fact *High Noon* is a very good but not a truly great film.[9]

Something like the same analysis applies to Stevens' *Shane*. Whereas *High Noon* humanizes the legendary Western hero while still insisting on his essential virtue, *Shane* offers what Lee Clark Mitchell calls "a distillation of the Western itself" (193) by retelling the classical story of the ex-gunfighter's decision to return to a life of violence on behalf of homesteaders who represent the future of civilization in their quarrel with western ranchers. The problem with this fine film is not, as so many allege, the un-heroic presence of Alan Ladd in the title role. Indeed, the smallish Ladd seems very much the kind of gentle, soft-spoken figure Stevens wanted in this realistic incarnation of the classic homesteaders-versus-ranchers Western tale, and Ladd as gunfighter is ultimately more believable than the extraordinary heroics of John Wayne or Clint Eastwood.

What the film fails to do more than suggest is the depth of this character's commitment to the lawless life he is trying to put behind him. Shane's attraction to his new family, the Starretts, is nicely rendered in scene after scene, and one is tempted to forgive Stevens' sentimental excesses in depicting Shane and Joe Starrett's (Van Heflin's) fistfight against what seems a cast of hundreds (in reality a dozen or so men). What the film needs is more of what we see for just a moment when Shane provokes the final gunfight by taunting his counterpart Wilson (Jack Palance) as a "Yankee liar," much as Wilson challenged ex–Confederate hothead "Stonewall" Torrey (Elisha Cook, Jr.) into drawing on him. What it especially needs is development of the insight into Shane's character which emerges when he twirls his guns proudly after shooting Wilson and his boss Rufus Ryker (Emile Meyer). Like Wilson, Shane is the sort of man who knows how to manipulate his enemies, and he obviously derives great personal satisfaction from his shooting skills, as we also see earlier when he delights in showing little Joey (Brandon De Wilde) how to shoot. The Shane captured in these brief moments is a man with hints of tragic complexity, torn between personal pride in his dazzling skills as a gunfighter and his love for the Starretts and their community of friends. In his doubleness Shane most resembles Gregory Peck's Jimmy Ringo in Henry King's *The Gunfighter*, a film about an authentic tragic hero destroyed by his internal divisions, as Shane is not. Shane is a man Stevens could have made the vastly more complex subject of his film had he been less concerned to "distill" the essence of the formulaic Western, or had he simply been more comfortable with the conventions and plotlines of a form he had never practiced before.[10]

We do not mean to suggest that either *High Noon* or *Shane* is a failed tragedy. Warshow objects to the bleak social realism of *High Noon*, its "vulgar anti-populism," because it has the effect of reducing Will Kane to "a pathetic rather than tragic figure" (119). But Kane is neither pathetic nor tragic. The man who faces four adversaries by himself and survives is hardly pathetic, but it is also true, as Phillip Drummond points out, that it is Amy, Kane's new wife, whose Quaker principles are compromised by her efforts to save her husband (76), whereas Kane's values and self-image are unchallenged by his ordeal. Kane does suffer profound disillusionment because of Hadleyville's refusal to help him, and he is no doubt embittered by what he goes through before throwing down his marshal's badge and leaving town with Amy. But he does survive, with his principles intact, so it is misleading to characterize his experience as tragic. The undiminished Will Kane, reunited with the courageous Amy, leaves town with a genuine future before him.

Shane comes somewhat closer to being a tragic action, especially for those who believe (mistakenly, we think) that Shane is fatally wounded as he rides away from the community he has protected by killing Wilson and Ryker. It is clear that Shane, burdened by the inescapable "brand" of his violent past, has no role to play in the new social order — which is no doubt why he rides through the town's graveyard as he makes his way up into the mountains after saying goodbye to little Joe — and that his love for Joe Starrett's wife Marian (Jean Arthur) will forever be unrequited. But these things are true because Shane is a gunfighter with near-mythic powers, not a farmer or a lover. The man who taunts Wilson before killing him and who takes professional pride in his deadly handiwork is hardly a tragic figure, especially as he manifests his skills for once in a good cause and manages to survive as well. In the course of Stevens' film, Shane realizes his potential as a certain kind of man, one who cannot leave his history altogether behind him but who can finally act on behalf of others rather than himself. This is a moving story, but not the kind of narrative which arouses the emotions of pity and fear.

It is no crime for these films to be something other than tragic. Peckinpah admired both films, especially *Shane* ("the best Western ever made" [Seydor 1997, 353]), despite the fact that neither embodies the tragic knowledge Adrian Poole has described as well as anyone. "In tragedy," Poole notes, "man does not get off so lightly; the difference is permanent, the damage irreversible.... Tragedy affirms the ruthless truth that hearts must break, that the cords that bind people to each other and that hold the heart together must all in time fail" (1987, 114, 230). Very few Western filmmakers have been willing to structure their stories to express such insights. *High Noon* offers perhaps the best example, for the makers of *High Noon* allowed Will Kane to live and go off with his new bride despite the fact his counterpart is killed in the film's source, John Cunningham's short story "The Tin Star" (Drummond 61). Similar strategies are at work in most of the best Western films, whether those of Ford, Mann, Zinnemann, Stevens, Budd Boetticher, Howard Hawks, Sergio Leone, or Clint Eastwood. We have previously argued that the major Western filmmakers made virtually no tragedies, and we would reach the same conclusion if the field were expanded to include Boetticher, Hawks, Leone, and Eastwood. Boetticher's revenge Westerns have been described by Kitses as "comedies, deeply ironic works, but comedies all the same" (2004, 177). In one of the best essays ever written on a Western, Gerald Mast's "The Genre Epic: *Red River*," Mast demonstrates how thoroughly Hawks structured *Red River* (1948) to avoid tragic expectations and therefore to justify the happy (or satisfying) ending so many have disparaged. (It is to Peckinpah's credit that he nonetheless thought *Red River* one of the great Westerns [Seydor, 1977, 353, n.37; Sragow 186].) And Eastwood's *Unforgiven* (1992) ends with his William Munny vanquishing the town of Big Whiskey *and* starting a happy new life with his children in the ultra-domestic dry goods business in San Francisco (leading some critics to comment on the "coincidence" that Munny reportedly begins his "new" life in the city of Dirty Harry). We view this as irony, somewhat forced, but not tragic irony. Indeed, any plausible list of the greatest Westerns should include almost no tragedies except Peckinpah's best films, those in which the damage — emotional as well as physical — is nothing less than permanent and irreversible.

III

Unlike John Ford and the other major Western directors, Peckinpah possessed a tragic vision and periodically embodied it in his films, especially those he was allowed to write or rewrite. This vision derived from his personal and literary experience, as we will document later in this chapter. Here we want to review the five films to which we will devote subsequent chapters, so as to highlight the contrast with Peckinpah's peers and to suggest the rich variety of his engagements with the tragic mode.

Peckinpah's movement toward the tragic Western can be seen in crucial decisions he made in each of his first feature films, *The Deadly Companions* and *Ride the High Country*. With *The Deadly Companions*, Peckinpah was not allowed to rewrite anything in the script or even to give direction to the female lead, Maureen O'Hara (Weddle 1994, 197–98).[11] Nonetheless, he chose to go outside the script near the end of the film by having his protagonist, Yellowleg (Brian Keith), shoot in cold blood a character named Billy (Steve Cochran) in what Peckinpah once characterized as "a brutal, realistic act" (Simmons 38).[12] Peckinpah has said he meant to undercut the film's happy ending, in which Yellowleg renounces vengeance against his primary antagonist and ends up romantically linked with O'Hara's character, Kit Tilden (Seydor 1997, 36). In doing this, Peckinpah did not convert the film into a tragedy, but he did make clear his distaste for the conventional Western. With *Ride the High Country*, Peckinpah was allowed to rewrite much of the dialogue (more than 80 percent [Seydor 1997, 44]) and to alter the plot in certain respects. As everyone has noticed (Simmons 44; Seydor 1997, 44; Weddle 1994, 203), Peckinpah's key alteration was to decide that Steve Judd (Joel McCrea) would die at the end rather than Gil Westrum (Randolph Scott). Steve is the film's protagonist and moral conscience, whereas Gil is an old friend who tries to rob Steve in the course of the action and only belatedly reverts to the spirit of their former friendship. Gil is the sort of character who dies at the end of countless Westerns, morally redeemed but punished as well for his transgressions. In killing off Steve rather than Gil, Peckinpah was effectively announcing that his Westerns would differ radically from the standard fare. Indeed, he was announcing that his films would be formal tragedies.

With his first Western features, after years of writing and directing Westerns for television, Peckinpah was already deeply suspicious of conventional Westerns. "I have never made a Western," he once said. "I have made a lot of films about men on horseback" (Schrader 25). Even a film such as *Ride the High Country*, with its exemplary hero Steve Judd, does not offer the classical "Westerner" as defined by Robert Warshow. For Warshow, this conventional figure rides faultlessly, draws his gun faster than others, and exhibits as well "an apparent moral clarity which corresponds to the clarity of his physical image against his bare landscape" (109). Steve Judd approximates this type more than any other Peckinpah protagonist, but his physical powers are hardly "faultless" and his "moral clarity" is qualified somewhat by his stubbornness and his tendency to preach, his tinge of moral certainty ("All I want is to enter my house justified," Steve says at one memorable moment). The aging Steve Judd is not very self-reflective, in fact, which both qualifies his status as paragon and suggests why he seems to lack the complexity of Peckinpah's later protagonists, Pike Bishop (William Holden) and Pat Garrett (James Coburn).

In this early film it is Steve's old friend, Gil Westrum, who embodies a more complicated (though not tragic) mixture of good and evil qualities. It is Gil and not Steve who recalls that the good old days were hard, even unyielding, as well as the occasion for Gil's and Steve's most impressive performances as lawmen (very poorly paid lawmen, as Gil reminds his nostalgic friend). It is Gil who feels acutely the embarrassment of working in Western shows as a kind of relic from the past. And it is Gil who crosses all moral lines by plotting to steal the money Steve has hired him to help guard. The film deals very effectively with this transgression on the part of a "good" man, someone Steve Judd thinks of as an equal. Ultimately, Gil recaptures his former sense of moral obligation and is rewarded with Steve's assurance that he always knew Gil was the honorable man of their common past. The film thus develops the story of a good but vulnerable man's inner conflict, but Gil is not the protagonist and his choices are not as severe as those we associate with tragedies based on the hero's mistakes. This is perhaps appropriate in a film filled with realistic elements masterfully orchestrated by an important new director, but a film which does not aspire to the more complex tragic structures of Peckinpah's later works. Indeed, Steve Judd's story becomes the occasion for Peckinpah's one venture into the form of Christian tragedy, with its emphasis on heroic sacrifice and the effects of such sacrifice on the fallen world the hero occupies and to some extent redeems.

Peckinpah's next tragic film is *Noon Wine*, the 1966 television production he wrote and directed for *ABC Stage 67*, an anthology series which debuted that fall. Based on Katherine Anne Porter's short novel, which deals with life in a south central Texas farm at the beginning of the twentieth century, *Noon Wine* is treated in Paul Seydor's 1997 "reconsideration" of Peckinpah's Western films and also seems to us a domestic Western. *Noon Wine* was Peckinpah's first directorial credit since his unhappy experience with *Major Dundee*, a film severely cut by executives at Columbia Pictures and released in 1965 to unusually negative reviews. When asked by Daniel Melnick in the summer of 1966 if he wanted to direct an adaptation of Porter's story, Peckinpah was probably prepared to accept almost any invitation to return to his career as a director. He seems to have been especially eager to accept this particular job, however, for *Noon Wine*, a work he already knew and admired, represents the kind of modern tragedy Peckinpah favored in his training in the University of Southern California drama department. This production allowed Peckinpah to resume the tragic experimentation begun in *Ride the High Country*, but in a form quite different from the latter's version of Christian tragedy. Indeed, *Noon Wine* is superb evidence that Peckinpah understood the values and requirements of a tragic action outside the conventions of the traditional Western.

Seven years separate *Ride the High Country* from *The Wild Bunch*, and in this period Peckinpah — rather like Ford as he moved toward the creation of Ethan Edwards— apparently came to believe that the most powerful Western film would offer as protagonist a man who combines Steve Judd's and Gil Westrum's more crucial features. The protagonist of *The Wild Bunch*, Pike Bishop, is not as pious as Steve, but he is also inclined to lecture or preach, as when he warns his men that they are nothing but animals if they don't stick together. It is crucial to the film's ultimate effect that we appreciate Pike's commitment to the values of loyalty, comradeship, and professionalism, precisely the values Steve Judd espouses and more or less embodies. But we cannot help but see the darker, Gil Westrum–like side to Pike, as when he abandons the unreliable Crazy Lee (Bo Hopkins) to simplify the Bunch's retreat from the embattled town of Starbuck, or when he shoots the blinded Buck because the Bunch cannot afford to stop and take care of their friend, or when he joins sides— however briefly — with the monstrous Mexican "general," Mapache (Emilio Fernandez), attracted by the prospect of challenging work but also the fee of $10,000 for stealing guns which may lead to the deaths of innocent families in small villages ("Ten thousand cuts an awful lot of family ties," as Pike proclaims). Pike's moral failures litter the film, in fact, from his overconfident decisions which lead to the imprisonment of his closest friend Deke Thornton (Robert Ryan), to his carelessness in protecting — or failure to protect — the one great love of his life, Aurora (Aurora Clavel), who is killed by her estranged husband even as Pike is wounded for life in his thigh, to his late decision to let his longtime friend Freddy Sykes (Edmond O'Brien) fend for himself against an attacking posse while Pike leads his men back to Agua Verde, Mapache's military garrison. In short, Pike Bishop is a real outlaw, not an older Ringo Kid, and his moral failures are of the essence in Peckinpah's tragic story.

Later, in 1973, Peckinpah returned to the subject of outlaw-as-hero with his controversial treatment of the Billy the Kid saga, *Pat Garrett and Billy the Kid*. Despite its flaws and the unforgivable interference of Peckinpah's masters at MGM, who cut 18 minutes from the film and refused to let Peckinpah edit the released version, this great if difficult film amply confirms the notion that only veteran Western filmmakers are in position to incorporate highly complex protagonists within the structures and conventions of the Western. We are thinking especially of Peckinpah's Pat Garrett, even though his Billy the Kid (Kris Kristofferson) is a much more complicated character than we are used to in the many reinventions of this legendary figure. It is Garrett who makes this film a memorable experience, as Peckinpah traces Garrett's conflicted efforts to survive in the new, post-outlaw West by becoming a lawman himself and purging New Mexico of its worst renegade, Garrett's friend and former colleague, the anachronistic "outlaw hero," William Bonney. The film's best moments capture Garrett's intense self-hatred as he doggedly works out his new commitment to the established order by tracking down the Kid and finally killing him. The portrait which emerges, that of a "hero" who violates his real values and inner self by surviving at any cost, is stunningly rendered by Peckinpah and his lead actor, James Coburn.

Pat Garrett and Billy the Kid is an extraordinarily grim film, very much in the mood of bitter irony and despair which characterizes so many American films of the 1970s. In some ways it takes us back to the spirit of such anti–Westerns as Arthur Penn's *Little Big Man* (1970), Frank Perry's *Doc* (1971), and Kaufman's *The Great Northfield Minnesota Raid*. The film is hard to cuddle up to or even engage through normal spectatorial involvement. Perhaps the complex Pat Garrett is ultimately too unlikable, too deeply encased in his mid-life crisis. Certainly he achieves nothing like the cathartic reassertion of self — or moral awareness — embodied in Pike Bishop's final moments. Even at its best, *Pat Garrett and Billy the Kid* may be a film for Western aficionados who appreciate its uncompromising portrait of moral ambiguity no matter how painfully dark the product. Yet we should also keep in mind that *Pat Garrett and Billy the Kid* is a different kind of tragedy from Peckinpah's earlier films. Its protagonist is very unlike those in *Ride the High Country* and *Noon Wine*, and while he resembles Pike Bishop in his history, strengths, and especially his faults, he is ultimately different from Pike in failing to acknowledge these faults, even as we know that he is aware of them, and he senselessly perpetuates them to the end of his life, which is radically different from the cathartic conclusion to *The Wild Bunch*. Rather than repeat himself in this later film, Peckinpah has in effect challenged Heilman's belief that tragedy must lead to the hero's redemptive self-knowledge, the "larger wisdom" he achieves at the cost of his life. In Chapter Five, we will assess Peckinpah's success in forging this innovative tragic form.

Peckinpah's final tragic film, *Bring Me the Head of Alfredo Garcia*, is almost as revolutionary as *Pat Garrett and Billy the Kid*. Seydor points us in the right direction(s) with this vastly underrated film, first by labeling it "an authentic revenge-tragedy" (1997, 35), then by describing it as "a remarkable film whose submerged sexual tensions and guilts have little precedent in American films" (1997, 366). Seydor does not discuss *Bring Me the Head of Alfredo Garcia* as a Western, but it shares much with Western films, especially its initial setting of El Jefe's (Emilio Fernandez's) huge Mexican horse ranch, defended by vaqueros who look and act like cowboys; its subsequent settings in remote, rural Mexico; its revenge motifs, indistinguishable from those we associate with the nineteenth-century American West; and its pervasive lawlessness (not unlike the world of the gangster film, another genre it recalls). We believe *Bring Me the Head of Alfredo Garcia* is as much a modern Western as David Miller's *Lonely Are the Brave* or Martin Ritt's *Hud* (1963) and more so than John Huston's *The Treasure of the Sierra Madre*. The greatest challenge Peckinpah undertook with this film was to elicit tragic emotions concerning his heroine, Elita (Isela Vega), and especially his hero, Bennie (Warren Oates), almost certainly the least commanding character Peckinpah built any of his films around. In Chapter Six, we will try to show how Peckinpah does this by imposing the conventions of Elizabethan and Jacobean revenge tragedy on his all too contemporaneous hero and heroine ("Peckinpah's tragic lovers," as they are astutely labeled in a photograph included in Garner Simmons' *Peckinpah: A Portrait in Montage*).

Peckinpah's career resembles that of John Ford in its broad pattern of development. Relatively early each director made films in which the protagonists are interesting, even fascinating, but still cast in the traditional mold which also produced Will Kane and Shane. Then, in a later, more mature period, both made films of increasing complexity, with heroes sufficiently morally ambiguous to elicit widespread controversy about their real nature. And finally, in films such as Ford's *The Searchers* and Peckinpah's *Pat Garrett and Billy the Kid*, they offered the kind of tragic complexity only the most ambitious artist even aspires to depict. Unlike Ford, however, Peckinpah produced formal tragedies at all points in this progression, from *Ride the High Country* and *Noon Wine* to *The Wild Bunch* to *Pat Garrett and Billy the Kid* and *Bring Me the Head of Alfredo Garcia*. It may tell us something about the restlessness of the tragic sensibility that while Ford confidently shot very little footage for his films and seems to have known exactly what he was doing as an artist, Peckinpah obsessively shot thousands of feet of film, as if like Orson Welles' Charles Foster Kane (*Citizen Kane*, 1941) he was looking for something he had lost and couldn't find, and which he only tentatively discovered in the editing room. This is especially true of the more radically open-ended tragic Westerns, which reveal a deeper level of uncertainty and a latently religious longing for the infinite, shadowed always by the alluring specter of death. David Thomson, perhaps invoking another great tragedian, Joseph Conrad, tellingly captures the difference between the two great Western directors: "[I]t was in looking that Peckinpah seemed most open or uncertain; *he looked to see*— whereas Ford looked to discover what he knew already" (2002, 672; our emphases). Gill Dennis, a screenwriter and Peckinpah's son-in-law, told David Weddle that "what [Peckinpah] was doing was putting things on the screen that he did not understand" (Weddle 1994, 402), things he carefully assembled in his films but could not claim to have mastered. Dennis once asked Peckinpah what he wanted written on his tombstone. Peckinpah responded in language which unconsciously recalled Ford's masterpiece: "I suppose the fact that I never stopped looking ... searching" (quoted in Weddle 1994, 13).

As we shall see, Peckinpah's tragic life prepared him best for making tragic films. Before exploring these films in individual chapters, we would like to conclude this chapter by reviewing the sources of Peckinpah's career as a tragic filmmaker in his life, his reading, and his formal training in drama and film.

IV

> T. S. Eliot has pointed out that a number of Shakespeare's tragic heroes have this trick of looking at themselves dramatically; their true identity, the thing that is destroyed when they die, is something outside themselves— not a man but a style of life, a kind of meaning.
>
> — Robert Warshow, "The Gangster as Tragic Hero" [103]

It can be argued that Peckinpah, a product of the authentic but rapidly modernizing American West, was destined to work within the tragic mode, to feel ironically "at home" and artistically engaged in the most personal, painful, and dislocating of genres, the tragic Western. Peckinpah's subjects always seem to involve the poetics of loss— the erosions of time, the irrevocable loss of the old West, the passing of the childhood he loved so deeply because it seemed to dissolve before his eyes as he desperately sought to hold onto it. It is this sense of a disappearing world which leads Peckinpah's most memorable character, the aging outlaw

Pike Bishop, to brood over his vanishing past, diminishing present, and desolate future: "We gotta start thinkin' beyond our guns. Those days are closin' fast." But there is no "beyond" for the doomed Wild Bunch. The persistent theme of lost time, of days closing fast, resonates to varying degrees with Pike and all the rest of Peckinpah's tragic heroes. "The people, the places in that area! It's mostly all gone now," Peckinpah once said. "Fresno's like a little L.A. today, and the country around it is chopped up with new roads and resort facilities and overrun with all these shit-ass tourists and campers. My brother Denny and I were in on the last of it" (William Murray 72). Like F. Scott Fitzgerald's Nick Carraway in *The Great Gatsby*, Peckinpah longed for the decidedly feminized "warm center of the world" (3) in a past which was already dead or dying, and which was perhaps less real than his Wordsworthian yearnings for a lost youth made it seem. Yet Peckinpah's ecstatic "remembrances" of an idyllic boyhood in the Sierra Nevada Mountains above Fresno are countered by a much darker, often repressed family history which was anything but blissful. Indeed, the family strife Peckinpah experienced in his youth combined with his intense nostalgia to produce the odd mixture of savage realism and lyrical longing which galvanizes his highly personal, intensely conflicted art.

Born in 1925 and raised in the rapidly growing agricultural city of Fresno, David Samuel Peckinpah was most at home on Dunlap's Ranch, the high-country spread of his maternal grandfather Denver Church, or at nearby Bass Lake and Peckinpah Mountain, the site of a lumber mill built by the Peckinpahs in the nineteenth century.[13] There he would hunt and fish with his father David, a highly successful lawyer and judge who had driven a stagecoach as a young man, Denver Church, a lawyer and United States Congressman, his brother Denver ("Denny"), and the old cowboys and saddle tramps, many of them crude but fascinating storytellers, who worked for Denver Church. Small, slender, and somewhat frail, artistic and literary from an early age, Sam nonetheless wanted very much to be accepted by his grandfather, his father, and their friends. This was the True West and the "true identity" (Warshow 103) of Peckinpah's youth, the one he told interviewers he had really inhabited, though his childhood was much more complicated, and far less idyllic, than the stories he spun. The mountains, the ranch, and Peckinpah's boyish joy at being in the company of men do not tell the whole story of his divided childhood because they omit his intense, troubled relationship with his mother, Fern Church Peckinpah.

The wealthy Peckinpahs lived just outside of Fresno in "a sprawling suburban-style ranch house, with twenty-four acres of exquisitely landscaped property for his playground" (Weddle 1994, 14), a creek running through it and room for half-a-dozen saddle horses and range for them to graze on. Sam's mother Fern, a difficult, self-centered, and domineering woman who held her husband's "lesser born" family in contempt, never really wanted to have children and insisted that her first born, Denny, be sent off to her own parents to be raised (Simmons 10). Like a character out of Tennessee Williams, a Blanche Dubois or Violet Venable, the histrionic Fern would feign serious infirmities or indulge in private delusions in order to draw attention to herself (Weddle 1994, 26–27). All the members of her family feared her, even David Peckinpah, a tall, strong man of stern disposition and imposing probity, who would fight with his wife but was nearly always reduced to humiliated silence by her controlling moods and would never allow his children to disagree with her or resist her authority in any way. Early in the marriage — rather like Hemingway's mother — she converted from the Episcopal Church to the anti-materialist religion of Christian Science and this seemed to create an even greater tension within her already fractious family. David, who also converted to Christian Science at his wife's behest, was himself a deeply religious man, and all of his children grew up reading the Bible. This would have a profound influence on young Sam, who would later use his biblical knowledge to help forge his cinematic tragedies of sin, expiation, and the complex forms of grace.

Peckinpah was born nine years after his brother Denver. Although his mother had not wanted a second child, Sam became her "favorite," and she fawned over him even as she appointed Denny the official caregiver of his much younger brother. Fern may have loved her children, and the "baby" Sam most of all, but he always felt manipulated by her mood swings, her narcissistic self-obsession, and very soon he came to distrust her love for him. As he entered a troubled, rebellious adolescence — at one point he was shipped off to a military school — young Sam "grew to detest his mother's grim dictatorship," her suffocatingly controlling personality (Weddle 1994, 27). This was the beginning of Peckinpah's life-long distrust of women, and his equally powerful desire to be loved by them at the same time. We see this in his personal life, as he married five times, three times to the same woman, Begonia Palacios,[14] and in the conflicted, ever-shifting manner in which he represents women in his films. Peckinpah was no misogynist, as many of his critics have charged, but women often emerge in his films as textually repressed, displaced or overly allegorized, at worst almost completely marginalized. There are exceptions (Amy Sumner in *Straw Dogs* [1971], Hildy in *The Ballad of Cable Hogue*, Elita in *Bring Me the Head of Alfredo Garcia*, perhaps Carol McCoy in *The Getaway* [1972]), but they are all too rare.

Peckinpah would see his mother less and less, especially when she committed the primal sin of selling Dunlap's Ranch, the boys' favorite place on earth, after her father's death in 1950, without consulting Sam or Denny, or, we would guess, her own husband. As Fern Lea, Sam and Denny's adopted sister, remembers it, "They sold it, my mother sold it, and this broke Sam and Denny's heart. They wanted that ranch very badly" (*Sam Peckinpah's West*). Sam and Denny viewed their mother's act as selfish and vindictive, as she knew how much the ranch meant to them and her late father. At this moment Sam absorbed one of the great and troubling obsessions of his tragic films, betrayal. After this genuinely traumatic event, followed 10 years later by his father's death in 1960, Sam rarely saw his mother unless he had to. Even so, whenever her name came up or something about her came to his attention, he would often become so upset he was rattled and distracted for hours. This went on for another 23 years, until Fern died in 1983, and even continued after her death. Unfortunately, her younger son was to follow her a year later, in 1984, when a pacemaker implant malfunctioned in Puerto Vallarta, Mexico, and he died in an airplane on the way back to Los Angeles for treatment. One might view this as Fern's revenge from the grave, a theme Peckinpah would explore brilliantly in *Pat Garrett and Billy the Kid* and *Bring Me the Head of Alfredo Garcia*, as well as in his powerful cinematic rereading of the conclusion to Porter's *Noon Wine*.

Fern Peckinpah had one saving talent: she was, after her fashion, an artist, both in the home and in nature. Fern possessed a dramatic sense of style and a "strong visual intuition" (Weddle 1994, 22). Outdoors she artfully planted throughout Fresno many magnificent still-standing trees and was above all an expert gardener. Young Sam, whose love of flowers and painterly imagination would later infuse his life and films, worked as a boy in the blazing summer heat tending to Fern's expansive gardens, where he nurtured and "developed his mother's eye for color and composition" (Weddle 1994, 22), as well as her passion for meticulously exacting detail. Fern created "an artificial brook, powered by a water pump, [which] weaved its way among the roses, irises, lilacs, pansies, and petunias. There were miniature waterfalls, tiny bridges, and castles. In this fairyland, Eden before the bitten apple, the shimmering red and yellow and blue flower petals held the dark undercurrents and disturbing ambiguities of Fern's life at bay" (Weddle 1994, 23). But in truth Fern's enchanted garden was Eden before and *after* the Fall, as she played both adoring Eve and deceitful serpent to her loving but wary son. Sam was coming to know and understand Paradise and Paradise Lost as simultaneous, contradictory emotions in his young life. Peckinpah's tragic sense of life came to him early in his childhood.

Perhaps Fern was emulating on a less grand scale her great uncle, the aptly named Moses Church (one thinks of *Chinatown*'s water magnate *Noah* Cross), who constructed his own Promised Land in the 1880s, "more than a thousand miles of canals [which] had transformed the [central California] valley into wheat fields, groves of fig, peach and walnut trees, and vineyards. Moses had fathered the greatest irrigation system ["Church's ditches"] in the world" (Weddle 1994, 15). With this kind of formidable legacy, it is no wonder that water discovered in the desert, indeed, water wherever it was found, was to figure prominently in all of Peckinpah's films. From the pond in the desert where Kit (Maureen O'Hara) bathes in Peckinpah's first film, *The Deadly Companions*, to the more artificial though no less significant swimming pool of John Tanner (Rutger Hauer) in his last film, *The Osterman Weekend* (1983), water comes to define a highly significant, often mythic, perhaps maternal and life-affirming space in Peckinpah's fictional world. It symbolizes a timeless vision of wholeness, of peace and harmonic flow, the romantic quest for permanence Peckinpah could never achieve in his own life.[15] And yet its inception comes from the profoundly ambivalent figure of the mother, the complex, mercurial Fern Church Peckinpah, a woman Peckinpah loved deeply but deeply feared.

Fern was also the seemingly omnipotent creative center of her son's imaginary Eden, its flowing streams, its gorgeous gardens, and ultimately young Sam's extravagant visual genius as a filmmaker. That he should feel so distrustful about beauty, associating it with his mother's "creation," adds another element of agonizing doubleness to a man, a writer, and a director who saw everything as inextricably "mixed" (Harmetz 173), who never experienced anything in his life as whole and complete, who longed for perfection but found brokenness everywhere, and who could within the same film create images of spectacular, even transcendent beauty, while contrasting them with grotesquely repugnant scenes of humiliation, suffering, and violent death, often directed at women, whom Peckinpah seemed to love and hate with equal passion. Fern's legacy to her son was a confusing, disturbing one, but it was a perfect seedbed for an aspiring tragic artist. Her decision to sell the family ranch recalls once again Orson Welles' young Charles Foster Kane, who is expelled from his vision of paradise, the wintry snow field on the Colorado prairie where he fought his imaginary Civil War battles, and the abandoned sled ("Rosebud") he cherished so much, both taken away from him by a mother he could never comprehend, whose passionate love and perplexing coldness would torture him for the rest of his tragically lonely life. Peckinpah's own Kane-like glass ball vision of Paradise shattered early, yet he spent the rest of his life in pursuit of lost time, trying to get back into the world of Dunlap's Ranch and Peckinpah Mountain. We see this quest in the beauty of the Sierras in *Ride the High Country*, the harvest joy that Mr. Thompson and Mr. Helton share in *Noon Wine*, the pastoral peace of Angel's village in *The Wild Bunch*, the conviviality of Pat Garrett and Billy the Kid riding together or sharing drinks as younger men in *Pat Garrett and Billy the Kid*, and the idyllic oneness of Bennie and Elita enjoying a romantic picnic under a sheltering green tree in *Bring Me the Head of Alfredo Garcia*.

His mother's overweening influence was one of two powerful tensions in Peckinpah's youth. The other was the often brutal, altogether masculinized world of his grandfather and father's friends. Peckinpah loved his father deeply, but he was always trying to prove that he was as tough as any of them, even though he was undersized (the "runt of the litter," as he was known) and equally happy staying in his room, reading books, or going to the movies. Reflecting on Peckinpah's childhood, his adoptive sister Fern Lea says, "Sam was basically a woman, emotionally. I think of a man as being systematic in his reasoning, to come to a certain point. Sam would get to the answer emotionally—the way he felt about it, the way he visualized it. I think he was embarrassed by it because in our family, 'By God, the men are men'" (Weddle 1994, 23). Between his father's rigid legal reasoning and belief in stern justice, and his grandfather's harsh, often sarcastic criticisms (he was not averse to humiliating his grandson if he thought the boy was being too "soft" or "feminine"), Peckinpah often felt lonely and alienated among the men of his family, even as he longed to be one of them. His was not so much a question of gender confusion about his sexuality, but rather what it means to be a man whose sensitivities were coded "feminine" and therefore found to be wanting by his grandfather and father. "They never accepted Sam the way they had accepted Denny," Betty Peckinpah (Sam's sister-in-law) says of the older men in the family. "David was not so openly hostile, but he never understood Sam's theatrical ambitions, his writing. For me, the tragedy of Sam was that he spent his life trying to find acceptance from that family. The macho posturing ... that wasn't Sam. It was, but it wasn't. That was him trying to win approval from his family. He spent his life trying to do that and it tore him apart inside. He never did get acceptance. It made him one of the saddest people I ever knew" (Weddle 1994, 37). It was young Sam's dream, and his damnation, to recapture the lost bliss of his childhood, a "bliss" we now know to be tainted from the beginning by the crushing reality of his demanding family.

Peckinpah's confusions about his personal identity were to help make him a great director with an acute sense of the painful divisions within human nature, fragments of his own broken nature he daringly put up on the screen, but they also made him a tormented and tormenting human being. His sister Fern Lea once remarked that Peckinpah, like his vain and selfish mother, "never grew up" and felt dispossessed and homeless all his life (Weddle 1994, 26). While the fundamental questions of identity formed the basis of his great and troubling art, especially his ability to achieve his own version of Keats' Negative Capability by completely entering the lives of his characters, it did not help him to grow and mature as a person. Always the lonely outsider, the emotional orphan, he never reconciled himself to his wrenching antimonies, and to the end of his life he remained a superannuated *enfant terrible*, the best and worst of friends, lovers, husbands, and fathers, the most "deadly" of companions. One minute soft-spoken, talking in a voice barely audible, with weary, sad eyes and a sweet, angelic smile, the next minute angry, vicious, and violent, often fueled by alcohol, then later by alcohol and cocaine, Peckinpah lived his life on a very high precipice, always threatening to fall into the abyss, never to return.[16]

Even the positive elements in Peckinpah's life ultimately found their way into the tragic structures of his films. A good example is his favorite country, Mexico. In the early 1970s Peckinpah, so clearly modernist in his sense of rootlessness and exile, described himself as an "expatriate" (Yergin 91) while wandering like Jack Kerouac through Mexico (William Murray 192), a country where, paradoxically, he always felt most at home, having lost his original home in the now vanished West of his childhood and the contemporary America of assassinations, riots, the Vietnam War, and the corrupt Nixon administration. For him Mexico was a country of wild and striking contrasts, gentle and harsh, beautiful and cruel, a mirror image of the conflicts within himself, his desire for peace, his need for war. Mexico was also Peckinpah's source of renewal, a place where people wore their emotions openly and didn't play Hollywood power games such as his bitter struggles with the money men of the studios. "Mejico lindo" evoked the long lost West of Old California, the visionary American past of the nineteenth century, Peckinpah's true home in history. Referring to Pike Bishop and the Wild Bunch, but in terms which apply to their creator as well, Paul Schrader says that it is in "the nature of their lives to go to Mexico to escape the new century. So there was that sense about having to go to Mexico to keep the West alive for one last suicidal hurrah" (*Sam Peckinpah's West*).

In going to Mexico, as Schrader says, Peckinpah was not just moving through space but back in time. Once asked to define what Mexico meant to him, Peckinpah described a place not unlike his mother's garden, with its brilliant flowers, or the mountains above Fresno, Dunlap's Ranch, Peckinpah Mountain, the lost world of his boyhood: "Everything important in my life has been linked to Mexico one way or another. The country has a special effect on me.... In Mexico it's all out there — the color, the life, the warmth.... In Mexico they don't worry so goddamn much about saving the human race or about the wheeling and dealing that's poisoning us. In Mexico they don't forget to kiss each other and water the flowers" (William Murray 192). Always the pariah, the Prodigal Son who knows, like one of his own rootless, romantic characters, Junior Bonner (Steve McQueen), that "home" has disappeared, Peckinpah experienced a permanent state of exile in Mexico, yet it was there he seemed most comfortable, fell in love many times, and made a number of his best films. Mexico was for Peckinpah a dreamscape of Proustian possibilities where he could relive and re-create an American past which had been wantonly destroyed by a century to which he owed scant fealty. Mexico's contradictory extremes of love and violence, beauty and terror, were the substance of Peckinpah's life and art, and as he lived the one he invented the other.

Peckinpah's Mexico proved the perfect context in which to dramatize his characters' tragic plights. In all the tragic films we witness Peckinpah's heroes at war with themselves but also their environments. That they feel trapped, that they don't *fit* anymore, makes them claustrophobic, angry, and ultimately violent. Mexico enables them to explore their American alienation within a different landscape, in effect a different temporal as well as spatial realm. The Mexican *topos*, as we might call it, points to a powerful element of anachronism, or displacement in time, in Peckinpah's tragic films, perhaps in all tragic actions. Tragic protagonists experience a form of temporal "doubleness" while living inside "several tenses and moods all at once, in [their] sense of what was and will be," all of this taking place "in moments of crisis in time" (Poole 2005, 99, 107). This vertiginous sense of "time out of joint" leads, as with Hamlet and Peckinpah's tortured protagonists, to moments of profound doubt and confusion, ultimately culminating in acts of terrifying violence.

By way of analogy, Peckinpah's Mexico leads us to major Shakespearean characters such as Hamlet and Macbeth. These figures often struggle to understand their actions within conceptions of time which run counter to conventional notions of temporality. As Emily R. Wilson notes, "Hamlet himself also has a distorted relationship to time; he cannot accept that time passes and one generation succeeds to another, that 'all that lives must die/Passing through nature to eternity.' Hamlet wants to stop time, to defer indefinitely the proper moment to act" (7). Hamlet seeks to recover his lost innocence, in particular his loving and relatively conventional relationship with his mother and the then living King Hamlet. Unbearably, Claudius and his mother have taken all of this away. By contrast, although he is no less obsessed with time, Macbeth "finds time too slow and tries to leap over it: for him, the right moment has always already slipped by" (Wilson 7). But what Macbeth really seeks, in an eerie anticipation of Peckinpah's Pat Garrett, is to deny the murder of Duncan by denying the existence of actual Time. If Time does not exist, then even though Duncan dies, he never really existed, in some metaphysical sense he did not die, and Macbeth is free to become king, a putatively guiltless man. But murder can never be "done quickly" enough, and there is no "be-all and end-all" in a bloody deed which reverberates throughout the kingdom of Scotland. Macbeth becomes a spectral being who witnesses the horror he has created in the return of the murdered Banquo, for in his tormented consciousness Macbeth haunts himself and can only kill and kill again in order to erase the reality of what he has become. It is a hopeless venture which tries to deny "the temporal order of human generations" (Wilson 7), one in which sons kill their "fathers" (Claudius, Duncan), their wives (Lady Macbeth, de facto), and their mothers (Queen Gertrude, who drinks the poison intended for her son). Hamlet defers and delays and Macbeth acts rashly, yet each clings to a notion of time which jars the conventional relationship between present and past, present and future. Time is the traumatic element in the great Shakespearean tragedies, perhaps in all tragedies. As Rebecca Bushnell writes, time "is at the heart of the tragic experience, as it tempts us with the dream of escaping time altogether.... Tragedy exercises its power over us because of both the enigma of the future and the absolute nature of the past: once an act has been done before us, it cannot be undone" (30). Time is what we cannot take back. It is irrevocable, irreversible, and ultimately linked with death. Peckinpah experienced time's complex, contradictory nature more profoundly in Mexico than anywhere else.

Peckinpah's ties with Shakespeare should remind us that he drew on more than his own life in making his films. Peckinpah's difficult life informs the films in ways large and small, but we would not want to argue that a tragic life necessarily leads to tragic works of art. Peckinpah bestowed many of his experiences on his most tragic characters and films, but he did much the same thing in non-tragic films such as *The Ballad of Cable Hogue* and *Junior Bonner* (1972) (arguably the most "autobiographical" of Peckinpah's works). Peckinpah's reading and his training in drama and film are also relevant to his tragic forms, for they led him to value very highly the theory and practice of tragedy. The man who made *The Wild Bunch* experienced most of Pike Bishop's sexual and professional failures, but he also read and admired Aristotle's *Poetics* and Shakespeare's tragedies.

By all accounts Peckinpah was an avid reader in his youth, his tastes ranging from cowboy novels to Tennyson's *The Charge of the Light Brigade* to *Moby-Dick* (retold in a children's book) to Shakespeare and many modern dramatists, especially Tennessee Williams ("easily America's greatest playwright" [Weddle 1994, 69]). His first wife, Marie Selland, recalls that during his years at USC Peckinpah read widely in writers such as Hemingway ("That man was my Bible" [Jenson 73]), Fitzgerald, Thoreau, Faulkner, Dickens, Camus, and various Greek philosophers, especially Plato and Aristotle (Seydor 1997, 341). In the late 1940s he spent six months in Mexico reading almost nothing but Shakespeare's major plays, as David Weddle reports: "He developed a great affinity for the Englishman's towering but much-flawed heroes. Haunted by guilt, torn between impulses noble and base, fated to tragic ends—and when they finally fell there was a grandeur to their descent. The tales often ended in orgies of bloodshed and destruction, bodies littering the stage, yet you felt oddly uplifted, exalted" (1994, 71). With Shakespeare, we would suggest, Peckinpah felt more than an "affinity." He learned from Tennessee Williams (among others) that tragedy was still possible in a "modern" age, but from Shakespeare he learned the secrets of a passionate and often violent kind of tragic action. Those bodies littering Shakespeare's stage inevitably remind us of *The Wild Bunch*, but the key to Peckinpah's experience with Shakespeare is that he felt "oddly uplifted, exalted" at the bloody end. We are reminded of Peckinpah's oft-cited comment about the conclusion of *The Wild Bunch*: "The strange thing is that you feel a great sense of loss when these killers reach the end of the line" (Farber 42). We hope to do something like justice to the Shakespearean elements in Peckinpah's tragic films, for they are the most important literary influence on his works.

Peckinpah's most important intellectual influence is not the modern anthropologist Robert Ardrey, as some have claimed, but Aristotle's *Poetics*. Marie Selland tells us that "Aristotle's *Poetics* is something that seemed to grab him and he was constantly referring to it" (Seydor 1997, 341); as Seydor says, "He knew Aristotle's *Poetics* cold" (1997, 345). Seydor also notes that Peckinpah originally wanted to write his master's thesis at USC on "some aspect of the theory and practice of tragedy from Aristotle to the moderns," though circumstances led him to write a more "practical" 1954 thesis about the director's role in producing and directing a one-act play, Williams' *Portrait of a Madonna*, for the stage and for a closed-circuit television broadcast (1997, 342). Throughout his career as a director, Peckinpah continued to refer to concepts he first encountered in the *Poetics*. We might well ask what drew Peckinpah to this ancient document.

We noted earlier that Peckinpah must have been impressed by Aristotle's emphasis on the emotional effects generated by tragic plays and his focus on the acts of the primary characters. We believe these features of the *Poetics* account for Peckinpah's sense of kinship with the text, but it must be acknowledged that most of his later references to Aristotle concern the specific concept of *catharsis*. As Weddle concludes, "Aristotle's *Poetics* gave him the foundations for dramatic writing, and he became a strong believer in the philosopher's theory that great drama provides an audience with a catharsis through which they can purge their own pain, rage, and fear" (1994, 73). Whether Aristotle meant *catharsis* to be this kind of purgative experience for the audience has been endlessly debated, but there can be little question that Peckinpah thought he did. Peckinpah once said of the violence in *The Wild Bunch*, "[M]y idea was that it would have a cathartic effect" (Prince 1998, 108), and he felt that violence in *Straw Dogs* worked much the same way: "It serves as a cathartic effect" (Weddle 1994, 12). He made it clear that the effect to which he referred was purgative in nature: "I'm a great believer in catharsis.... Look, the old basis of catharsis was a purging of the emotions through pity and fear" (William Murray 68). Interestingly, Peckinpah even invoked *catharsis* and the tragic emotions of pity and fear in discussing *Straw Dogs*, a film we do not consider tragic despite its many intense, potentially tragic elements: "I intended it to have a cathartic effect. Someone may feel a [strange] sick ex[u]ltation at the violence, but he should then ask himself, 'What is going on in my heart?' I want[ed] to achieve a catharsis through pity and fear" (quoted in Fine 192).[17]

It would seem that Peckinpah intended his films to be therapeutic in addition to whatever else they achieved. Stephen Prince has argued that in this regard Peckinpah misunderstood Aristotle and the effects of violence as depicted in film as opposed to violence as reported in Greek drama (1998, 108–12, esp. 110–11). Prince may be right about this (though his book seems largely intended as a social treatise against violent movies, an argument which has little to say about the artistry of Peckinpah's films). Ultimately, in our view, it doesn't matter very much whether or not Prince is right. What matters is that Peckinpah designed his films to elicit the emotional responses of pity and fear, which Peckinpah followed Aristotle in identifying as the effects appropriate to tragedy. This means that Peckinpah intended at least some of his films to be tragedies in the sense Aristotle first formulated well over 2,000 years ago. We conclude that Aristotle was in theory what Shakespeare was in practice: a guide to how Peckinpah might channel his own painful personal experiences into his art.

An influence study would consider a good many figures other than Aristotle and Shakespeare even if it were confined to drama and dramatists. Peckinpah's connections with Tennessee Williams, for example, would make a very interesting essay if not something longer. Even relatively minor works such as *Portrait of a Madonna* helped Peckinpah understand what would be required in his own art. In his master's thesis on the production of this one-act play, Peckinpah notes two discoveries about what must occur if audiences are to respond appropriately to Williams' tragic intentions. The first is that the heroine, Lucretia Collins, must be presented as positively as possible early in the play: "the audience must understand her beauty and potential as a human being subjectively in order to feel her personal tragedy" (11–12). The second is that genuinely affecting tragic figures must "meet their fate with courage and dignity" even if they are shown to be "defeated and broken by society and their own inadequacies" (12). These lessons were obviously remembered when Peckinpah made *Ride the High Country* and *The Wild Bunch*, and it would be an interesting study to see how they apply to later works such as *Pat Garrett and Billy the Kid* and *Bring Me the Head of Alfredo Garcia*. To know what Peckinpah read or saw and especially what he liked is to appreciate how crucial drama was to his evolution as a tragic filmmaker.

The same point can be made about Peckinpah's training in film. Indeed, Simmons, Weddle, and Seydor provide rich accounts of Peckinpah's apprenticeship in film, his likes and dislikes among individual films, and what Peckinpah apparently learned from his experience with other films. Simply to list the films and directors we know to have been among Peckinpah's favorites is to provide the basis for a meaningful study of his understanding of film as a medium, its history, and his own place within that history: *The Ox-Bow Incident, My Darling Clementine, The Treasure of the Sierra Madre, Red River, Viva Zapata!, High Noon, Shane, The Bridge on the River Kwai, Rashomon, Henry V, The Left-Handed Gun, Bonnie and Clyde*, Ford, Kazan, Bergman, Fellini, Kurosawa, Antonioni. (Seydor offers a longer list of films and directors "culled from several interviews Peckinpah gave during the last twenty years of his life" [1997, 388, n.46].) We know more about Peckinpah's tastes in Westerns than in other genres, so we think there is good evidence for one important conclusion about Peckinpah's relationship to the world of Westerns: that he saw himself as going beyond the excellent works of his predecessors (most of whom he knew and judged very fairly) in order to realize their tragic potential.[18]

It should be clear that we mean to argue Peckinpah did just that whether or not he understood himself to be doing so. Along the way we will have more to say about the personal, literary, and cinematic influences on his films, as well as their surprising connections with works of European and American art. But our focus will be on the form Peckinpah fashioned for each of his tragic films so that we can generalize about his tragic practice in our conclusion. Lest this agenda seem narrowly formalistic (as it may in fact be), we should add that the following topics will be engaged as we proceed: the journey motif; religious iconography; mirrors and doubles; doors and doorways; domestic spaces (bedrooms, kitchens, dining rooms); water (rain, rivers, lakes, ponds, streams, oceans); deserts (wind and sand); fiestas and celebrations as rituals of renewal; wounds (real, symbolic, and both); men with women; men without women; women alone; woman as the Other, the often occluded source of so many of the tragic emotions in the films. If all goes well, these topics will come to seem highly relevant to Peckinpah's tragic films as well as interesting for their own sake. Like everything else in Peckinpah's best works, they achieve their point and effect by contributing to the emotional experience Peckinpah understood as tragic.

We should conclude this chapter by acknowledging that the films we will be analyzing are the products of a thoroughly collaborative process, perhaps more collaborative than any other modern art form. When we speak of what Peckinpah did in making these films, especially when we address his role in revising the screenplays of others, we realize that we cannot always say — indeed, we may never be able to say — whether the relevant idea or language came from Peckinpah or others involved in the production. We do assume that Peckinpah made the final decision as to what should ultimately go into his films, unless we have credible evidence that his studios altered their released versions or limited his role during production. We realize this makes us advocates of the so-called auteur theory of filmmaking and accept the label as more or less accurate.

Chapter Two

The Double Vision of Tragedy in *Ride the High Country*

> [T]ragedy is born in the West each time the pendulum of civilization is half way between a sacred society and a society built around man.
>
> —Albert Camus [305]

> In the last day, that great *day* of the feast, Jesus stood and cried, saying, If any man thirst, let him come unto me, and drink. He that believeth on me, as the scripture hath said, out of his belly shall flow rivers of living water.
>
> —John 7: 37–38[1]

> [California] is a tragic country—like Palestine, like every promised land.
>
> —Christopher Isherwood as quoted in Iyer [109]

In Chapter One we briefly describe Peckinpah's efforts to make his first feature film, *The Deadly Companions* (1961), more believable and interesting than the script he was ordered to follow without any changes. Those writing on Peckinpah have dutifully evaluated these efforts, often concluding that Peckinpah made the film much better than it deserved to be, but they have understandably been reluctant to treat the film as if it truly embodied Peckinpah's intentions. In this regard Peckinpah's second film, *Ride the High Country* (1962), is an entirely different enterprise. As we noted earlier, Peckinpah was allowed to rewrite most of the dialogue, to make important structural changes (although he did not make many), to change the film's title from *Guns in the Afternoon* (subsequently used as the title abroad) to *Ride the High Country*, and to put together the final cut of the film as it was in fact released.[2] We have suggested that the decision to have Steve Judd (Joel McCrea) die at the end rather than Gil Westrum (Randolph Scott) virtually announced Peckinpah's intention to make a tragic film rather than the more conventional story he inherited. The larger point to be made is that *Ride the High Country* is the first of Peckinpah's films to embody almost 100 percent of what he wanted on the screen. In this sense *Ride the High Country* is both Peckinpah's first tragic film and the first which could be rightly designated "a Sam Peckinpah film."

I

Peckinpah has described *Ride the High Country* as a film about the "salvation and loneliness" of its solitary hero, Marshal Stephen Judd (William Murray 74). At another, though related, level this classic Western centers on the concept of tragic sacrifice and an equally tragic theme, the threatened death of the American West. In an act of sacrificial surrender,

Steve Judd dies so that a blighted land may be redeemed, restored to new life symbolized by Steve's regenerated friendship with his old partner, Gil Westrum, and the imminent union of two young people, Elsa Knudsen (Mariette Hartley) and Heck Longtree (Ron Starr).

Although a tragedy, *Ride the High Country* fails to conform to Aristotle's classic definition as it is usually understood because Steve Judd, while imperfect, lacks the requisite "tragic flaw" which leads to his undoing and eventual death.[3] But as Northrop Frye points out in his *Anatomy of Criticism* (1957), it is a reductivist fallacy to assume that all tragic actions are based on a rebellious hero's "violation of moral law," or that "Aristotle's hamartia or 'flaw' must have an essential connection with sin or wrongdoing" (210). Instead, Frye adduces various kinds of tragic actions, among these the disputed genre of "Christian tragedy." In spite of its apparently anti-tragic denial of the Greek — and Shakespearean — notion of the shadowy complicity of good and evil, and the even more resolutely untragic Christian promise of eternal life, this particular dramatic form remains tragic for Frye because of its focus upon the life-pattern of its protagonist. Specifically, Frye argues that Christian tragedies are those which symbolize the Passion, "as do all tragedies in which the hero is in any way related to or a prototype of Christ" (1957, 220). Additionally, these tragedies emphasize "the success or completeness of the hero's achievement" (1957, 220), that moment of "full rich serenity" which "is often a sequel to a previous tragic or heroic action, and [which] comes at the end of a heroic life" (1957, 221). By choosing to emphasize the Christ-like sacrificial nature of the protagonist over the central Christian paradox of death and resurrection, a theme taken seriously but left open-ended and ambiguous at the end of *Ride the High Country*, Frye avoids one of the key sticking points in the debate over the possibility of Christian tragedy.[4] Frye's tragic model, then, informs the archetypal design of the life, death, and eventual "salvation" of Stephen Judd.

That Peckinpah should employ the literary model of Christian tragedy to depict Steve Judd's life and death should surprise no one who knows anything about Peckinpah's childhood growing up in Fresno, a youth dominated by questions of law (his grandfather, father, uncles, and brother were all lawyers) and "a Bible which was very big in our family" (Whitehall 173). Peckinpah, a lifelong student of the Bible, eventually rebelled against the rigid strictures of his religious upbringing, but this did not preclude his absorbing — and remembering — the Bible's stories, parables, and miracles which he had heard as a boy, while subsequently making them his own. Peckinpah's actual religious beliefs seem far less important than his persistent use of the Bible as an organizing frame of reference for his writing and for the visual iconography of his films. Finally, what makes Peckinpah's relationship to Christianity and Christian tragedy interesting is not, as W. H. Auden has written, that artists like Peckinpah "necessarily believed the Christian dogmas, but that their conception of man's nature is, historically, derived from them" (164).

Contrastingly, if one were to read *Ride the High Country* within a more traditional definition of the tragic flaw, and view it once again from the prism of Peckinpah's personal past, then we believe the *hamartia* "figure" would be an America whose all-too-human fall from grace and whose tragic history Peckinpah depicts at a time of turbulent national change. Steve Judd and the old West he so venerates function as victims of America's westward expansion, its simultaneous betrayal both of its people's deepest dreams and of its magnificent natural resources. Rapacious yet repressive, acquisitive yet nihilistic, the turn-of-the-century West we witness in *Ride the High Country* effectively seeks out the ruin and death of men like Steve Judd, men whose commitment to law and justice, to community, and to the sanctity of nature renders them useless and anachronistic. Peckinpah's films nostalgically — and often bitterly — rue the near extinction of the pastoral West, especially the California Peckinpah knew as a child, a California of small farms and ranches, of mountain hunting trips, of solitary and unsullied high-country lakes and forests, now almost obliterated by an advancing "civilization." In an interview Peckinpah laments his riven childhood, regrets the passing of an older, better world, and decries the changes: "Today the [family] ranch is gone. There are motels. It's all gone" (Whitehall 174). The "all goneness" of Peckinpah's past functions as a crucial metaphor in *Ride the High Country*'s dialectic between presence and absence, climaxing in the double disappearance (dead and "gone") of Steve Judd at film's end. For Peckinpah, enduring human values, "[o]utdated codes like loyalty, friendship, grace under pressure, all the simple virtues ... have become clichés" (William Murray 72). If people practice those virtues in Peckinpah's romantic-pessimistic world, they must, like Steve Judd, die for them, but die in such a way as to keep their values alive in others.

To summarize, what makes *Ride the High Country* so rhetorically and artistically satisfying lies in its shifting back and forth between the double discourses of Christian and Aristotelian — more particularly, historical — tragedy. Never choosing one over the other, but rather opting to represent both of them at once, and often in conflict, the film brings each to rich and complex expression. Thus it is a mistake to opt for one vision of the West over another, as David Weddle does when he writes of a Western "mythology that Sam Peckinpah and his generation could no longer believe in, no matter how much they might have yearned to" (1994, 221). Both Wests are present in *Ride the High Country*. In this respect it resembles a number of 1960s Westerns—*The Misfits* (1961), *The Man Who Shot Liberty Valance* (1962), *Lonely Are the Brave* (1962), *Monte Walsh* (1970)—all of which lament the passing of a heroic way of life. Like these other films, *Ride the High Country* mixes praise-song and threnody, faith and fact, preserving in its tortured oppositions a complex, multifarious vision of tragic experience. Like Scott Fitzgerald, Peckinpah fulfills "the test of a first-rate intelligence" in his "ability to hold two opposed idea in the mind at the same time, and still retain the ability to function" (1945, 69). That we are dealing here with contrasting definitions of the tragic genre makes Peckinpah's achievement in *Ride the High Country* all the more aesthetically impressive.

Finally, more than any director of Westerns other than John Ford, Peckinpah refashions the biblical Fall in the Garden of Eden, itself the originary tale in any definition of Christian tragedy, as the historical fall of the American West. In so doing he recasts the heroic attempt to redeem the dying West as an imitation of Christ's sacrificial death upon the cross. In what follows we propose to explore Peckinpah's binocular vision of tragedy by tracing it through the iconic figure of Steve Judd in his tragic confrontation with a ruthlessly secularizing, ardently modernizing America.

II

We first see Steve Judd as he rides into the foothills town of Hornitos. This ride, preceded by the stunning credit sequence in which the film's eponymous "high country" is depicted in all its autumnal splendor, establishes at once the relationship between Steve and the natural landscape. Although we do not see Steve during the credits, as we see Shane riding down out of the Tetons toward the Starrett ranch during the credits for George Stevens' *Shane* (1953), the final fixed image we behold is of a golden aspen grove which, like the mountains, trees, lakes, and streams of *Ride the High Country*, comes to represent certain values associated with Steve Judd. We sense that these values are under assault, however, even before the credits cut to the jarring first shot of the film's narrative, the carnival at Hornitos. Through the technique of overlapping sound, a favorite Peckinpah device, film composer George Bassman's lofty and pastoral "high country" theme is invaded and eventually drowned out by the squealing music of a sideshow hootchie cootchee.

Unlike John Ford, who loved parades and patriotic displays, and who filled his films with spectacles of national pride, Peckinpah presents civic celebrations of dubious origin or suspect worth. Working in a more cynical time, Peckinpah borrows from Ford, but with a difference. It is not at all clear why people have gathered in Hornitos to decorate and festoon their buildings in the traditional trappings of Memorial Day or the Fourth of July. American flags and red, white, and blue bunting adorn the town for some reason, but we never learn what it is. Therefore the carnival, and the horse and camel race into which Steve Judd rides, seem divorced from a specific historical moment, severed from any significant social context. No wonder the town treats one of the West's founding figures as if he were an intruder, an alien presence. Thinking the cheering townspeople have perhaps come to honor him, Steve pauses on his horse, poised at the center of the film frame between patriotic rolls of bunting, to smile and tip his hat in acknowledgment, the word "America" written on a sign above his head, as if to indicate his iconic significance to a grateful populace. Instead, Steve is hectored by a policeman, told that he is "in the way," and finds himself the object of angry ridicule from a crowd eager to follow the finale of what we learn is a corrupt race.

Later, it is obvious that Peckinpah depicts the hideously deformed and denatured landscape of the mining camp at Coarsegold as an Eliotic waste land. It is less obvious that he intends much the same thing with the more conventional and refined town of Hornitos. As Paul Seydor points out, however, their relationship is symbiotic: each feeds the other, and both serve the money machine (1997, 54). Nothing seems real or connected with a living tradition in Hornitos. Nor is there anything "carnivalesque" about the midway shooting gallery where somberly-dressed Steve Judd encounters his old friend, Gil Westrum, decked out like Buffalo Bill in fringed buckskins and a fake red wig and calling himself "The Oregon Kid," tamer of the feared "Omaha Gang," even though both are completely fictional. "Carnivalesque" is Mikhail Bakhtin's term for the festive, perhaps sacred time when "life is subject only to its own laws, that is, the laws of our freedom. It has a universal spirit; it is a special condition of the entire world, of the world's revival and renewal, in which all take part. Such is the essence of carnival, vividness felt by all its participants" (7). Vividness hardly rules the midway. Westrum cheats his customers, and his young compatriot Heck Longtree races a camel against a group of horses he knows cannot win at that distance. An angry mother harshly pulls her two young sons away from the exotic dancers by grabbing their ears. The "revival and renewal" evoked by Bakhtin, a celebration allowing for the temporary "return of Saturn's golden age upon earth" (7–8), is nowhere to be seen in Hornitos.

The season is autumn, and traditionally in small towns around America and Europe this is the time of year for fairs and festivals honoring the harvest. Richard B. Sewall, following the suggestive theories of the Cambridge anthropologists, argues that tragedy itself may have been born out of such events as "the dance of mourning in the fall festival at the death of the old year or (as some think) the ritual sacrifice of propitiation," for such religious ritual "was in itself an action, a response to a condition, a kind of answer to the question of existence. It was an answer in terms of gesture and action rather than language, and represents, perhaps, man's first attempt to deal creatively with pain and fear" (5–6). But in Hornitos we see no evidence of the earth's cornucopic riches, no sign that such a denatured town connects in any way with the fertile land which surrounds it. Hornitos serves as Peckinpah's representative modern godless city — mercenary, meretricious, and severed from its vital past; noisy, crude, and corrupt, its raucous automobiles and newfangled bicycles harbingers of the even more mechanized age to follow, an age to which Steve Judd, in the autumn of his life, does not belong.

Steve has come to town to negotiate a job transporting gold from Coarsegold, a mining camp on the crest of the Sierras, to the bank in Hornitos. Too old to hold down a regular marshal's job and fallen on impecunious, threadbare times, Steve hopes to win back some of his former self-respect by performing his duties with integrity and professionalism. His meeting with the bankers, a father and son named Samson, is comical in many ways, as the elderly Samsons (who seem to be much the same age, equally balding and effete) tell Steve they expected a younger man and that the gold to be transported will not be worth the $250,000 they have mentioned in a letter but something like $20,000. (Indeed, the gold turns out to be worth closer to $11,000.) Nonetheless, Steve handles the potentially humiliating situation with firmness and even grace. His clothes tattered, his age showing, his reputation as a lawman a vague memory (if not forgotten entirely), Steve is motivated to overcome the Samsons' doubts and his disappointment at the diminished assignment because he has been reduced for years to working as a bartender or bouncer. For him, the proposed job is not altogether unlike his former efforts as a lawman. The strength of character Steve shows with the Samsons reinforces the impression of the Hornitos scenes that Steve is an exceptional figure whose values contrast more or less absolutely with everything and everyone in Hornitos.

This contrast includes Gil Westrum, Steve's former deputy and longtime friend. Steve hires Gil and Heck Longtree, Gil's partner in carnival con games, to assist him in the task of bringing gold from Coarsegold to Hornitos. It is soon clear that Gil and Heck intend to win Steve over to their plan to steal the gold or to kill him if he refuses to join them. As others have noted, Gil Westrum functions as a Mephistophelean figure to tempt Steve Judd away from his ethical commitment to honor his contract with the bank. Gil wears suitably — and comically — Satanic red long-johns and remarks to Heck that even if "the Lord's bounty is not for sale, the devil's is." The first time he encounters Steve in the film, Gil, looking like a grotesquely comic version of buffalo-slaying Bill Cody, expresses his surprise by saying, "I'll be damned!" An older man like Steve, Gil too has fallen on ragged times. But Steve refuses to compromise his principles despite his reduced situation, while Gil is only too willing to compromise all of his. Twice they journey through the Knudsen farm on their way to and from Coarsegold. In language which underscores the double nature of tragedy we want to highlight, Seydor describes this journey as "a kind of passage — moral, ecological, [and] mythical" (1997, 52). It is also a journey which leads to the film's deepest tragic revelations.

Gil Westrum's role is to tempt Steve Judd as they ride through the realistic as well as allegorically charged High Sierras. Gil assails Steve's lack of resources after so many years of loyal service in bringing law and justice to the West. He also remarks on Steve's loneliness in the absence of his one true love, a woman with the suitably pastoral name of Sarah Truesdale, who, fearing Steve's dangerous profession, rejected his proposal of marriage years ago when he refused to abandon the law. When Gil compares Sarah's smile and general demeanor with Elsa Knudsen's, Steve, clearly affected, attempts to brush aside the comparison. But it has left its mark on the solitary old man, who has no money, no home, no spouse, no children or grandchildren, unlike Sarah Truesdale, now living on a ranch in Idaho with her husband and children. While moved by memories of Sarah, Steve also seems to intuit Gil's darker intentions. He communicates with his old companion in such a way as to make it evident he has pierced Gil's verbal and physical disguises, and that through suggestive language and parable-like actions he intends to return Gil to spiritual health.

The Knudsen farm cited above is ultimately more central than Hornitos or Coarsegold to the film's action. *Ride the High Country* is shot through with biblical language and imagery, but at the same time the film is highly critical of its most putatively religious figure, Swedish farmer Joshua Knudsen (R. G. Armstrong), the smugly self-righteous father of an innocent young daughter, Elsa. Nevertheless, the Knudsen farm looms as the film's geographical, structural, and symbolic focal point. Like the Garden of Eden, and so many other mythic visions of paradise, it lies "at the 'center of the world'" (Eliade 166) in *Ride the High Country*. The farm, ablaze with autumnal colors— the seasonal colors of tragedy in Frye's theory — is ringed by golden trees and adjoined by majestic mountains. Almost allegorically, it is situated between two contrasting locations: the foothills town of Hornitos, with its corrupt carnivals and pinched, puritanical society, and the physically devastated mountain mining camp of Coarsegold, a virtual Sodom and Gomorrah. In its purest essence, the farm, mediating between nature and society, embodies the classically American version of a pastoral Eden which Leo Marx defines as "a mythic idea, an all-encompassing vision that converts the ethic of the middle link into the 'true and only' philosophy for Americans" (112).

But the Knudsen farm is not what it seems to be from a distance. It first appears up close as grim and foreboding, photographed from deep within a dark and dirty barn in which Elsa Knudsen, figuratively buried alive and dressed like a man, gendered as a woman, bends and toils over mounds of filthy hay. Her father, gloomy and Plutonic, jealously harbors repressed incestuous desires for his daughter. Knudsen's wife is named Hester, a name which is surely no accident, though Peckinpah has said he was less conscious of the Hawthornian connection than that of the rather strained biblical connection to the book of Esther (Seydor 1997, 51). Five years ago Hester was driven from the farm by her sin-crazed, sex-obsessed husband's rigid, authoritarian ways. Whether she entered the harlot's trade, as her husband's inscription on her grave indicates, or whether her escape from the farm has been perversely interpreted in that manner by her husband, we cannot tell. We do know that a similarly grim fate awaits Hester's daughter, who, though independent and strong-willed, cannot save herself alone. She needs help, and only Steve Judd, a surrogate father-figure, will be willing to give it to her. In a series of intricate symbolic dissolves, Peckinpah makes it clear that Elsa's hope for a new life, and the concomitant restoration of natural and human harmony to the Knudsen farm, rest with the salvific figure of Steve Judd.

Critics conditioned to discuss Peckinpah's films as the works of an insidiously ironic, angry, and apocalyptic iconoclast may miss the manner in which *Ride the High Country*, though suffused with its creator's inveterate sense of irony, paradox, and self-awareness, affirms at the same time basic Christian values. This paradox within a paradox should become apparent in the following close analysis of two key scenes in *Ride the High Country*, scenes which anticipate the extraordinarily inventive montage sequences of Peckinpah's later, more technically innovative films.

On the night before the Judd party leaves the Knudsen farm during its first visit there, Joshua Knudsen quarrels bitterly with his daughter Elsa over Heck Longtree's amorous attentions toward her. Knudsen catches the two of them taking in the night air by a hay wagon in the barnyard and angrily sends Elsa into the house. There the father, furious at Elsa for implying that he wants her all to himself, strikes her violently. Confused, Joshua goes to his knees before Elsa, begging her forgiveness, then retreats to his own bedroom. Angry and rebellious, her hands covering her face, Elsa sinks to her knees on the floor, vowing that this is the last time her father will ever hit her. Next follows a remarkable dissolve, in which technically "two images blend in such a way that their union constitutes a symbolic equation" (Dick 61): the stricken figure of Elsa slowly fuses with and is briefly juxtaposed over a shot of her mother's grave. Then, in a moment of Poe-like terror, Elsa sinks, literally dissolves, and finally disappears into that same grave, its daunting wooden cross inscribed, as was traditional in ancient crucifixions, with her father's biblical injunction against his "fallen" wife: "Wherefore, O Harlot, hear the word of the Lord. I will judge thee as women that break the wedlock and shed blood are judged. I will give thee blood in fury and in jealousy." Ultimately, Joshua Knudsen will pay for destroying Hester in the very "blood in fury" to which he has sentenced her. For now the camera indicates his bloody complicity in that death when it slowly dollies back and simultaneously pans, left to right, to reveal the cause of Hester Knudsen's early death: the kneeling figure of Joshua, hands tensely clasped and seeming to form a large fist, silently praying, eyes closed, beside his wife's grave.

These tightly framed, weakly lit images, static in their depiction of a blindly fixed and obdurate soul, suggest not the prayer of forgiveness or trust in divine mercy, but rather the "fury" of judgment and retribution. For this is the twisted misreading of Old Testament patriarchal law favored by a so-called Christian, but decidedly uncharitable, father. Joshua Knudsen is a latter-day Roger Chillingworth who has sentenced *his* Hester to eternal damnation. The scene horrifies because it foreshadows Elsa's fate. On account of the father's cruel actions, driving both mother and daughter away from what is no longer a "home," Elsa may be doomed to repeat the apparent "sins" of Hester Knudsen. This cinematographical burial scene can also be linked to the Elsa we first encounter *buried*, entombed deep inside her father's barn.

In his 1955 essay "The Garden of Eden and the Deacon's Meadow," Perry Miller argues that for American artists and writers of the early nineteenth century, "the biblical vision out of which these particular examples come was so predominantly, almost exclusively confined to the Old Testament" that "[t]here are hundreds of Edens, Josephs, Elijahs for every rare Crucifixion or still more rare re-creation of the Manger, while Madonnas are, of course, nonexistent" (113–14). Joshua Knudsen, named after one of the great warrior generals of the Old Testament, fits Miller's description perfectly. His wilderness pioneer's sense of the world derives almost exclusively from his perversely narrow readings of the Old Testament, which he quotes liberally while virtually ignoring the New Testament. Steve Judd draws generously from both books of the Bible, although his spiritual credo derives from the New Testament, specifically Christ's parable of the Pharisee and the tax collector (Luke 18: 9–14). (Seydor provides an excellent discussion of this parable and its application to *Ride the High Country* [1997, 47].) Paraphrasing a passage from Luke 18: 14 and reflecting a favorite quotation of Peckinpah's father, Steve says, in opposition to Gil Westrum's materialism, "All I want is to enter my house justified." Scripturally, "justified" means "accepted by God," or "right with God" (May and Metzger 1272). The heavenly "house" Steve enters when he dies at the end of the film is presided over by a high mountain, traditionally associated with the spiritual world.

If the brutal confrontation in the Knudsen house and the image of the praying father's face offer virtually no hope, Peckinpah provides a second dissolve, which completes the montage, to radically oppose the preceding sense of enclosure, terminus, and death. As the figure of Joshua Knudsen begins to vanish, the screen fades into a closeup of two feet, Steve Judd's as we come to learn, soaking in a rapidly moving clear mountain stream. Peckinpah prepares for this transition in the previous graveyard shot by moving the Judd party, in deep space left to right, through a sunlit avenue of trees, out beyond the praying Knudsen. As they cross the film frame, they pass by the ranch's windmill and trough and seem to emerge in the distance from the crude wooden cross, seen in closeup, above Hester's grave. This draws the viewer's eye into the following dissolve, prepares him or her for the cinematic transition which occurs, and adumbrates, as we shall see, the theme of life coming out of death which is key to this entire sequence and to *Ride the High Country* as a whole.

In a moment of ironic daring typical of Peckinpah, the former scene, so sanctimoniously reverential in the apparent image of the grieving husband praying beside his wife's grave, represents at bottom a perverse adherence to the fundamentalist letter of biblical law. But why then in the subsequent shot does the camera focus in closeup (from a medium high angle) upon those soaking feet? On a story level, Peckinpah obviously intends his audience to respond to the naked humanity of his aging hero, Steve Judd, who welcomes such casual comforts as cooling his trail-sore feet in a mountain stream. But on a discursive level, and as part of an intricate montage sequence, those feet will come to symbolize a larger, potentially tragic action, more specifically the Christian "mimesis of sacrifice" (Frye 1957, 214) at work in the film.

As the camera dollies outward and pans slightly to the right (a camera movement parallel to Knudsen at his wife's graveside), it reveals the entire figure of Steve Judd, gazing at his feet in the flowing water and obviously enjoying the sensation. This is one of several important moments in the film where the man of law, Steve Judd, also expresses an abiding attachment to the western landscape. It is also one of those moments in which the tragic man and the tragic land are seen in relation to each other. The director then cuts to something — and someone — quite different, a smirking young man, Heck Longtree, fully clad and sitting on the bank beside the sliding stream. Steve looks over and remarks, "In about thirty years you'll like the feel of it, too!" Heck is sizing Steve up, preparing for the moment he and Gil Westrum will strike, seizing the gold from the seemingly helpless older man. Heck interprets Steve's actions as signs of weakness. He then pulls a sandwich from his saddle bag, unwraps it, and tosses the wrapper away. "Pick that up," commands Steve, "these mountains don't need your trash!" Once again the film emphasizes that Steve Judd's ethical and spiritual being is allied with his veneration for nature. At a literal level the stream interlude, written and filmed unobtrusively so as not to draw attention to its symbolic artifice, unfolds as a serio-comic moment along the trail, articulating certain differences in values between Steve Judd and Heck Longtree. But a more complicated interpretation arises from this scene of instruction when the sage older man attempts, indirectly, to impart knowledge and wisdom to a reluctant young disciple. Foolishly, Heck refuses to comprehend Steve's actions and words. Bearing in mind that this moment cinematically mirrors Joshua Knudsen's grim vigil at his wife's grave, Joshua's spiritual blindness and Heck's related failure to see what Steve is teaching him directly complement each other.

Reading more deeply into this crucial moment, it becomes apparent that the lesson bears a close resemblance to a pivotal scene in the New Testament Gospel according to John, the scene in which a humble Christ startles his disciples by endeavoring to wash their feet (John 13). Michael Bliss suggests as much when he relates Steve's foot-washing to a "pleasurable self-baptism" (1993, 47). Thus a seemingly mundane event expands into biblical meaning through the conversion of lush foothill terrain into a moral and religious landscape. In Breughelesque fashion, the trees of Eden and the Jordan River suddenly manifest themselves in the indigenous California mountains. This form of symbolically charged realism produces what Leo Braudy describes, in reference to several contemporary Roman Catholic directors, as a kind of "incantatory moment, a mode of suprarealistic perception that I would like to call a sacramentalizing of the real, not so that it be worshipped but so that its spiritual essence ... inflect[s] what is otherwise a discrete collection of objects in space" (18). This "sacramentalizing of the real" is what Peckinpah intends in an iconographically rich montage sequence, foreshadowed the night before at the Knudsen dinner table when Steve Judd and Joshua Knudsen engage in a contest of dueling biblical quotations.

The New Testament passage to which we refer tells us that "when Jesus knew that his hour was come that he should depart out of this world unto the Father, having loved his own which were in the world, he loved them unto the end" (John 13: 1). In a related manner Steve knows, and has probably suspected from the beginning, that Gil and Heck intend to betray him. Imitating Jesus with his disciples, Steve never completely loses faith in Gil and Heck. In John the most sincere but prosaic of Christ's disciples, Simon Peter, cannot understand why Christ should commit such a humble and self-abasing act as washing the feet of his followers. Ever impetuous and headstrong, Peter misunderstands as usual and interprets Jesus' actions on a superficial level. Christ replies, in language which echoes Steve's advice to Heck, "What I do thou knowest not now; but thou shalt know hereafter" (John 13: 7). In time Peter will comprehend, and so too will Heck Longtree, significantly by another waterside, a mountain lake where he is forced to choose allegiances between Gil and Steve. In the gospel Peter goes so far as to tell Christ that his hands and head also require washing. He is baffled when Jesus replies, "He that is washed needeth not save to wash *his* feet, but is clean every whit: and ye are clean, but not all" (John 13: 10). This may explain why Peckinpah frames a closeup of Steve Judd's feet in the water for the initial shot of this conclusion to the montage. Those talismanic feet give the lie to the hypocritical picture of Joshua Knudsen's praying hands. Like Heck Longtree and Gil Westrum, Knudsen is unclean in his spiritual being, unwilling to allow the Bible's genuine message of faith and forgiveness to wash over him.

Steve Judd must, of course, gather at his own river and cleanse his own feet, for no one joins him in the sacred western stream, though he intends through his homely example to "cleanse" the spirit of young Heck Longtree. But Heck has, unwittingly, chosen another biblical path, and as Gil Westrum's corrupt companion, he ignores Steve's exhortations. We have already seen the manner in which Peckinpah depicts the smooth-talking seducer Gil as the devil incarnate. If that is so, then Heck Longtree, the youthful betrayer, fulfills the role of young Judas, reflecting similar events from the book of John. This is probably why Peckinpah depicts Heck in the act of eating, for John locates the story of Christ's betrayal in the Last Supper, just prior to the Feast of the Passover, "the devil having now put into the heart of Judas Iscariot, Simon's *son*, to betray him" (John 13: 2).

As noted above, the stream carries baptismal implications as well, if Heck would allow himself to enter its revivifying waters and be cleansed/saved. This should surprise no one familiar with the life and films of Sam Peckinpah, Westerner and inveterate hydrophile, who invariably "found baptisms where he could, in tacky hotel showers, in the free flow of wine and tequila, in momentarily Thoreauvian ponds [and streams, one might add], and always in the blood of his much fallen and fragmented heroes" (Murphy 1985, 74). Water runs through all of Peckinpah's films, and its presence is always noteworthy.[5] When, for instance, Elsa Knudsen first observes the Judd party riding through the trees toward her father's farm, dominating the foreground of the film frame stands a horse trough, symbolically analogous to the windmill and trough noted earlier in the graveyard scene. Peckinpah uses this homely domestic association to link Elsa and Steve through the practical and unobtrusive watering trough. The relationship between mutable water and renewed life for this young girl imprisoned beneath her father's stifling control alerts us to her potential rescue by Steve Judd. We would add that the stream in which Steve bathes his feet is also an ambivalent symbol, exemplifying both the Christian and historical versions of tragedy employed by Peckinpah in *Ride the High Country*. On the one hand the flowing water "signifies fertility and the progressive irrigation of the soil; and on the other hand it stands for the irreversible passage of time and, in consequence, for a sense of loss and oblivion" (Cirlot 274). Thus, in addition to its baptismal implications, the stream also indicates the tragic movement of time, the Heraclitean flux which leads ultimately to death. Both Steve Judd and the West he cherishes are doomed unless some miraculous transformation takes place, a transformation for which Peckinpah holds little hope.

Water figures in other scenes in which Steve Judd is not present. The first strains of genuine feeling between Elsa and Heck occur the first evening after dinner when Heck, standing outside the kitchen window, offers to dry the dishes Elsa has been washing. Here Heck, though only temporarily, seems less the aggressive Lothario than an attentive, affectionate young man. Similarly, when Heck and Elsa first exchange a tender kiss up in the high mountains, the kiss takes place beside a cerulean blue lake. Here, once again, Heck's sexual demons seize him and he attempts to force Elsa down to the ground. Thus it is little wonder that the crudest member of the odious Hammond brothers, Henry (Warren Oates), whose character failings—as well as first name—parallel Heck's, refuses to bathe before his brother Billy's wedding to Elsa.

Baptism in the Christian church symbolizes a spiritual cleansing, the remission of sins and the promise of eternal life through Christ. Its meaning centers on death and death overcome. In that sense it parallels the sacrament of Holy Communion. Kathleen Murphy suggests the connection between these two most important Christian rituals in her comparison of baptismal water to the sacrificial blood of Peckinpah's heroes. It is not by chance that Steve Judd dries his feet with a blood/wine-red, though slightly faded, western bandanna, thus linking Baptism and Holy Communion.[6] As the Johannine exegete in the *Harper's Bible Commentary* writes, "many interpreters believe that John deliberately replaced the Lord's [Last] Supper with his distinctive portrayal of Jesus's washing the disciples' feet," since "the words of the [Eucharistic] institution interpret Jesus's death, just as the foot washing does" (Mays 1066). Heck Longtree, a Judas figure and devil's disciple, affirms only the value of money and the sensual pleasures of the body. His is a material soul, given over to his appetites and wholly resistant to the spiritual blandishments of Steve Judd. Baptism and Holy Communion thus act as two related sacraments promising redemption and new life. Heck cannot understand this, and instead prefers to litter the venerable high-country mountains with unclean "trash," a word which once again links him to the "white-trash" Hammond brothers.

Heck's crude act of mastication, a clutter of crumbs strewing his shirt front, parallels the Johannine text. In John 13: 18, after he has bathed the disciples' feet, Christ figuratively conflates the foot-washing with the eating of bread, saying, "He that eateth bread with me hath lifted up his heel against me." Not knowing of whom Jesus speaks, the disciples ask him to name his betrayer, and Jesus replies, "He it is, to whom I shall give a sop [morsel] when I have dipped *it*." John continues: "And when he had dipped the sop, he gave *it* to Judas Iscariot, *the son* of Simon" (John 13: 26). Then, after Judas eats the morsel, Satan enters him, "so that the Eucharistic bread appears in the demonic inversion [paralleling the same sacred/profane inversion in the Knudsen-praying/Steve Judd–washing scenes], and Satan, the Opponent/ Helper, is incorporated into the human agent" (Kermode 1979, 92). Life becomes death, salvation damnation, through Judas/Heck's violation of the sacraments.

At this point Peckinpah again joins the theme of the tragic betrayal of the human spirit to the tragic abuse of the land, and particularly America's self-betrayal as a nation. Returning to the streamside, Gil Westrum pauses to lift one of Steve's boots, within the sole of which he finds a gaping hole. Unaware that he too, like Heck, is enacting a greater biblical drama, Gil ironically mimics John the Baptist. Responding to the Pharisees when they question his authority to baptize, John, who has not yet encountered Christ, responds, "He it is, who coming after me is preferred before me, whose shoe's latchet [sandal] I am not worthy to unloose" (John 1: 27). Gil, of course, sees only the literal boot (confusing sole with soul), which enables him to comment sardonically on the historical theme of contemporary society's ingratitude toward those who have suffered and sacrificed to settle the West.

Thinking of footwear, Gil invokes the memory of a mutual acquaintance of theirs, "old Doc Franklin," who wore fancy-toed boots he ordered from Boston. Now dead and forgotten, Doc, who "gave 30 years of his life to make the West safe for decent people," could attract only three people to his funeral, says Gil: "The mortician, the gravedigger, and me." Historically self-conscious, *Ride the High Country* is filled with references to a forgotten or fallen America. The film begins with the travesty of a (John) Fordian patriotic celebration which culminates in a rigged horse and camel race which mocks an authentic hero, Steve Judd. In a film so concerned with true and false fathers, it is possible to infer that "old Doc Franklin," like most names in the Peckinpah canon, has not been chosen randomly. Rather, it is onomastically intended to evoke one of our nation's genuinely iconic figures and founding fathers, an inventor who helped to "invent" America, Benjamin Franklin. Though not literally a medical man, Franklin was in his later years known by the honorific "Doctor." Born, as we know, in Boston, where Doc Franklin purchased his boots, Ben Franklin helped write the U.S. Constitution, was an ambassador to France, and at his death was the most famous and revered

American in the world. Gil Westrum's Doc Franklin, on the other hand, has died in obscurity, having given, like Steve Judd, "30 years of his life" to an ungrateful West.

It is difficult to ignore the multiple uses of the number three in a film so richly suffused with biblical references. Earlier, Steve tells Heck that in "about 30 years" the boy will appreciate the soothing comfort of water on his aching feet. Then, more relevantly, we learn that Doc Franklin, like Steve Judd, labored "30 years" to make the West a better place to live. Finally, Gil, who has been teaching young Heck his duplicitous trade for "better than three years," tells Steve that only "three people" attended Doc's funeral. Even those who are unfamiliar with the Bible know enough to associate the number 30 with the "30 pieces of silver" Judas was given to betray Christ, and that Christ was 30 when he began his mission. Peckinpah prepares the viewer to make this connection when, in a brilliantly ironic stroke, he has the covetous and essentially materialistic Joshua Knudsen, twisting and perverting the Bible, instruct his daughter, whom he has just struck, to "[r]eceive my instruction and not silver, knowledge rather than choice gold." And at the dinner table that night, Steve Judd, responding to Joshua's accusation that he is "trafficking" in gold, replies that he is "transporting," not "trafficking," and that, quoting the Bible himself, "A good name is rather to be chosen than great riches, a loving favor rather than silver or gold." Finally, of course, the number three is even more loaded in its biblical range of reference: to the triune nature of the Godhead, to Christ's crucifixion on Golgotha between two thieves, and to Christ's resurrection on the third day after his death. Such biblical parallels can hardly be accidental coming from a director-writer as steeped in Old and New Testament texts as Peckinpah, whose film is rife with biblical quotations and allusions.

In the same exchange about Doc Franklin, Peckinpah's irony reaches its climax as Gil, the most Cain-like of friends, employs a pastoral metaphor to entice Steve into casting off his deepest principles. Gil comments on the public's repudiation of Doc Franklin, its lack of "gratitude, the fairest flower that grows within the human heart." Throughout *Ride the High Country*, Peckinpah demonstrates that the betrayal of the human world and the violation of the natural world are one, that Steve Judd and the film's "high country" are finally the same redemptive entity, and that each is desecrated on the altar of greed and corruption, all in the contradictory name of "progress." While Steve Judd's life bears striking parallels with Doc Franklin's, Gil's story of Franklin's sad fate also fits into the secondary pattern of historical tragedy which parallels its Christian counterpart. That a country dedicated to the ideals propounded by its Founding Fathers should at the same time betray those ideals helps make *Ride the High Country* a genuinely indigenous tragedy.

The Judd group departs this Edenic oasis and resumes its journey up the mountainside to the physically brutalized — and spiritually brutalizing — mining camp of Coarsegold. Steve leads the way with Gil and Heck following. Peckinpah chooses to film their departure from behind and above in an overhead shot, employing a Chapman crane to create an arresting effect. About this important moment in the film Garner Simmons writes:

> Of the many memorable shots involving the Chapman there is one that begins at a river bank by a stand of aspen trees as Steve Judd mounts his horse and rides on ahead, leaving Heck and Gil to exchange comments on the likelihood of Steve joining them to steal the gold. As Heck and Gil mount up, the camera begins to crane some thirty feet into the air allowing us to look beyond the aspens, golden in the autumn sunlight, to where Steve is joined by his companions. Uniquely coupled with the beauty of this shot is its impact from the way it visually parallels the relationship between these three men: Steve rides ahead, alone and pointing the way, while Gil and Heck must pass over the same ground in order to reach him [45].

Simmons' language seems strikingly Bunyanesque, especially in its reference to Steve's "pointing the way," as in Christ's charge to his disciples to "Follow me." Gil and Heck, two lost pilgrims, climb a Calvary of conscience, and ultimately consciousness. With Steve, they again number a biblical trio, two thieves and a guiltless man. Add to this the spectator's visual sensation, through the use of the ascending crane, of rising above the spatio-temporal continuum into a God's-eye view of the events below, thus imparting a kind of omniscient perspective to the shot. Some higher force seems to stand outside and above the immediate action and guide the film's subsequent events.

In a like manner George Bassman's musical score reflects the contest between earthly—or material—wills and a divine—or numinal—perspective. Initially, as the crane begins its ascent, the music becomes brooding and sinister; Gil and Heck ride behind Steve, and we already know they intend to do him harm if he refuses to help them steal the gold. But as the camera boom concludes its movement above the stream, the aspens, and the three riders, its lens comes to rest upon the resplendent high mountains off in the distance. At this point the film's dominant "high country" nature theme, its only memorable musical motif, and one we associate with Steve Judd, reasserts itself, overlapping and then engulfing the previous musical motif. Here too we find a biblical parallel. On the day Christ comes to John to be baptized, the heavens open and a spirit like a dove descends upon Christ (Mark 1: 10; John 1: 27).

This scene can best be understood as a reprise of the first (credit) shot in *Ride the High Country*. There cinematographer Lucien Ballard focuses upon a remote high-country lake. Then, in a sudden and dramatic tilt, the camera thrusts vertically upward to reveal a mighty granite mountain. We would suggest that the lake (more generally, water in all its metamorphic forms) and the mountain establish an ontological bond. Like the baptismal stream which Steve Judd enters, the lake assumes archetypal significance in a film suffused with natural symbols of the earth's seasons. Primordially identified with nature's generative cycles, the lake embodies the archetypally feminine "mystery of creation; birth-death-resurrection; purification and redemption; fertility and growth" (Guerin 157). The primarily masculine mountain, rising in the sky toward the heavens, contrastingly symbolizes the religious theme of transcendence, the "idea of meditation, spiritual elevation and the communion of the blessed" (Cirlot 221). Peckinpah, famous for integrating his credit sequences into the plots of his films, dramatically links the two natural symbols, water and mountain, with which he frames this important scene, thus suggesting a form of mythic marriage between Heaven and Earth, or Eternity and Time, a marriage which, like *Ride the High Country* itself, is simultaneously Christian and pagan. Steve Judd, so human and yet so god-like, a man of the law and yet connected to a higher law, stands in the middle, binding all the film's waters and mountains.

Although *Ride the High Country* embodies an allegorical journey toward salvation, its vertical ascent into the primitive and corrupt waste land of the Coarsegold mining camp exposes how polluted even the sacred Sierra mountains have become. Wintry and barren, pocked and pitted, devoid of any signs of vegetative life, Coarsegold is Peckinpah's anti–Paradise, his symbol for the tragic death of nature. Gil says as much when the Judd party, now accompanied by Elsa Knudsen, arrives in the camp and laughing women throw their night's slop in Elsa's path. "Lovely place," remarks Gil. "A beauty spot of nature—a Garden of Eden for the sore in heart and the short of cash." Coarsegold's center of lovelessness and sterility is an enormous red-haired Irish madam named Kate (Jenie Jackson), who runs the town's true gold mine, "Kate's Place." Like so many of the characters and locations in *Ride the High Country*, grotesque Kate fits Frye's description of the natural "mythos of tragedy" in literature: "The sunset, autumn and death phase. Myths of fall, of the dying god, of violent death and sacrifice and of the isolation of the hero. Subordinate characters: the traitor and the siren. The archetype of tragedy and elegy" (1963, 16). In *Ride the High Country*, whether or not Peckinpah was conscious of it, every aspect of the tragic mythos unfolds schematically. The film takes place in autumn, Steve Judd is the dying hero/god, Gil and Heck are traitors, and

Kate represents Frye's Circe–like "siren," a woman capable of reducing men to debased states of bestiality. In archetypal criticism, Frye writes, "the individual and the universal forms of an image are identical" (1963, 19). This applies to Kate, who, in addition to her "siren" identity, falls under the heading of "the harlot, witch and other varieties of Jung's 'terrible mother'" (Frye 1963, 19).

The themes of love and marriage (with its implications of maternity) dominate the Coarsegold section of *Ride the High Country*. Elsa has come here to marry a miner, Billy Hammond (James Drury), who works in Coarsegold with his four semi-savage brothers. Elsa's mother Hester may have lived and died in a terminal place like "Kate's." The film's tragic pattern seems to indicate that Elsa will share her mother's fate unless rescued. Her wedding march, atop a horse, to the profane "church" which is "Kate's place" resembles an ancient sacrificial procession rather than the restoration to fertility of a blighted land. Coarsegold is wintry and snow-streaked, whereas weddings are traditionally associated with springtime and seasonal renewal. In Frye's scheme spring is associated with romance, but Elsa rides off to her own funeral, as suggested by the processional song the Hammonds sing, "When the Roll Is Called Up Yonder."[7] Dressed (ominously enough) in her mother's white wedding gown, a garland of flowers wreathing her head, a meager bouquet in her hands, Elsa participates in a ritual as devoid of spiritual dimension as the mysterious patriotic "celebration" in Hornitos.

Elsa's engagement to Billy Hammond suggests how desperate she is to escape from her father. Her wedding descends from the vulgar details just mentioned to the attempted rape of the new bride by all four of Billy's brothers, who obviously take Elsa to be a family prize. With help from Heck, Steve manages to rescue Elsa from the Hammonds, but only after the marriage ceremony has been performed. The Hammonds are therefore able to pursue Billy's claim on Elsa with the only certified "law" in Coarsegold, a miners' court. Steve has often been criticized for accepting the jurisdiction of the court and presumably its verdict, while Gil has been praised for intervening with Judge Tolliver (Edgar Buchanan) to insure a legally doubtful but just verdict which allows Elsa to leave with Steve, Gil, and Heck. We think it is wrong to assume that Steve would have left Elsa with her legal husband, however, regardless of the miners' verdict. To have done this, Steve would have to have been as inflexible and legalistic as Joshua Knudsen, precisely what his critics allege but the film everywhere denies. Earlier, when relativistic Gil assails Steve for adhering to a rigid conception of the law, an "ironbound code of ethics," Steve responds that his "code satisfies pretty easy, partner," then tells of his own youthful lawlessness, a parable aimed at convincing Gil not to steal the gold and destroy their friendship. Thus, when Steve refers to his boyhood self as "slicker 'n a snake and twice as mean," we know that the real referent of his tale is Gil, the slippery-tongued seducer (and perhaps "that boy," Heck Longtree). Steve was rescued by Marshal Paul Standiford, who was right, Steve says, even as Steve was wrong. This modest wisdom is repeated when Steve later acknowledges to Elsa that, contrary to her father's simplistic belief that "there is only right and wrong, good and evil," moral judgments are far more complicated than this would imply. "It's not that simple, is it?" Elsa asks Steve. "No, it isn't," he replies. "It should be, but it isn't."

Each of us would like to experience a reduction of life's endless ambiguities and occupy a privileged position above the struggle from which we can gaze down on human folly. But Peckinpah's tragic vision refuses to allow such a self-assured point of view, even for himself. He subjects his characters, and himself, to ruthless scrutiny. Thus, when critics such as Colin McArthur, Jim Kitses, Neil Fulwood, and Terence Butler argue that Steve is Knudsen-like because of his "inflexible belief in the value of right and wrong" (Butler 40), they ignore the Christian element in Steve's nature, specifically his acceptance of humankind's fallen condition, the capacity for sin in all of us. Christ came to overcome the harsh strictures of the

Mosaic Law; he came not to destroy Hebraic law, but to "fulfill" it on a higher, transcendent plane (Matthew 5: 18). Therefore, Seydor is almost certainly correct when he suggests that Steve's "agreement to abide by the [miners'] court is provisional, predicated less upon any inflexible devotion to legality at the expense of justice than upon a willingness to exhaust every possible alternative to violence" (1997, 54). Indeed, as Seydor says, it is Gil who, in one of Peckinpah's most telling inversions, acts out of an "ironbound" relativism and "becomes almost brutally inflexible" (1997, 55). Like the Satan-figure in a medieval morality play, Gil plays the already inscribed role of "tempter-devil-whore [like Kate, he substitutes gold for friendship, or love]" (1997, 56), wholly resistant to Steve's attempts to prevent him from destroying himself, and their friendship, through the theft of the gold.

It is therefore no surprise that Gil and Heck attempt unsuccessfully to steal the bank's gold on their first night away from Coarsegold. This precipitates a double death in the film, of the friendship between Steve and Gil, and of nature itself. Suddenly, the beautiful Sierras are transformed, through a cinematic use of the pathetic fallacy, into an extension of the waste land imagery we saw in Coarsegold. Dry, cold mountain winds blow up obscuring clouds of thick dust; grays and browns predominate over greens and blues as nature responds to a profound rift in a human relationship by mirroring that split. Frye's vision of the mineral world in its tragic phase directly parallels Peckinpah's. Frye describes a landscape of "deserts, rocks and ruins, or of sinister geometrical images like the cross" (1963, 20), all present, in various forms, in subsequent scenes of *Ride the High Country*. The spring and summer worlds which love and friendship make possible in Frye's literary and mythic cosmogony now dissolve into the pervasive imagery of chaos and doom.

The following night, as the party prepares to bed down beside a still mountain lake, a Poe-like tarn with its stripped and fallen trees and its haunting bird cries, Gil pleads with Steve to untie the straps which now bind his hands. Steve complies and Gil proceeds to run off into the night, in search of the horse and six-gun of the slain Silvus Hammond (L. Q. Jones), who has been killed by Heck when the Hammond brothers attack the Judd party after it leaves Coarsegold. Water again figures prominently in an adequate reading of this scene. The mottled lake contrasts markedly with the bright and lively stream beside which Steve Judd lectured Heck Longtree on "these mountains," as well as the shining blue body of water beside which the Judd party was intercepted by Elsa on her trek to Coarsegold to marry Billy Hammond. A death-like calm pervades this place of betrayal. The site provides another visually complex montage, first Gil preparing to bed down between two dark and portentous pine trees, then Steve standing, center-frame, between two dead naked pines when he learns the following morning of Gil's flight. As Frye points out, "sinister geometrical images like the cross," as well as imagery of the dense forest, "a heath or wilderness, or a tree of death," are common features of the tragic *mise-en-scéne* (1963, 20). It may be obvious why the doomed tragic figure, Steve Judd, should be poised, Christ-like, between two denuded poles in the water, for his symbolic crucifixion has been prepared for from the beginning of the film. But Peckinpah also films Gil between two live pines. Of course, the irony is that Gil is no Christ, for his soul is moribund and the living trees comment on his spiritual deadness. Steve, on the other hand, exemplifies a life of faith in others despite Gil's treachery, and that faith is rewarded in Heck's belated turn toward Steve and Elsa after he gets the drop on the old man, then has second thoughts and gives him his gun. Still, something in nature dies when Gil turns on his friend, though something else offers hope for renewal. The sequence insists upon its ambiguities. The "trees" of Golgotha between which Steve stands and the living trees of resurrection and renewal between which Gil beds down promise rebirth or renewal for the fallen friend, but only through the ultimately sacrificial death of Steve Judd.

This scene beside a spooky mountain lake prepares us for the climactic events which

Heck Longtree (Ron Starr) gets the drop on Steve Judd (Joel McCrea) beside a gloomy mountain lake in *Ride the High Country*, as Elsa Knudsen (Mariette Hartley) gazes on. Out of love for Elsa and respect for Judd he soon gives his gun up to the old marshal.

occur at the Knudsen farm at the end of *Ride the High Country.* That Peckinpah chooses to return to this geographical and structural center, the Axis Mundi of the film, indicates once again its importance. The farm, so deceptively pristine and pastoral, has never been what it should be. This is especially so now, for the surviving Hammonds have reached the farm before Steve, Heck, and Elsa. The Hammonds have already slain Joshua Knudsen and propped him up on a fence beside his dead wife Hester's grave in a mocking mimicry of prayer. From a distance, his limited eyesight failing him, Steve signals Heck and Elsa to ride in because he thinks the ranch is safe. When Elsa remarks that her father never prays by his wife's gravesite in the afternoon, Steve realizes something is wrong and they race for a ditch in a hail of Hammond gunfire. Peckinpah depicts this scene so as to project a maximum sense of disorder and disequilibrium. Amidst the gunfire, he trains his camera, in medium closeup, on the nervous, herky-jerky movements of the farm's chickens as they wander randomly looking for food around the fence where open-eyed Joshua Knudsen is propped. In addition, Peckinpah directs our attention to Henry Hammond's jet-black pet raven, a Poe-esque carrion-eating and eye-plucking symbol of death which adds to the troubling air of menace as it pecks violently at the chickens.

The superficially calm Knudsen farm has always been a "lawless wilderness" (Seydor 1997, 59), for both Joshua and the Hammonds are sources of a radically anti-pastoral disharmony and perversion. This opens the way to tragic experience, for as Joyce Carol Oates has written, tragedy thrives on the shock value of "making ... domestic landscapes into wilderness," as "passion breaks its dikes and flows out into nature" (8). In *Ride the High Country* the themes of lawlessness and the tragic wilderness anticipate a more radical, less realistic redefinition of the film's spatio-temporal universe, its movement onto another plane. This begins with Gil Westrum's one-man cavalry charge toward the ranch after he sees the Hammonds open fire on Steve and the two young people. This kind of action, witnessed countless times by Western filmgoers over the years, initiates a high degree of self-consciousness about Westerns, especially when we consider how closely the careers of Joel McCrea and Randolph Scott were identified with the genre. It also prepares for the resacralization of the farm within the literary and mythical contexts of the pastoral mode.

Both the Hornitos and Coarsegold sections of *Ride the High Country* feature forms of rituals gone wrong, demythologized, crudely secularized, devoid of both historical and national memory, deprived of a genuine contact with a living past or a sustaining body of beliefs. They lack, in short, any vestige of the religious or mythic imagination. Both Gil's familiar ride and the final, highly stylized/ritualized showdown between Steve and Gil and the Hammonds partake of forms derived from the legendary past of the West, a West in which Steve and Gil actually participated. Friends once again, they are rejuvenated, reconnected with their shared memories by the experience of fighting against a common evil, the way it "used to be." They meet the Hammonds "head on, just like always," as Steve says. We have seen these rides and classic Hollywood face-offs so many times that the accumulated body of meanings they carry establishes continuity with a living tradition, the partly historical, partly mythical West as well as its corollary, the cinematic West. This archetypal "journey into the past" (Seydor 1997, 59) enacted by Steve and Gil provides an entrance into the ultimately religious experience with which the film concludes.

Lying in a ditch, two old friends now reunited, Steve Judd (Joel McCrea) and Gil Westrum (Randolph Scott), prepare to defend the Knudsen farm in *Ride the High Country*, while the young couple, Elsa Knudsen (Mariette Hartley) and the wounded Heck Longtree (Ron Starr) wait nearby.

As Mircea Eliade writes, the past can become the present in special circumstances because, unlike the irreversible temporal process of classical tragedy, "*by its very nature sacred time is reversible.*" Both in the founding of the old West and in its filmic tradition, we witness a "*primordial mythical time made present.*" This new conception of time as mythical "represents the reactualization of a sacred event that took place in the mythical past, 'in the beginning'" (68–69). Through the revitalizing process of ritual, one passes from the sheer temporality and literalness of a carnal or profane world to a spiritual and symbolic understanding of time, experienced as infinite possibility (cf. Kermode 1979, 1–21). For the religious person, as for Steve and the revitalized Gil, "neither space nor *time* is ordinary. There are times as well as places set apart for festivals and holidays that break the unvarying and meaningless time of ordinary temporal duration" (Livingstone 63). At the end of *Ride the High Country,* the Knudsen farm opens itself up to deeper spiritual meaning and ultimately becomes a sacred "place."

In devising this effect Peckinpah may have drawn on another "sacred" place in a film he no doubt saw only a year before he began shooting *Ride the High Country.* David Weddle reports that in the 1950s and 1960s Sam and Marie, his first wife, "went to see all the new foreign films; [Sam] drank them in voraciously" (1994, 106). Doubtless he saw Ingmar Bergman's acclaimed *The Virgin Spring* (1959), which won the Academy Award for Best Foreign Film in 1960. Bergman, "that bad Swede who keeps laying down those great films" (Peckinpah as quoted in Macklin 152), was one of Peckinpah's favorite filmmakers, and *The Virgin Spring* bears many striking similarities to *Ride the High Country.* It deals with the brutal rape and murder of an innocent young girl by two shepherds, while Peckinpah's film explores the possible multiple rape and degradation of the equally innocent Elsa Knudsen, a Swedish-American girl/woman. Each film highlights symbolic natural imagery, and each features the closeup of a menacing raven. Finally, the struggle in the Knudsen barnyard, within the shadow of a towering tree, culminates in the sublime surrender to death embodied in Steve Judd's act of tragic sacrifice. This recalls Bergman's depiction of a trickling spring which begins to flow miraculously from beneath the head of the dead girl (Birgitta Pettersson) in a forest glade where the grieving father (Max von Sydow) discovers her body beside a rushing stream. The divine appearance of this "virgin" spring is not matched in Peckinpah's more naturalistic, less allegorical conclusion, but we should remember the windmill and watering trough, and earlier the beautiful mountain stream which is the site for the potentially violent encounter between Steve and Gil and Heck, and also the story in the Book of John in which holy water mixed with blood flows miraculously from Christ's side as it is penetrated by the centurion's sword, a biblical episode we will discuss momentarily. As in Bergman's great film, Peckinpah's aqueous images all participate in the sacralizing transformation which underscores the spiritual dimension of Steve's final passage to death.

Ride the High Country's most celebrated moment, which represents a completion and culmination of the scene beside the mountain stream, centers on the emotionally charged and cathartic death of the old marshal, Steve Judd, at film's end. Here, having been reconciled to his friend Gil Westrum, and assured of the safety of Heck and Elsa, Steve at last, to use his own chosen biblical term, enters his earthly and heavenly house "justified." Steve dies to rise, falling down below the film frame to enter the seasons of the earth, yet leaving a towering mountain, traditional symbol of spiritual transcendence, in his place. Entwined with the Christian themes of death and resurrection, but also a more temporal and elegiac "sense of loss, [the] feeling that an era has ended" (Skerry 14), this moment climaxes the double vision of tragedy in *Ride the High Country.* It is therefore possible to experience *both* a permanent sense of loss and the spiritual ascendance of Steve Judd, enduring beyond the grave. Depending on one's own religious predilections, *Ride the High Country* ends with either the paradoxical, and overtly Christian, triumph of life emerging out of death, or the tragic finality of death alone, and with it the imminent vanishing of the old West. We would suggest that Peckinpah, inveterately ambiguous, wants us to experience both emotions. We should recall that Peckinpah described his film as about "salvation and loneliness," terms which equate perfectly with its Christian and historical views of tragedy.

Gil Westrum has already begun his regenerative process when, after deserting the Judd party the night before, he comes charging into the Knudsen farm in order to save Steve and the two young people from the Hammonds. For Steve, this process begins (and perhaps ends) with one of the most memorable deaths in Western films. In the printed script we learn that Steve, in attempting to rescue the gunshot Heck, is wounded, "much more seriously, in his side," having been "nailed ... good" by Elder Hammond (John Anderson) (104). Both details seem crucial to us because of their close relationship to the story of Christ's crucifixion. The crucifixional reference to "nailing" Steve Judd is obvious. Less apparent is the idea that Steve is shot in the side, and that in the ensuing shootout the Hammonds manage to put all their bullets "in one place," as the script indicates (109). The script describes Steve as holding onto his "midsection," but clearly in the film Peckinpah shifts Steve's mortal wound to his left side.[8]

Within the traditions of Renaissance art, Christ's redemptive wound is usually depicted as being on his right side, though the Book of John does not indicate upon which side the centurion's wound is inflicted. Since the right side is normally associated with righteousness, the left with duplicity, or something "sinister," it is interesting to speculate why the painterly Peckinpah, very likely aware of these associations and the traditions of western art, locates Steve's wound on his left side. One answer may lie in Peckinpah's own ambivalence about Steve's *human* capacity to redeem a doomed American West, the director's belief that finally nothing and no one is strong or virtuous enough to make that possible. The wound's location may be another indication of Peckinpah's growing pessimism about the West as dream or ideal, a pessimism which plunges toward much darker depths in later films such as *Major Dundee* (1965), *The Wild Bunch* (1969), and his most despairing Western, *Pat Garrett and Billy the Kid* (1973). The fault lies not with Steve Judd, but with the historically represented America which Peckinpah depicts in all his Western films. Another and quite different answer to why Peckinpah locates the fatal wound on Steve's left side is that left-sidedness came in the Renaissance and after to represent "human love, the passage of time, and the feminine" (Hall 6), qualities we associate with Steve's feelings toward the young lovers Heck and Elsa and toward his redeemed friend Gil Westrum. Nor should we forget the relatively "unknown woman," Sarah Truesdale, Steve's first and only *true* love. Thus Peckinpah seems to confirm the legitimacy of both the masculine *and* feminine sensitivities Steve Judd demonstrates throughout *Ride the High Country*. Even in the placement of Steve's wound Peckinpah engages a complex set of possibilities.

One is impelled, especially within the context of significant symbolic wounds in films such as *The Wild Bunch* and *Pat Garrett and Billy the Kid*, to read the placing of Steve's wound as an oblique reference to St. John's description of the expired Christ on the Cross. In John 19: 34, a Roman centurion, attempting to determine whether Jesus has died, "pierced his side, and forthwith came there out blood and water." In the First Epistle of John 5: 5–6, the writer describes Christ as "the Son of God" who "came by water and blood." Allegorically, John conflates Christ's death and the centurion's action with the promise of new life as envisioned in the ceremony of baptism as well as in the ritual of Holy Communion. We have earlier argued that these two rites are intertwined in the mountain-stream scene. Here at the end of *Ride the High Country* Peckinpah reprises one of the film's crucial moments. In the First Epistle of John 5: 6–8, we are told that Christ is "he that came by water and blood ... not by water only, but by water and blood. And it is the Spirit that beareth witness, because the Spirit is truth.... And there are three that bear witness in earth, the Spirit, and the water, and the blood: and these three agree in one." If we read for "Spirit" the distant mountain toward which Steve, his body transfigured by light, gazes just before he turns toward the earth to die, for "water" the barnyard windmill and watering trough which appear in the immediate distance in Steve's place as he sinks to the bottom of the frame, and for "blood" that which pours into the ground from the one central wound of humanity, it is not difficult to understand why this is a memorable death, why Seth Cagin and Philip Dray suggest that the violence in *Ride the High Country* is "pointedly cathartic and even sacred" (17).

To Cagin and Dray's tragic and religious terms, "cathartic" and "sacred," we would add "sacrificial." For Steve Judd dies not just for an idea of himself, but also for his friend, Gil Westrum, and for the future of the West as embodied in Heck and Elsa. As Gil kneels and bends almost Pietá-like over his fallen comrade, he tells Steve not to "worry about anything," that he will get the gold to the bank in Hornitos. Steve replies in language the newly-repentant Gil surely understands: "Hell, I know that. I always did. You just forgot about it for awhile, that's all." Steve always knew who the real Gil Westrum is, which is why he was so hard on him when Gil forgot. Their last words to each other, Steve's "So long, partner," Gil's "I'll see ya later," are among the most emotionally rending in this or any other film. And doubly so because when Gil says, "I'll see ya later," at some deeper religious level he means it. For as he rises from the dying Steve, who would prefer to "go it alone," behind Gil, absorbing his body at the center of the screen, stands a soaring cottonwood tree, the mid-afternoon sun dappling through its leaves and branches and illuminating Gil's body almost as if it were a medieval painting. The Tree of Death becomes the Tree of Life through the redemptive power of Steve's sacrificial surrender. While Gil glows in the late-afternoon autumn sun, Steve lies prone, as Kitses remarks, "the old man alone in the shadow of [that] great tree in the yard" (2004, 210).

As sight is such an important metaphor in *Ride the High Country* and the New Testament, the mortally wounded Steve's comment to Gil, "I don't want them to see this. I'll go it alone," hardly seems unusual. But it is sight as vision which is so metaphorically crucial (see Bliss 1993, 35–36). Earlier, in the graveyard scene, we watch Elsa disappear, in that disturbing dissolve, into her mother's grave. Now we witness Steve Judd's disappearance from the film frame, with only the rumpled ridge of his buckskin jacket — analogous perhaps to the high-country mountains with which we identify his spirit — barely rising above the bottom of the frame. For Paul Seydor, in the commentary to the 2006 DVD edition of the film, "the movie finally becomes metaphysical at the very end when Steve Judd drops down," for "his body is literally supporting the entire landscape" in an "almost Whitmanesque" moment of transcendence. We would augment Seydor's apt description by proposing that the *mystical* body and blood of Stephen Judd sacramentally bless the hallowed ground beneath the tree where he dies. Cinematically, we are witnessing a sacrificial death in which Steve Judd substitutes his body for Elsa's in the earlier graveyard montage, dying so that Elsa and the genuine West she stands for might survive. But this is only one part of the final equation in a highly charged, remarkably complex scene. As Steve speaks his last words to Gil, between them, in mid-to-deep space, stands the same romantic hay wagon in which Heck and Elsa began their courtship in earnest. In the earlier tableau Peckinpah photographs in closeup the future lovers, a fragile Adam and Eve, aureoled by the surrounding hay from the wagon. It is a ritual moment, like a scene out of rural, pastoral romance, or a painting by Constable, which culminates in the rustic hay wagon, recast as a symbol of their unity and imminent marriage, heralding once again new and fertile life emerging from the tragic but redemptive death of Steve Judd.

At the end of *Ride the High Country* Steve Judd, a martyr to the virtues and meanings of the old West, as both land and idea, dies his hero's death, and when his body touches the ground the words THE END, in gold, flash suddenly across the screen.[9] As Frank Kermode has written in *The Sense of an Ending*, "THE END" is a figure for death (7). Here that figure seems doubled, for both the hero and the film die simultaneously before us. Does this apparent finality indicate that Peckinpah wants us to experience the complete disappearance of the true Western hero at film's end? This seems unlikely, for Steve Judd's legacy both to the characters in the film and to the audience is too lasting, too *enduring*.

Finally, it would appear that for Peckinpah Steve Judd's death places the burden of the future upon those who would profit from an act of tragic sacrifice and those who would not, upon those who care about what was for Peckinpah, ever paradoxical, the *real*, as in *mythic*, West, and those who do not. We know, from our perspective in the first years of the twenty-first century, that the world Steve Judd stands for no longer exists and will never return. Steve's death incorporates "the two elements of sacrifice" Northrop Frye perceives in a tragic death: "One of these is *communion*, the dividing of a heroic or divine body among a group which brings them into unity with, and as, that body" (our emphasis). This we experience in the collective love and hope for the future which Gil, Heck, and Elsa feel toward Steve Judd. The second mode of sacrifice is "*propitiation*, the sense that in spite of the communion the body really belongs to another, a greater, and potentially wrathful power" (1957, 214; our emphasis). In *Ride the High Country*, as well as the other tragic films considered in this study, that "wrathful power" may represent the dark and indelible spirit of tragedy and its primordial Nietzschean counterpart, nature itself, as Steve gazes off toward the mountains of the high country just before he enters the sacred ground, his last vision of an earthly paradise now vanishing before his eyes, and ours. As Garner Simmons remarks in the 2006 DVD commentary on the film, "The original script calls for Steve Judd to stare off into the sunset. He doesn't. He stares off into this incredible landscape. He is part of it. This is really who he is." It would have been sentimental if Steve *had* died gazing wistfully at the sunset, but the majestic mountains, so close to the spirit of the romantic sublime, convey complex meanings which embrace both beauty and terror, grandeur and "wrath," as Frye would say.[10] *Ride the High Country* ends as it began, unwilling, unable to resolve the double vision of tragedy which the personally triumphant — and historically traumatic — disappearance of Stephen Judd so brilliantly limns.

III

We have emphasized the importance of Peckinpah's decision to have Steve Judd and not Gil Westrum die at the end of *Ride the High Country*, thus moving the film from a more conventional structure to one which is tragic. What Peckinpah did is not unlike Shakespeare's decision to end *King Lear* with the old king's death (as well as the deaths of other notable characters, most especially Cordelia), for as Stephen Booth has pointed out, all previous versions of the Lear story end more or less happily, with Lear restored to his kingdom and Cordelia alive and sometimes paired with Edgar, as in Nahum Tate's notorious (but popular) eighteenth-century redaction of Shakespeare's tragic play (17, 57). Like Shakespeare, Peckinpah insists on a tragic conclusion by taking material almost always employed for comic or at least non-tragic effect and restructuring it to conclude with the hero's tragic death.

It remains to be pointed out that *Ride the High Country* is an unusual if not unique form of Christian tragedy, distinctly modern in its underlying assumptions. As it happens, *King Lear* is one of Sewall's two major examples of Christian tragedy. For Sewall, Marlowe's *Doctor Faustus* is "the first 'Christian tragedy'" (57) and *King Lear* "define[s] Christian tragedy in its full development" (68). These plays are Christian because of the values embodied in the dramatic action and the spiritual conflicts dramatized in the tragic protagonist, whose "guilty and remorseful soul" is the dramatic (and tragic) subject (52). Faustus and Lear suffer in the context of Christian values and a Christian world view, but as in nearly all tragedies they suffer because of their own mistakes (thus their guilty and remorseful souls). Similarly, W. H. Auden points to the hero's errors (if not sins) when he says that at the end of a Christian tragedy we are made to feel, "What a pity it was this way when it might have been otherwise" (143). And Northrop Frye suggests in the same vein that Aristotle's *anagnorisis* typically provides "the recognition of the determined shape of the life [the tragic hero] has created for himself, with an implicit comparison with the uncreated potential life he has forsaken" (1957, 212). For Sewall, Auden, and Frye, Christian tragedy depicts the extreme consequences of the hero's moral lapses, about which he comes to feel remorse and we come to feel regret because it could have been otherwise if he had not chosen to act as he did.

In *Ride the High Country*, by contrast, Steve Judd acts more or less precisely as we want him to act. His mistakes are real enough, as when he trusts Gil and Heck, fails to load the guns before leaving Coarsegold ("an inexcusable oversight," in one critic's view [Bliss 1993, 55]), and rides too confidently into the Knudsen farm at the end of the film. These are hardly "errors" for which Steve should feel remorse, however, especially his judgments about Gil and Heck, for these are ultimately validated by the film as a whole. Unlike the heroes in most Christian tragedies, indeed, most tragedies of any kind, Steve Judd is guilty of no moral lapses and in fact always behaves with exemplary moral character as events unfold.

In this regard Steve differs somewhat from other examples of this kind of modern tragic protagonist. In Ernest Hemingway's *A Farewell to Arms*, for example, Frederic Henry is first depicted as a somewhat cynical participant in World War I who perceives Catherine Barkley as nothing more than a convenient target of seduction. Eventually, Frederic comes to love Catherine sufficiently to make his "separate peace" with the war, which he deserts in order to be with Catherine and the baby they are expecting. We are made to understand and in fact support Frederic's desertion, which is presented as exemplary behavior in the world of this novel. Frederic suffers enormously at the end of the book when Catherine dies in childbirth, but by this point we understand his pain to be the inevitable outcome for one capable of loving someone as deeply as he loves Catherine and willing to act on his wholly admirable feelings. Steve Judd does not become more admirable in the course of *Ride the High Country*, but like Frederic he suffers because of who he is in a world which does not reward virtue and is in fact hostile to those who try to maintain their moral character in a fallen world. Like Frederic, then, Steve Judd is the protagonist in a tragic action which does not turn on the hero's "flaw" or even his "mistake," an action in which the hero's demise comes about because he acts precisely as we want him to act.[11]

This kind of tragic structure is unusual even in the modern period, as Sewall suggests in adducing the seriously flawed Ahab, Hester Prynne, and Raskolnikov as his primary examples (62). Nor is it typical of Peckinpah, whose subsequent films center on protagonists who are deeply flawed and whose faults are essential to their tragic deaths. In these later films, Peckinpah continues to experiment with various tragic structures, ranging from *The Wild Bunch*, in which the protagonist ultimately acts as we want him to act but who nonetheless brings about his own demise because of decided character flaws, to *Pat Garrett and Billy the Kid*, in which the protagonist acts at all times against his better self (much as Macbeth acts) and struggles to suppress his overwhelmingly painful awareness of the moral suicide he commits throughout the film. Indeed, it is hard to imagine tragic protagonists more different than Steve Judd and Pat Garrett, characters who testify to the remarkable range of Peckinpah's tragic experimentation. Having achieved the exemplary version of Christian tragedy we experience in *Ride the High Country*, Peckinpah was to move on to very different tragic models, perhaps better, perhaps worse, but in any case always pointing up his commitment to the tragic Western as his principal genre.

Chapter Three

Noon Wine: A Tragic Pastoral

Antiquest felt at Noon
When August burning low
Arise this spectral Canticle
Repose to typify
— Emily Dickinson, "Further in Summer Than the Birds," 11. 9–12 (485–86)

There are people all over the place, dozens of them, I'd like to kill, quite literally kill.
— Sam Peckinpah as quoted in William Murray (74)

Peckinpah enjoyed a good working relationship with everyone involved in *Ride the High Country* (1962) until the very last moment in postproduction, when MGM's president Joseph Vogel saw the film, disliked it intensely, and barred Peckinpah from the studio. This seems to have had no real effect on the finished product except that Peckinpah's producer, Richard Lyons, handled the musical score, which Peckinpah disliked (Weddle 1994, 216–18). This late contretemps was to be the second of many such episodes, some quite serious, with producers and/or studio executives, and Peckinpah's next project, *Major Dundee* (1965), was to be one of the worst instances. The story of Peckinpah's travails with Columbia Pictures and his producer, Jerry Bresler, is almost better known than the picture itself, and legend has it that this is the first Peckinpah "masterpiece" all but destroyed by studio cuts to the film Peckinpah wanted to release. We will briefly review the unhappy history of *Major Dundee*, with special attention to the question of why the film did not continue Peckinpah's exploration of tragic form(s).

Major Dundee is often seen as a trial run for the much more successful *The Wild Bunch* (1969), a film in which Peckinpah develops situations and motifs he first introduced in *Major Dundee*. There is a great deal of truth to this notion, as any review of the specific parallels confirms. From a formal point of view, however, the interesting thing about the earlier film is that it was first conceived as a tragedy but became something very different. As we hope to show, the formal precursor to *The Wild Bunch* is not *Major Dundee* but a fifty-minute television adaptation Peckinpah wrote and directed one year after the debacle of *Major Dundee*. This television show, *Noon Wine* (1966), is Peckinpah's first tragic work after *Ride the High Country* and the next significant step toward *The Wild Bunch*. We hope to justify our view that *Noon Wine* is Peckinpah's first venture into modern forms of tragedy and one of his finest works in any genre.

I

With *Major Dundee*, Peckinpah was barred from the studio before the film was properly cut, so his producer, Jerry Bresler, worked with several Columbia editors to establish the final cut. This involved shortening the film Peckinpah wanted to release, a film variously said to be 180 minutes, 161 minutes, 154 minutes, or 150 minutes.[1] Bresler's cut seems to have run 134 minutes when previewed in early 1965, at which time the studio decided to cut further to the 122-minute version which was finally released. In 2005 Sony released an "extended version" of *Major Dundee*, which appears to be the Bresler cut with 12 minutes of material restored.[2] Peckinpah always denounced the "mutilated" version of the film Columbia first released, and he was appalled by the Bresler version as well. David Weddle has formulated Peckinpah's central objection to both "reduced" versions of *Major Dundee*: "Whole scenes and sequences—mostly those that lingered on the subtleties of Dundee, the demons that drove him, and his inner conflicts—were ripped out of the film" (1994, 251). All of Dundee's motivation was gone, Peckinpah claimed (Cutts 6). Virtually every critic of *Major Dundee* has lamented what Columbia did to Peckinpah's film, though many have questioned whether *Major Dundee* would have been a great or even a good film at any length.

It has been obvious for some time that we will never see anything like the director's final cut, for Peckinpah never made such a cut and many of the scenes cut by Bresler have never been seen by anyone. The extended version restores three scenes from the eight deleted scenes Jim Kitses first identified, but two of these scenes are still missing material Kitses describes and his list suggests that at least five scenes are still missing or were only partially filmed.[3] We can only guess at what these scenes would have added, just as we can only guess how many of these scenes would have been retained in Peckinpah's final cut. Nonetheless, despite the obvious problems in evaluating the several versions of *Major Dundee*, we think it is possible to reach a definite conclusion about Peckinpah's claim that Dundee's characterization was destroyed by the studio. To assess this claim, or to evaluate the relevance of the scenes restored in the extended version, or to judge the likely impact of the scenes still missing from the film as we have it, we need to return to the question of what Peckinpah was trying to do in *Major Dundee*.

The story of *Major Dundee* was first conceived by Harry Julian Fink, whose "treatment" of the subject is succinctly described by Weddle:

> [Jerry Bresler] came upon a thirty-seven page treatment by Harry Julian Fink (who would later write *Dirty Harry*) called *And Then Came the Tiger!* It told the story of a Union cavalry officer, Major Amos Charles Dundee, who is banished to a remote outpost in New Mexico during the closing days of the Civil War to look after a prison full of captured Confederate soldiers. When a rampaging Apache war chief, Sierra Charriba, wipes out an entire company from Dundee's regiment, the major decides he's tired of being a jail keeper. He throws together a makeshift army of Union regulars, Confederate prisoners, and local cutthroats and thieves, and takes off after the Indians. Dundee becomes so obsessed with his quest for vengeance that he leads his men across the Rio Grande on a 2,400-mile trek over the mountains and deserts of Mexico, which is embroiled in one of its many revolutions. The Juaristas are battling the 70,000 French troops that have occupied their country, and Dundee soon finds he must also fight the French, who consider his incursion a violation of international law. By the time he leads a ragged group of survivors back across the Rio Grande ten months later, he has not only caught and killed the Apache, but met and beaten Europe's finest on the field of battle, and carved his name in history [1994, 229].

We quote Weddle at such length because his summary of *Major Dundee* confirms that the story was originally conceived as one leading up to and climaxed by Dundee's military successes. To put it mildly, this initial conception underwent dramatic sea changes as the project went forward.

Fink was signed to write the film script from his own treatment, but shortly before the film was to begin production Peckinpah read Fink's lengthy but unfinished script, rejected it as a hopeless starting point, and hired Oscar Saul to work with him in drafting a more workable script (Weddle 1994, 232). Saul brought a very different view of the story, believing that it depicted Dundee and his men as "indistinguishable from the savages they chase." Peckinpah may not have agreed altogether with Saul, but he clearly saw *Major Dundee* as a darker tale than the one Fink outlined. When the actor R. G. Armstrong read the script Saul and Peckinpah put together, he pointed out that it represented "*Moby-Dick* on horseback," and Peckinpah agreed (Weddle 1994, 233). Seydor also cites a letter now housed in the Peckinpah Collection in which Peckinpah says, "Actually, it was *Major Dundee* where I tried to take on Melville" (1997, 83). Peckinpah may never have firmly committed to a tragic, *Moby-Dick*-like version of *Major Dundee*, but he apparently considered several dire conclusions to the film. The most calamitous of these endings—and the one most like the conclusion of *Moby-Dick*—would have seen Dundee's men wiped out one by one by the Apaches as the troops tried to retreat to the U.S. border (Seydor 1997, 83). Alternatively, Peckinpah is said to have considered an ending in which Sierra Charriba was neither taken nor destroyed, an anti-climactic resolution which would have shown "that the quest was an end in itself" (Combs 21). These endings hardly square with the film Fink first imagined or Peckinpah finally tried to make.

Seydor's chapter on *Major Dundee* (1997, 63–89) explains how Peckinpah changed his mind about Major Dundee the character and therefore *Major Dundee* the film. At first Peckinpah shared Saul's desire to show "how men in war soon forget their ideals and become lost in the lust for blood and glory" (Seydor 1997, 69), a revisionist stance which seems to have temporarily given way to a more tragic conception in which Dundee repeats Ahab's obsessive quest and the film climaxes in one kind of catastrophe or another. In Seydor's view, however, Peckinpah came more and more to identify with Dundee, perhaps because of his own ongoing problems with his "superiors" at Columbia (1997, 80), and his conception of the character and the film changed radically. James Coburn, who plays the scout Sam Potts, tells of asking Peckinpah what in the character of Dundee led Peckinpah to want to make this film. Peckinpah's response confirms his later if not his original view of Dundee: "Because he continues. I mean through all the shit, through all the lies, through all the drunkenness and the bullshit Major Dundee goes through, he survives and continues" (Simmons 67). Whether or not the shit, lies, drunkenness, and bullshit Peckinpah refers to are of Dundee's own making, Peckinpah admired Dundee's resilience, his commitment (if only to his self-conception, Robert Warshow's heroic touchstone resurrected), and apparently his performance as an officer as well. We take this final point from a memo Peckinpah wrote to his co-editors on *Major Dundee*: "I think we should all remember *Major Dundee* is the story of the making of a great officer" (Seydor 1997, 81).

Virtually every critic of *Major Dundee* has rejected Peckinpah's reading of his own character. Weddle speaks of Dundee as "driven not by any sense of justice or ideals, but by his own ruthless ambition and corrosive demons" (1994, 230); Michael Bliss laments "the monomaniacal nature of Dundee's quest" (1993, 58) and argues that Dundee pursues Sierra Charriba because of "raging racism" (1993, 61); Kitses concludes that "[b]efore he is through, the major, not a pretty character, decimates his command, destroys a Mexican village, provokes a war with neutral French forces, and leaves behind a bloody trail of death and destruction stretching far behind him" (2004, 213); Matt Wanat follows Bliss in speaking of "Dundee's egomaniacal quest" (90) and his "goal" of "racist extermination" (94); and even Seydor cannot see Dundee as anything but "wrong for pursuing the expedition long after the [Rostes] children have been reclaimed" (1997, 82). In effect, Peckinpah's critics have responded to his portrait of Dundee's obsessive quest for professional redemption (much like that of Colonel Thursday in John

Ford's *Fort Apache*, as Seydor points out [1997, 75]), the portrait of a deeply flawed "hero" not unlike Melville's Ahab but hardly that of a great officer. In his memo to his co-editors, Peckinpah acknowledges that his hero's inability to admit personal failure "almost" breaks him, that he reaches "the bottom of personal degradation" before finally recognizing his weaknesses and becoming "the Commander he thought he was at the beginning of the picture" (Seydor 1997, 81). Peckinpah obviously felt that Dundee's final military successes, depicted in the last 15 minutes, were sufficient to reverse the film's many tragic forebodings and the strong impression of Dundee's egotism and disastrous misjudgments. The critical record suggests that Peckinpah was as wrong about this as his hero proves to be again and again until the film's final moments.

We are obviously suggesting that Peckinpah, and not the executives at Columbia, is primarily responsible for the flaws in Dundee's characterization and therefore the film as a whole. Seydor argues that Peckinpah is in part at fault but the studio must share the blame because its cuts diminished Peckinpah's efforts to develop a more complex and ultimately redeemed Dundee. Indeed, commenting on Peckinpah's claim that he "shot about forty-five minutes of Dundee under the microscope," precious minutes ruthlessly cut by Bresler and the Columbia executives, Seydor remarks, "There is no reason to doubt Peckinpah" (1997, 82). We think there is no reason to doubt that *Major Dundee* would be a better film with the cuts restored, but we do in fact doubt that 45 minutes of Dundee under the microscope were cut. Moreover, even if 45 minutes were deleted, there is no evidence that more than three minutes came from the post–Durango scenes in which Dundee supposedly redeems himself and emerges a great officer.

No one can prove how many of the deleted minutes presented Dundee under a microscope, but the evidence suggests that Peckinpah's claims are exaggerated. The 12 minutes restored in the extended version do add to the overall portrait of Dundee (Charlton Heston), whose competence is displayed in recapturing Captain Tyreen (Richard Harris) and four of his Confederate soldiers, whose agonies at Durango are significantly enhanced by more than five minutes of additional footage, and whose renewed soldierly skills are exhibited in the one originally-deleted scene after Durango, in which we observe Dundee devise new strategies for the pursuit of Sierra Charriba (Michael Pate) and finally accept Potts' demand that Dundee climb up a tree and bring down the crucified body of Riago (José Luis Ruiz), the Apache scout whose loyalty Dundee has questioned repeatedly. This humbling moment adds a great deal to Peckinpah's scheme to redeem Dundee at the end of the film, and if there were other additions like this one, either in the extended version or in the still-missing footage, we would be moved to share Seydor's confidence about Peckinpah's claim. But there seem not to be any other examples. All of the other deleted scenes identified by Kitses come before Durango and either do not include Dundee (as in the deleted or only partially-filmed opening scenes of the Halloween party at the Rostes ranch followed by the massacre of all those present) or present Dundee comically or ironically (as in the "long" scene in which the men laugh at Dundee trying to mount a mule after the Apache ambush at the river, or the end of the knife-fight between Potts and Sergeant Gomez [Mario Adorf], a fight Dundee mistakenly takes to be in earnest and therefore breaks up). (The descriptions in this paragraph all derive from Kitses 2004, 211–12.) We conclude that Peckinpah's microscope did not fall on Dundee's redemption except in the three-minute scene climaxed by the audience's discovery of Riago's body, so the three-hour version of *Major Dundee* may well have seemed even more abrupt in "depicting" Dundee's redemption.[4]

The scenes restored in the extended version should assure everyone that the restoration of all deleted scenes would make for a better and not just a longer film. But the other deleted scenes described by Kitses do little to justify Peckinpah's revised conception of Dundee, so we must again regret that Peckinpah came to believe in this later reading of his own character. Moreover, we say this despite the fact we believe Dundee's critics have exaggerated the major's faults. As both Kitses (2004, 211) and Seydor (1997, 72) note, Dundee's motivation for pursuing Sierra Charriba would be rather more credible if the film opened as Peckinpah intended, with 10 minutes of footage depicting the Halloween party and the actual massacre. Indeed, these missing scenes and other materials still in the film seem to us to justify Dundee's almost universally deplored decision to continue his pursuit of Sierra Charriba after the Rostes children are returned. Dundee's errors and misjudgments elsewhere (reminiscent of Pike Bishop's in *The Wild Bunch*) reflect on Dundee's character but do not justify the more extreme criticisms of his egomaniacal and racist tendencies. Rather, they point to the richly suggestive parallels with Ahab Peckinpah unfortunately abandoned in the last one-third of the film, in which he effectively gave up his pretensions to tragic form in order to pursue the all-too-abrupt rehabilitation of Dundee as officer and man.

We think Peckinpah needed to stick to the tragic conception which shapes the first half of the film or to revise it altogether in order to justify his later notions about Dundee, presumably by adding a good deal of relevant material after Dundee leaves Durango. Ultimately, Peckinpah did neither of these things, so the failure of *Major Dundee* seems to be of his own making. If this analysis is correct, the studio's primary sin was not the cuts it made, bad as those were, but the pressure it put on Peckinpah to finish filming before he could add the additional scenes needed to flesh out his new conception of Dundee. Would these scenes have made *Major Dundee* into the masterpiece critics continue to evoke in discussions of the film? One can only guess. Given our thesis in this study, it is tempting to argue that *Major Dundee* would have been a better film if Peckinpah had stuck to his tragic project and realized a form as close to the *Moby-Dick* analogy as possible. Seydor believes that the scene in which O. W. Hadley (Warren Oates) is executed is supposed to be "the film's watershed," after which, logically, there is a "seal of doom upon the whole expedition" (1997, 79). But the most Seydor (or we) can plausibly claim is that if Peckinpah had gone on to fulfill the expectations aroused by this scene, he would have made a film which is more "coherent and unified" than the one he in fact made (1997, 83). A tragic *Major Dundee* may have been a great film, but we will never really know.

We do know it was providential for all concerned when Daniel Melnick contacted Peckinpah about a year after the release of *Major Dundee*. Melnick's invitation to adapt Katherine Anne Porter's *Noon Wine* (1936) allowed Peckinpah to direct again and to engage a modern tragic work for the first time since his years at USC. Peckinpah was drawn to the tragic conception Porter expressed in a passage Peckinpah underlined twice: "[*Noon Wine*] is a story of the most painful moral and emotional confusion, in which every one concerned, yes, in his crooked way, even Mr. Hatch, is trying to do right."[5] As Seydor notes (1997, 102), Peckinpah himself was soon to remark, "Things are always mixed. We're all guilty to some extent" (Harmetz 173). In Porter's short novel, Peckinpah found a story which embodied his own understanding of life, and in this film, unlike *Major Dundee*, he would do full justice to the tragic possibilities of his material.

II

> The experience of the dead as a living force is intrinsic to tragic form.
>
> — Sir Arthur W. Pickard-Cambridge as quoted in Padel (346)

For both Porter and Peckinpah, *Noon Wine* is essentially a tragic work. In her 1956 essay "*Noon Wine*: The Sources," Porter traces the story of Royal Earle Thompson and his wife Ellie to Porter's childhood memories of growing up on a farm in south central Texas near the turn of the century (the short novel's dates—1896–1905—approximate Porter's childhood years in the area). Two memories stand out: (1) of a rural tale of violence and murder Porter heard as a little girl; (2) of a wife, whom Porter actually saw, forced by her husband to lie about the manner of his victim's death in order to exonerate him. The second memory is especially relevant to *Noon Wine*, for Porter recalls that while the wife lied for her husband, "she did it unwillingly and unlovingly in bitter resignation to the double disgrace of her husband's crime and her own sin" (1970, 476). In *Noon Wine,* Porter shaped these memories of murder and the coerced defense of a husband by his wife into a dark, ultimately tragic tale. As we shall see, Peckinpah had good reason to respond to such a story and adapted it in such a way as to emphasize even more clearly its tragic elements.

Not everyone has read Porter's *Noon Wine* as a tragedy, but Porter once referred to the Thompson marriage as "tragic" (1990, 377) and described the story with interviewers in terms which make her tragic intentions plain. In one such interview, Porter asserts, "Any work of art has got to give you the feeling of reconciliation—what the Greeks call catharsis, the purification of your mind and imagination—through an ending that is endurable because it is right and true. Oh, not in any pawky individual idea of morality or some parochial idea of right and wrong. Sometimes the end is very tragic because it needs to be" (Thompson 15). Here Porter goes on to defend the conclusion of *Noon Wine* against readers who object to Mr. Thompson's suicide at the end:

> ... and I would say, "All right, where was he going? Given what he was, his own situation, what else could he do?" Every once in a while when I see a character of mine just going toward perdition, I think, "Stop, stop, you can always stop and choose, you know." But no, being what he was, he already *has* chosen, and he can't go back on it now [Thompson 15].

Porter's remarks about *catharsis* and the inevitability—the rightness—of Mr. Thompson's suicide complement her sentiments in an important essay she wrote defending Thomas Hardy's passionate, rustic tragedies against the attacks of T. S. Eliot, who dismissed them as not sufficiently "edifying":

> With no disrespect to conventional piety, may I venture that in the regions of art, as of religion, edification is not the highest form of intellectual or spiritual experience. It is a happy truth that Hardy's novels are not edifying. The mental and emotional states roused and maintained in the Reader of *The Mayor of Casterbridge* or *The Return of the Native* are considerably richer, invoked out of deeper sources in the whole human consciousness, more substantially nourishing, than this lukewarm word can express. A novel by Thomas Hardy can be a chastening experience, an appalling one, there is great and sober pleasure to be got out of those novels, the mind can be disturbed and the heart made extremely uneasy, but the complacency of edification is absent, as it is apt to be from any true tragedy [1970, 6–7].

The true province of tragedy, Porter continues, resides in that "intransigent, measureless force, divided against itself, in conflict alike with its own system of laws and the unknown laws of the universe," and this was Hardy's "genuinely tragic theme in the grand manner, of sufficient weight and shapelessness to try the powers of any artist" (1970, 10). This "shapelessness" is what drives Porter to find, in the best manner of modernist tragedy, a sufficient form for the chaos which lies at the heart of tragic experience. This is one of the reasons Peckinpah was drawn to Porter's highly formal yet richly ambiguous art, for Peckinpah was fond of saying that "things are always mixed" (Harmetz 173), a belief which informs the moral and thematic ambiguities of his films.

There is no evidence that Peckinpah knew anything about Porter's writings and interviews on tragedy, but his markings in the margins of both his copy of *Noon Wine* and his copy of "*Noon Wine*: The Sources" are extensive (see Seydor 1997, 101–102), and we suspect that Peckinpah, himself well-versed in classical Greek tragedy, would have been fascinated by her interpretation of tragic *catharsis* in light of his own well-known belief in the power of *catharsis* to affect a viewer profoundly.[6] We know that in his copy of Porter's essay Peckinpah underlined the section in which she writes of "the underlying, perpetual ominous presence of violence; violence potential that broke through the smooth surface almost without warning, or maybe just without warning to children, who learned later to know the signs" (1970, 472). Porter's meditation on her south Texas childhood should remind us of nothing so much as Peckinpah's major films. While Peckinpah, as would be expected, deals more specifically with questions of violence and the tragic emotions of pity and fear, his formulations are finally not all that different from Porter's:

> I'm a great believer in catharsis.... Look, the old basis of catharsis was a purging of the emotions through pity and fear. People used to go and see the plays of Euripides and Sophocles and those other Greek cats. The players acted it out and the audience got in there and kind of lived it with them [William Murray 68].

Peckinpah seems to be saying that "a purging of the emotions" can only occur when the artist has produced a drama, or in his case a film, which leads to a calming effect, the result of tumultuous, contradictory, and violent emotions passing through an audience on their way toward realizing that the work of art has explored a human problem, no matter how disturbing, in such a way as to suggest that with its conclusion the work has nothing more to do but much more to say to its audience as they continue to experience its artistry in a complex variety of ways. In this sense, endings are really beginnings in both Porter and Peckinpah. In what follows, we propose to read *Noon Wine*, short novel and film, different as they may be in certain ways, as genuine tragic actions in which Porter and Peckinpah embody unusually compatible notions about tragic art.

Noon Wine is the story of Royal Earle Thompson, a proud, foolish, and indolent Texas dairy farmer who is married to a weak, valetudinarian wife, Ellie, a woman of firm if almost inhumanely strict moral principles who wears dark smoked glasses as if to enable her to keep the things of this world she fears, or deplores, at bay, who keeps her bedroom suffocatingly closed even during torrid Texas summers because she suffers from the sun and bad eyesight, and who is physically and emotionally of little help in managing the deteriorating, dilapidated family farm. The Thompsons have two young sons, Arthur and Herbert, who seem, as we first meet them, untrustworthy troublemakers. Neither of the parents seems particularly close to their children; indeed, Porter describes Mrs. Thompson as looking upon her children "as if they were rather troublesome nephews on a prolonged visit" (228).[7] The Thompsons' lot is not a happy one, but Mr. Thompson maintains an air of false superiority based solely on a superficial "feeling for the appearance of things, his own appearance in the sight of God and man. 'It don't *look* right,' was his final reason for not doing anything he did not wish to do" (233). For "it" to "look right," Mr. Thompson's work on his farm must be limited to such self-proclaimed masculine pursuits as slaughtering livestock and going to town to sell the products of his somewhat limited "labor."

This kind of masculine self-deception extends to a theme both Porter and Peckinpah explore brilliantly: the false dichotomy between a man's area of responsibility and that of his wife. "It was his dignity and his reputation that [Mr. Thompson] cared about, and there were only a few kinds of work manly enough for Mr. Thompson to undertake with his own hands" (233–34). He feels let down, emasculated by his infirm wife, and even blames her for making him run a dairy farm, for he perceives his efforts on this farm as "woman's work" which involves chores such as milking cows, caring for hens ("cackling, clutching, hatching out when you least expected it" [233]), and gathering eggs, tasks which leave him "unmanned," a feeling the unexpected arrival of his nemesis Homer T. *Hatch* will reinforce (233). He thinks he is a "failure," someone who "knew, without putting it into words, that he had been going steadily down hill" (234), and he is not at all reluctant, in language bordering on misogyny, to blame his sickly wife for his own predicament. This poseur's respect for "appearances" and his lack of genuine insight, or vision, perhaps the most venerable of tragic metaphors, prevent him from changing his situation into something more positive.

One fateful day a mysterious stranger appears at Mr. Thompson's collapsed, half-open gate, moving "steadily, like a man following a plow, as if he knew the place well and knew where he was going and what he would find there" (222).[8] He says simply, "I need work." Tellingly, in both Porter and Peckinpah, he adds, "You need a man here?" (222). His name is Olaf Helton, and he is a Swede, not an Irishman as Mr. Thompson initially thinks, and Mr. Thompson, working slowly "back and forth" at a butter churn in the short novel (223) or, in Peckinpah's version, sitting even more idly, chewing tobacco, staring at the unused churn, surely looks like he could use some help.

As in all his films, Peckinpah's attention to his beginning, including the credit sequence, is extraordinary. The arrival or advent of Mr. Helton is preceded by a series of three still shots, connected by dissolves, of the Thompson farm: first, its barn, more specifically what seems to morph into the farm's crucially important springhouse, its dark door ominously open, with star Jason Robards' name superimposed across the screen; second, the farm house, with co-star Olivia de Havilland's name blazoned across that domestic scene; and third, a second shot of the farm house, looking bright, sunny, and airy with grass, trees, and a picket fence. All three shots are from relatively the same angle and distance, so why two shots of the farm house? Upon repeated viewings, one notes that in shot two Peckinpah has substituted a not-too-convincingly idealized painting of a farm house for the "real" farm house, out in the country somewhere, which he photographs in shot three. Since "Olivia de Havilland" is superimposed across the screen, and since she plays a character whose sense of reality is seriously compromised by her rigidly idealized sense of right and wrong as well as a kind of pictorialized faux romanticism about what a lady-like life should be, we encounter here in a credit sequence the element of artificiality in her future presentation. Peckinpah is setting up a Tennessee Williams–like sense of the imagined, unreal world Ellie Thompson inhabits and is not likely ever to leave.

Peckinpah then focuses more specifically on farm life itself. In a fourth shot he shows the two children, Arthur and Herbert, climbing down a ladder from the barn, undressing and leaping happily into a large, circular water trough next to the barn. Helton, entering the farm, ignores the boys (in Porter's short novel they are digging in the dirt and do not see Helton) who call out to him, "Hello! Hello!" as if he doesn't hear them. The boys' youthful joy may be a reminder of the happy childhood Helton has lost forever by the time he appears at the farm. This is underscored by Peckinpah's emphasis on the water being splashed into the air by the frolicking boys (now unseen in the frame) as Helton makes his way past the farm fence toward Mr. Thompson. While the fence intercedes almost with a kind of limiting legal force, separating Helton from the boys, it is nevertheless startling to see the water rise as if from nowhere and embrace Helton in the frame, for his identity seems to be merging, within the composition of his moving body, the fence, and the water, with the spray. Peckinpah, whose obsession with water's cleansing and revivifying powers is in full force in this film, uses the water to establish a bond between the naked boys at play and Helton, now lost in his deeply personal self, a prisoner of the past, of memories both happy and sad.

Peckinpah adds a third element to Helton and the boys playing in the water by introducing composer Jerry Fielding's first variation on Mr. Helton's harmonica motif. Earlier, Fielding employs violins and a piano to introduce the film's first scenes/shots. Olaf Helton's arrival at the Thompson farm is foreshadowed by the harmonica, but his actual appearance is underscored by the more somber, wistful, and perhaps even tragic sounds of an oboe. Helton's presence will ultimately raise important questions about the nature of both life and death for the Thompsons and their sons. None of them will "see" their world in the same way after his portentous arrival. This is why it is so important, and one of Peckinpah's trademarks, that when his own credit is flashed on the screen, "Written and Directed by Sam Peckinpah," we see Mr. Helton, right after he passes the boys in the trough, framed by the natural branches of a tree as he leaves behind the limiting and human-made farm fence on his way in to talk to Royal Earle Thompson.

Immediately upon his arrival at the Thompson farm, Olaf Helton, a man with few possessions except several elegant and prized harmonicas, goes to work transforming this failing venture, seemingly a case study in entropic collapse, into a happy and modestly successful enterprise. Because his success is so sudden and welcome, bringing new life to the dilapidated farm, both Thompsons soon learn to ignore Helton's eerie, alien appearance. To them he is, as Edward Groff describes him, an "opaque mystery—a 'furrin' blank-eyed ghost who plays a haunting tune on his harmonica and is not manly, by Mr. Thompson's standards, because he is perfectly willing to do the sort of work Mr. Thompson disdains as women's work" (42). Indeed, were he not such an energetic worker, one would think that Helton, his watery "blue eyes so pale they were almost white, looking and not looking at [Mr. Thompson] from a long gaunt face, under white eyebrows" (223), comes from some kind of underworld land of the dead, a sort of half-human, half-alien zombie, a wandering, "disembodied spirit" (236), according to Mrs. Thompson, who in her own fashion identifies with him, repeatedly calling him "a stranger in a strange land."

Everything about Mr. Helton, an emissary from the lands of the living and of the dead, conjures up its opposite. He becomes a key to the tragic theme of doubling, the Aristotelian theme of "pity and terror," the Nietzschean tragic pleasure which emerges through tragic suffering in the "spirit of music" which runs throughout the short novel and film, and his sinister/benign presence ultimately evokes his own double, Mr. Homer T. Hatch. Taciturn, expressionless Helton, with his dark and unknown past, "speaks" primarily through the musical tune he plays on his precious collection of harmonicas, a tune neither Thompson is familiar with nor wants to know about until it is too late. A key to Helton's enigmatic nature lies in his music, the "pretty tune" which Mrs. Thompson finds alternately "merry and sad": "Slowly she realized she had been hearing a new sound even in her sleep" (226). As Keats might ask, does Mrs. Thompson wake or sleep? The music seems to speak to her from another realm, and she responds to its siren song positively. A nine-year dream has begun, finally to end in a nightmare from another, more terrifying world.[9]

Not only can Helton evoke both joy and sorrow in a single rendering of his obsessive tune, he has different harmonicas, some of which "were in different keys, some lower and sweeter than the others, but the same changeless tune went on, a strange tune, with sudden turns in it, night after night, and sometimes even in the afternoons when Mr. Helton sat down to catch his breath" (236). Helton's halting, reticent speech, like the rendering of his tune, seems to be "wandering up and down" (229); as if suspended in water, his words "wavered slowly up and down, and the emphasis was in the wrong place" (225), as is perhaps the homeless, placeless, Cain-like "stranger" Mr. Helton. All of this descriptive language conveys the feeling that in his mind, and perhaps in his actions, Helton moves, ghost-like, between the worlds of light and darkness, heaven and hell. Fielding's rendition of Helton's song captures its pure "sweetness," but also the deeper strains of melancholy and longing sadness which accompany it. In listening to this music, we feel the presence of an existence, now blocked, which once knew some kind of exquisite joy, but which can now only experience that joy—and its loss—in the song he plays, over and over again. Adrift in his life and seemingly "dead" in the present, Helton has reached the point where his whole emotional and spiritual existence is concealed in his song, which is all that holds him to some kind of human connection.

In searching for a visual/aural correlative to the oxymoronically sad sweetness of Helton's tune, Peckinpah works forward from the initial image of Mr. Helton arriving in south Texas on an arid August day, like a water god, seemingly bathed in deep focus by the flashing Botticellian spray of the boys at play in the trough, and finds what he needs in one of the most complex symbols of both short novel and film, the springhouse, which doubles as the dairy farm's milk house and seems to represent the real hope for the Thompsons' fortunes in the steady flow of its ever-trickling, deep underground source. Surprisingly little has been written about the springhouse, but it is clear that Peckinpah responded to it profoundly when he read the short novel and made it a key symbolic location, more so than Porter, in his adaptation. Porter's description of the springhouse/milk house is almost Hawthornian in its veiled but vivid allegorical richness:

> The milk house was only another shack of weather-beaten boards nailed together hastily years before they needed a milk house; it was meant to be temporary, and it was; already shapeless, leaning this way and that over a perpetual cool trickle of water that fell from a little grot, almost choked with pallid ferns. No one else in the whole countryside had such a spring on his land. Mr. and Mrs. Thompson felt they had a fortune in that spring, if they ever got around to doing anything with it [226–27].

The double nature of the springhouse tells us a good deal about *Noon Wine* as a tragic action. Here Porter describes a secret source of future happiness for the Thompsons in the ancient, "perpetual" flow of that "cool" trickle of life-giving water as it falls from a seemingly ancient, primordial grot, or grotto. The language is mutedly if also richly romantic, a rustic American version of Coleridge's caverns measureless to man, and evocative enough to suggest the possibility of a special kind of oasis, a potential vision of paradise, within the bleak setting we encounter in the searingly oppressive late summer heat of rural Texas. The springhouse suggests another nature, though, one closer to death and its silent sources, when Porter writes that the "little grot" is "almost choked with pallid ferns." Can we not make a paradoxical connection between the soft life-music of the "cool trickle" of spring water and the metaphorically violent language of the "little grot, almost choked with pallid ferns"? And do not these suggestions of life and death link perfectly with the strange and ambiguous persona of Olaf Helton? Helton, like the life-giving spring, holds the key to the family's "fortune" and, unknown to them, their dark and tragic fate. Porter alludes to the relationship between death and cold water, like the springhouse pool, when she mentions two previous workers on the farm (analogous to Mr. Helton and his antagonist, Mr. Homer T. Hatch), who got into a fight in which one killed the other with a knife and ended up incarcerated in the hoosegow at *Cold Springs* (223; our emphasis).

For nine years, however, Helton's extraordinary effect on the Thompsons seems entirely benign. It is Mrs. Thompson who first discovers the fruits of Mr. Helton's creative labors in the springhouse:

> Rickety wooden shelves clung at hazard in the square around the small pool where the larger pails of milk and butter stood, fresh and sweet in the cold water. One hand supporting her flat, pained side, the other shading her eyes, Mrs. Thompson leaned over and peered into the pails. The cream had been skimmed and set aside, there was a rich roll of butter, the wooden molds and shallow pans had been scrubbed and scalded for the first time in who knows when, the barrel was full of buttermilk ready for the pigs and the weanling calves, the hard packed-dirt floor had been swept smooth. Mrs. Thompson straightened up again, smiling tenderly [227].

The weak, infirm Mrs. Thompson seems almost reborn by the sight of what Helton has accomplished. "Smiling tenderly," one might say maternally, a word we rarely associate with her feelings toward her own sons, she seems to look upon this new and fruitful creation with a loving mother's gaze. Here in this rejuvenated, hopeful space, both "spring" and "house" take on new and reverberating meanings.

The positive nature of Helton's effect on Mr. Thompson is less obvious but no less dramatic. Peckinpah establishes through two different work montage sequences just how joyous the Thompson family is watching Helton and the boys work, as Mr. Thompson prepares to haul the produce and dairy products to market. Peckinpah superimposes closeups of Mr. Thompson and Helton with a montage of work on the farm, or rather with Helton's work on the farm, as if to show a genuine relationship, even a kind of nascent friendship, between the two men. Seydor argues that Peckinpah sentimentalizes the second of these sequences (after the first shows moments of shared feelings between Mr. Thompson and Helton) when the director has Mr. Thompson and Helton grin at each other over all that has been accomplished and Mr. Thompson proudly takes an apple from a crate Helton has filled. For Seydor, this is false because "Helton is obviously schizophrenic, incapable of this or any other normal social relationship" (1997, 99). But Porter strongly disagrees with such a limited view of Helton. For her, Helton would be pointless were he not someone who has been profoundly wounded by life, as we eventually learn a man who has killed his own brother and suffered incarceration in a mental hospital, but still sentient enough to know he has lost something precious and to experience it again in his music, alternately "merry and sad," as well as in those flashes of life which materialize when he and Thompson are together, each "working" in his own way and exhibiting elements of genuine friendship.

In a letter discussing the complex symbolic meaning of the title *Noon Wine* and the song from which it comes, Porter argues that for Mr. Helton, "the song stands in his mind for the time when he was innocent, and his constant playing of it is the symbol of his constant brooding and remorse ... so you see, it really has a number of meanings.... For of course he is not mad, never was; a dislocated being, warped, out of balance, but not mad" (1990, 173). This important quotation underscores just how and why both Thompsons, but especially Royal Earle, identify so profoundly with Helton. If he is a lost sheep, unable to find his way back to a home which is no longer there, so too, ultimately, are they. In the last analysis, each of them is a stranger in a strange land, the phrase Mrs. Thompson uses twice in Peckinpah's film, which is another way of describing the particular kind of tragic experience embodied in Porter's short novel and, perhaps more so, Peckinpah's adaptation. Thus Peckinpah picks up on Helton's humanity as most of Porter's critics have not, and turns what might seem a sentimental depiction of affection between the two men into a profound insight into both Mr. Helton and Mr. Thompson. This is the true meaning of the work montages, in which Peckinpah captures Helton's almost miraculous effect on Mr. Thompson as economically as Porter renders Helton's effect on Mrs. Thompson when she sees the transformed springhouse.

The connection between Helton and Mr. Thompson is ominous as well, however, as we see well before the arrival of Homer T. Hatch and the devastating events which follow. Porter and Peckinpah highlight the early scene in which Helton flies into a silent rage when he encounters Arthur and Herbert besmirching his only links to a lost, presumably happy past, his harmonicas. Silently shaking both boys, as Mrs. Thompson observes from her kitchen window, Helton pours out much of the murderous rage he feels against those who would steal his most precious possessions from the past, his memories, as re-experienced in his harmonica tune. Mr. Thompson, a man given to temper tantrums, expresses a similar rage when he returns home, learns what his boys have done, and threatens to take a calf rope to them, thus revealing the less benign features he shares with Olaf Helton and anticipating the blind rage he feels toward Homer T. Hatch later in the action. Peckinpah, who gives Helton a moment of dialogue with Mr. Thompson, depicts Helton's sense of outraged violation when Thompson goes to his shack to apologize for his boys' behavior. "They play game with my music, Olaf Helton's music!" Helton cries while throwing his harmonicas to the floor in disgust. Mr. Thompson picks them up, places them delicately on Helton's table, and walks out. Helton looks at them a moment, then lovingly holds them to his breast, almost as if they were cherished dolls, or indeed his children. This scene, not in Porter, humanizes Helton even as it exposes the violence beneath his intensity. In the scene which follows, Mr. Thompson, his titanic temper all too clearly on display, threatens to knock his boys down and break their ribs.

Porter speaks of this troubling tie between Helton and Mr. Thompson in the letter concerning the origins of the song from which she takes her title:

> First let me explain about "Noon Wine." Maybe that title was a mistake, though it seemed so clear to me. Don't you remember the song is about a man who drank all of his wine in the morning and had none left for the rest of the day.... Maybe I went too far for my symbol, but it was for me a symbol of recklessness, of any rash act that would mar, even spoil, the future of a man. And by extension this is true of Mr. Helton, and later, of Mr. Thompson, too. Even if the reckless and unconsidered act in both cases was the extreme one of murder.... It *is* a little hard to explain, though the connection still seems clear in my mind ... but the song carries a double symbol, for Mr. Helton is obsessed by the memory of his act, and the song stands in his mind for the time when he was innocent, and his constant playing of it is the symbol of his constant brooding and remorse... [1990, 173].

Strangely, Helton has murdered in order to preserve, through the perfect music of his harmonica tune, the memory of what he has already lost. The murder of his brother did not lead to his retreat from life; that began before his brother took his harmonica and may have been even more traumatic than the killing of his brother. But the brother's theft and his murder led to Helton's incarceration and left him with only his music to keep alive the memory of a previous, happier life. If Helton is "not mad," but rather "a dislocated being, warped, out of balance," as Porter says, then his real problem is that he cannot have back what he has irrevocably, irreversibly lost, some form of perfect bliss he knew in the past, the kind of bliss we may all have known but have learned to accept as forever lost. Helton cannot do this. His harmonicas and the tune he plays endlessly are his only connections to the one "life" he has ever truly affirmed. Porter may see the song as emblematic of that previous view of paradise, but because it is both "merry and sad" we must wonder if both the possession of that world and its subsequent loss are not embedded in the song's mysterious double nature. In any event, as Porter suggests and Peckinpah dramatizes, Helton and Mr. Thompson are fatally linked by rash acts from which they can never fully recover.

Everything changes for the Thompsons with the arrival of a second, vastly more dangerous mysterious stranger, Homer T. Hatch. It is again oppressively hot and dusty in August, the same month in which Olaf Helton first appeared, amidst a restorative spray of flashing water. Mr. Thompson is fast asleep in a rocking chair, but he will awake from his pleasant dreams into an appalling waking nightmare in which the grotesque "stranger" (as Porter calls Hatch at least 11 times) sets out to destroy everything Mr. Thompson has held onto so precariously in the years following Helton's arrival. Bounty hunter and pursuer of Olaf Helton, Hatch is anything but the "savior" of the Thompson farm. Indeed, his arrival marks *Noon Wine*'s decisive turn toward tragedy, as the smug, proud, and self-important Mr. Thompson, living within the falsely earned illusion of his own success, is about to confront his own nature in the starkest, bleakest of terms. Singularly unprepared for the test he is about to undergo, Thompson will nonetheless arrive at a kind of provisional illumination which renders him a tragic figure in ways both Porter and Peckinpah work very hard to authenticate.

Homer T. Hatch has come to uncover the uncannily "hidden" or repressed aspects of Olaf Helton, his fratricide, his incarceration in a mental hospital, his flight from this hospital, but it is Mr. Thompson whom he exposes. Irritated but fascinated, Mr. Thompson hates Hatch almost as soon as he first sees him. With his filthy brown rabbit teeth, his sudden changes of expression, and his fits of loud raucous laughter when nothing apparently funny has been said, Hatch throws Mr. Thompson entirely off his guard. Hatch seems a person in pieces, and yet "[h]e certainly did remind Mr. Thompson of somebody, or maybe he really had seen the man himself somewhere" (224). Could this man be the devil, as Glenway Wescott has suggested (39), or perhaps, closer to home, a laughing, cackling, grotesquely distorted funhouse mirror image of Mr. Thompson himself? There is an aspect of the Freudian Unheimlich or "uncanny" in Hatch which makes Mr. Thompson feel that Hatch is someone he has known or seen before, a hideous repetition and repression of things in Mr. Thompson's past he cannot confront and has kept locked up most of his life: his own capacity for lying to himself and others, especially his wife, whom he seems to love and yet resent in equal measure; his exploitation of Helton by paying him low wages even though he knows Helton is worth much more; his own sudden blasts of nervous, unmotivated, and excessive laughter, well beyond the situation at hand; his smug belief in his own personal rectitude before the law and society, a belief which allows him to see himself as a good and honest citizen of his community, precisely the self-image Hatch projects. Mr. Thompson can't get a focus on Hatch because he can't get a focus on himself. While Homer T. Hatch may not be Mr. Thompson's psychological double in the sense Otto Rank develops in his classic account, Hatch is close to being a projection of everything Mr. Thompson cannot face up to in himself, what he will finally confront at the tragic conclusion of both short novel and film.

Peckinpah's hot, sweating, intrusive Hatch is a superb representation of Porter's character, as Peckinpah seems even more conscious of the latent threat Hatch represents with his big knife and his handcuffs. Everything begins to fall apart when Mr. Thompson invites Hatch to join him for a chaw of tobacco in his side yard, next to the chopping block where, in the film, the ominous ax embedded in a tree trunk splits the film frame in two and seems to bring Thompson and Hatch closer to a violent tipping point. Mr. Thompson is shocked to learn from Hatch that Helton was last seen in North Dakota singing his one song while sitting in a "lunatic asylum," wrapped in a straightjacket, and this revelation is followed by an even greater shock: Helton was in the mental hospital because he had slain his own brother, run him through with a pitchfork when the latter took one of Helton's cherished harmonicas, lost it, and then refused to replace it right before his own marriage. But as Hatch and Mr. Thompson sit down to have a chaw, Hatch goes beyond educating Mr. Thompson about Helton's past to challenge everything Mr. Thompson believes or values, even the kind of tobacco he chews. Serpent-like, Hatch keeps striking at Mr. Thompson's feelings of ownership, husbandly manliness, even his sense of selfhood.

Earlier, Mr. Thompson has alluded to Ellie's sickliness and weak eyes, and Hatch, whose own wife has died early of too much hard work, seizes upon this moment to talk about Ellie as if she were a worthless domestic animal: "I never had much use for a woman always complainin'. I'd get rid of her mighty quick, yes, sir, mighty quick. It's just as you say: a dead loss, keepin' one of 'em up" (248). Mr. Thompson is "baffled" by Hatch's response because "[t]his was not at all what [he] had heard himself say" (248). He begins to feel even more protective toward Ellie and, by extension, Mr. Helton, and resentful toward Hatch. His rage begins to rise, "climbing from somewhere deep down in him, climbing and spreading all through him" (250). Mr. Thompson's anger only increases as Hatch continues to go after Ellie, who in one respect resembles Katherine Anne Porter, a lover of flowers who once wrote "The Flower of Flowers" (1950), an extravagant rhapsody to the sweet red roses of her childhood (1970, 145–

The fatal moment in *Noon Wine*. Mr. Thompson (Jason Robards) and Mr. Helton (Per Oscarsson) poised before the murderous ax.

53). As he continues the critique of "sweetenin'" leveled against Mr. Thompson's favorite tobacco, Hatch squirts a stream of juice at a "dry-looking little rosebush that was having a hard enough time as it was, standing all day in the blazing sun, its roots clenched in the baked earth." He then declares that "sweetenin', even a little ... is the sign of—" before Mr. Thompson interrupts him with a strident defense of Helton (260). This association of "sweetenin'" with Helton and the rose with Mrs. Thompson's frail condition is deliberate, as Hatch has set out to destroy Mr. Thompson's friend and wife. While Peckinpah does not have Hatch squirt tobacco at a rosebush, he alters Porter's story slightly by showing Mrs. Thompson out gathering flowers in a basket while Mr. Thompson and Hatch are first talking, then later shows her arranging the flowers in a vase just as she hears the crack of the ax on Hatch's head.

How does it come to pass that Mr. Thompson kills Homer T. Hatch with an ax? In both Porter and Peckinpah the catastrophe is precipitated by Helton coming around the corner of the house and rushing at Hatch, who is prepared to defend himself with his "long bowie knife in his hand" (255), but in Porter events are filtered through Mr. Thompson's fevered consciousness. We never learn just what happens ("something has happened" is as close as Porter comes to an explanation [255]), for Porter enters into Mr. Thompson's seemingly deranged vision of things:

> He saw the fat man with his long bowie knife in his hand, he saw Mr. Helton come round the corner on the run, his long jaw dropped, his arms swirling, his eyes wild. Mr. Helton came in between them, fists doubled up, then stopped short, glaring at the fat man, his big frame seemed to collapse, he trembled like a shied horse; and then the fat man drove at him, knife in one

> hand, handcuffs in the other. Mr. Thompson saw it coming, he saw the blade going into Mr. Helton's stomach, he knew he had the ax out of the log in his own hands, felt his arms go up over his head and bring the ax down on Mr. Hatch's head as if he were stunning beef [255–56].

As Seydor reminds us (1997, 104–105), we are not certain Hatch has the handcuffs in his hand, nor can we tell whether or not Helton actually ran *between* Mr. Thompson and Hatch, which would have given Thompson an excuse to defend his "good" double against his "evil" double. It is all mysterious and enigmatic, subjectively rendered through Porter's prose and Mr. Thompson's severely skewed point of view. Eventually we learn that Helton has no knife wound, though he runs from the Thompson farm after Hatch is killed and dies from a beating inflicted by the posse which tracks him down.[10] Did Mr. Thompson fantasize the knifing and the other details of the Helton-Hatch confrontation? Neither we nor Mr. Thompson himself can finally answer this question.

In Peckinpah's film the composition is significantly altered, for of course Peckinpah must visualize the scene. He provides extreme closeups of the ax in the tree stump, of Mr. Thompson's face, of his shoulder moving back, but we never actually witness the act of killing Hatch, never see the ax in his hand, as if some unseen force is moving within him, like a devilish Greek deity, to cause this disaster. All is confusion, and Thompson's act, experienced in Porter through free indirect discourse, is depicted in Peckinpah not just in Thompson's "fragmented perceptions but in some sense [the camera work which] actually embodies them" (Seydor 1997, 105). This captures the sense in which Mr. Thompson is both a murderer and an innocent man, contradictory notions which will madden and perplex him, and alienate his wife, with her desire for order and moral clarity, for the sanctity of her word and always speaking the truth. In Seydor's eloquent formulation, it is as if Mr. Thompson "has *willed* the killing of Hatch rather than actually done the deed, which is crucial to the full understanding of his claim to innocence" (1997, 105)—as if forces within his body and his subconscious mind strike out against Hatch in a series of broken, jagged, and rapid camera shots, culminating in that horrible sound which Ellie hears in the moment Peckinpah cuts to her. This cut to Mrs. Thompson implies as well some of the husband's profoundly ambiguous feelings toward his wife. Not that Mr. Thompson would ever kill Ellie, even in his most murderous rages, but rather that there are times when her withering judgment of him makes him hate her, especially her unequivocal sense of morality, so like that of Joshua Knudsen in *Ride the High Country*, her absolute, implacable values insisted upon despite the wildly varying contingencies and "mixed" nature of human behavior. She is so judgmental, so unforgiving, and he hates her for judging him, and hates himself even more for hating her. It is a vicious circle, not unlike Peckinpah's deeply conflicted feelings for his own mother, or for his "law and order" father.

It soon becomes clear that Mr. Thompson will never get to the heart of what happened, that it will never come "straight" for him because his newly-discovered confusions reveal his tragically divided nature in ways he has effectively masked for years, both in his marriage and in his unexplored relationship with Helton. Homer T. Hatch has set loose the tragic machinery latent in *Noon Wine* from the beginning, for as Thomas F. Walsh remarks, the short novel is not just a "tragedy of circumstances," but also "a tragedy of character in that only Mr. Thompson could be destroyed by Helton and Hatch because they symbolize ingredients in his character which make for self-destruction" (88). We would add that eventually they also make for a kind of self-enlightenment, fragmentary and incomplete perhaps, but this is true of most great tragedies. Complete self-illumination and self-understanding are more common in Greek tragedy, almost nonexistent in Shakespearean tragedy, and virtually alien to the skeptical vision which informs most modern tragedies.

When Mrs. Thompson finally does come around the corner of the house and sees Hatch on the ground, his head bashed in, and is told by her husband that Hatch has struck a knife into Mr. Helton, it is clear that Mr. Thompson has imagined what he wanted to see, has come to the rescue of Mr. Helton because he was in mortal terror for Helton's life. Now Mr. Thompson stands there beside his wife, his hand on the ax handle, bent over "a man Mrs. Thompson has never seen" (256). This language suggests the abyss which will separate the Thompsons irreversibly, rendering them permanent "strangers," as the tragedy continues to unfold. Mark Schorer captures perfectly the new and terrible world of suffering and death the Thompsons have entered: "After all the easygoing years, the sudden unexpected *horror* of the present, the horror whose truth one could not know until one was inextricably *in* it, when it proves to be an absolute doom to which one's own nature, however trivially expressed before, now commits us; this is what [*Noon Wine*] is about. One man's present, the wine bottle, and the time not yet noon" (174). The perfect family has been destroyed and Mr. Thompson must face his fate alone, with no help from his wife, his children, his neighbors, or anyone else. He may be exonerated at his trial, but the insight he gradually achieves is that, like Helton, he has become a stranger in a strange land.

Mrs. Thompson begins to experience her own sense of "strangeness" when she is asked to corroborate Mr. Thompson's version of events even though she has not seen what happened. When she is asked to lie for her husband at his trial for the murder of Hatch, it rends her soul. She lies, but her lie opens a permanent rift between her and her husband. In language which anticipates the moral complexities of *The Wild Bunch*, Mr. Thompson, who is not even certain his wife would be lying, since he cannot conceive of himself as a murderer, pleads with her before they go to court: "It ain't what I *want* you to do, Ellie, it's what you *have* to do." The language here is not in Porter and is very close to the tormented Deke Thornton's "What I like and what I need are two different things," a similarity which should remind us of the importance attached in *The Wild Bunch* to Thornton's "giving his word," even if it is given to a railroad. It is surprising to see the similarities between Mrs. Thompson and Deke Thornton (Robert Ryan), a tortured, conscience-riven outlaw who betrays his friend Pike Bishop (William Holden) (as indeed Pike betrays him). Whatever the reason it is invoked, Kantian morality may seem to have little place in Peckinpah's "mixed" moral universe, but in *The Wild Bunch* it becomes a crucial issue. Writing at the top of his form, Peckinpah inserted here the crucial, despairing request from husband to wife, reminding us

Beneath a menacing tree Mr. Thompson (Jason Robards) pleads with his frightened wife (Olivia de Havilland) to perjure herself in a court of law in *Noon Wine*.

that Porter's achievement is not at all compromised by Peckinpah's skillful alterations in her greatest work.

Peckinpah captures brilliantly the widening gap between the Thompsons when, after the trial is over and Mr. Thompson has "won" his case, we see him all alone in the darkening courtroom, his wife and children cut off from him, his sense of helpless isolation enhanced by a high angle shot, to be followed by an agonizing series of montage shots as Mr. Thompson forces Ellie to ride with him, like some far more conflicted version of Coleridge's ancient mariner, while he explains his version of the story to mostly well-mannered but, like Ellie Thompson, disbelieving neighbors (see Seydor 1997, 101). Porter covers all of this as a flashback, whereas Peckinpah deals with the problem by filming the events in real time, and the effect on both Thompsons is, if anything, even more devastating. In Porter, husband and wife are described as moving through "thick" late-summer dust which covers their clothes and gets in their lungs (262). The effect of the Thompsons' gradual descent into the living hell of their life together is movingly conveyed by Peckinpah's camera work. In another superb montage, Peckinpah juxtaposes the faces of husband and wife on their buckboard in separate shots, for we almost never see the two of them in the same shot, the distance between them has grown so great. Throughout these visits we see there will be no new life for the Thompsons, as Ellie seems to know when she stands before an icebox Helton has helped them purchase and feels in her despair "the sweet coldness flow out of it" (258). Now the thick blanket of death-like dust covers her, and she senses that her life has become "all one dread" and does not know if she can go on (257).

Peckinpah combines this powerful reflection with another piece of writing, Wordsworth's "Tintern Abbey," in which we find the same phrase Porter and Peckinpah use in slightly different ways. In Porter the relevant passage reads: "There was a time, she said to herself, when I thought I had neighbors and friends, there was a time when we could hold up our heads, there was a time when my husband hadn't killed a man and I could tell the truth to anybody about anything" (259–60). Peckinpah shortens this speech but retains its central poetic significance, its overwhelming sense of loss and regret for a world now dead, and he incorporates the key speech in which Mrs. Thompson defines life as "all one dread" as she sits beside her husband in the agonizing, fruitless visits with their neighbors in which Royal Earle over and over again invokes "My wife" in defense of his innocence.

For Mr. Thompson, life is no less "dreadful." In the buggy ride home from their last disastrous visit to a neighbor, Mrs. Thompson draws farther and farther away from him. In Porter, it is now clear that Mr. Thompson has given up; "his eyes hollowed out and dead-looking" (258) tell us all we need to know about his future. Mr. Thompson argues with his wife, but he knows it is too late. He feels like "a dead man": "He was dead to his other life, he had got to the end of something without knowing why, and he had to make a fresh start, he did not know how. Something different was going to begin, he didn't know what. It was in some way not his business. He didn't feel he was going to have much to do with it" (265). The language of fatality is dominant here, much in the spirit of the Greeks, or for that matter the last act of *Hamlet*. Mr. Thompson "knew the end had come" (264), and all he can do is give himself over to it. His boys look at him as if he is indeed a stranger, his wife barely speaks to him. He still runs those awful events over in his mind, trying to find the "straight" of it, but he cannot do so. Everything becomes so "thick" that this word, used repeatedly in the short novel, comes to underscore the obscure origins of the tragic events Mr. Thompson must endure but will never understand. The irrational outburst of violence against a man he barely knew says so much about the lies and self-deceptions which characterize his life, yet nothing really explains why he killed Hatch in an act which, as written by Porter and filmed by Peckinpah, still feels hallucinatory rather than real.

Peckinpah is famous for his brilliant and enigmatic endings. One might say that the way he ends *Noon Wine* sets the stage for the later superb endings. The conclusion consists of two scenes which culminate in the climactic death of Mr. Thompson. The first scene begins with Mr. Thompson lying in bed on his final night, exhausted, defeated, but awake and tossing violently. The events which have precipitated his ruin run through his mind. In a high angle shot which recalls the sense of entrapment we experience with the capture of Helton in a corral, Mr. Thompson lies enfolded by darkness in a room "so claustrophobic it feels airless, conveying an almost unbearable impression of a couple trapped in a dynamic that is destroying them" (Seydor 1997, 107). Ellie lies next to Mr. Thompson, silent, still, perhaps feigning sleep, "her arms crossed over her breast and holding herself so rigid she suggests a cadaver laid out in a coffin" (Seydor 1997, 107). One wonders who is really being crucified here, the crucifying wife or the crucified husband? Both are suffering in their own ways. This room, like their life together, has become their tomb. Peckinpah will pick up on this idea once more, to devastating effect, in a radical change he makes at the end of the film.

His mind racing, Mr. Thompson is still trying to "straighten out" what happened. In voiceover he thinks, "Maybe everything about my killin' that Hatch was wrong from start to finish. Dammit, I did. Maybe not the right thing but the only thing I could do. But did I have to kill him? By God, I never saw a man I hated more. When I first laid eyes on him I knew in my bones that fella was just here for trouble. Why didn't I just tell that Hatch to get out before he ever got in? Ay, yah, why didn't I do a lot of things? All I had to do was, well, maybe I had to hit him, or just grab him and put the handcuffs on him and take him over to the sheriff for disturbin' the peace. But what about that knife...?" He looks over at his wife and asks, "You asleep, Ellie?" as we dissolve to images of Hatch's face, then his hands, his knife, his cuffs, and Mr. Helton racing around the corner of the house only to find himself trapped between the two men before running off, all of these nightmare images superimposed in montage on a closeup of Mr. Thompson writhing in bed. His voiceover continues, "But if I hadn't killed him, nothing would a happened to Mr. Helton. Oh God, God! He would be playing his tune right now about feelin' so good in the morning and drinking all the wine so he needn't feel bad, and Hatch would be safe and ready to listen to reason and repent his meanness." Suddenly, Thompson rises out of bed and speaks aloud, "You comin' around ready to persecute an innocent man, ruinin' a whole family for...?" And he blindly swings an imaginary ax, as if reliving a waking nightmare. His face is distorted by genuine rage as he reenacts the very murder he has denied committing. This is a moment of pure self-indictment, as Thompson catches himself in a "confession" of how much he hated Hatch and wanted to kill him.

At the same time Ellie awakes, terrified, and watches her husband make those very real murderous ax swings into the air. She screams and then cries out, "Oh, oh, don't! Don't! Don't!" (266). Her scream seems to duplicate Helton's stifled scream, almost an animal screech, which Peckinpah added when he depicted Helton caught in the corral like a trapped animal. The boys rush into the room, thinking their father has struck their mother, and Arthur, the older son, cries out, "Momma, momma, don't die." Mother and sons gather on one side of the room, Royal Earle on the other, his head down, turned aside, having reached the absolute depths of aloneness. Arthur looks at him as if he were a "dangerous wild beast" (266), language recalling the sheriff's description of Helton near the moment of his death, when "he fought like a wildcat" (259). Arthur cries out, "What did you do to her? ...You touch her again and I'll blow your heart out" (266–67). But the abject Royal Earle Thompson has no more "heart" to be blown out. He tells the boys, "Don't you get any notions in your head. I never did your mother any harm in my life, on purpose" (267). That final comma or pause (prolonged in Peckinpah's adaptation), that moment of doubt on Mr. Thompson's part, must be perceived as a partial acknowledgment of the repressed anger he feels toward Ellie. And yet we know he would never have done any real harm to his wife. What he did to Hatch was in fact a genuine aberration, if no less lethal. Yet part of what went into that murder was aimed at Ellie, as both Thompsons seem inchoately to know.

Alfred Hitchcock once remarked, in discussing Norman Bates in *Psycho*, that there is a kind of scale which all of humankind falls along, from least to most violent, and in certain situations the scale may alter radically. This is true for Mr. Thompson. Once he had everything with Mr. Helton. Then Hatch came along and because Mr. Thompson was so desperate to hold onto what he had, he was willing to kill to preserve it. His actual murder of Hatch and his frustrated guilt and anger before Ellie are of a piece, though distinguished by the significant act of killing itself. Mr. Thompson claims he "never did nothin' to harm your mother in my life ... on purpose," but when that same phrase, "on purpose," is used again at the end of the short novel and film, it takes on an even more complex meaning, as Peckinpah subtly alters Porter's distinction between Mrs. Thompson and Hatch, as viewed by Mr. Thompson, by having Mr. Thompson use the same phrase and again pause before it (unlike the same passage in Porter) to create an even more perplexingly ambiguous view of the Thompson marriage, a view which we believe helps to explain Peckinpah's decision to change the place where Mr. Thompson chooses to end his life.

Standing in the doorway, Mr. Thompson essentially tells his family farewell, for he knows that he is not coming back. He speaks his final words to his wife and children while half in light and half in darkness, the perfect cinematic "space" for a character who is completely torn, unable to inhabit either the realm of the domestic or the abyss-like world of pure darkness. Mr. Thompson has no other options. "What else could he do?" Porter has reminded us. In a double sense, there can be no return to things as they were. Things were never completely real during the time Helton lived with them, and the cruel reality of Mr. Thompson's having killed/murdered Homer T. Hatch only serves to enhance the terrible awareness of what can never be recovered within the Thompson family.

Peckinpah films Mr. Thompson's brief but final nocturnal journey to the springhouse using a very high crane shot, in which we see the Thompson farm house, its picket fence gate open, at the right side of the film frame, and the springhouse at the other. Peckinpah then films Thompson's entrance into the springhouse, using a low angle shot to catch his entry. The springhouse seems even gloomier than usual, its play of shadows which surround Thompson creating a more deeply-interiorized sense of what is to follow. We hear the steady running of spring water into the dark pool which lies just beyond Mr. Thompson, but those green ferns we associated earlier with the transformative power of Mr. Helton are now absent, hidden perhaps in the thickening shadows Peckinpah employs in filming this altered space. Helton is now dead, and Thompson sits down at a crude table to begin composing his suicide note.

In Porter, when Mr. Thompson decides to take his own life, he walks through the night, a kerosene lamp in one hand, a loaded shotgun in the other, to "the farthest end of his fields" (267), where he "could almost see in the dark" (268). Mr. Thompson's going so far from home, away from his wife and children, may indicate his desire not to take his life anywhere near the house, to keep this terrible last act as far away from his already suffering family as possible, but it may also indicate just how distanced he now feels from his family. His aloneness is so complete, he must get as far away as he can while remaining on his own land. Much to Porter's anger and chagrin, which she expressed in a letter to Peckinpah after the film of *Noon Wine* ran on ABC, Peckinpah follows a symbolic line of thought and imagery which begins with the first shot of the film by choosing to have Thompson take his life in the film's most symbolically loaded space, the springhouse. Why does Peckinpah choose this location for the film's climactic scene? We suspect that Mr. Thompson's feelings for Helton and their odd but genuine friendship may have drawn Thompson to the site identified with the one person in the world for whom he still feels some kind of human bond. The springhouse is where Mrs. Thompson first witnessed the Helton "miracle" at work, its waters flowing coldly and purely, its butter cooling in the pristine pool (258). Ever drawn to and entranced by water, intensely aware of the central significance of water to the history and meaning of the West, Peckinpah once made an entire film dealing with this theme, *The Ballad of Cable Hogue* (1970), a fable about a man who found water — and love — where there wasn't any. In *Noon Wine*, from the film's first shot of Helton moving along the Thompsons' fence, the spray of water from the boys at play in the trough seemingly guiding Helton to Mr. Thompson, we know that water and its central source, the springhouse, will loom large symbolically.

Mr. Thompson has lost everything — wife, children, community, his good name — with the murder of Mr. Hatch, but also the death of Mr. Helton, for which, following his wife's admonition, he takes equal responsibility. Peckinpah leaves an important reference to Helton in Mr. Thompson's suicide note even as he omits a good deal of the note as written by Porter:

> I Royal Earle Thompson do solemnly swear that I did not take the life of Mr. Homer T. Hatch ... on purpose. I did not aim to hit him with the ax, only to keep him off Mr. Helton, who would have done the same for me. I've told all this to the judge and jury, and they let me off, but nobody believes it. My wife...[11]

In these brief sentences, especially the final, unconcluded sentence, we may have the answer as to why Peckinpah goes on to alter the ending. Mr. Thompson seems really to believe that Helton would have done anything to "save" him, but his wife would not do so. Yes, she lied for him, but transparently and without passion, conviction, or love. And it destroyed their marriage, almost more than the actual death of Hatch, for her to violate her principles and tell that lie. But in Peckinpah's version more than in Porter's, Helton may very well have come to Mr. Thompson's rescue, though we can never know, even in the film where there is more evidence that a relationship has grown up between Mr. Thompson and Helton. The real point is that to the end Mr. Thompson *believes* in Helton's coming to his rescue, perhaps because he knows no one else would have done so. This may be a saving fiction, a Eugene O'Neill "pipedream," but Mr. Thompson feels compelled to affirm it because the truth which counters it is too dark and despairing.

In his conclusion Peckinpah alters Porter's subtle distinction between Mr. Thompson's important pause before he says "on purpose" in speaking of his wife and Mr. Thompson's written confession: "I did not take the life of Mr. Homer T. Hatch on purpose" (268). It is unbearable for Mr. Thompson to think that he ever struck out against his wife "on purpose." Thus the hesitation, the pause. With the murder of Hatch, however, Porter's Mr. Thompson is emphatic, with no need to pause. Here, sans the crucial pause, and yet employing the same phrase he used to defend himself against any charge that he deliberately intended Mrs. Thompson harm, he argues even more emphatically for his innocence: "I did not take the life of Mr. Homer T. Hatch on purpose." And yet we know Mr. Thompson "hated" Hatch from the first moment he saw him. The tragic irony here is that he seems to feel the need to deny any kind of doubt, to eliminate the pause, but we know that there was plenty of anger, of real will in the death-blow he dealt Hatch. And he also feels the necessity to deny he ever *deliberately* intended to cause his wife harm. This distinction does not work for Peckinpah, who inserts the same pause Porter creates for Mr. Thompson's claim about his wife in order to imply the same level of doubt on Mr. Thompson's part about his slaying of Hatch. The connection between the two claims reinforces the doubt about his feelings toward his wife. Perhaps this is why Peckinpah's Mr. Thompson kills himself so close to "home." It may be for a purpose he does not fully comprehend, but this is a crucial aspect of tragic doubt, partial understanding, the confusion of motives at the very heart of virtually all great tragedies.

It would be too extreme to call this an act of revenge against Mrs. Thompson, but it certainly brings out more conflicted feelings toward her than Porter registers. When Mr. Thompson proceeds to cross out "My wife" from his note, we are uncertain about his motivation. Earlier, he has insistently evoked Ellie in his defense, always beginning his appeals to his neighbors with the claim "My wife will tell you the truth." "My wife... My wife...": the phrase haunts the short novel. When Mr. Thompson obliterates his wife's name, he does so in equally charged language: "He wet the pencil point with the tip of his tongue and marked out the last two words. He sat a while blacking out the words until he made a neat oblong patch where they had been, and started again" (268).[12] Is Mr. Thompson blacking out the reference to his wife because he no longer wants to invoke her name to lie for him? Perhaps. But is he not also blacking out her name because he knows their relationship is dead? In essence, he is "burying" her before he buries himself.

It is interesting that we do not see in the film the results of Mr. Thompson's blacking out Mrs. Thompson. Rather, the internalized voiceover ends here, with Mr. Thompson's act of "silencing" his wife. Now Thompson begins to speak aloud what he writes and concludes his note with a final condemnation of Hatch: "It was Mr. Homer T. Hatch who came to do wrong to a harmless man. He caused all the trouble and deserved to die, but I am sorry it was me who had to kill him." In Porter, his note finished, Mr. Thompson "licked the point of his pencil again, and signed his full name carefully" (268). "Carefully" is the word Porter uses earlier to describe the manner in which Royal Earle Thompson, so "unmanned" by his "woman's work," tries to preserve his artificial dignity: "All his carefully related fields of activity were related somehow to Mr. Thompson's feeling for the appearance of things, his own appearance in the sight of God and man" (233). This may help us to understand why he signs his full name "carefully," then arranges himself in that far field so that he can take his own life in a dignified fashion, even as he "fumble[s]" for the trigger with his "great toe" just before pulling it (268). The scene may feel a bit comic in the midst of Mr. Thompson's tragedy of misunderstanding, but it conveys a poignant sense of dignity which prevents it from being comically crude or cruelly ironic. In his own bumbling fashion, as Porter once said, Mr. Thompson is trying to do the right thing.

Peckinpah's ending is even more complex and painful in other ways. David Weddle remarks that, after Mr. Thompson blacks out his wife, speaks his final lines, and looks "off into the shed's dark hollow space," he places his suicide note "carefully under a lead weight, then picks up the shotgun, pulls back both hammers, and, after a moment's hesitation, brings the barrels to his forehead" (1994, 293). But Mr. Thompson is not just in the barn, he is in the film's most important symbolic space, the springhouse. Also, it is not a simple "dead weight" he picks up, it is a butter stamp, used no doubt to stamp and identify as Mr. Thompson's the cooled butter formed in molds in the cold spring water and sold at market. This makes the stamped butter an object of pride for Mr. Thompson, something which honors his feelings for Helton as he places the butter stamp on his final note. This works once again to demonstrate just how much Mr. Thompson's attachment to Helton has come to supplant his feelings for his wife. As Walsh notes, "Mr. Helton ... does displace Mrs. Thompson on the farm and accentuates Thompson's ambivalence toward her. He is Thompson's wish-defense against destruction" (84). Here at the end, as throughout the film, Peckinpah extends Porter's insight into Helton's significance for Mr. Thompson.

We would note another change from Porter, who emphasizes that Mr. Thompson cocked both hammers so that "the twin barrels pointed towards his head" (268). In Peckinpah, despite Weddle's assertion, only one hammer is cocked, and we see it in closeup, as if Peckinpah wants us to know he is subtly altering Porter. Though clearly Thompson does not understand what he is doing, he may be subliminally suggesting, by pulling back just one hammer, his allegiance to what is still good and alive in him based on his genuine fellow feeling and friendship for Helton. In a darker vein, Mr. Thompson may also be indicating that the second loaded barrel, figuratively if not literally, is reserved for his wife. For as Mr. Thompson raises the shotgun to his head, Peckinpah cuts to the same overhead crane shot he used initially when Mr. Thompson made his way across the barnyard to the springhouse. We hear, from this high angle, the sound of a single shotgun blast as it roars and reverberates like a memory throughout the farm, a sound very much like Pat Garrett's gun as he kills Billy the Kid in *Pat Garrett and Billy the Kid* (1973), a sound which feels like the death of more than a single person. Indeed, in the act of slaying the Kid (Kris Kristofferson), Garrett (James Coburn) seals his own fate as well as his young friend's. In his wife's words, Garrett is already "dead inside," and one wonders if Mrs. Thompson does not feel much the same way about herself.

As the shotgun blast echoes across the farm, Peckinpah cuts swiftly to Mrs. Thompson, sitting alone in bed at the left side of the film frame, staring at the other half of the frame, once filled by her husband, now empty and dark. We are reminded of the coffin-like spaces which enveloped Mr. Thompson in the springhouse, and the claustrophobic darkness which surrounded Mrs. Thompson and her husband as they lay in bed earlier. While the sound of the gunshot resounds through her mind, she makes a quarter turn toward the camera, revealing an ambiguous expression which does not easily give up its meanings. Is she relieved that it is finally over? If so, she also looks startled and perhaps aggrieved, guilty and relieved at the same time. The turn of her head away from the darkness and the lowering of her eyes are the same expressions we have seen her husband make whenever he felt guilty or rejected before her critical, self-righteous judgment. She makes no sound while gazing off, and within a few seconds the screen fades to black, which implies, it would seem, not just the end of the film, but the end of both Thompsons.

It seems perfectly natural that Katherine Anne Porter, who liked Peckinpah's film even though she complained about the commercial interruptions over which he had no control, was upset about the ending because it was not *her* ending, because she knew, at some deeper level, that Peckinpah had changed her conclusion in ways she found disturbing. Seydor has provided an excellent account of Peckinpah's ending and Porter's reaction to it:

> This closeup [of Mrs. Thompson], it is said, left the audience at the cast and crew screening absolutely devastated. Yet Porter strenuously objected to it in a letter she later wrote to Peckinpah, protesting that Mrs. Thompson "was not alone, her sons were with her trying to soothe her terror and grief." But the setup is obviously close enough that it doesn't preclude the presence of her sons offscreen; just as obviously, Peckinpah, taking a cue from Porter herself, wanted to allude to the murder for one last time, which he also played offscreen except for the sound of the death instrument over a somewhat looser closeup of an equally uncomprehending Mrs. Thompson [1997, 112].

Seydor goes on to say that "[t]he final closeup is Peckinpah's way of suggesting she has failed her husband as much as he has failed her." As Seydor notes, "the composition at once freezes Mrs. Thompson in a bleak present and posits an equally forlorn future, leaving her as isolated as her hapless husband, as confused, and as deluded about her own complicity in the dark chain of events that has brought them both to this place of desolation and despair" (1997, 112). This positioning of Mrs. Thompson alone, isolated in the Dantean darkness of their bedroom, seems another way of equating her spiritual death with her husband's literal death, implying, through the still-loaded chamber of the shotgun, a place for her in this terrible skein of miscommunication, of love gone terribly wrong, of the vast chasm which has separated the tragically doomed Thompsons in both life and death.

Earlier, we spoke of Peckinpah's decision to end with Mrs. Thompson's response to the shotgun blast as a radical change from Porter. Perhaps it is better to say that this moving finale illustrates Peckinpah's extraordinary ability to alter Porter's text in order to reproduce or even magnify the tragic effects of this great short novel. Peckinpah's fifty-odd minute adaptation of *Noon Wine* lacks the scope of his greatest films, *The Wild Bunch* in particular, but nothing he was ever to do exhibits so thoroughly, in every detail, his mastery of the filmmaker's art.

III

Seydor rightly describes Peckinpah's adaptation of *Noon Wine* as "exceptionally faithful without being literal" (1997, 99). Nonetheless, there are significant differences between Porter's and Peckinpah's versions of this tragic tale. As Seydor himself notes, Peckinpah surpasses Porter in conveying what it costs Mrs. Thompson to lie for her husband (1997, 101). Indeed, despite his reputation for seldom developing his women characters, Peckinpah expands Mrs. Thompson's role to powerful effect, especially in those parallel moments when she hears the ax striking Hatch and the shotgun blast signaling her husband's suicide. Some would say Peckinpah characteristically implicates Mrs. Thompson in the guilt which properly belongs to Mr. Thompson, but it seems to us Peckinpah is simply extending Porter's insights into the "tragic" marriage between Mr. and Mrs. Thompson. Peckinpah departs from his source more clearly (though not altogether so) in expanding the role of Helton, his relationship with Mr. Thompson, and the importance of the springhouse as it relates to Helton and the Thompsons' fortunes. As we have argued, Peckinpah follows Porter's characterization of Helton in her text and her letters concerning the text, but he goes farther than Porter in heightening the dramatic life of all the principal characters by humanizing Helton and therefore the people with whom he interacts. By expanding the portrait of Helton's divided nature, Peckinpah expands as well the tragic dimensions of both Mr. and Mrs. Thompson.

Peckinpah enhances these tragic relationships in part by assembling an extraordinary group of actors for his adaptation. The minor parts are played by important recurring figures in Peckinpah's films such as L. Q. Jones and Ben Johnson; the crucial parts of Helton and Hatch are flawlessly performed by Per Oscarsson and Theodore Bikel, respectively[13]; and the Thompsons are of course played by Jason Robards and Olivia de Havilland, among the finest actors of their era. De Havilland manages to generate a great deal of sympathy for a character who could have seemed a satiric caricature, and her responses to the film's violent deaths are almost unbearably moving.[14] Except for Peckinpah, however, no one is more responsible for the film's tragic depth than Jason Robards, the preeminent O'Neill actor of his time who immortalized Jamie Tyrone in *Long Day's Journey into Night* and Theodore Hickman, or "Hickey," the guilt-tormented husband who murders his all-too-loving wife in *The Iceman Cometh*. Whether or not Peckinpah was aware of it, Robards' depiction of Mr. Thompson blindly swinging an imaginary ax as he relives the murder of Hatch is eerily reminiscent of Robards' celebrated portrayal of Hickey.[15] Throughout, Robards embodies a Mr. Thompson whose fatally divided character is simply more complex and compelling than Porter's creation.

Seydor has also paid rich tribute to Peckinpah's "dream cast" (1997, 99), another example of the insight he provides everywhere in his chapter on *Noon Wine*, the most significant commentary on this key film. Earlier, we said that Peckinpah had good reason to respond to Porter's short novel, and Seydor amply justifies this claim by devoting fully half of his chapter to the parallels between the Thompsons and Peckinpah's parents (1997, 113–34). The biographical connections do not fully account for Peckinpah's scrupulous attention to Porter's text, however, and we would argue that the one thing missing in Seydor's chapter is appreciation of Porter's tragic form and Peckinpah's commitment to honoring this form. In part this may derive from Seydor's views on Helton, for Seydor a schizophrenic incapable of normal social relationships and therefore hardly a fit participant in a tragic action. In part, however, Seydor simply seems not to take the film's devastating moments (described so well throughout his chapter) as adding up to a tragic action. We would like to conclude our own discussion of this great film by reviewing the kind of tragedy it represents.

Groff has previously traced the tragic elements in Porter to the origins of Greek tragedy in the myth of Dionysus, for whom the first tragedies were performed in public:

> In the enigmatic character of Dionysus, the ancient Greeks expressed their understanding of the human capacity to feel joyous transcendence in the psychological ground where the tragic vision of suffering is nurtured. The wine god, who represents the power of spiritual intoxication to transcend mundane realities, has his terrifying aspects, as well; for in this state of sublime intoxication, irrational forces which go beyond the mind's power to order its world are unleashed. Hence, the persistent prayers of Sophoclean choruses for moderation, forbearance, and humility. Reverencing maturity of judgment, reason, stability, and tolerance — all Apollonian virtues in support of a safely established society — the ancient Greeks were not so naïve as to trust that the gods were in their heaven and all was right with the world [43].

In Groff's view, Porter's *Noon Wine* embodies the ancient "Dionysian spirit of tragedy" (45) in its reincarnation of the unending conflict between Dionysian and Apollonian forces in nature, the Dionysian elements appropriately captured in Helton's drinking song and the violence which ensues at what Friedrich Nietzsche would call "noontide."

Groff does not in fact cite Nietzsche, whose writings on tragedy and "noontide" could easily serve as a brilliant gloss on tragic form in both Porter and Peckinpah. Nietzsche's first book was entitled *The Birth of Tragedy* and he wrote on the subject often. In *Thus Spake Zarathustra*, he describes his eponymous hero-wanderer's quest for a perfect transcendent union of his conflicting selves:

> About the hour of noon, however, when the sun stood exactly over Zarathustra's head, he passed by an old gnarled and crooked tree which was embraced around by the abundant love of a vine and hidden from itself.... Then he felt a desire to relieve a little thirst and to pluck himself a grape, but when he had already extended his arm to do so, he felt an even greater desire to do something else: that is, to lay [*sic*] down at the hour of perfect noon and sleep.... In falling asleep, however, Zarathustra spoke thus to his heart: "Soft! Soft! Has the world not just become perfect? What has happened to me? ... Just see — soft! Old noontide sleeps, it moves its mouth: has it not just drunk ... an ancient brown drop of golden happiness, of golden wine? Something glides across it, its happiness laughs. Thus does a god laugh.... Precisely the least thing, the gentlest, lightest, the rustling of a lizard, a breath, a moment, a twinkling of the eye — little makes up the quality of the best happiness. Soft! What has happened to me? Listen! Has time flown away? Do I not fall? Have I not fallen — listen? Into the well of eternity?" [Hough 94].

Sheridan Hough refers to the experience captured here as "the moment in which all differences vanish" (94), something like the Dionysian spirit of complete union with nature in which the self escapes from its conflicting dualities with a momentary state of intoxicated bliss in which one is "rescued from this painful self-awareness by the ecstatic (and perfectly unshadowed) moment of 'noon'" (xix). It need hardly be said that for Nietzsche this state, whether embodied in Helton's song or Mr. Thompson's contentment with his family and farm, is transitory and certain to be followed by the ceaseless and death-obsessed flow of time. At this point a violent burst of energy is set loose, to be followed, inevitably, by pain and suffering.

We think it is useful to see Peckinpah as looking for a story in which such tragic forces are unleashed by the protagonist as much as by the world in which he lives. Peckinpah's first great tragedy, *Ride the High Country*, embodies the uniquely Christian tragic form in which an imperfect but morally unblemished hero suffers for others, redemptively, and need confront no personal demons in the aftermath of his confrontation with evil. Though Peckinpah chose to avoid developing *Major Dundee* as a more traditional tragedy in which the hero's mistakes—and demons—are crucial to the action, it was inevitable that he would eventually be drawn to such a story as reflecting his own experience of the world. Peckinpah found this story in Porter's treatment of Mr. Thompson's "high noon," what Emily Dickinson calls the day's "antiquest" hour in "Further in Summer than the Birds," her depiction of our primordial meeting with death, a time without illusions or shadows. One might object that Mr. Thompson never fully faces his situation and in fact continues to displace all guilt onto his antagonist, Homer T. Hatch. But Mr. Thompson's suicide registers a very different verdict, one in which he judges and even executes himself in the manner of Othello, another tragic protagonist who never altogether understands his role in the tragic catastrophe but who does understand, at the deepest levels of his being, that he has become someone or something he can never justify or transcend. In his next film, *The Wild Bunch*, Peckinpah would devise a tragic structure in which the hero is more culpable than Mr. Thompson and yet manages to act redemptively at the end (at least in part) despite his guilt. Here, in *Noon Wine*, Peckinpah sticks to more traditional territory, as if working through the more established tragic patterns before moving on to his greatest contribution to modern film and modern tragic practice.

We wish to close with an appeal for the restoration of *Noon Wine*, for the unavailability of one of Peckinpah's finest works is an absurdity. It is no accident that no one has written at length about Peckinpah's *Noon Wine* except Seydor, for Seydor notes there are only two color copies of the film made from the original, one in the Museum of Broadcasting (New York City) and one in the private collection of the late Jason Robards (the print used in retrospectives of Peckinpah's works) (1997, 106). We ourselves know the film in a version presumably copied from one of the two color copies and now housed at the Museum of Television and Radio, Beverly Hills, California. With the recent restorations of *The Wild Bunch* (1995), *Major Dundee* (2005), and *Pat Garrett and Billy the Kid* (2005), it seems inevitable that someone will eventually undertake this necessary work on what remains the least-viewed of all Peckinpah's films. We hope that those who care about Peckinpah will eventually find a way to make this crucial film widely available.

Chapter Four

The Tragedy of Love in *The Wild Bunch*

> Modern romance, like Greek tragedy, celebrates the miracle of dismemberment, which is life in time.
>
> —Joseph Campbell, *The Hero with a Thousand Faces* (25)

> An emotion cannot be checked or destroyed except by a contrary emotion which is stronger than the emotion which is to be checked.
>
> —Spinoza, Proposition IV.7

> The sparrow has found her a house and the swallow a nest where she may lay her young;
> By the side of your altars, O Lord of hosts, my King and my God.
>
> —Psalm 84: 3

The Wild Bunch (1969) is widely perceived to be Peckinpah's best film and "one of the great masterpieces of world cinema" (Seydor 1997, 147). Indeed, film historian David Cook compares it with Orson Welles' *Citizen Kane* (1941): "Like *Kane*, *The Wild Bunch* will remain an enduring work of American art—vast and explosive, vital and violent, with something very dark and very noble at its soul"(130). There are many reasons for this extravagant praise: Pike Bishop (William Holden) is Peckinpah's most interesting and affecting character, the most traditionally tragic of his protagonists but also the most complex; the rest of the cast is uniformly excellent; the scope of the film is unrivaled in Peckinpah's oeuvre, ranging from the passing of the old West in early twentieth-century America, to the civil war in Mexico between the Hueristas and forces loyal to Pancho Villa, to the dawn of the First World War (1913); the film's emotional range, from earthy humor to the most compelling tragic moments in all of Peckinpah, is the greatest and most finely integrated in all the films. The vast criticism on *The Wild Bunch* has covered most of the relevant topics with great but not uncritical skill, as we see most clearly in the two volumes of essays published on the film—Michael Bliss' *Doing It Right: The Best Criticism on Sam Peckinpah's* The Wild Bunch (1994) and Stephen Prince's *Sam Peckinpah's* The Wild Bunch (1999)—and Paul Seydor's magisterial 75-page chapter on *The Wild Bunch* in the second edition of his *Peckinpah: The Western Films—A Reconsideration* (1997).

Seydor's lengthy chapter covers a remarkable number of important topics: how the film came to be made and how 10 minutes of crucial footage were deleted, most of them after the film was first released; how the film was restored in the 1995 re-release by Warner Brothers; the nature and relevance of the flashbacks deleted until 1995; the common but mistaken accusation "that all the women are wholly unsympathetic" (1997, 159); the elements of Peckinpah's past reflected in the film; the ideas embodied in the dramatic structure; and the film's generic connections with forms as diverse as tragedy, comedy, romance, and epic. We are surely not alone in sometimes feeling that Seydor has said everything worth saying about this great film. Inevitably, however, there have always been reservations about even this splendid critical treatment. Seydor's final section on the ending is especially debatable, in particular his claim that "Peckinpah takes a dramatic structure that has been tragic for most of its length and at the last possible moment deflects it away from the tragic toward the comic" (1997, 212). This is the sort of thing one might say of Shakespeare's *The Winter's Tale*, not the most tragic of Peckinpah's films. And when Seydor deals with the film's structure and content, defining Pike Bishop's tragic dilemma at the end as well as anyone has done, he says much about Pike's mistakes and omissions with the rest of the Wild Bunch but little about his lost love Aurora (Aurora Clavel) and the other women in the film who represent another, perhaps more important failure on Pike's part.

Seydor acknowledges the value of the Aurora flashback and rejects the charge of misogyny so often leveled against the director and his film, but we think he does not go nearly far enough in recognizing the theme of unrealized sexual love in his account of Pike's tragic situation. We mean to focus on this subject, building upon the many insights Seydor and others have offered about *The Wild Bunch* but proposing a more complete account of the psychological forces which underlie the film's tragic action. The notions about men and women Peckinpah dramatizes in *The Wild Bunch* may seem to some unfashionably dated, even stereotypical, but we think this objection could be made to every major writer, including Shakespeare, and every filmmaker of note in the twentieth century. We would argue that what matters here is Peckinpah's ability to bring his "ideas" on this subject to rich dramatic life, especially in his crucial portrait of Pike Bishop, perhaps the most interesting tragic protagonist in all of American film.

I

Who are the Wild Bunch? From their incongruous name—"Wild" implying anarchic freedom, and "Bunch" a tenuous grouping[1]—to their brutal deaths in which these bad men are ennobled, even elevated to the status of legendary heroes, Peckinpah's strangely virtuous villains confound "safe" interpretation. To understand them, we must rid ourselves of the notion that Peckinpah is a simpleminded maker of macho films. Rather, as Ernest Callenbach says, Peckinpah is "a truly obsessional artist, struggling for clarity on issues that upset and confuse him" (1980, 21). In this chapter, we want to discuss the Wild Bunch's baffling contradictions, their roistering, profane lives versus the surprising sensitivity they are also capable of expressing. These contradictions arise, we believe, both from Peckinpah's "obsessional" concerns and from his dual perspective as a resolute romantic and an unblinking tragic artist, a man who knows that for every act of idealism, every invented dream, we are rent by the real and pay for our polarities in flesh, blood, and spirit.

George Bernard Shaw once said, apropos of Shakespeare, that the "lot of the man who sees life truly and thinks about it romantically is despair" (Sarris 184). "Despair" implies a kind of fixed grief, the soul's immobilization and the self's incapacity to create—or destroy. Peckinpah knows this emotion, as does Pike Bishop, Peckinpah's heroic protagonist in *The Wild Bunch.* Pike's solution to the problem of grief centers on violent action, ambiguous and always fraught with contingencies, but necessary. Violence in Peckinpah's best work becomes a means of self-exploration and self-definition, a way of understanding our complexities. Jim Kitses captures the violent core of Peckinpah's turbulent vision when he describes the struggle for self-definition which characterizes the classic Peckinpah hero: "above all, it is the quest for personal identity that provides the dramatic action of [Peckinpah's] films, a quest seen both in terms of a meaningful confrontation or dialogue with the past, and a tortured struggle to achieve mastery over self-annihilating and savage impulses" (2004, 212). While we are in essential agreement with Kitses' conclusions regarding the role of violence in Peckinpah, we nevertheless believe that it is only through violence of a certain kind — which we shall explore later — that his characters come to the tragic realization of their identity in the world. This paradox dominates Peckinpah's art: self-revelation comes through self-immolation.

The "past" to which Kitses refers assumes an especially important, densely lyrical quality in *The Wild Bunch*, in which the explosively violent, paradoxical nature of Peckinpah's artistry is expressed most brilliantly. Here many antagonistic elements conflict with each other: the past versus the present; age versus youth; spirit versus flesh; ideals versus actualities. The list could go on and on, but we want to concentrate on a theme which absorbs all the dichotomies cited above and which dramatizes the full range of Peckinpah's moral and aesthetic imagination. We refer to the theme of male-female love, especially to the clash between archetypal male and female sensibilities. Peckinpah pours the full measure of his art into this most fundamental human confrontation, and in the process he demonstrates a complex sensitivity to women his critics seldom acknowledge.[2]

Near the beginning of *The Wild Bunch*, as the gang, disguised as government soldiers, enter the starched southwest Texas town of Starbuck in order to rob the railroad bank, Pike Bishop, their outlaw leader, accidentally bumps into an older woman as he and his men cross the street to the bank. Within the amassing tensions of the moment — the anticipated robbery, a band of bounty hunters and railroad men waiting to ambush the Bunch when they make their escape — the scene functions as a suspenseful contretemps, delaying the imminent shootout. But there is more to the scene than its dramatic function. It represents the first encounter between men and women in the film, and significantly this encounter involves a violent collision. Thus from the beginning of *The Wild Bunch*, even within its superb juxtaposition of action sequences and credits frozen into newsprint (the contrast between history and myth, temporality and timelessness, established from the film's initial moments), Peckinpah sets up the difference between the world of the outlaw, dominated by coarse males, and the civilized domestic world of females. But the scene reverberates with other possibilities. After the surprised Pike Bishop strikes the woman, knocking her load of packages to the ground, he immediately apologizes ("I beg your pardon, ma'am") and offers his arm to escort her across the street ("May I?"), while his lieutenant, Dutch Engstrom (Ernest Borgnine), volunteers to carry her packages ("Allow me, ma'am") to the other side of the street. Dutch's action is purely a stratagem, but Pike's is not. His courtliness is best understood as both a strategic maneuver and a gentlemanly response, for he is, as we shall learn, a man whose tender solicitations toward women are too often opposed by the destructive consequences of his relationships with them.

This moment may seem secondary, but it provides our first insight into the tragic doubleness which haunts and perplexes Pike Bishop. If he is an outlaw, and a rather vicious one at that, he is simultaneously a man dedicated, though haltingly, to a code of behavior, an ideal notion of right conduct toward others and toward himself. In short, he is not like the feral Gorch brothers, who comprise the most disruptive element of the Wild Bunch. Forms interest Pike as much as actions. And it is those forms which lead to moments of introspective silence within the ceaseless turmoil, the mad motion of Pike Bishop's life.

Although the scene with the woman and her packages lasts for only a moment, Peckinpah weaves it into the unfolding male-female motif. As the gang leave the woman, who veers off to the right while they march in twos toward the bank, we first hear the voice of the bank manager haranguing one of his tellers. In the context of the film's mounting action, especially the imminent robbery, what he says seems of little consequence. But if we consider his speech in connection with Pike's collision with the woman on the street, the two events begin to form a meaningful pattern. The young teller has botched an important transaction with a woman customer, and what his manager tells him will reverberate throughout the film, for it points to the conflict between intention and action, conception and actuality. It also underscores one of the central differences between the male and female worlds as Peckinpah understands them. "I don't care what you meant to do," rails the manager, "it's what you did I don't like." Peckinpah cuts immediately from the banker's speech to the crouched figure of Pike Bishop's estranged partner and friend, Deke Thornton (Robert Ryan), now waiting to ambush Pike from a rooftop. The action freezes to another newsprint credit, and when it resumes we watch the Bunch approach in a shot made from within the bank, while the manager continues to berate his employee. We hear him in mid-sentence: "...to this lady, you made a fool of yourself and this railroad in the bargain. Now, I want you to apologize to this ... yessir, can I help you?" Just as he is about to use the word "lady" once more, the gang enter the bank. Instead of invoking her name, the manager speaks to Pike, who thus fills the ellipsis left by the omission of the woman's name. This is not an accidental conjunction of interrupted events in this superbly edited film. It is meant to suggest a connection between the "lady" standing there awaiting the teller's apology and Pike Bishop's first really planned utterance: "If they move, kill 'em!" Next comes another newsprint freeze frame and the words "Directed by Sam Peckinpah." The fatal clash between the male outlaw and the civilized female is thereby identified with Peckinpah himself.

It all happens so fast, and is so nearly obliterated by the subsequent slaughter of Starbuck citizens, when the bounty hunters and railroad men open fire upon the Wild Bunch, that we tend to forget just what has been said, and why it is so significant. Only much later do we realize that it is not just Pike's violent occupation which occasions his difficulties with women, but also his personal nature, torn between principle and compromise, word and deed. Pike has always harbored dreams of love, of marriage and of settling down to a peaceful, respectable life. But when Aurora, the woman he loves, is slain by her vengeful estranged husband, who also wounds Pike, his hopes are shattered. This brief description of Pike's true love does not do justice to the psychological factors which culminate in Aurora's death. As we learn from Pike's flashback narration much later in the film, he bears a heavy burden of responsibility for this death. Having promised to meet Aurora at an appointed time, he callously, and for no apparent reason, delays their rendezvous for two days. He arrives at her door, clean-shaven (which tells us this must have taken place some time in Pike's more youthful past, for we never see him elsewhere without a moustache), his arms laden with groceries and a bouquet of conciliatory red roses, in a possibly self-conscious parody of a penitent spouse's peace offering. A proud woman, insulted by Pike's casual indifference to her needs, Aurora slaps Pike hard across the face, knocking his groceries to the floor. The scene comically ridicules Pike's feeble attempts to placate Aurora. But it is her dignity versus his comic buffoonery which gives the flashback its dramatic edge, for she has far more at stake than Pike Bishop. She is especially worried about her estranged husband, as she fears he will come back and do harm both to her and to Pike, though she says he has gone for good.

That night, as they prepare for bed, Pike and Aurora are interrupted by the husband's appearance with a gun in the bedroom doorway, where we see him first in Aurora's mirror, across from Pike, before he kills her and wounds Pike in the left thigh, which, in the spirit of our discussion of Steve Judd's (Joel McCrea's) wound on his left side in *Ride the High Country* (1962), seems to anticipate the guilty, repentant Pike's growing sensitivity toward women and toward love after Aurora is slain. After all, he is responsible for her death, and the wound

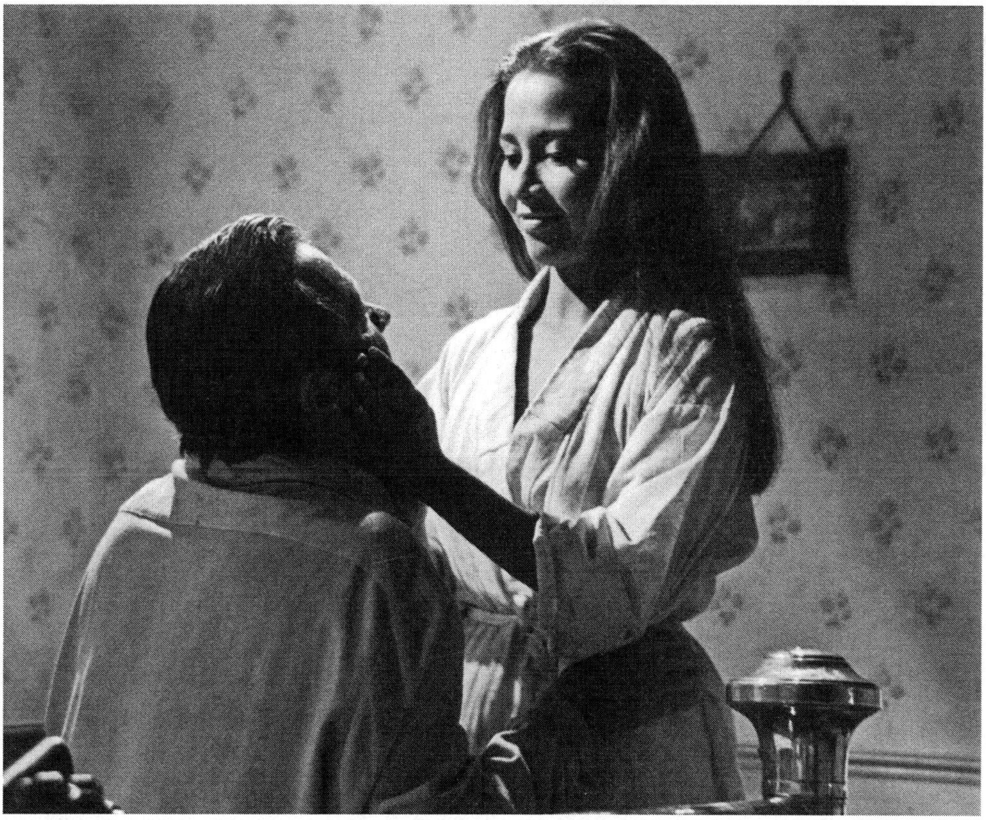

In the bedroom. Pike Bishop (William Holden) and the woman he loves, Aurora (Aurora Clavel), in a final embrace in this production still from *The Wild Bunch.*

serves to remind him every day, every minute, of what he has done. This scene destroys any comfortable assumptions of conventional devotion we may have formed about Pike and this woman he purports to love. For when a man as good at his work as Pike Bishop says he is, when a careful, meticulous planner of jobs, whose life, and the lives of others, depend upon constant wariness and vigilance, neglects his responsibility to the woman he loves, we realize he is expressing an unconscious conflict within his nature, a conflict between the outlaw's love of freedom and the would-be husband's desire for a civilized, settled life. In addition there is a fundamental, almost unappeasable sense of isolation in Pike which may be impossible to bridge, in spite of his yearnings toward love and friendship, and which may bring us closer than anything to the tragic core of Peckinpah's world.[3]

This crucial scene, omitted from all commercial prints of *The Wild Bunch* when it was first released to a mass American audience in 1969, is absolutely necessary to our argument. Indeed, the restoration of this scene is the single most important contribution of the 1995 re-release of *The Wild Bunch.* Without it we cannot possibly imagine Pike Bishop as a tragic hero, nor can we comprehend the many small but significant details which seem pointless outside the larger frame of the male-female theme.[4] Consider two key moments in Starbuck, during the mêlée precipitated by the Wild Bunch's attempt to escape from the railroad's hired killers. In this bloody shootout, filmed, as Seydor has indicated, as if we the audience, like the Wild Bunch and the trapped citizens of Starbuck, are in the midst of its chaos and destruction (1997, 139), Pike Bishop's horse, crazed by gunfire, rears and tramples a defenseless woman to death. At the same time his boot hooks her shawl and pins it to the side of his horse. Later, after the gang have ridden to the outskirts of town, Pike discovers the white shawl and succeeds, after considerable effort, in shaking it loose from his boot. The subtle image of the clinging shawl points to Pike's failure to free himself from his own inner conflicts as well as from the memory of the woman he loved and in effect betrayed. Peckinpah stresses the poignancy of the shawl by foreshadowing its appearance in an action sequence in which one of the gang members is shot and crashes on his horse through a dress shop window and topples two clothed female mannequins, their hats the colors—black and red—of the woman Pike bumped into at the beginning of this sequence. Moreover, by crosscutting the slow-motion scene of the rider falling into the dress shop with normal-motion scenes of the random devastation throughout Starbuck, Peckinpah ties this specific violation to the larger destruction inflicted on the town as a whole.

Thus we witness within this elaborate sequence first the relatively harmless collision between Pike and the older woman, then the trampled lady who falls under the hooves of Pike's horse while he tries to avoid crushing her, then the mannequins knocked down brutally by the falling horse and rider, and finally, the subtlest image, the fallen woman's clinging shawl. All of these images of violence are tied to the troubled identity of Pike Bishop. They will be reinforced by similar images even before we get to the Aurora flashback about halfway through the film. After this flashback, the entire sequence of related incidents and characters falls firmly into place, to be augmented but not materially altered by important scenes involving women later in the film. Pike's failure to reconcile his identity as an outlaw with his need for female love leads inevitably, tragically, to the terrible events we have described. Pike is a man divided against himself, but "division," as Robert Heilman has written, can become the salutary "occasion of self-awareness or self-knowledge" in the tragic protagonist. Out of "the inconsistent and the contradictory" can emerge the hero's desperate, ultimately unsuccessful attempt to render his life whole again (248). By the end of *The Wild Bunch* Pike Bishop has made his journey to self-awareness, and he chooses to fight those divisions which fill him with regret for his own existence. His moment of illumination comes in a woman's room, as it should. Before this can occur, however, Pike needs to pass through the progressive stages of aloneness, community, and self-knowledge which will free him to choose life and to die.

Pike's journey "home" begins on the trail, as the Bunch retreat into Mexico, in flight both from an advancing posse—led by Pike's best friend, Deke Thornton—and a pursuing past. It becomes evident how fecklessly Pike avoids the latter in a scene amidst a barren stretch of desert waste land. When Freddy Sykes (Edmond O'Brien), whom we know as one of the two remaining members of the original Wild Bunch, foolishly allows the horses to tumble over a high sand dune, he arouses the anger of one of the Gorch brothers, Tector (Ben Johnson), who draws his gun and threatens to "get rid of [Sykes]." Pike leaps to Freddy's defense in a celebrated speech: "You're not getting rid of anybody. We're gonna stick together, just like it used to be. When you side with a man you stay with him, and if you can't do that, you're like some animal. You're finished. We're finished—all of us." This eloquent speech is pure Peckinpah, written by a man who believes in all those values which now embarrass us, "[o]utdated codes like courage, loyalty, friendship, grace under pressure, all the simple virtues that have become clichés" (William Murray 72). But the speech unwittingly exposes the gap which has opened between Pike's principles and the expediencies of the moment. For Pike is a man who has already betrayed, in spirit as well as in deed, a number of those close to him, including the woman he loved and his best friend. As we noted in Chapter One, the list of those sacrificed to the needs of the moment is quite long: before the film begins, Aurora and Deke Thornton; during the escape from Starbuck, Crazy Lee (Bo Hopkins) and Buck, the blinded gang member Pike must shoot because he cannot ride anymore; after the Bunch arrive in Mexico, Angel (Jaime Sanchez) and Freddy Sykes, whom Pike leaves to Deke Thornton's posse just before the film's final events. Appropriately, perhaps, Pike's stirring speech meets with sniveling contempt from the odious Gorches, "*Brother* Tector" and "*Brother* Lyle" (Warren Oates), who "side" only with each other.

What follows this near-fatal confrontation between members of the Wild Bunch underscores Peckinpah's sense of a world never at rest, resistant to language, to stasis, to any kind of enforced order. It is natural for the audience to relax momentarily following a scene as charged as the one between Pike and the Gorches, but Peckinpah's tragic world keeps relentlessly turning, and the false calm he creates leads to a crucial moment which enlarges our understanding of what has gone before. His speech concluded, his command to "Mount up" uttered, Pike reaches for his horse, but as he mounts, his left stirrup snaps and he falls hard to the ground. While the Gorches scorn Pike's pretensions to leadership when he cannot even get on a horse, he painfully picks himself up from the ground and with an excruciating effort manages to mount. He rides off alone, up and across the harsh, hot desert, while in a rear shot, using a telephoto lens, Peckinpah and cinematographer Lucien Ballard film his solitary departure from the group, to the exquisitely melancholy accompaniment of Jerry Fielding's extraordinary score. Nothing moves except Pike, and the cameras lens, in a slight zoom, "seemingly boring into Pike's back, further emphasiz[es] his isolation" (Mast 1977, 294). Or so Gerald Mast writes in an otherwise brilliant analysis of the composition of this scene. But why would the camera's motion toward Pike, as if it were drawn to him, enhance our sense of his "isolation"? We believe the opposite is true. The remaining members of the Bunch, even the Gorches, sense the fundamental loneliness of the man and briefly extend themselves to him. So does the audience, as it experiences Pike's pull on the camera. But Pike's back is to the Bunch, as well as to the audience, and finally his private solitude seems inviolable as he begins to vanish from the film frame.

The sudden surge of sympathy Peckinpah manages to create for Pike Bishop, a sympathy for which the film's events to this point have not really prepared us, looms large in our growing acceptance of the possibility of Pike's heroic status. This shot, perhaps the most extraordinary in the entire film,[5] merits further discussion. For a moment, while the camera remains fixed on Pike's almost vanishing figure, his loneliness, his diminished dignity, and his pain seem so overwhelming that even the cruel sun-blasted landscape disappears from the frame as Pike appears to be moving, like a weary god, through shimmering, white-hot space. Thus the shot becomes dream-like, almost hallucinatory, setting the stage for future anti-realistic moments, such as the transcendentally romantic, almost surreal beauty of the exodus from the village of their youngest and only Mexican comrade, Angel, as well as the orgiastic, virtually Artaudian shootout at the film's conclusion. This shot therefore establishes the possibility for mythic grandeur in a film too often dismissed for its overt violence or grimy realism. These elements are vital to the larger meaning of *The Wild Bunch*, but unless they are seen in the context of the visionary brilliance of the scenes cited above, *The Wild Bunch* may seem a splendidly orchestrated but gratuitously bloody "action" film.

It is important to remember that the desert scene begins with Pike's injury to his already maimed leg, specifically his left thigh, where he was shot by Aurora's left-handed and almost stereotypically "sinister" husband. We think it is obvious why Peckinpah locates Pike's wound, now a permanent scar, on his thigh. Both in its origin on Pike's left side and in its location, it is emblematic of a sexual scar, thus reminding us of Pike's contradictory responses toward women, who would simultaneously love him and yet deprive him of his outlaw's anarchic freedom, draw him into the social and communal responsibilities which inevitably attend marriage. This duality characterizes adventurer-fighters such as Pike Bishop and John Ford's Ethan Edwards. While attractive as an ideal, the predominantly feminine world cannot ultimately satisfy the outlaw's ingrained need for male camaraderie, for the sheer exhilarating thrill of moving fast and fighting furiously through vast — though now diminishing — western space. Paul Zweig addresses this conflict in his book *The Adventurer* (1974), in which he expands on the adventurer's ties with females:

> The unrelenting masculinity of adventurer literature — from the *Iliad* to James Bond — has often been remarked. What has not been remarked is the enveloping influence of the feminine which haunts adventurer tales in subtle but definite ways. The adventurer cannot be contained by situations. His life is a flight into danger, as if he were pursued by an enemy which he feared more than danger itself. And this appearance of flight is altogether apt, for the adventurer does have such an enemy. The adventurer is in flight from women. Because he cannot cope with the erotic and social hegemony of women, he flees them even into death [61].

Within the context of *The Wild Bunch*, Zweig's remarks suggest the manner in which Pike's paradoxical relationships with women exemplify men of his profession, masculine adventurers who, whether warriors or gunfighters, dwell within a morally ambiguous realm insofar as they are, in Robert Warshow's phrase, "killer[s] of men" (112), cut off from the feminine, maternal source of life, and yet simultaneously "envelop[ed]" by it, as Zweig argues. These men traffic in death and this leads to calamitous results, as we have already seen, in their relationships with women.

In a number of ways, allowing for necessary historical and psychological variations, Pike resembles the most celebrated of warrior-heroes, Odysseus, whose identity also centers on a thigh wound he incurred as a child when he killed a boar. The name "Odysseus" means "to cause pain and to suffer for the pain we cause." Odysseus kills the boar, but he is also gored by it. Therefore he comes to know, as George Dimock says, "subjectively and objectively what it is to persecute" (55). Like Pike Bishop, Odysseus suffers a wound which morphs into a psychological scar. Torn by dual commitments to war and adventure on the one hand, home and family on the other, Odysseus, though he longs to return to Ithaca and to Penelope, tarries 10 long years—constrained, and captivated, by women — in reaching his destination. And once he arrives home, weary, nearly sea-broken, he still manages to display himself most effectively, even most comfortably, as a supremely vicious warrior, vanquishing his wife's suitors in an exceedingly violent massacre. In addition, we know that although Odysseus is happy to be home and reunited with Penelope and his son, Telemakhos, his wanderings are not over, for he is destined to die at sea, the true and terrible home of this peripatetic Homeric adventurer. This is why Dante assigns Odysseus-Ulysses a special place among the "evil counselors" of his *Inferno*. Dante's Ulysses can never curtail his endless journeying forth, nor his advising others to do the same. "[N]ot fondness for my son, nor reverence / for my aged father, nor Penelope's claim / to the joys of love, could drive out of my mind / the lust to experience the far flung world / and the failings and felicities of mankind," intones Ulysses from his static circle in Hell (223). If Penelope represents "nostos," or the object of return, for her husband, she also symbolizes a kind of death-like terminus, the end of his very modern compulsion to explore the "far flung world," as well as himself.

While Homer does not seem to view Odysseus as a tragic hero, Dante comes closer to interpreting Odysseus/Ulysses' "flaw" or "mistake" as a deep-driven compulsion to move rootlessly through the world. But Peckinpah creates a truly tragic hero in Pike Bishop, a man who had love but who carelessly neglected it for a lonely career of fighting and adventuring across the treacherous desert (a sandy sea, more or less equivalent to the Homeric ocean). In addition, like Odysseus, Pike is named in such a way as to reflect the contrarieties within his nature, as well as those within his creator, Sam Peck/Pike/enpah. If he is a bad man, pike-like, piercing and dangerous, Pike also possesses spiritual, even bishop-like qualities, emotions he rarely permits himself to express and which always emerge during those sudden silences which punctuate the film's frenetic action. Pike Bishop resembles Odysseus—and all heroic adventurers, including the archetype of the male-female split in American literature, Cooper's Deerslayer—in his inability to resolve, except destructively, the warring male and female impulses which co-exist within him. Only in the film's final moments will he attempt to redress or reconcile the oppositions in his tragically divided self. We cannot begin to understand that calamitous finale unless we study its complementary opposite, the view of life presented in Angel's village, for there the film's feminine sensibility is expressed most profoundly.

Like an earthly paradise, a green world of frame-filling trees, Angel's village, despite its recent pillaging by the army of the Huerista mercenary, General Mapache (Emilio Fernandez), thrives with abundant human and natural life. Although the first sight the Wild Bunch have of the town includes bleak, abandoned adobes and a panting, starving dog, these are, we soon learn, signs of Mapache's ravishment of the village and do not reflect the pueblo itself. Once they enter, the Bunch are captivated by its festive vitality. Women and children abound, there is plentiful food and drink, and later in the evening a fiesta, with music, drink, and dancing, is celebrated for the gang. Meanwhile, giggling girls draw water from a well with the aid of the amazingly courteous Gorches, while children swim and dive happily in a pond, a moment of innocent, youthful bliss straight out of one of Peckinpah's favorite films, John Huston's *The Treasure of the Sierra Madre* (1947). Later, the tamed Gorches play a children's game, cat's cradle, with the laughing senoritas. Pike is dumbfounded by all of this because he knows how brutal the Gorches can be. He is educated by a wise village elder, Don José (Chano Urueta), who remarks of the Gorches' play that it is "not so surprising. We all dream of being a child again, even the worst of us. Perhaps the worst of us most of all." Pike, who longs "most of all" to forget his past and enter a time-negating pastoral world, nods in assent. It should be added that Peckinpah thwarts the potential sentimentality of this scene by portraying Don José as not just another benevolent Mexican peasant, but rather a man whose insight derives from his own experience. "Then you know who we are?" Pike asks Don José, but then laughingly adds, "And you too!" Indeed, at the end of the film Don José will reappear as a full-fledged bandit who recruits Freddy Sykes and Deke Thornton to a new version of the Wild Bunch.

Why does the village welcome the Wild Bunch so fulsomely into its midst? On one level it is because they ride with Angel and should be treated with hospitality because they are his "friends." But the deeper reason, we suspect, lies in the village's ancient origins. In *The Hero with a Thousand Faces* (1949), his examination of the disappearance of myth and ritual in modern life, Joseph Campbell argues that, unlike ancient cultures, the modern "social unit is not a carrier of religious content, but an economic-political organization" from which the "dream-web of myth" has fallen away (387). But this is untrue of Angel's village, where the myth of the hero and the festive ritual which celebrates the hero—and the guest—are brought to full expression. The village seems classless as well, devoid of the strict hierarchies which overdetermine one's place and status in Mapache's Agua Verde, where the rank-obsessed German officers advise the general on the proper conduct of his murderous affairs. The village is communal, not hierarchical, ritualistic rather than regimental, spontaneous rather than ordered. The village is a perfect representative of what the anthropologist Victor Turner calls "liminality" in his studies of the Ndembu people of Africa. During ritual celebrations, Turner argues, the people undergo a radical change in their social status, as they "momentarily exchange their established place in the social structure for a condition of 'communitas.'" In this state of community their links to each other are "anti-structural in that they are undifferentiated, equalitarian, direct." They are living, if only temporarily, "outside the categories of ordinary social life" (21). Turner calls this state "liminality," or "thresholdness." Liminality becomes a way of abandoning the structures of everyday social life, but it also re-fuses those structures with ancient tradition.[6]

Angel's village welcomes the gang members into its communal life, even allows the Gorches the erotic freedom to sleep with their young women (the morning after the fiesta Lyle retrieves his hat from a senorita who will obviously miss him), but it also gives them a hero's farewell when they depart from the village. This double vision, absorbing both egalitarian and heroic qualities, establishes the value matrix of the village as crucial to the film's moral vision, and argues as well that to affirm that matrix the village—like the rest of us—needs its heroes, revolutionaries such as Angel. We think that the village and what it stands for are at the center of Peckinpah's world view. Like so many other twentieth-century artists—Joyce, Faulkner, Wallace Stevens, perhaps even Hemingway—Peckinpah depicts the religious quest within an irreligious age, thereby expressing the secular longing for the infinite which underlies so much modernist/romantic writing. The communal values of Angel's village also symbolize the fusion of male and female principles. This explains why the village is able to effect an almost miraculous transformation—and especially feminization—of the ruthless gang. Because the village verges on myths of pastoral bliss, perhaps even the myth of the Garden of Eden before the Fall, an obsessive image which can be traced back to Sam Peckinpah's own childhood, it cannot be seen as part of the strictly objective texture of *The Wild Bunch*. Instead, it looms within the film as a kind of romantic, idyllic retreat, an island out of time, an oasis hovering somewhere between reality and dream (unnamed, it opens to greater imaginative interpretation), a sort of actualized ideal which mediates between the arid, etiolated Protestantism of Starbuck, with its sin-crazed, alcohol-condemning citizens clothed in funereal black, and the lurid debauchery of Mapache's drunken, whore-filled Agua Verde.[7] Between these falsely dichotomized versions of sacred and profane existences—for it is evident Peckinpah believes one cannot exist without the other—Angel's village moves through imagined space, synthesizing rather than compartmentalizing spiritual and earthly values.

Although it has been damned by those who deplore its sentimentality, the Wild Bunch's overtly romanticized exodus from Angel's village seems perfectly apt within Peckinpah's portrait of the village and his film's larger purposes. Photographed with slow forward and side tracking shots, from the point of view of both the Bunch (seen from low angles, against a background of trees) and the villagers who line and garland the gang's departure, the scene celebrates and memorializes a future of which the Bunch themselves are unaware: their subsequent destruction of Mapache's army. While the brilliant morning sun riffles through the village's bright green trees, and families gather along the way, girls lavish flowers on these unlikely "heroes" (a bemused Dutch Engstrom holds a rose in his meaty hand). There is also music, "La Golondrina" ("The Swallow"), a lonely wanderer's song of separation from his beloved native land. Graciously, Pike tips his hat to Don José, and Angel kisses his mother farewell. The scene swells with extravagant emotions, and rightly so, because it elucidates a central paradox of the warrior's existence: in order to sustain (both in the world and in our imaginations) Edenic retreats like the village, havens from history's nightmare, we must fight for them, violate their underlying feminine or maternal principles of home, family, and community, so that those principles may be preserved. Intuitively, without a trace of irony, the villagers seem to understand the Wild Bunch better than the Bunch understand themselves.

We cannot begin to comprehend why the Wild Bunch rise to the fallen Angel's rescue in Agua Verde unless we understand his roots and what those origins mean to the gang and to Pike Bishop in particular. When he chides Angel in the latter's village for vowing revenge against Mapache for killing his father and "molesting" his sweetheart Teresa, Pike realizes, as Seydor acutely remarks, that he can scarcely hold in check his own combustive emotions over the loss of Aurora (1997, 165). "Either you learn to live with it or we'll leave you here," he warns the headstrong youth, even as we sense Pike's own difficulties in achieving self-control. This is confirmed in his several facial expressions during the fiesta, especially the dancing.

Seated on the ground, bottle in hand, Pike declines to dance with an attractive woman who seems to be with Don José. This is less because of his wounded leg than because of the psychologically painful source of his wound. When Dutch offers to dance with Don José's companion, and then is cut in upon by the grimy, toothless Freddy Sykes ("I'm gonna steal his girl!"), Pike laughs, but his expression quickly turns to an ironic, self-examining gaze, then narrows to a silent introspection. He is no longer quite present to the dancing, the drinking, the general merriment, but rather transported back to the woman with whom he should be dancing, Aurora. This occurs as evening falls, a time of memory and inwardness. There can be, of course, no certainty as to what Pike is thinking — or feeling — but because of Peckinpah's technique of dissolving from one scene to another, here from meditation to movement, from night to morning, we can deduce a close connection between Pike's painful memories and the morning ride out of the pueblo. We begin to hear the initial strains of "La Golondrina" as Pike stares off into space that night, then we dissolve to the departure the following morning. Utilizing this technique of overlapping sound, astutely analyzed by Richard Gentner and Diane Birdsall (36), Peckinpah is able to connect evening with morning, Pike's inner world of solitude and memory with the outer world of love and shared action.

While Peckinpah is, by his own admission, nothing if not romantic,[8] it is equally true that his is a kind of very modern, self-questioning romanticism. Pike's advice to Angel, to learn to "live with" the loss of Teresa, underscores Peckinpah's implicit critique of romanticism's obsession with the Ideal or Absolute, the notion of Woman as archetype rather than flesh and blood. Angel lost Teresa because, as Don José tells Pike, he worshipped her from a celibate distance, treated her as if she were a virginal goddess. Mapache, on the other hand, won her over ("She went with him because she wanted to," says Don José) when he offered her the pleasures of food, wine, and carnality. For Mapache, Teresa was no goddess but a fruit ripe for the picking. Angel's subsequent slaying of Teresa echoes Pike's responsibility for Aurora's death, and in Pike's half-comic, half-sardonic remark, "Angel dreams of love and Mapache eats the mango," he may be unwittingly commenting on his own inability to fuse idealistic commitments to love and friendship with his imperfect actions toward Aurora and Deke Thornton, as well as others he has had to shoot or abandon on the trail when the necessity of the moment required it. When Pike and the rest of the Wild Bunch march off to rescue Angel in Agua Verde, they do so not just for their maimed comrade but also for the values his village implicitly affirms, and especially for those communal, feminine values from which Pike feels so tragically separated. For once at least they fuse action and idea, the warrior's destiny to die on the battlefield with his commitment to a life antithetical to war.

II

After the Bunch leave Angel's village, they make their way to Agua Verde, Mapache's town, where they eventually reach a pact with the devil, so to speak, a $10,000 commission to steal guns and ammunition from an American army train. The women of Agua Verde are depicted as "chattel" (Seydor's term for what Teresa represents to Mapache [1997, 160]), and the scene in which Angel shoots Teresa takes the earlier images of violence against women to a logical extreme characteristic of Mapache and his town. The Aurora flashback follows a few moments later, reminding us of the larger pattern traced throughout the first half of the film. Immediately thereafter, however, with the Bunch's complex operation against the American train, Peckinpah initiates a kind of middle "act" or section of his film in which the Bunch finally demonstrate their physical virtues in the execution of Pike's masterful plan. Thematically, the shift is to camaraderie or even friendship, captured throughout the sequence in such moments as Angel saving Dutch's life on the train, the exquisite performance of every detail in first robbing the train and then blowing up the bridge on which Deke and his posse are standing in their pursuit of the Bunch, and the elaborate drinking scene at the end as the Bunch celebrate (if only momentarily) the virtuosity and excellent outcome of their escapade. Here it almost seems as if the Bunch finally come together to realize, in the flesh, the values of solidarity and comradeship merging into genuine friendship.

Even here, in the midst of the film's most high-spirited moments, we must note the uglier realities on display: the American soldiers killed by the Bunch as they take the train, the youthful American troops shot at (and in one instance, killed) rather than the Wild Bunch, the fact that all of this physical dexterity and excellent planning advance the political and military "cause" of Mapache and the German officers who advise him. Moreover, this middle section of the film brings Deke Thornton to the fore in scene after scene, reminding us of the other face of friendship, one which may ultimately not be tragic but which certainly comes very close. Early in the film we have seen Deke Thornton lead the rag-tag posse which the railroad official Pat Harrigan (Albert Dekker) has organized to pursue the Wild Bunch. We have noted in particular Deke's reluctance to shoot Pike Bishop during the gunfight in Starbuck. Soon thereafter Deke recalls an earlier event which explains his relationship with Pike, who is shown elsewhere at the same time thinking back to the same night five years ago when Deke was captured by the Pinkertons because of Pike's arrogant miscalculation. In this shared flashback, Pike and Deke are shown in a brothel only hours after they have pulled off one of their jobs in the same town. A careful, circumspect man, Deke questions the wisdom of Pike, who is drunk and surrounded by prostitutes, in hiding from the police in a town they have just robbed. Deke asks Pike how he can "be so damn sure" they are safe from their pursuers. Pike's response, "Being sure is my business," is to be the film's most ironic utterance, and echoes here in Deke's memory, as it echoes throughout the rest of the film. For if there is anything which tragedy teaches us, it is that "being sure," any form of cognitive certainty, is a feckless stance to take within a tragic world. Almost at once the Pinkertons break in, Pike escapes as Deke is wounded, and Deke is sent off to the blazing hell-hole of Yuma Prison to serve a 25-year sentence.

It is not just the prison itself, or the fact that Deke is tortured (in the Yuma flashback, we see him being whipped, wrists bound together) which leads to Deke's profound need to get out of prison; rather, it is the larger theme of suffocating entrapment which drives Deke to seek his provisional release. In order to secure his freedom from prison, however, Deke must agree to give Harrigan his word that he will lead the posse to track down Pike and the Wild Bunch. As he performs this hateful task, Deke seems no less entrapped and constrained than he was in prison. As we first see him, he is leaning against the wall of a roof in Starbuck, waiting for the Wild Bunch. He appears to be sleeping, or lost in thought, his head down, reflecting, as we shall see, his great discomfort at the trap in which he finds himself, indeed, his shame at being coerced into betraying his best friend. Shamefaced, excluded from the group he longs to rejoin, Deke seems to find it intolerable to even look at what has become of his life. He hides his face, covers his hands in dark leather gloves, and, Grecoesque, agonizes over his fate. The agony derives from being forced to do something which runs completely against his ethical sensibility. An early draft of Walon Green and Sam Peckinpah's screenplay describes Deke's situation as we see him for the first time: "DEKE THORNTON SITTING NEXT TO HIM [Harrigan], his back against the wall. Thornton is a hard-bodied, quiet-spoken man, with a lined face and the embittered manner of someone who has changed sides to stay alive and while part of his life has gone out of him with the change, the personal integrity by which he has lived is still intact" (5).[9]

Deke is truly a man whose back is against the wall, and the source of his dilemma is precisely his personal integrity. Peckinpah is careful, in a way he will not be with Pat Garrett, a character who resembles Deke both physically and situationally, to insist upon Deke's integrity despite the circumstances of his life at present. Deke is an honorable man of his word, a man driven by a form of inner necessity to define who he is and to respect whatever verbal or personal commitments he makes, no matter how much he hates the person to whom he gives his word or the task he is thereby assigned. When Harrigan taunts him for wanting to bolt from the scrofulous band of bounty hunters to rejoin Pike and the Wild Bunch after the massacre at Starbuck, Deke replies, "What I like and what I need are two different things." For Deke, the pleasure principle gives no pleasure. He would "like" to rejoin Pike, yes, but his "need" is to honor his word, his commitment to his own Kantian "inner core of moral personhood we all carry within us" (Rosen 9), even if he gives his word to someone like Harrigan who has allowed an entire town to be shot up in order to capture or kill Pike Bishop, with whom he has a personal grudge, as we later learn from Pike.

It is quite possible that this well-known line—"What I like and what I need are two different things"—derives from Robert Ryan himself. Peckinpah is famous for taking the suggestions of his own actors. Perhaps he took Ryan's advice and borrowed this line from a different but related context in Anthony Mann's *The Naked Spur* (1953). There Ryan plays a character completely unlike Deke Thornton. Famous at the time for his psychotic villain roles in numerous films noir of the 1940s and 1950s, Ryan plays a character named Ben Vandergroat in *The Naked Spur*. A red-clad, slick-talking embodiment of serpentine evil who tries to persuade the virtuous but overwrought hero, Howie Kemp (James Stewart), not to play the bounty hunter and return him to Kansas where he is wanted for murder, Ben rides with an innocent young woman named Lina Patch (Janet Leigh), who willingly does his bidding. At one point, his hands still tied, he asks Lina to scratch his back. He repeatedly beckons Lina with the same lubricious phrase, "Will ya do me?" and she always complies. This time she remarks, "I don't know whether I'm doing this for you because you need it or just because you like it." Ben's response, "A man needs what he likes," captures perfectly the merging of the reality principle and the pleasure principle in the vile Ben Vandergroat. For people such as Ben, inner conflicts do not exist. What he likes is precisely what he needs. It is completely otherwise with Deke Thornton, whose whole life seems to turn on the unresolvable contradiction between desire and necessity, the craving for freedom and the need to follow certain codes of right behavior. For Deke, what he likes and what he needs are very different things.

Deke's dedication to his word—rather like Steve Judd's in *Ride the High Country* and Ben Tyreen's (Richard Harris') in *Major Dundee* (1965)—has always been problematic for viewers and critics. Indeed, it is questioned within the film by Dutch Engstrom, who has joined the gang after Deke's capture and cannot understand why Pike is so forgiving toward the ever-pursuing Deke Thornton. "Damn that Deke Thornton to Hell!" Dutch cries out. "What would you do in his place?" Pike replies. "He gave his word." Dutch responds that Deke gave it to a railroad, Pike reiterates, "It's his word!" and Dutch seemingly caps the argument by insisting, "That ain't what matters—it's who you give it to!" This exchange is famous enough to have attracted the attention of the well-known literary critic, student of American jurisprudence, and neo-pragmatist, Stanley Fish, who begins his book *The Trouble with Principle* (1999) with a discussion of the Pike-Dutch debate:

> I read the scene as a profound and concise analysis of the great divide in political theory. On the one side is the man of principle for whom a formal contract must be kept irrespective of the moral status of the other party; when you give your word, you give your word and that's it. On the other side is the man who varies his obligations according to the moral worth of the persons he encounters; some people have a call on your integrity, others don't, and the important thing is to determine at every moment which is which.

> There is, I think, no doubt which of these two visions is today the more generally approved. The Holden character speaks in the accents of Enlightenment liberalism; what he says is in accord with the maxims many of us have long since internalized: "A man's word is his bond." "Ours is a government of laws, not men." "You can't justify the means by the end." "Respect for your fellow man must be extended to all and not selectively" [1–2].

Fish is not very helpful on Pike's role in this "debate."[10] Pike defends Deke for some very complicated reasons, perhaps including Pike's "Enlightenment liberalism," even though he would not know the phrase, but also a deep sense of guilt for betraying Deke's belief in him as a good leader, a good man, and a loyal friend. After all, Pike's endorsement of Deke's principles is very much bound up in his own sense of honor and his duty toward his men. How else are we to understand his famous "When you side with a man" speech except as a statement of Pike's absolute principles as a leader? That Pike betrays those principles renders his actions, but not his convictions, ironic. Pike shares Deke's belief in "a man's word [being] his bond" (Fish 2), a view which recalls Steve Judd giving *his* word to a bank in *Ride the High Country.* But Pike knows all too well that he has not lived up to his ideals. Pike's typical response to changing situations is nothing if not pragmatic and situational, and often fatally wrong. Whether he is leaving old Freddy Sykes' grandson Crazy Lee behind to be captured or killed in Starbuck, abandoning the severely wounded Sykes, a genuine friend, in the hills, or allowing Angel to be tortured to death by Mapache, Pike acts within the moment, often disastrously, and Pike's even more grievous mistakes with Aurora and Deke Thornton are not so much pragmatic as thoughtless or careless, thus adding to the irony of Pike's principled stand in his argument with Dutch. Like the rest of us, but even more so, Pike functions within a world of moral ambiguities and moral compromises. *The Wild Bunch* is a genuine tragedy, not a philosophy text, and tragedy never offers easy ethical answers.

This brings us back to Dutch Engstrom. First, Dutch never knew Deke personally, as Fish says he does (1). Dutch began riding with the Bunch after Deke's capture due to Pike's negligence. Second, for Fish to say that Pike stands for "abstract principle," regardless of context or situation, while Dutch upholds a person's worth as the sole criterion for his allegiance, could not be further from Peckinpah's point. Pike defends Deke, a man of his word, both because he admires his old friend for his principles and because Pike has been so tragically lax in following those principles. Moreover, who is to say that Dutch's sense of a person's "moral worth" is not itself an "abstract principle"? Fish wants us to believe that Dutch always responds to situations from practical considerations rather than inveterate principle. Yet it is Dutch who takes an a priori stand for Angel because he believes in Angel's rather abstract and surely quixotic cause of liberty, a position very much in "the accents of Enlightenment liberalism" (Fish 2). Earlier, in the loggia at Agua Verde where the Bunch confront the thieving, murdering Mapache for the first time, Pike laughingly compares his own gang of thieves with Mapache's. Dutch's indignation is ardent and instantaneous: "We ain't nothing like him, Mr. Bishop. We don't hang nobody." This distinction may seem both sophistic and casuistical, but it is clear what Dutch is saying: the Wild Bunch are an anarchic band of outlaws who rob banks and trains and do, indeed, kill people; but they do not engage in the viciously sadistic, mass-murdering, near-totalitarian actions of Mapache, who is a willing instrument of the all-corrupting state power embodied in General Huerta and the German Imperial Army.

When the Wild Bunch finally confront Mapache's army in the battle of Agua Verde, with which we will deal more extensively later, their actions reflect an extraordinary mix of personal and political motivations which cannot be easily separated. Both Pike and Dutch hate to see what is being done to the tortured Angel, and both detest Mapache and the seemingly pristine, white-suited German officials and officers. When Pike and Dutch rise to defend Angel, it is not just Angel they wish to liberate but ultimately an entire people, Angel's village writ large, and a set of ideals these people embody. This helps to explain why we come to admire Dutch for his convictions. As Fish notes, Dutch "varies his obligations according to the moral worth of the persons he encounters" (1), but this leads him to make firm moral commitments. It is Dutch who most clearly identifies with Angel's revolutionary cause, itself based on firm moral principles, but also with Angel the man because Angel rescued Dutch from certain death during the train robbery. For both reasons, or "sides," to use Fish's term, Dutch asks for and receives from Pike the promise of a case of ammunition for Angel and his "puro indio" comrades so they can continue their revolutionary struggle against Mapache. Ironically, it is because of this altruistic act, born of Dutch's contempt for the general and his affection for Angel, that a massacre ensues. Angel is captured, tortured, and murdered by Mapache, who learns about the theft from Teresa's mother. The Bunch are subsequently destroyed during their massacre of Mapache, his army, and the town of Agua Verde. Acting out of profound philosophical and personal convictions, Dutch precipitates a mass catastrophe. Peckinpah does not judge him for his choice, any more than he judges the more Kantian Deke Thornton for unswervingly keeping his "word." Tragedy is a genre which proffers no answers to the human plight, only the most probingly intelligent and emotionally arresting questions.

To return to Pike and Deke, it is Pike whose experience is ultimately tragic, while Deke emerges relatively unscathed from his trials at the end of *The Wild Bunch.* Without rehearsing Deke's final actions at this time, it can be said that, unlike Pike, Deke does not undergo something like Aristotle's *anagnorisis* because he has nothing much to learn about himself or the world, which he understands all too well from the first. The distinction between what Deke likes and what he needs may torment him, and he is certainly loath to fulfill his pledge to Harrigan; but he never doubts that it is what he *needs* which must be honored. He is Fish's despised man of principle, nor has he ever been anything else. We can judge him, if we are so inclined, for saving his life by accepting Harrigan's coercive offer, but we should also see that Deke has entered into this pact with eyes open and consequences understood. Nor is he tormented by what Pike Bishop has done to create his dismal situation. Indeed, Deke remains devoted to his friendship with Pike, even as it exists in absentia. Pike's dereliction of leadership in getting Deke caught seems of little weight to Deke, who continues to speak of Pike as a true professional, a good leader of his men, and, strangely, his own friend. "What kind of men are we up against?" the bounty hunter Coffer (Strother Martin) asks. "The best," Deke replies. "They never got caught." Deke, clearly not a born leader, seems to view Pike as a projected ideal leader of the Wild Bunch, whatever his faults, and to assume that Pike shares his values—which the Pike-Dutch debate confirms, insofar as Pike's declared values are concerned.

Deke Thornton's fidelity to Pike Bishop, even as he hunts him down in Mexico, points toward future possibilities, and can be understood, at least in part, through a brief glance at classical tragedy. In his *Shame and Necessity* (1993), the late English philosopher Bernard Williams, who throughout his career was concerned with bridging the gap between ancient tragedy and modern tragedy, argues that for the Greek tragedians and historians, in their seemingly quite different ethical system, the condition of shame (mixed invariably with a less lethal degree of guilt) produces on the part of the ashamed person a sort of quasi-fictional but quite real "imagined other" who looks upon the person living in shame with an equally "imagined gaze" (82). Deke Thornton, who hates his predicament in leading his "gutter trash" bounty hunters in pursuit of his friend, views Pike not as a former friend who has betrayed him but as a sort of "imaginary" projection of the ideal leader of the Wild Bunch. In Williams' terminology, Pike, a natural leader, becomes for Deke an idealized "internalized other," or superego, who must be "identified in ethical terms. He ... is conceived as one whose reactions I would respect; equally, he is conceived as someone who would respect those same reactions if they were appropriately directed to him" (84). But is the supposed "internalized other," the impossibly exemplary Pike Bishop, for instance, in any sense *real*, especially when it is Pike whose very un-ideal actions led to Deke's humiliating, shameful plight? Paradoxically, the answer seems to be yes. Williams writes that it is a "mistake" to view both the real and the ideal other as somehow unrelated to each other: "Those alternatives leave out much of the substance of actual ethical life. The internalized other is indeed abstracted and generalized and idealized, but he is potentially somebody rather than nobody, and somebody other than me. He can provide the focus of real social expectations, of how I shall live if I act in one way rather than another, of how my actions and reactions will alter my relations to the world about me" (84). This is why, when Pike and the rest of the Bunch have destroyed Mapache's army, Deke's faith in Pike as friend and "imaginary" but real leader is justified.

This way of thinking about Deke and his feelings for a redeemed Pike can be illustrated imagistically and symbolically as well. For the more outer-directed man of shame like Deke, "the most primitive experiences of shame are connected with sight and being seen," while for the guilty man like Pike, "it has been interestingly suggested that guilt is rooted in hearing, the sound in oneself of the voice of judgment; it is the moral sentiment of the word" (Bernard Williams 89). As noted earlier, we first *see* Deke Thornton as he sits silently, head down, eyes closed, apparently asleep, leaning against a wall atop a building in Starbuck.[11] Throughout the film, the gaunt Deke consistently wears dark leather gloves and dark or ashen clothes and hat, as if trying to hide or conceal himself from the sight of others. Conversely, Pike is haunted by words, echoing voices from the past and his own exaggerated statements of his personal worth: "Being sure is my business"; "When you side with a man you stay with him, and if you can't do that, you're like some animal"; "What would you do in his place? It's his word!" Pike can find no release from his sins because he cannot forgive himself. Deke, on the other hand, looks outside of himself and eventually achieves a form of spiritual reconciliation with Pike, now dead, through his reunion with old friend Freddy Sykes and the oddly reconstituted Wild Bunch.

Bernard Williams effectively explains the differences between Deke and Pike in his discussion of the relationship between shame mixed with a kind of forgivable guilt and the tragic figure's purer form of guilt, which bears little or no relationship to any kind of social redemption: "If we come to understand our shame, we may also better understand our guilt. The structures of shame contain the possibility of controlling and learning from guilt, because they give a conception of one's ethical identity, in which guilt can make sense. Shame can understand guilt, but guilt cannot understand itself" (93). By the end of the film, as we shall see, Deke becomes conscious at some level of his being of the "structures of shame" which contain the potential seeds of freedom from both the shame and the guilt he has known. With Pike Bishop there is no real release from actions for which he cannot forgive himself. Shame moves us outward into the world through its centrifugal motion toward others. Guilt moves the tragic figure more deeply and centripetally inward toward the isolation of the self, and ultimately toward cataclysmic, if ever-conflicted, death.

Deke Thornton is a wonderful character whose final fate — to be addressed in due time — is crucial to the film as a whole, for it helps us to appreciate and value Pike's very different fate; indeed, Deke's function is to define by contrast Pike's divided nature and his tragic decision at the end of the film. But Deke is not a tragic character, not at any time in Peckinpah's detailed portrait of the man. This helps to explain why the theme of friendship, though obviously important in *The Wild Bunch*, never quite rises to the tragic level of the theme of love. Pike feels guilt for what he has done to Deke, who no doubt concerns him more than Crazy Lee, or Buck, or Angel, or even Freddy; but the guilt he feels for all his fellow gang members derives more from his tattered self-image than any depth of feeling toward the men concerned.

Deke is a partial exception, perhaps, but only partial. As we shall see, it is the memory of Aurora which finally moves Pike to redemptive action, not the memory of his best friend.

In Agua Verde, after the Wild Bunch have robbed the American arms train for Mapache, Angel is taken prisoner and tortured when Mapache discovers that Angel has saved a case of arms for his people. Pike and his men ponder the situation while watching from a hilltop overlooking Agua Verde. Here Pike and Dutch debate Deke Thornton's behavior and Dutch implores Pike to return to Agua Verde to rescue the captured Angel, invoking the opinion of Freddy Sykes: "Sykes thinks that we ought to go back after him." Ironically, the Bunch watch helplessly as the wounded Freddy is himself pinned down by Deke Thornton's pursuing posse in the valley below them. As if ashamed of his own failed leadership, Pike turns away from the camera and from his men, effectively hiding his face and acknowledging there is nothing they can do for Angel or for Freddy. Pike elects to return to Agua Verde to avoid Deke's posse and to try (unsuccessfully) to buy Angel back from Mapache. Reduced to four men against an entire army, the Bunch find themselves powerless to rescue Angel. For the first time in the film — other than in the bordello flashback which centers on Deke Thornton's capture — the noticeably chaste Pike Bishop, still in flight from the haunting memories of Aurora and Deke, chooses to vent his helplessness and disgust at Angel's torture in another brothel.

The beautiful, dark-skinned prostitute with whom Pike sleeps, though younger, resembles the equally striking Aurora more than the haggard whore the Gorches share. Pike first saw the young woman in one of the film's most extraordinary scenes, the shooting of Teresa. Wearing a softly colored blue and white checked dress (blue is the color of the Virgin Mary in the Catholic Church), the young woman is first seen smiling at Pike. Enter Teresa (Sonia Amelio), dressed in expensive (virginal) white satin. Then what Seydor calls Peckinpah's "prodigious sense of irony" goes to work (1997, 189). The young prostitute, as we discover, is really virginal in her authentic nature while Teresa, once the symbol of uncorrupted purity for Angel, has become, in Don José's words, the true "whore of Mapache." In this role-reversal, accomplished cinematically through a series of blinding cross-cuts between Teresa's awful death while seated on Mapache's lap and the young woman in blue's terrified reaction, we are invited to identify the young woman with Teresa's fate, while simultaneously she begins to take Aurora's place in Pike's imagination by incarnating both the Teresa of Angel's dreams and the proud, sensual, loving Aurora of Pike's tortured memories.

This symbolic transposition of roles/selves becomes clearer in the late scene between Pike and the young woman in her room. We first see her there photographed over Pike's right shoulder, as a cross glows over his other shoulder. Pike, dressing, turns and looks at her while she, wearing a clean white slip, quietly moistens her neck and her breasts with a cool cloth. We are reminded that water is associated throughout *The Wild Bunch* with the cleansing, regenerating process. We think again of the children in Angel's village swimming naked in the pond, the village itself so verdant and un-desert-like. Even the scene in which the Gorches bathe in huge water/wine vats built 300 years ago by Spanish dons indicates their salutary scorn for class and hierarchical tradition. The Gorches, irrepressible as always, cavort among the vats like happy children, and their drunken revelry culminates in a sauna where the other members of the Bunch laugh and playfully throw water at each other. It is here that Pike, prodded by Dutch, grants Angel his case of rifles, and here as well that Lyle, water-drenched and drunkenly formal, introduces his "fiancée," one of the whores. This comic mock-marriage motif also sets the stage for what follows next, Pike's voiceover reminiscence to Dutch about Aurora, including his intention "to marry her."[12]

Dealing with the traditionally virgin birth of the hero, Joseph Campbell writes of the mother, "She is a personification of the primal element named in the second verse of Genesis, where we read that 'the spirit of God moved upon the face of the waters'" (297). If the mother (virginal because she has coupled with God) is to be identified with "the face of the waters," and if Peckinpah focuses our attention on the young woman washing her neck and breasts, we think the water here, as elsewhere in *The Wild Bunch*, should be identified with childhood (and thus baptism), and with innocence in particular. The young woman's breasts are both erotic and maternal, linked to our conception of her as lover and mother, while the whiteness of her slip — ironic only if associated with her profession, prostitution —connotes a virginal purity, quite different from the flashy satin dress Teresa wore. The young woman never speaks. Nor should she, for as we have seen elsewhere, silence within the roiling present of *The Wild Bunch* invariably provokes powerful retrospective emotions, echoes from the mournful world of Pike's past. Pike's own silence is hardly exceptional either. Immobilized, confronted by the tragedy of his life, of his lost love, he can only stare dumbly at the ruins of his ever-present past. For Pike keeps running into what he loves or has loved, and like most people — outlaw or intellectual — he cannot talk about this at all. In a related context Eudora Welty writes of the doomed traitor and weary outcast Aaron Burr, "a man could be so alone in his heart that he could not even ask a question. In such silence as falls over a lonely man there is a childlike supplication, and all arms might wish to open to him, but there is no speech." Pike's pain and "childlike supplication" will eventually open him to the possibility of youthful transformation, but for now he is, like Welty's protagonists in "First Love," unable to "find names for the places of the heart and the times for its shadowy and tragic events" (165).

When the camera finally rounds to Pike's tired face, we see that it limns the suffering, the rue, and the loss he has known, all elicited by the presence of the young woman, who, though she is in the same room with Pike, seems distant from him. She then enters the expanded tableau of the cross, herself, and her baby sitting in its crib. Since we view each of them from Pike's perspective, his back turned to us and thus looking at them much as the audience does, they assume a kind of triptych-looking, frieze-like fixity. (Pike appears, back turned, in separate frames with all three.) Like the audience, Pike gazes at cross, mother, and child as if they inhabit a plane of reality he cannot share except as a spectator. This scene rouses and recapitulates, in synoptic fashion, Pike's memories— though probably at an unconscious level — of Angel's village, the young girls, their mothers with their babies, the naked boys swimming in the pond. It also brings to the surface Pike's agonized remembrances of Aurora undressing in her bedroom, as well as the scene in the brothel when Deke is taken prisoner and Pike escapes.

Many critics, in particular Mark Crispin Miller, have written intelligently about this crucial scene. Miller rightly emphasizes the "helpless sadness" etched on Pike's face as he gazes at the woman and child, "at something that could have made him a different person" (4). But we believe that Miller, though acutely sensitive to the *mise-en-scène* in the young woman's room, misses the opportunity to expand his interpretation beyond Pike's sorrow. Nevertheless, Miller points us toward the larger implications of this scene when he draws our attention to a very significant detail: "[Pike] hears a baby cry, and turns to see the infant lying on the other side of the cot. The camera zooms in slightly, accentuating the infant in a sequence otherwise made up of lingering stationary shots" (4). We would emphasize the difference between the static, motionless silence in the room and the slight zoom inward toward the crying baby. For this subtle shot energizes the shadowy room, propels us subjectively — again it is his vision we share in this room — into Pike's dawning awareness of the baby's existence — and promise. In a similar vein William Butler Yeats writes that in observing, as Pike Bishop does, the specific "tragedy of love, we renew, it may be, some loyalty of our youth, and go from the theatre with our eyes dim for an old love's sake" (241). When we "renew" our now tarnished youthful loyalties, by extension we become youthful again — perhaps even like a baby. This, we believe, is the process in which Pike slowly begins to participate.

If we find ourselves identifying with Pike as the would-be father of this child, at a deeper level something more expansive is also taking place. "We all dream of being a child again." Don José's profound and pregnant words prepare us for Pike's rebirth into heroic action. He does not just stare at the baby; rather, in that slow zoom shot, he subjectively enters its new life, its pastlessness, its guiltlessness, its freedom. Pike makes love with the young woman, recapitulates his physical and spiritual love for Aurora, and becomes at once a new man and the father of his reborn self. And because he has evolved into the hero, he can commit himself to vital action (the zoom shot), lifting himself from the lonely passivity and stoicism of despair. We must add, however, that this does not mean Pike can rewrite his tragic fate. Indeed, the "action" or fresh start to which he is now committed is certain to end with his own death. This is the tragic logic of *The Wild Bunch*, a film in which full commitment to one's better self is an act of suicide as well as moral redemption.

One way of describing what takes place in *The Wild Bunch* is to say that the film embraces a process in which images, such as the woman and her child, are constantly expanding toward the archetypal, then contracting toward the literal. At their best these images should be felt simultaneously in their immediacy *and* in their larger dimension. We think it is spurious to argue that mythic experience detracts from our response to characters as people in a specific situation. As A. E. Dyson has said, "In many great tragedies, it is true, we are taken beyond a sense of the hero's personal identity to his archetypal role as sacrificial victim, fisher king or dying god; and this, to some degree, modifies response. But such suggestions do not subtract from personal involvement though they may enrich it" (138). This is certainly true of *The Wild Bunch*, and especially true of the scene in the young woman's room, where profoundly felt emotions expand beyond their immediate setting to suggest a larger area of significant experience.

The subtle picture of the Madonna and Child (though she is also a woman, and the baby a baby) within a bordello (virgin and whore, spirit and flesh united in one identity) embodies Peckinpah's desire to unite within a single person the sacred and profane sides of Pike Bishop's divided nature. Unlike the austere, flesh-denying Puritanism of Starbuck (its very name an attempt to transcend earthly experience) and the soulless depravity of Mapache's Agua Verde (with its connotations of green, slimy water), the young woman, so representative of the authentic spirit of Angel's village, synthesizes warring polarities. No wonder Pike pines for what he feels in her presence, then realizes in some inchoate manner that it will be out of her being that his own transformation can take place. In a literal sense it is clearly too late for this aging bandit to move forward, for he is already an anachronism in a new, mechanized age, perched on the edge of world cataclysm. It is 1913, and if Pike is to begin again, it must be on new ground, though paradoxically derived from the old ground of this violent man's former existence. It is time, as his lover's/friend's/hero's code dictates, to affirm his ideals in action and to embody his principles, even if he must die for those principles.

Angrily, disgustedly, Pike, holding an almost empty bottle in his hand, looks from the woman, the cross, and the child into the next room, where the seemingly unregenerate Gorches are haggling with their whore over her prices, until, hurling the bottle down, Pike moves to the doorway and looks into their adjoining room. Pike rests his hands against the walls of the door and stares at the sordid Gorches. Those arms, partially stretched in an understated imitation of a weary Christ on the Cross (we should remember that directly behind Pike is the illuminated cross on the wall), create an image of Pike standing between two worlds. Finally he becomes the two worlds, those of flesh and spirit, when he makes his only utterance here, his call to action throughout the film, "Let's go!"

The Gorches, especially the mercurial and dangerous Lyle, stare back, not knowing what to make of Pike's look or his command. Tector lies on a makeshift bed, a nervous, chirping

"Let's go!" In a bordello Pike Bishop's (William Holden's) final exhortation to the sordid Gorches (Warren Oates as Lyle, shown with his back to the camera, and Ben Johnson as Tector), to pick up arms and defend the honor of *The Wild Bunch*.

bird, probably a sparrow, playing between his fingers but struggling as well against an entangling string which prevents it from flying away. The scene and the bird may remind us of Angel's earlier sparrow-like taunting of the Gorches, "cheep, cheep, cheep," in the village where they learn the stolen gold is nothing but washers, of the courageous Angel who in Dutch's words has "played his *string* out to the end" (our emphasis), and of Angel, tethered and pulled on a rope around the walls of Agua Verde by Mapache's automobile. For the Gorches the scene repeats the cat's cradle game the brothers played with the girl in Angel's village, but this time with a difference. The cat's cradle is a symbol of infinity,[13] chiefly because it is capable of innumerable combinations. Here, though, the string entwined within Tector's fingers appears frayed, almost broken, as the bird flutters futilely to free itself. The bird finally falls to the earthen floor as Tector rises to join Pike and Lyle in battle. The men leave the room and we are left with another extraordinary zoom-in closeup image of the panting bird, lying on its side, its life slowly ebbing away. This seems to represent a kind of archaic omen, possibly Homeric (Penelope dreams of an eagle ensnaring a serpent just prior to her husband's return), possibly biblical (cf. the ironic epigraph from Psalm 84: 3 at the beginning of this chapter), more probably Shakespearean (Hamlet's "There is special providence in the fall of a sparrow"), and it also conjures up the more immediate image of the warrior as wanderer, far from home, who envies the migratory bird ("La Golondrina") in its homeward flight. Birds are often identified with the spirit or soul, so it would seem that the tethered sparrow (swallow) is linked in its physical death to the higher destiny of those who will die and be reborn through heroic actions in the battle of Agua Verde.

In response to Pike's "Let's go!" Lyle gradually begins to comprehend the meaning of Pike's command. His "Why not!" seems to be less an interrogative than an imperative, for he reverses the implications of Pike's exhausted, cynical "Why not?" uttered earlier when, helpless before the torture of Angel, Pike agrees to go to the bordello. That both Gorches leave off fighting over how much to pay their whore to go off to fight against a tyrannical dictator, for someone other than themselves, seems almost miraculous, and indeed it is, much like this whole scene in the brothel. As Pike says earlier while watching the Gorches play with the cat's cradle, "Now that I find hard to believe." Then as now, however, the Gorches' form of redemption is tied to Pike's rebirth and the theme of the innocence and freedom of childhood. Before he goes to meet Dutch and the Gorches, now outside, Pike returns to the room, to the young woman and her baby, and by extension to the softly illuminated cross. He gazes at the young woman one last time, then reaches into his pocket and throws his remaining gold coins onto the table before her. She seems disappointed, perhaps insulted, because her affections toward Pike obviously transcend a prostitute's financial transactions. But Pike does not throw the money down out of scorn for the young woman. In part he feels a corrosive self-contempt, born of the tragic realization that the new life she proffers comes too late for an aging man so burdened with the mistakes of his past, and of his own nature, he can no longer live with himself. But equally powerful is the tragic knowledge of what he must do, and why, and for whom.

Seydor's description of Pike's dilemma could not be improved upon:

> The next woman will only remind him of the one killed beside him long ago; at the bottom of the next bottle he will find only the same desolation; and solitude will not bring him even the cold comfort of isolation, for he will always be haunted by the voices of the past that live in his heart, whispering of debts unpaid, words broken, and friends abandoned because all he cared about was saving his own skin and making another good score. It isn't enough, it cannot sustain, and so it places him in a situation as authentically tragic as any a man can know: walk away, his life's a fraud; stay and fight, his life is over [1997, 169].

Seydor also sees that "[t]he prostitute and her baby are an ironic reminder of the family [Pike] might have enjoyed had he been, once in the past, just a little more careful." And he sees as well that Pike's present concern for Angel is linked to Aurora, for Angel is a "member of the only family [Pike] has left" (1997, 169). But Seydor's moving account of what Pike is feeling as he comes to his momentous decision focuses almost entirely on his betrayals of the Wild Bunch: "At this point Angel is no longer just Angel; he is Thornton asking, 'How can you be so damn sure?'; he is Crazy Lee saying, 'I'll hold them here until hell freezes over or you say different'; he is Old Sykes wounded and left to die; and he is Angel after all, near death yet playing his string right out to the end" (1997, 169). The centrality of Pike's failure with Aurora and all the other women in his life, missing here in Seydor's otherwise splendid treatment of the turning point in Pike's life, is strongly suggested by the fact Peckinpah develops Pike's decision around the scene with the young woman and not his male comrades. Pike's several failures with his fellow gang members are of course relevant, excruciatingly so, but it is Aurora who dominates his thoughts and feelings in the form of the young woman, Aurora's touching surrogate.

As one man, equal in the purpose which unites them — they walk four abreast, not in military, hierarchical twos as they did at the beginning of the film — the Wild Bunch begin their slow progress through Agua Verde, indifferent to the heavily armed hordes of soldiers who surround them, to the plaza where the drunken Mapache waits with the hideously maimed Angel. Intensifying drum rolls punctuate the Bunch's movement toward certain death, but counterpointed to these martial drum beats is "La Golondrina," the song Angel's people sang for the Bunch as they rode out of the pueblo. Here, though, it is slurringly rendered by the drunken soldiers and their women, who are so stupefied by alcohol they seem indifferent to the song's melancholy message. But the audience, by now sympathetic with the gang if the film is working for them, cannot miss the significance of this song. Nor can they ignore another talisman of Angel's village, the tall green tree of life — so out of place in this dry and dusty town — toward which the Bunch move as they set out to rescue their doomed comrade.

That four men destroy an army of over 200 soldiers, a feat of fantastic, even legendary magnitude far exceeding any attempts to "understand" it (for it is, to use Thomas Keneally's phrase, "truer than truth itself" [232]), elevates the film's final cathartic action to mythic status, for which we have been suitably prepared by the "realism past realism" (Kauffmann 267) of the Bunch's exodus from Angel's village and Pike's newfound commitment to heroic action experienced in the young woman's room. Peckinpah utilizes telephoto lenses to track — front and rear, coalescing past and future in the mythic, timeless present of their moving forms — the Bunch's walk through Agua Verde, and because of this, while the camera remains focused on them, their surroundings appear progressively more smoky, vapory, insubstantial, as if they constitute a realm *less* than real. It is as if the Bunch move in such a way as to punch a hole in whatever spatio-temporal system holds the rest of "reality" in check. This is particularly evident in a startling montage built on precise dramatic cutting. Just before the Bunch reach the plaza and Mapache, we observe the corner of a wall, with nothing but space and a few random background buildings filling the rest of the frame. The Bunch enter the frame, photographed in a rear tracking shot, as they are about to turn into the plaza. Suddenly, in a brilliant cut, they round the corner as one, almost as if they materialize out of empty air. Of course, this is not really what happens. We first view them in the rear tracking shot moving toward the building corner, then, in a forward tracking shot, we watch them enter the plaza. The effect of these two cuts is arresting and even menacing, as directly behind Pike the flames and smoke of a burning fire seem to rise up and penetrate his physical and symbolic being. This sets the scene for the apocalyptic events which follow.

The specifically female motif appears once more when, after Angel's throat is cut, Mapache is slain, and the fierce fighting begins, Pike Bishop veers into a woman's room off the plaza. In a dramatic zoom-in, zoom-out shot, we view the woman doubled as she is both standing before Pike and reflected in the wardrobe mirror. This is Pike's nightmare moment, the return of the never wholly repressed, for it recapitulates the scene in Aurora's bedroom when she was murdered and Pike was shot by her husband. Pike's hesitation before the woman and his refusal to shoot her contrast with the massive carnage of the battle, a bloodbath in which soldiers are mowed down in machine-gun fire like rows of wheat and other members of the gang, particularly Dutch, use women indiscriminately to shield themselves from Mapache's *federales*. The scene repeats Aurora's death, but it also gives us one final indication of Pike Bishop's ambivalent feelings about women. The doubled mirror image of the woman, reflecting what for Pike is her virgin/whore, lover/betrayer nature, plus the presence in the room of another man, a half-clad soldier hidden behind the wardrobe, perplex Pike as he stalls for a moment within the battle's swirling action. Instead of killing the woman he turns his gun on the wardrobe, shoots and shatters the mirror, perhaps killing the soldier, perhaps firing at his own image, perhaps in a memory flash shooting at the image of Aurora's murdering husband who first "appears" in the bedroom framed in her dresser mirror.[14] It is never clear just what Pike sees or knows, what is real or unreal, in this brilliantly realized mimetic maze. If he is firing at his own image, this may be another instance of this sad bad man's yearning for the peace of death. And if he is indeed reenacting the death of Aurora, it is he who takes the place of the murdering husband, a psychological displacement which can only increase the guilt of this already guilt-ridden man.

Moments later this same woman, a vengeful leer across her face, shoots Pike in the back, reflecting once again the agonizing doubleness he has always experienced with women.[15] Furious, he turns toward her, cries "Bitch!" and shoots her in the breast.[16] At the moment of his death Pike is shot once more in the back, this time by a child, a little boy dressed in an ill-fitting simulacrum of the dead Mapache's uniform. Pike Bishop dies at the hands of a woman and child, representatives of the very world he longed for and yet fought against, a world symbolized first by Aurora, then later by the young woman in the room with her baby and her cross. This is the world Pike has alternately desired and denied. Therefore it is appropriate, even just, that this doomed warrior-hero should die for what he has loved—and feared.

Pike expires with his finger poised on the trigger of a machine gun, the gun's nose seemingly pointing proudly, arrogantly, into the air. It is a troubling image, one we are not likely to forget, and reminds us of the paradoxical account of a tragic death we apply to Steve Judd's demise at the end of Chapter Two (see Frye 1957, 214). What can this image mean? We would suggest that in a film filled with so many signs of entrapment—the walls and roofs of Starbuck and Agua Verde, canyon walls ringed with Mapache's double-crossing henchmen, a thatched enclosure for scorpions built by children who have learned evil only too well—the gun arched upward toward the blue sky implies an act of defiance, a rebellious opening toward freedom—even in death—and a kind of romantic transcendence. On the other hand, we would stress the brutally insistent, perhaps even obvious, nature of a gun phallically pointed up, its defiant, murderous energy contending with the other pole of its symbolic possibilities. Does not the gun, within its paradoxical capacity both for creation (Mapache's army destroyed, Angel's villagers taking arms and ammunition—even the machine gun itself—out of Agua Verde to feed the revolution) and destruction (so many dead, so many weeping wives and mothers, the line of refugees departing the ruined garrison a harbinger of wars and displacements to come in this bloodiest of centuries), underscore the general theme of relationship, made specific here through the engendering violence of love which bonds both the spiritual and carnal capacities of mankind, forging a unity which Pike Bishop could act upon but which he perhaps only intuited, never quite comprehended?

Like the *Iliad*, and because it deals with warriors, adventurers, men of action, *The Wild Bunch*, as Alaisdair MacIntyre has written of Homer's great poem, "lays claim to the form of understanding which it denies to those whose actions it describes" (121). But this does not mean that Pike understands nothing in his final moments. Otherwise he would be neither heroic nor tragic, and he is both. Pike's manner of dying helps us to understand why, out of frustrated but obdurate love, he merges his own self-annihilating but life-creating impulses in the shattering holocaust which concludes this wrenching film.

That spirit and flesh, myth and reality, potency and destruction should be so tenuously allied; that good and evil, female and male, indeed, bishops and pikes, should lodge so precariously in one man, points explicitly, at film's end, to the terrible grandeur of human nature as it is depicted in *The Wild Bunch.*

III

The events which follow the deaths of Pike Bishop, the Wild Bunch, and something like 200 *federales* have generated a critical debate almost as interesting as that concerning what leads up to this massive confrontation. These events center on Deke Thornton, who has been observing the fight from a distance through his binoculars. Deke arrives at the scene of the slaughter as the friends and family members of the soldiers begin to deal with the horrific aftermath and Deke's vulturous posse begin to lay claim to the still-valuable bodies of the Wild Bunch. Deke dismounts from his horse, backlit by the sun in scintillating golden dust, and seems to enter a more mythic than human realm as he makes his way through the all-too-human carnage which has recently taken place. We watch him move straight toward Pike's fallen body, Pike's back turned to us and to Deke, again suggesting the overwhelmingly complex guilt and desire for expiation which have marked Pike's final days. In an extraordinary slow zoom we see Deke, gloved as always, reach down and remove Pike's traditional Colt revolver from its traditional gun belt. There has been no indication in the film that Pike ever used any guns but the modern machine gun and his modern hand gun, no doubt stolen from the U.S. Army. It is as if Pike also reveres his old six-shooter and what its associations with the past mean to him as well as to Deke. Deke lovingly cradles the gun in both hands before he walks off with it, the single memento he takes from his old friend.

Seydor suggests that Deke's gesture is "a symbolic farewell, but the way in which the music softly, almost imperceptibly, reprises the lyrical main theme reminds us that it is also a moment of reunion. Both Peckinpah and [Jerry] Fielding were in especially close accord on this effect; in one of their earlier conferences they discovered that each had independently come to feel that the entire film built to this moment" (1997, 185). We suggested earlier that Deke's faith in Pike leads to a kind of redemption as their friendship is reestablished here at the conclusion. In this "reunion," as Seydor calls it, Deke no longer feels ashamed once he sees what Pike and the Wild Bunch have done in Agua Verde. Pike has lived up to Deke's expectations of an idealized leader, indeed, Deke's faith in Pike as friend and leader has been amply "justified," as Steve Judd might say, while Deke himself has stuck to his principles but has not been required to capture or kill Pike. When Freddy Sykes and the men from Angel's village ride into Agua Verde, Deke first joins Freddy in ironic laughter at how things have turned out, then in more genuine laughter which links him to Freddy, Don José, and the men who ride with Don José, but also with the old Wild Bunch whose laughter has rung throughout the film and will return once more in the film's closing shots. Deke then joins Freddy, Don José, and this new version of the Wild Bunch with a smile we have not seen before in this tortured man's life. As we remarked earlier, Deke Thornton's fate is hardly tragic and might even be seen — within limits— as triumphant.

By contrast there can be no such release for Pike Bishop, since what he feels is entirely directed toward his own guilty self and the things he has done for which there can be no forgiveness. He cannot take these things back, nor somehow cancel them out. He can say, in effect, there will be no more failures, no more evasions, no more expediencies for which his friends and lovers must pay. He can do more than this; he can act accordingly, whatever the consequences. It is much the same for Dutch, who is eager to go for Angel, and even the Gorches seem to participate voluntarily in this climactic assertion — if not reassertion — of the values by which the Wild Bunch have presumed to live. Ironically, then, Pike can offer Dutch and the Gorches a final opportunity for redemption, and his example will live on for Deke and Freddy, the leaders of the new Wild Bunch, but for Pike himself there is no viable alternative but the most meaningful form of self-annihilation.

This is to insist again that Pike is a tragic character, unlike Deke, Freddy, or the revamped Wild Bunch who ride out of Agua Verde at the end. The impact of Pike's death has been reduced in value by readings which highlight the comic/romantic elements of the film's final moments. As we suggested at the beginning of this chapter, it is Seydor who has expressed this position most memorably. Seydor embellishes the positive nature of the new Wild Bunch by referring to Don José and his men as "revolutionaries" (1997, 211), as many of Peckinpah's critics have done, though he does see that Freddy and Deke are not moved by revolutionary fervor: "what is left in the world of time and circumstance, which is to say the world of history, are two old men, survivors off to fight for a cause they don't believe in because it gives them another chance at something they do believe in, which is to stay on the run, on the move, on the *go*" (1997, 210). Earlier, however, Pike has identified Don José as a bandit, not a revolutionary, and while we have previously seen the impressive Indian revolutionaries who come for Angel's case of rifles, the only thing we see Don José and his men do is murder Deke's posse when they start back to the United States to collect the bounties on the Wild Bunch.[17] To associate Don José and his colleagues solely with a "cause" is wishful thinking.[18]

But this is not to identify the new Wild Bunch with Deke Thornton's sordid posse. If the new Bunch are not committed revolutionaries, they display much of the spirit which informs the old Bunch in their final moments. Freddy Sykes is not a tormented figure like Pike Bishop, but there are symbolic echoes of Pike in Freddy's bandage on his left thigh, the location of Pike's wound, and his humorous and uplifting invitation to Deke to join the new Bunch: "Me and the boys got some work to do. Wanna come along?" Here Peckinpah employs one of his most audacious anti-realistic touches. When Freddy rides into Agua Verde after the battle is over, he is bandaged on his left thigh, whereas we have seen him shot by Coffer in his right thigh. The transposition of Freddy's wound from his right thigh to his left can hardly be considered a mistake in continuity in such a brilliantly edited film and suggests that Freddy preserves Pike's spirit within the newly reconstituted Wild Bunch. Deke Thornton is even more obviously renewed by Pike's stirring example at the battle of Agua Verde, and it is not hard to imagine Deke as a less-conflicted but even more competent replacement for Pike as the leader of the Wild Bunch. Moreover, Don José is obviously a bandit of real substance, a man whose earlier judgments about Mapache, Teresa, Angel, and the Gorches have been adopted by Pike himself. A man who earlier ran from Mapache and his so-called soldiers, Don José is now committed to a course of revolutionary action against the Hueristas which may eventually recall Pike's call to action against Mapache and his 200 *federales*. Like the old Wild Bunch, the new Wild Bunch will have to make their way through a lawless terrain, no doubt engaging in violent and morally-conflicted acts, but who is say the new version of the Wild Bunch will not match or even exceed the spiritual legacy of the old Wild Bunch?

Far more important is Seydor's position on the film's famous conclusion. "The Bunch's villainy is left to perish in the dusky and lurid glow of the windswept desert when Pike, Dutch, and the Gorch brothers are carried off head down over a saddle as society's outlaws," Seydor claims. "When they are next seen, it is as heroes of some legendary adventure, illumined by a radiance if not celestial, then at least transcendent, emanating from the faithful if factitious folk imagination of the people of Angel's village" (1997, 211–12). Seydor refers to Peckinpah's use of the old B-Western device of reviewing the major cast at the end by showing each in turn as he appeared earlier, in this case laughing at one of the several occasions where laughter is abundant (after the debacle in Starbuck, at Angel's village, after the successful raid on the arms train),[19] followed by the exit from Angel's village reprised.[20] As the film concludes with these joyous images, Seydor argues, Peckinpah abruptly shifts a dramatic structure which has been tragic throughout and "deflects" it toward the comic, toward "the world of romance" (1997, 212). As we remarked earlier, we are apparently supposed to think of *The Winter's Tale* or *The Tempest*, plays typically characterized as romances and not comedies because of the heavy dose of tragic materials similarly "deflected" at the end of Shakespeare's magical performances.

We think the echoes here are indeed Shakespearean, but from Shakespeare's tragedies rather than his romances. At the end of many of the tragedies, after the death of the hero, a new order is established, however precariously, led by the men (always men) who will take the kingdom forward after its recent catastrophe(s). The survivors are such characters as Horatio (*Hamlet*), Edgar (*King Lear*), and Macduff (*Macbeth*), philosophers or statesmen of intelligence and moral rectitude who testify to the greatness of the dead protagonist (Horatio, Edgar) or the immense waste represented by the dispatched "hero" (Macduff). We are made to see that the death of the hero, however painful, is not the end of things, not even for a brief period; but we are also made to feel the diminished state of the kingdom and the dramatic world Shakespeare has created. The loss of Hamlet or Lear is enhanced, not diminished, by the survival of such "leaders" as Horatio (or Fortinbras, the political leader to come) or Edgar, whose excellences do not adequately compensate for what has been lost with the death of the protagonist.

Macbeth is the best and perhaps the most relevant example, for in most respects Macbeth is the play's villain and Macduff its heroic victim, and the death of Macbeth marks the restoration of order ("The time is free") after the anarchy Macbeth has loosed on Scotland. But the greatest loss dramatized here is Macbeth himself, a man whose poetic greatness has registered throughout the play even as his moral lapses make it more than appropriate that he should die at the end. Pike is not Macbeth's equal as a poet or a villain, but we are made to care about his soul more than any other in his dramatic world, and his death, though redemptive, is not to be neglected in the presence of the new Bunch's laughter, images of the old Bunch's happier moments, or even the oddly prophetic celebration of the Wild Bunch as they leave Angel's village. The film's overwhelming tragic effect is enhanced, not "deflected," by the contrast between the final fate of the Wild Bunch and their more joyous moments in the past, much as Pike's tragic fate is accentuated by the contrast with Deke's good fortune.

Stephen Prince goes so far as to say, "The Bunch's entrance into Valhalla at the end of the film subscribes to what Richard Slotkin has argued is a defining American cultural mythology of violence" (1998, 225).[21] Gabrielle Murray has rightly replied that "the Bunch do not enter Valhalla — they die — and those images that we see incarnated at the film's conclusion are retrospective highlights of moments of joy and laughter in their lives" (61). These "highlights" and Deke's gesture in taking Pike's gun are the filmic equivalent of Horatio's final praise of his good friend Hamlet and Edgar's devastating invocation of the cosmic loss which should be felt with the demise of King Lear and his one true daughter, Cordelia. Seen in this light, as in so many others, *The Wild Bunch* is indeed Shakespearean, but the model is Shakespearean tragedy, for the death of the tragic protagonist is as crucial to Peckinpah as it was to Shakespeare.[2]

Chapter Five

Pat Garrett and Billy the Kid: The Tragedy of Pat Garrett

The reversal of a focused, unitary intention, in which the whole life of a man may be concentrated, is at the very heart of tragedy as Aristotle conceives it.

—Gerald Else 1967, 91

I have lived long enough: my way of life
Is fall'n into the sear, the yellow leaf,
And that which should accompany old age,
As honor, love, obedience, troops of friends,
I must not look to have; but in their stead,
Curses, not loud but deep, mouth-honor, breath,
Which the poor heart would fain deny, and dare not.

—Macbeth, in *The Tragedy of Macbeth*, V.iii.22–28

Pat Garrett is about people just waiting around to die. If the West is a wide-open country, Peckinpah sees it as a prison from which almost every decent person is trying to escape, without success.

—Maximilian Le Cain (3)

At the beginning of Chapter Four we refer to Pike Bishop (William Holden) as the most traditionally tragic of Peckinpah's protagonists. This may seem an odd judgment, for Pike is a professional bandit who hardly seems better than the average person, Aristotle's famous criterion for a tragic protagonist (Else 1967, 18). Indeed, Shakespeare's practice suggests that, like Aristotle, he could not imagine a central tragic part for anyone not among the play's ruling class. (*Romeo and Juliet* offers a possible exception.) For Peckinpah, as for most modern tragedians, the hero's character is far more relevant than his social status, and we have already argued that Peckinpah presents Pike as a warrior rather than a thief, a man committed to "[o]utdated codes like loyalty, friendship, grace under pressure, all the simple virtues [which] have become clichés" (William Murray 72). In *The Wild Bunch* (1969), Pike's failure to live up to these "codes" leads to the tragic catastrophe, but Peckinpah works very hard to persuade us that Pike believes in these traditional values, lest we not take seriously Pike's failure to live up to them or his rededication to such values at the film's conclusion.

In *The Wild Bunch* Peckinpah remains committed to the insights about tragedy he first formulated in his 1954 M.A. thesis on his production of Tennessee Williams' *Portrait of a Madonna*. There he argues that "the audience must understand [Lucretia Collins'] beauty and potential as a human being ... in order to feel her personal tragedy" (11–12), and he praises "the ability of [Williams'] characters—defeated and broken by society and their own inadequacies—to meet their fate with courage and dignity" (12). Pike's potential as a human being, dramatized throughout, and his courage and dignity in meeting his fate are precisely the features which mark the film as tragic. No less traditional is Pike's acute and painful awareness of the choices he has made, the "self-knowledge" Robert Heilman and others require of a tragic protagonist (Heilman 248, 251). Indeed, *The Wild Bunch* admirably illustrates "the theory of choice and responsibility implicit in the *Poetics*" (Kerrigan 13), as Pike and his men deliberately choose to die in defense of their comrade Angel (Jaime Sanchez) and the values embodied in Angel's village. Peckinpah has noted that the events just after the Bunch shoot Mapache (Emilio Fernandez) reinforce the element of choice in their final actions: "they can get out, and they know it, and they look at each other and they start to laugh, because this is the end and they want it all" (quoted in Weddle, "The Making of *The Wild Bunch*," 51). If *The Wild Bunch* is "a romantic tragedy focused on the theme of redemption," as David Weddle has said (1997, xvi), it is because Pike Bishop is made to understand the irrevocable mistakes he has committed and to choose the courageous, dignified response to this knowledge embodied in the film's unforgettable conclusion.

If Pike Bishop is an oddly modern embodiment of the traditional hero, Pat Garrett (James Coburn) must seem an extremely untraditional version if indeed he is tragic at all. The protagonist of *Pat Garrett and Billy the Kid* (1973), Garrett occupies the traditional position of moral authority in Westerns, that of sheriff or marshal, but his decision to become the sheriff of Lincoln County, New Mexico, is precisely the mistake or error which generates the film's tragic action and hardly points to his moral or ethical authority. Indeed, Pat Garrett is no Steve Judd (Joel McCrea), the exemplary lawman and moral conscience of Peckinpah's first great Western, *Ride the High Country* (1962). Unlike Steve Judd, Garrett has not given his adult life to securing the peace in a lawless territory, and in fact he turns to the role of lawman only because it serves his personal interests. The price he must pay for this decision includes hunting down and killing his former friend William Bonney or Billy the Kid (Kris Kristofferson), an action more or less the opposite of Steve Judd's efforts to redeem his old friend Gil Westrum (Randolph Scott). As we will see, Garrett is reviled throughout the film, by virtually every other significant character. Nor does he die at the end of the film, the only Peckinpah protagonist to survive the tragic action in which he participates.[1] It is not hard to see why many viewers have either denied that Garrett is tragic or, like Brad Stevens, argued that "as a tragic hero, he is more Macbeth than Hamlet" (270).

The comparison to either Hamlet or Macbeth may seem fanciful, but the parallels point to Garrett's central role in Peckinpah's most unusual modern tragedy. Garrett shares little with Hamlet except that each faces a horrifying task, worthy of Greek tragedy, to kill someone close to himself, a father figure (Claudius) or a son figure (Billy the Kid). The real parallel here is structural, for both Hamlet and Garrett procrastinate throughout the work in question, delaying the violent action each feels he must perform. The parallels with Macbeth are much more significant, for Macbeth is Shakespeare's most damned and doomed tragic protagonist, one who inspires revulsion not unlike the calumny visited upon Garrett throughout Peckinpah's film. The crucial parallel is that both Macbeth and Garrett bring disaster upon themselves by their own fateful decisions. This is more obvious with Macbeth, whose murder of Duncan, his relative, guest, and king, is one of the most awful crimes in all tragic literature, but we hope to show that Peckinpah places almost equal dramatic weight on Garrett's decision to become sheriff of Lincoln County with the assistance of ranchers such as John Chisum (Barry Sullivan) and business interests collectively known as the Santa Fe Ring, a decision which obliges him to hunt down Billy the Kid and turn his back on everything and everyone in his former life, most especially his Hispanic wife Ida (Aurora Clavel).

The dramatic structures of *Macbeth* and *Pat Garrett and Billy the Kid* may seem very different as Macbeth's murder of Duncan comes at the beginning of his play and Garrett's assassination of Billy the Kid comes at the end of Peckinpah's film, but both works are structured around an initial mistake which leads to the disastrous consequences traced throughout the action. At various points in this chapter, we will elaborate the parallels with Macbeth which make Garrett anything but the "tragic victim" Raymond Williams identifies as the typical protagonist of modern tragedy (87). Indeed, it is very much to the point that none of Peckinpah's tragic heroes is a victim of anything but his own choices. In this crucial sense, all of Peckinpah's tragic protagonists, even Pat Garrett, derive from a relatively traditional view of what constitutes tragedy.

Not everyone has seen Pat Garrett as a tragic character, traditional or nontraditional. Jim Kitses is the latest to reject the notion that Garrett is even the film's protagonist, preferring instead to see Garrett and Billy the Kid as equally central to a story Kitses finds harshly revisionist rather than tragic. Kitses specifically rejects Paul Seydor's reading of Peckinpah's film as Pat Garrett's tragedy, arguing that "the film is balanced equally on the shoulders of both men" (2004, 230) and that Garrett's tale is neither central nor tragic (2004, 246, n.6).[2] Our own view is that Seydor is right to see Garrett as the film's tragic protagonist, for virtually everything in this dark film elaborates the story of Garrett's fateful decision to join forces with Chisum and the Santa Fe Ring, men who represent the economic and corporate elite in the territory of New Mexico as of 1881. On the other hand, we also hope to demonstrate that Seydor's reading of Garrett's plight underestimates the role played by his wife Ida both in defining Garrett's tragic situation and in embodying the alternative he has effectively rejected in choosing to become sheriff of Lincoln County. Seydor believes that the film offers "a fairly complete picture of the paucity of options the environment opens for Garrett" (1997, 285), a view he repeats in the commentary to his 2005 Special Edition of *Pat Garrett and Billy the Kid*, where he again stresses the "paucity of options" available to Garrett. We feel that Seydor exaggerates "the theme of determinism" in Peckinpah's film, "its interlocking themes of casual violence and naturalistic determinism" (1997, 275), an approach which leads him to downplay the choice Garrett has made and to all but ignore Garrett's wife, whose crucial scene with her husband is discussed on one page of Seydor's 52-page chapter on the film (1997, 284).[3]

As we explore the tragic action of *Pat Garrett and Billy the Kid*, we also want to address Peckinpah's role in reshaping the script as well as directing this film. Many of his critics have seen Peckinpah as somehow tampering with Rudolph Wurlitzer's original screenplay, subsequently published by Wurlitzer after the release of the film.[4] For example, Neil Fulwood speaks of "the true genius of Wurlitzer's script" (107), and Bill Mesce agrees with Wurlitzer's complaint about "the deleterious effect [Peckinpah's] constant reworking was having on the screenplay" (136). Seydor rightly defends many of the changes Peckinpah made with the original script, but his account suggests that Peckinpah's alterations were not always for the best (see 1997, 265–66). Moreover, Seydor thinks "it is hard to determine how much actual writing Peckinpah himself did, because reports vary, as do memories" (1997, 262). Reports and memories no doubt vary, and it is sometimes hard to say whether Peckinpah drafted a particular change or instructed Wurlitzer to write the new lines, but we believe the available sources—Wurlitzer's published screenplay, the final shooting script dated November 3, 1972,[5] and the completed film — allow us to go well beyond Seydor's sympathetic but "balanced" account to reverse Fulwood's and Mesce's conclusions. We hope to establish that Peckinpah's role in recasting *Pat Garrett and Billy the Kid* was as extensive and as crucial to the film's success as Seydor has demonstrated in the case of *The Wild Bunch*.[6]

We do not mean to suggest that *Pat Garrett and Billy the Kid* represents anything but "a genuine collaboration" between Peckinpah and Wurlitzer, as Seydor describes it (1997, 265). The finished film includes many scenes adapted from Wurlitzer's original script and much of the dialogue is taken verbatim from Wurlitzer. Nonetheless, Peckinpah's additions, deletions, and alterations transformed Wurlitzer's characters, especially Pat Garrett and Billy the Kid, and therefore the film as a whole. As Weddle suggests, Wurlitzer's Pat Garrett is "a small-minded man troubled by few scruples and little guilt when he finally guns down the Kid" (1994, 454), and Seydor sees that Wurlitzer's Garrett "is portrayed as little more than a corrupt official who has 'sold out,'" whereas Peckinpah's Garrett is a "richer" character whose motives run "deeper" (1997, 282–83). Peckinpah's Garrett, as we have suggested, recalls the anguished and damned Macbeth, an altogether different kind of character. In creating this character, Peckinpah effectively "destroyed" Wurlitzer's script to good effect, as James Coburn once remarked (quoted in Simmons 171). To show how Peckinpah went about doing this should go a long ways toward establishing the tragic nature and achievement of Peckinpah's next to last Western.

We will be highlighting Peckinpah's contributions to the script in each section of this chapter. The first two sections will deal largely with Pat Garrett, the first examining how Peckinpah recast the opening scenes of Wurlitzer's script to establish Garrett as the protagonist, the second tracing Garrett's Macbeth-like descent into the violent and even dehumanizing consequences of his mistake in scene after scene from Garrett's visit with Governor Wallace (Jason Robards) and two representatives of the Santa Fe Ring to the climactic scene in which Garrett kills Billy the Kid. In the third section, we will explore Peckinpah's characterization of Billy, stressing the many ways in which Peckinpah transformed Wurlitzer's rather crude portrait into a more interesting and complex figure whose primary function is to contrast with the more central Pat Garrett. Finally, we will conclude with a fourth section on the several versions of *Pat Garrett and Billy the Kid*, a review not unlike the "epilogue" to Seydor's latest chapter on the film (1997, 298–306), but different from his discussion because it will focus on Seydor's own Special Edition of 2005. This section will clarify the differences among the four major versions of *Pat Garrett and Billy the Kid*, but its ultimate purpose will be to assess the several versions of the film by how well they dramatize the tragedy of Pat Garrett.

I

> Peckinpah got behind Garrett; he understands Garrett and he identifies with Garrett.
> —Rudolph Wurlitzer as quoted in Aghed (66)

> The idea of a "living death" looks like a modern complement to the old belief in ghosts, the haunters, the revenants, the undead. It's a vision of death-in-life, a life so drained of meaning, value, purpose, and joy that it seems like death, being dead before you are dead. It's a version of hell on earth, more inert, more soundproof, more blank than others.
> —Adrian Poole (2005, 39)

The originality of Peckinpah's choice of Garrett as protagonist has been slighted by everyone writing on this film. As Weddle notes, *Pat Garrett and Billy the Kid* is one of 46 films recounting the Billy the Kid saga (1994, 453), yet it is the first to tell the story of Billy's death with Garrett as the protagonist. Peckinpah may have been pushed in this direction by Wurlitzer's script, for Garrett is at least as important as Billy the Kid in this scenario, as Wurlitzer's title would suggest and as he remarks himself in the introduction to his published screenplay: "The shadowy figure of Pat Garrett, at first illusive and alien, became more and more luminous and dominating, even threatening to take over the dramatic form and change the title to one name" (1973, v). Wurlitzer's Garrett remains an undistinguished figure throughout, haunted by no demons and apparently guilt-free when he finally kills the Kid, but he does share center stage with Billy as no previous Garrett had done.[7] It remained for Peckinpah to see the potential in focusing on Garrett rather than his legendary victim.

We think it is important to see that Peckinpah orchestrated the essential changes in Wurlitzer's script before production began in Mexico on November 13, 1972. Weddle has provided an excellent 15-page account of how Peckinpah was brought into the project and the changes Peckinpah initiated before shooting began (1994, 453–67), and Seydor has concisely described the several scenes Peckinpah added or expanded at the beginning of Wurlitzer's script (1997, 261–62). Yet it seems to us that even Weddle and Seydor underestimate how thoroughly Peckinpah transformed Wurlitzer's script before production began in mid–November 1972. Weddle implies that Peckinpah came to see the story as essentially about Garrett during production: "As shooting progressed [Peckinpah] had grown more and more interested in Garrett and less and less in the Kid" (1994, 477); and Seydor agrees that Wurlitzer's script was primarily altered in Mexico: "The changes were made not all at once but were added individually throughout the shooting schedule, sometimes by Peckinpah himself, sometimes by Wurlitzer, and sometimes by Wurlitzer acting on Peckinpah's instructions" (1997, 262).[8] Seydor also notes that materials from Peckinpah's 1957 adaptation of Charles Neider's *The Authentic Death of Hendry Jones* (1956) were "interpolated into Wurlitzer's screenplay during shooting" (1997, 256).[9] In fact, however, materials from Peckinpah's adaptation, often taken directly from Neider's novel, are already present in the November shooting script. We think this script proves that Peckinpah did not so much improvise on the set as refashion Wurlitzer's original screenplay during preproduction to make it the story of Pat Garrett's tragedy.

Many of the changes we will be discussing were made in September and October of 1972 (see Weddle 1994, 457), a period in which Peckinpah apparently held many story conferences with Wurlitzer and Gordon Carroll, the film's producer. A summary of one such conference reveals that Wurlitzer himself came to see that Garrett would dominate the film because he had "more dimension" than Billy, was truly "ambivalent," and was in fact the film's "tragic man." Responding to Wurlitzer's—and Carroll's—comments about Garrett's tragic depth, Peckinpah offers his terse but enthusiastic agreement: "Yep!"[10] Wurlitzer sympathized with Peckinpah's reading of Garrett, then, but he was less enthusiastic about the changes Peckinpah made to embody his view that Garrett should be the film's protagonist. Indeed, the changes we will examine are all deleted in Wurlitzer's published screenplay, which strongly suggests they appear in the November shooting script because Peckinpah wanted them there and not because they are in any real sense Wurlitzer's. The process of altering the script continued during production, as Weddle and Seydor point out, and it is relevant that these later changes are also excluded from Wurlitzer's published screenplay, ample evidence that the published script is more or less Wurlitzer's original work restored. It is especially interesting that Wurlitzer rejected the scenes Peckinpah added or required Wurlitzer to revise at the beginning of the action, for Peckinpah redefined the nature of the entire project in these early scenes.

There are four such scenes: the prologue in which Garrett is himself assassinated in 1909, 28 years after the shooting of Billy the Kid[11]; the new opening scene in which Garrett visits Billy and his men at Old Fort Sumner five days before he is to become sheriff of Lincoln County; another new scene in which Garrett and a large posse capture the Kid while killing two of Billy's men; and the jailhouse scene in Lincoln which originally opened Wurlitzer's script, now revised to include Garrett, who was not present originally and who in fact never meets with Billy in Wurlitzer's script until the night he kills the Kid. Peckinpah and Wurlitzer agree that Peckinpah wrote the prologue (though not the epilogue which reprises Garrett's death), so it appears in the shooting script because Peckinpah handed it to Wurlitzer at some point before November.[12] Earlier, Peckinpah drafted the opening scene with Garrett and Billy at Old Fort Sumner. Peckinpah told Seydor that he wrote half of this scene (1997, 262), but

Wurlitzer gives Peckinpah full credit for a scene Wurlitzer scorned ("The director wanted their relationship in front, so that everyone would know they were old buddies" [Wurlitzer 1973, viii]).[13] Peckinpah recalls that Wurlitzer drafted the scene of Billy's capture and most of the new passages involving Garrett in the jailhouse scene (Seydor 1997, 262), but Wurlitzer did so at Peckinpah's insistence and, as we hope to show, Peckinpah added materials in the jailhouse scene which are in neither Wurlitzer's published screenplay nor the November shooting script. Indeed, Peckinpah's hand is all over these four early scenes which precede Billy's escape from the Lincoln County jailhouse and Garrett's crucial encounter with his wife Ida.

The prologue depicts Garrett's death on his ranch near Las Cruces in 1909 at the hands of John W. Poe (John Beck), Garrett's deputy at the time of Billy the Kid's assassination, and two other men associated, like Poe, with the Santa Fe Ring. Peckinpah noted to Jan Aghed that the same people who killed Billy later killed Garrett (Aghed 65), an historically dubious claim which required Peckinpah to invent most of the "facts" presented in the prologue.[14] In addition to the irony of Garrett being shot by the same men (or their representatives) who sanctioned the shooting of Billy the Kid, the prologue makes at least three points relevant to Peckinpah's revised understanding of his story. First, it immediately focuses our attention on Pat Garrett, whose "point of view" is established by the frame story, as Seydor has remarked (1997, 275). Second, it confirms for anyone familiar with the story of Billy's death that Garrett never does escape from the unholy alliance he forges with the Santa Fe Ring. Though he and not Billy survives the events of 1881, Garrett is still effectively trapped in the situation the film gradually reveals to us. And third, the prologue provides the first example of one of the film's strongest motifs, the insults to Pat Garrett which punctuate virtually every scene. Here, in the course of an argument about the use of land Garrett has leased to Poe, Poe says of the Santa Fe Ring, "I believe they elected you and paid you good wages for killing the Kid." Garrett responds by cursing Poe and reaching for his rifle, only to be shot by Poe and his associates before he can get off a shot. Garrett's irascible, violent response to Poe, so unlike his much more measured responses to those who insult him in 1881, suggests that he has not grown more serene or self-sufficient with the passage of time.

The prologue is followed by the new scene which takes us back to Old Fort Sumner, Billy's place, and a reunion of sorts between Garrett and Billy the Kid just before Garrett is to become sheriff of Lincoln County in 1881. Garrett has taken a two-day ride from Lincoln in order to warn Billy that once he becomes sheriff he will have to come after him if Billy is still in the territory. Garrett tells his old friend and colleague that "the electorate wants you gone," but Billy correctly interprets this to mean that Garrett has "sold out to the Santa Fe Ring," the first of Billy's several insults directed at Garrett in the three scenes prior to Billy's escape from the Lincoln jailhouse. Billy says nothing to suggest he will comply with Garrett's request that he leave the territory, Garrett warns Billy that he is serious, and the two part having come to no agreement about the future. Wurlitzer has dismissed Peckinpah's insistence on this scene as pandering to the audience by assuring them Garrett and Billy are "old buddies" (1973, viii), but Seydor has responded with an excellent analysis of the logical and dramatic reasons for including such a scene (1997, 263–65). As Seydor says, Peckinpah felt the need for "a true germinal scene ... in which there is a sense of promise and implicit fulfillment, of direction and implicit destination, of forces being set into motion that must inevitably and unavoidably collide in the way they finally do" (1997, 265). The "promise" here is tragic because Garrett has switched sides, as Billy will not do,[15] and there can be no compromise or peaceful resolution unless Garrett is willing to switch sides yet again, a possibility the entire film denies in its every detail.

The first scene embodies more than Peckinpah's departure from Wurlitzer's strategy of having his co-protagonists only meet at the end of the film. Ironically, perhaps, given his deviations from historical fact elsewhere in the film, Peckinpah goes back to something like the historical circumstances surrounding Garrett's *decision* to become sheriff of Lincoln County in order to emphasize the tragic consequences of this decision. Like all other versions of the Billy the Kid saga (including Peckinpah's), Wurlitzer's falsely assumes that Garrett and Billy were good friends who once rode together (see Weddle 1994, 456, and Metz 53). Wurlitzer's Garrett has been a lawman for many years, however, well before he captures Billy and eventually shoots him. In the late scene climaxed by Garrett's shooting of Holly (Richard Bright), the bartender/storekeeper Lemuel (Chill Wills) explains Garrett's aggressive behavior by pointing to "all that tight-assed law he done put inside himself all these years bustin' out" (Wurlitzer 1973, 80).[16] Earlier, in a scene direction, Wurlitzer writes, "[Garrett] has the bemused detachment and melancholy of a man who has experienced both sides of the law, leaving him with an awareness of the futility of all things" (1973, 15). Wurlitzer's Garrett did not recently become sheriff, he has no connections to the Santa Fe Ring (which does not exist in Wurlitzer's script), and he apparently comes across Billy in the normal course of events. This is to say he does not agree to take down the Kid as a condition of the business community's support for his election as sheriff, as the real Pat Garrett effectively did.[17] This makes all the difference, of course, for Peckinpah's Pat Garrett is precisely a man who has made the unhappy decision we learn about in the new first scene.

The ominous consequences of Garrett's decision become even clearer in the next scene, the capture of Billy at Stinking Springs. Wurlitzer did not include this scene, but had Billy describe his capture to J. W. Bell (Matt Clark), one of Garrett's deputies (1973, 3). Significantly, Billy's account does not include the killing of Billy's companions, Charlie Bowdre (Charlie Martin Smith) and Tom O'Folliard (Rudolph Wurlitzer); indeed, there is no shooting of any kind. Peckinpah presumably added the capture scene so that he could immediately render the violent consequences of Garrett's decision to become sheriff. Here Bowdre is shot as he steps outside the cabin Billy and his two companions occupy, with no warning of any kind, and soon O'Folliard is shot to death as well. Billy finally surrenders to Garrett and his posse, but he concludes the scene with another insult to Garrett as the new sheriff comes to take custody of him: "You're in poor company, Pat." By this relatively early point in the film, the pattern is already well established: Poe insults Garrett in the prologue, Billy's men openly ridicule Garrett when he visits them at Old Fort Sumner, and Billy accuses Garrett of betrayal (no doubt including self-betrayal) in the scene at Old Fort Sumner, the scene of his capture, and the jailhouse scene which immediately follows. Eventually, as we noted previously, the list of Garrett's insulters will include most of the film's cast.

The three scenes Peckinpah added at the start of *Pat Garrett and Billy the Kid* highlight Pat Garrett: his later death at the hands of the Santa Fe Ring, his alienation from Billy and his men because of his unexpected decision to turn to the law (and its wealthy champions), and his inevitable use of deadly force to embody his new commitments. By adding Garrett to the next scene, Wurlitzer's original opening in the Lincoln jailhouse, Peckinpah allows Garrett to explain more fully why he has changed his life so radically. In the opening scene at Old Fort Sumner, in response to Billy's dismissive "How does it feel?" Garrett replies, "It feels ... like times have changed." This is but one of Garrett's several "answers" to the question of why he has joined forces with Chisum and the Santa Fe Ring. Later, Sheriff Cullen Baker (Slim Pickens) tells Garrett, "I'd rather be on the outside of the law than packing a badge for that town of Lincoln and them that's a running it," and Garrett responds, "It's a job. Comes an age in a man's life when he don't want to spend time figurin' what comes next." In the jailhouse scene, Billy insults Garrett yet again ("I never figured on hearing you brag on being a working man. I never figured you for the law, either"), and Garrett's reply offers no fewer than three explanations for his fateful decision: "It's just a way of staying alive. No matter what side you're on, you're always right. And I aim to be rich, old, and gray."

Peckinpah added most of Garrett's response to a much briefer reply Wurlitzer drafted for the November shooting script (see 1972, 11). Peckinpah added other materials during production, including many of deputy Bob Ollinger's (R. G. Armstrong's) colorful exchanges with Billy,[18] but Garrett's self-defense or rationale is by far the most crucial addition. Garrett's earlier remark to Billy ("It feels like times have changed") rather weakly suggests Garrett has no real choice but to "adjust" to changing times and to adopt this particular adjustment. His reply to Sheriff Baker suggests he is prematurely retired from the business of making personal decisions. Garrett's response(s) to Billy in the jailhouse embodies a much more serious, even considered understanding of his condition and how it led to his decision to abandon the focused, unitary intention of his former self and embrace the reversal implicit in his new job. Indeed, Garrett's response is crucial to our sense that he is not simply an official who has sold out, but rather a man somehow compelled to embrace forms of survival and security he knows to be profoundly corrupt.

Garrett's first explanation, that his decision is "just a way of staying alive," reminds us of his reply to Billy's comment that Garrett is in poor company, "Yeah, I'm alive, though," as well as his later claim to Poe that, unlike Billy, he plans to grow old with the territory. Garrett's third explanation, that he aims to be "rich, old, and gray," is essentially a restatement of the first, though it adds the prospect of wealth to the original concept of physical survival, a significant acknowledgment that his reward for serving as sheriff will go well beyond his official wages. Both explanations derive from a passage in Neider in which Dad Longworth (Neider's version of Pat Garrett) says he wants to live "forever," and Hendry Jones (Neider's Billy the Kid) replies, "Well I won't be around to see you when you're old and gray" (38, 39).[19] As this third explanation suggests, Peckinpah's Pat Garrett aspires to more than the longevity and respectability of Neider's Dad Longworth, especially in his dealings with Chisum. These two explanations share a common concern for physical well-being and security, however, motives which hardly seem consonant with the analogy to Macbeth we have proposed. Even at the material level of existence, Macbeth's "vaulting ambition" (I.vii.27) in seizing the kingdom of Scotland dwarfs Garrett's much more modest concerns for breath itself and a measure of the wealth he has never known.

Garrett's ties to Shakespeare's tragic character are much more strongly suggested by Garrett's second explanation to Billy. As Bliss recognizes, Garrett's second assertion ("No matter what side you're on, you're always right") reveals he is fully aware that the law he now serves is wholly corrupt. Bliss' paraphrase here does not go far enough, however: "you're always safe if you have the power of legal authority on your side" (1993, 233). Garrett's concern for safety or security is real enough, as his first and third explanations prove; but his second explanation points to something in Garrett much closer to Macbeth's "black and deep desires" (I.iv.5), if not his vaulting ambition. Garrett understands that the authority of a corrupt law is virtually absolute, that one can *always* prevail in any dispute, that his new position provides not only survival and security but real power, the kind of power he has never known in his life as a bandit, a life distinctly on the outside looking in. We will see Garrett exercising this power more and more as the film progresses, in his shooting of Billy, of course, but even more starkly and intolerably in his execution of Holly, as we think the shooting of Holly must be called. These later actions will suggest a Garrett not unlike the Macbeth who finds he has stepped so far in blood he cannot make his way back to shore (III.iv.136–38). Macbeth's haunting soliloquies testify to the profound guilt he feels about his chosen course, even as he steps farther and farther away from his former self. Whether Garrett ever achieves this level of self-understanding is much harder to say, but he is not oblivious to what he has done and where he is headed, and the scenes which immediately follow, especially the confrontation with his wife, point up Garrett's uneasiness with the new life he has chosen.

Prior to these scenes, however, Peckinpah depicts Billy's violent escape from the Lincoln jailhouse while Garrett is absent. Wurlitzer's script begins with this escape, which naturally focuses dramatic attention on Billy. In Peckinpah's film, Garrett remains the principal figure established in the new opening scenes even when he is off-stage, collecting taxes in his new role as sheriff. Indeed, Garrett's "presence" during Billy's escape is especially telling if Seydor is right to suggest that Garrett has left the gun which Billy finds in an outhouse and subsequently uses to kill J. W. Bell and Bob Ollinger. Seydor cites the "proximity" of the scenes in which Garrett speaks with Billy about "staying alive" and Billy finds the hidden gun (1997, 294), but he might have cited as well the cumulative weight of the new or revised early scenes which make so much of a friendship now endangered. Seydor's suggestion would be inconceivable concerning Wurlitzer's script, but it is all too believable vis-à-vis Peckinpah's film. And if Garrett did in fact leave the gun for Billy, then the bloody consequences must be assigned to Garrett and are hardly "unforeseen," Seydor's adjective for the consequences of Garrett's actions (1997, 275).[20]

Peckinpah recast the scene of Garrett's return to Lincoln so as to emphasize these bloody consequences. In Wurlitzer's script, Garrett rides a horse into town "early" in the morning (1973, 14) and Ollinger's body is nowhere in sight (1973, 15). A horse Billy has stolen after leaving Lincoln has returned to town (1973, 19), so it appears to be at least one day later and perhaps two or three. In the November shooting script, Peckinpah adds Ollinger's body still lying in the middle of the street while Garrett speaks insultingly to the few townspeople in the vicinity: "Will some of you sons of bitches get him off the street and into the ground"(1972, 21A).[21] In production, Peckinpah retained the body and a less crude version of Garrett's request to the crowd ("Would some of you ... people get him up off the ground and into it?"), but he altered the scene in several crucial ways. First, he has Garrett ride into town in a buggy rather than on horseback, a brilliant detail pointing to Garrett's conspicuous efforts to embody the social role he has taken on as Lincoln's new sheriff (and tax collector). Then, with Ollinger's mutilated body, Peckinpah has Garrett confront the all too material consequences of his new life, and especially so if he left the gun for his old friend Billy. Finally, Peckinpah adds the surly response of one of the townspeople to Garrett's demand that they get Ollinger off the ground and into it: "Anything you say, Sheriff." Here Garrett is insulted for the first time by someone other than those personally involved in his quarrel with Billy, a brief but telling moment which reveals that Peckinpah's Garrett, unlike the historical Pat Garrett, has achieved no popular favor by bringing in the Kid and is in fact treated by the public as an object of contempt for siding with the powers that be against the ever popular Billy the Kid. For capturing Billy the historical Pat Garrett was a hero, "the best-known and most popular man in New Mexico" (Metz 89). The real Pat Garrett did antagonize both his patrons and the general public during his long career as a lawman, but at the time of Billy's capture, escape, and assassination, Garrett was a veritable folk hero. Peckinpah does not so much modify this fact as reverse it.

The image of Pat Garrett riding into Lincoln in a buggy is followed up in the next few scenes as Peckinpah continues to explore Garrett's troubled assimilation into respectable society. Dressed entirely in black, looking like an undertaker rather than a sheriff, Garrett leaves the scene of Ollinger's body to enter the local saloon/barbershop, where he instructs the barber to "do me up good this time, Giuseppe" and to "leave the moustache," as if in anticipation of future events (as when he visits Governor Wallace) in which his sartorial appearance will matter. This scene has been characterized as "a debased version of [Wyatt] Earp's visit to a barber shop in *My Darling Clementine*" (Butler 86), and, as we shall see, the contrast with John Ford's great Western of 1946 will continue beyond the saloon/barbershop. Here Garrett instructs a young boy (Sam Craven) to run down the street and "tell Mrs. Garrett that I'm gonna be home for dinner," then proceeds to finish his elaborate shave, have a bath, share a mid-day meal with his newly-appointed deputy Alamosa Bill (Jack Elam), and return to the Lincoln streets looking like the narcissistic dandy — or community leader — he aspires to be.[22] Garrett's stylish dress, so incongruous at the violent scene of Billy's capture, recalls a disenchanted nobleman's famous description of the newly-crowned Macbeth: "now does he feel his title / Hang loose about him, like a giant's robe / Upon a dwarfish thief" (V.ii.23–25). Unlike Ford's Wyatt Earp (Henry Fonda), Garrett is not simply awkward in his social transition but a Macbethian "thief."

Finally, after what must be several hours of preparation, Garrett initiates his solitary promenade toward home. As if on cue, we hear church bells, then suddenly we see several married couples and a man and two women, all well-dressed in their Sunday best and strolling past Garrett seemingly on their way to various Lincoln churches. The sounds of the church bells seem incongruous, almost surreal, in "lowdown" Lincoln, as Billy describes the town, but they make excellent sense as another allusion to Ford's *My Darling Clementine.* We are meant to recall the famous "wedding march" scene in which Marshal Wyatt Earp, like Pat Garrett fresh from the barber's chair and smelling like a desert flower (thanks to his cologne), escorts his "lady fair" Clementine Carter (Cathy Downs) to the dedication of the first, still incomplete church in Tombstone, which opens majestically onto Monument Valley's magnificent buttes and mesas, harmoniously complementing the burgeoning new town. Here we sense not just the union of man and woman, but of the surrounding desert, with its stately cacti and towering rocks, and the small but thriving frontier town. This is a place where the man of the West joins the woman from the East in a whirling dance through which John Ford celebrates the mythic marriage of nature and civilization in what may be one of the most joyously optimistic moments in all of American film.[23]

There is, of course, nothing at all "mythic" about Pat Garrett's solitary, hesitant march "home." Finally, after passing by several snorting pigs running wild in an alley, he arrives at his destination, where he gazes at the alien white picket fence which surrounds what Weddle nicely describes as "a huge, two-story white Victorian," a house which "tower[s] above the other colorless adobe structures of Lincoln, a hallucinatory icon of hearth and home embodying all the allure and horror of domesticity that American men run toward and away from" (1994, 478–89). Peckinpah has provided this house for the Garretts, for Wurlitzer's script describes "a simple adobe house" (1973, 19) very much like all the other buildings in pictures of Lincoln as of 1880 (see Utley 110, #3). Garrett's towering house testifies to his belated desire to realize a domestic and civic respectability we would properly identify as Victorian.[24] It fits all too well with the sounds of church bells which seemingly arise out of nowhere and couples apparently going to churches we do not see, not to mention the children chanting in indecipherable Spanish and circling in their own druidic dance behind the Garrett house. No wonder Garrett, who fears domestic life as much as his creator/director, halts as his decidedly white house comes into sight, looming like a mirage, then throws down his burning cigar and pauses for a long time before the surreal picket fence, so quintessentially "homey" and "American." Indeed, the great American photographer Paul Strand once remarked of his famous and eerily similar photograph *White Fence, Port Kent, New York* (1916), "You wouldn't find a fence like that in Mexico or Europe" (quoted in Dyer 141). Strand's comment prophetically contrasts things American and things Mexican, a contrast which soon proves essential to Pat Garrett's tragic situation.

With one reluctant finger Garrett pushes open the picket fence, lets it close, pushes it again, then pauses before he walks through. The house is shiny white, with a single green potted fern on the front porch. We have seen how the green ferns in Peckinpah's *Noon Wine* (1966) figure prominently in the springhouse scenes, giving new life to the Thompson farm, but this kind of transformation seems unlikely to happen here. Garrett enters his own home as if he were a stranger, an intruder. He first looks warily upstairs to see if his wife is there, then gazes anxiously around, a series of gestures which anticipate his ghost-walk through Pete Maxwell's house at the end of the film. Cautiously, Garrett edges toward the kitchen, where his wife is at work preparing the Sunday dinner we thought he was planning to share with her.

Peckinpah has constructed a magnificent *mise-en-scène* for our first impression of Ida. Standing in her kitchen, at once erotic and domestic, she is attired in a beautiful Sunday-best white dress and played by the sensual but dignified Aurora Clavel, whom we remember as the long-haired Malinche in the now restored *Major Dundee* (1965, 2005) and as Aurora, Pike Bishop's doomed lover in *The Wild Bunch*. Looking like a figure out of seventeenth-century portraiture, Velázquez, say, or one of Manet's beautiful women who are so completely enmeshed in their modernist blending together of figure and ground, Ida and her kitchen are a masterpiece of painterly form, for she exudes an exquisite sense of belonging, the pure oneness of her *being* in the world. The whole composition is unified by the traditional artist's touch of a sumptuous satin cloth, here wine-red, which sensuously adorns an ironing board. Although hers is a white "gringo" house, Ida's kitchen is Mexican-style, opulent with bright red peppers (*ristras)* hanging on the wall, small pastel paintings of children's clothing above the stove even though the Garretts are childless, an apple pie cooling on the table, and a Cezannesque bowl of bright colorful apples before which Ida is peeling green cooking apples for more pies. She is so inviting and so obviously at *home* here, while her stranger-husband, in a distancing deep focus shot, seems to draw farther and farther away from her. She terrifies him because she is so clearly, heartbreakingly open to a love he cannot reciprocate.

As Seydor says, in response to critics who see the misogynist Peckinpah in every film he made, "Sam's sympathies are with Ida, and not with Garrett," for Garrett is "a man truly at war with himself,"[25] caught between his past and a friend (the Kid) he has lost and no longer genuinely believes in, and a present, including his beautiful and sensual wife, he recoils against and sees in the context of the arid, life-denying world he has chosen for himself. For political reasons Garrett has staged a marriage, built an Ibsenian "doll's house,"[26] and constructed their marriage as if it were a theatrical display of Garrett's putatively successful integration into Lincoln's mixed white and Latino culture, respectively represented by the frame house and the Mexican wife.[27] But Ida has refused to play Garrett's game, has turned the house into a home, herself into a woman open to love and family. Perversely, Garrett seems to see all of this as a trap, Ida as noir spider and himself as helpless fly, and he can abide none of it, as Ida bitterly understands. Worse, as we see almost immediately, Garrett knows he is in this trap of his own making. His guilty awareness is rendered more clearly in this scene than anywhere else in Peckinpah's film.

In their confrontation, the first and last time they are together in the film, it is difficult for the guilty Garrett even to make eye contact with his wife, let alone touch her or hold her in his arms. In her presence he looks almost shy, clearly ill at ease. Ida smiles widely, for she has not seen Garrett in "over a week," but then, noticing his discomfort, she looks down sadly, mournfully. Garrett nervously grabs an apple and begins bouncing it in his hand, as if he were about to succumb to the biblical temptation to take a bite, but he puts it down. He stands at one end of the kitchen table, she at the other, the seemingly intimate domestic space metaphorically widening into the bleak emotional desert which ultimately gapes between them and which will consume him at film's end. And while there is real joy on Ida's part at seeing her husband, it quickly turns to sorrow as she sees that he does not plan to stay, that he cannot hide his shame over what their marriage has become. Ida seems to know intuitively why her husband is so restless. Her first words to him are, "They say William Bonney has escaped." To which he responds, "He has. And he's in Old Mexico, I hope. Where we should be, if I had any sense." Garrett sits down, caught in the closed film frame between the white outline of her breast on one side of him, a prominent green plant in the window on the other, both signs of life, but a life he rejects. "You might say that you are glad to see me," she finally says. "It has been over a week that you have been gone." He becomes even more distracted, looks down evasively, and finally responds: "I'm sorry." This crucial remark seems heartfelt, one of the most revealing statements Garrett will make at any point in the film, but in a moment he rises nervously and tells her he has to get back to town because there's "a drunk down there causin' a lot of trouble, goes by the name of Alamosa Bill. Said he rode with the Kid down in west Texas," which we know to be a complete fabrication. He then strides off toward their bedroom to remove a green scarf from the bureau, entering by a door on the right, while Ida enters through a door on the left, the door through which we see their immaculate, virtually virginal white bed.

The double door entrance into the Garrett bedroom recalls the stage of the ancient Greek tragic theater of the fifth century B.C. While the visible part of the stage, or *orkhēstra*, was in the foreground and part of the main stage, two doors which opened into an unknown darkness, called the *skēnē*, were characteristically placed at the center of the stage. As classicist Ruth Padel notes, Greek dramatists could "use the opposition between left and right to underline emotion hanging around a character and her [or his] fate" (343). And while we can "see" what lies inside the Garrett bedroom, unlike the "invisible space" of Greek drama, we are nevertheless struck by the impression Peckinpah creates that the bedroom represents for the doomed Pat Garrett a dangerously closed world, an alienating cul-de-sac or what Padel calls a "closed space": "There is no way out. What happens in there is the plot's trapped outcome and dead end, the image of inevitability" (343). Garrett cannot wait to escape from this room, but he will discover at the end of the film even more dangerous doorways. Indeed, Garrett never truly escapes from his own bedroom. As in Greek tragedy and virtually all of western culture, the two doors suggest domestic interiors, often coded female and meant to represent the inner feminine spaces of a house, like a kitchen or more pointedly a bedroom. These entities are threats to Garrett's already fragmented sense of self. Thus he ignores the bed and his wife and seizes an item of masculine attire, the green scarf, which we will come to associate more and more with his pursuit of Billy the Kid.

In language which eloquently but witheringly evokes the spiritual and physical desolation of their barren marriage, Ida, who clearly views the home as a sacred space, asks her husband if he will "be *blessing* this house with your *presence* for dinner?" (our emphases), and all he can say is that "it looks like it's going to be a long night." Her face turned away from Garrett, she replies, "It's been a long year."[28] Then she proceeds to the heart of her lament: "My people don't talk to me. They say that you are getting to be too much of a gringo since you have been sheriff, that you make deals with Chisum. You don't touch me. You are dead inside. I wish that you had never put on that badge." And Garrett, whose whole existence seems to turn on evasions of time, replies, "Not now." Angrily she cries out, "Si, ahora! Or I won't be here when you get back."

Then Garrett does something interesting. Standing in the entrance between the front room and the kitchen, he angrily lifts his leg and stomps his foot, a Johnsonian gesture which ironically proves nothing and avoids everything, while simultaneously he tears down one of the two green brocade curtains which divide the two rooms, their color and texture very like the scarf Garrett takes from the bedroom and wears in his pursuit of the Kid. It is as if they are theatrical curtains, with Garrett the trapped and tragic hero poised center stage between

In their kitchen Ida Garrett (Aurora Clavel) confronts her guilty husband (James Coburn) with their lifeless marriage in *Pat Garrett and Billy the Kid.*

them, desperate to escape his fate. This, we believe, is an example of the Hamletian play-within-a-play element which recurs throughout *Pat Garrett and Billy the Kid*. Peckinpah is a director who spent many years working on the stage, and one can still see remnants of his stage career transformed to film. He does much the same kind of thing with even more traditional "stage" curtains in *Straw Dogs* (1971), another film about a phony house and marriage in which the bedroom is a bloody Strindbergian battleground. Like David Sumner (Dustin Hoffman) under siege in *Straw Dogs*, Garrett tears down his artificially staged world, the "doll's house" he has built — the beautiful Mexican wife, the lovely American house, the false props of a settled life and a happy marriage.

The artifice is over, the game is lost, and both Garrett and Ida know it. When he says to her, "We'll deal with this when it's over," we read his thoughts in a doubled context: the death of the Kid, and Garrett's own emotional death. He is "dead inside," his life is "over," and one senses that, like Macbeth, he probably knows it at some repressed level of his being but cannot stop. Ida says of the Kid, "I hope he gets away." Garrett's response mirrors his own self-defeat and underscores the same theatrical metaphor: "He won't. There's too much play in him...." We emphasize Garrett's pause at the end of a sentence which hangs in aural space and does not seem to conclude as he speaks it. Garrett does not accent the word "play," followed by the downbeat of "in him," which would be the normal way of concluding the sentence; rather, he overtly accents the rising beat of the words "in him," then pauses, as if awaiting his wife's response which will complete, in effect, his (death) sentence. Ida's perfect rhetorical antithesis, "And not enough in you," completes Garrett's sentence and radically alters its meaning. It is as if Garrett expects Ida to put him down, to finish his own sentence as her own, to underscore his own defeat before her. Garrett is already "played" out, as Ida knows. Everything which follows in the film is a kind of postscript to this conversation between a husband and his abandoned wife.

No church bells ring in Lincoln when Garrett silently departs from his wife, who stands head down in the dining room, their empty bedroom and bed caught in the frame between them, enlarging the loneliness she feels. This is a perfect prefiguration of ghost-like Garrett's tragic absence in the doorway of Pete Maxwell's house, as the Kid's *novia* Maria (Rita

Coolidge), a double for Ida, gazes at an empty space. All we hear now, as Garrett leaves his "home," are the soft sounds of Bob Dylan's guitar and the now more faint and distant chant, a dying fall, of the children dancing in a circle behind the Garrett house.

Remarkably enough, this stunning scene did not appear in the film's theatrical release of 1973 and was also omitted from the Turner Entertainment version in 1988, even though Turner was attempting to distribute the so-called preview version of the film, the last one on which Peckinpah worked, and Garrett's scene with Ida was included in the preview version.[29] We will discuss later how the most important scene in Peckinpah's second-best film was first made available only 32 years after the picture's first release in 1973.[30] For the moment, we want to explore the bizarre consequences of the film's postproduction history. Most recent critical discussions focus on the 18 minutes deleted by MGM when Peckinpah's film was first released, and the effects of these many cuts are indeed a major subject for anyone interested in this film.[31] For us, however, it is even more important to see that most criticism of *Pat Garrett and Billy the Kid*, from its first reviews to subsequent chapter-length critiques, has been written by people who never saw the crucial scene with Garrett and his wife or who have given it only brief attention in their assessments. There is no evidence, for example, that well-known critics of the film such as Jim Kitses, Stephen Tatum, Michael Bliss, and Brad Stevens ever saw the scene, and we have previously noted that even Paul Seydor devotes little more than a paragraph to it. We believe that only those who have not experienced Garrett's encounter with Ida could say that its omission is "not crucial," as Kitses writes (2004, 233),[32] and that this powerful scene, among the best in all of Peckinpah's films, should be at the heart of any reading of the film's tragic action.

When the scene with Ida is discussed, it is sometimes viewed as evidence of Wurlitzer's crucial role in shaping the project. Seydor remarks, for example, that "the argument between Garrett and his wife" is "directed essentially as Wurlitzer conceived [it], with most of his dialogue left intact" (1997, 265). The scene does derive from Wurlitzer's original screenplay, in which Wurlitzer creates a troubled, insecure marriage rather unlike the historical marriage, which lasted 27 years until Garrett's death, was marked by eight children, and included Garrett's "long and affectionate" letters to his wife after more than 25 years of marriage (Metz 40).[33] Wurlitzer's marriage is not directly tied to Garrett's recent decision to become respectable, for Wurlitzer's Garrett is a longtime sheriff; but Wurlitzer does present the marriage as part of the package Garrett has bought into in turning away from his outlaw past. Peckinpah retains this crucial aspect of the scene, much as he retains 80 to 90 percent of Wurlitzer's dialogue. Nonetheless, no scene better illustrates Peckinpah's transformative powers as both writer and director, for the characters depicted here are very different from Wurlitzer's, and Garrett's tragic plight emerges as it does not in Wurlitzer's version of the scene.

Wurlitzer's Ida did suggest Peckinpah's Ida, for she challenges her inattentive husband, shrewdly notes his compromising involvement with such men as Chisum, and is quick enough to complete Garrett's sentence about the "play" in Billy exactly as Peckinpah's Ida will do (Wurlitzer 1973, 21). But her rebellious complaint about Garrett's behavior gives way when Wurlitzer's Garrett reasserts physical control over her, walking over to her and "holding her breast so that it hurts," reminding her that she is his sexual possession by saying, "Wait for me. I need that now." We are told that "[s]he nods, half-relieved, half-defeated" (1973, 21), a response Peckinpah's Ida could never have made. Peckinpah's Ida is more passionate, more committed, and clearly beyond such sexual bullying. She is given the scene's most memorable moment when she tells her husband, "You are dead inside," an insight Peckinpah added to Wurlitzer's somewhat revised version of the scene in the November shooting script. Peckinpah may have believed "that a woman's place was in the home, making her husband happy and looking after the kids," as Weddle has argued (1994, 159), but the home his Ida puts together is not simply "well kept up," as in Wurlitzer's script (1973, 19), but a rich, impassioned display of her taste and exemplary intelligence. All of the sumptuous details in Ida's house are Peckinpah's additions, and all add to his compelling portrait of this remarkably gifted woman. Gabrielle Murray has suggested that Peckinpah's women are "less complicated [than his men], with little desire for adventure, freedom, and intensity" (103), and we ourselves have previously noted that his women often seem marginalized, but Peckinpah's Ida is ample proof that Murray exaggerates when she argues that women in Peckinpah are without "longings, yearnings, and desires" (104).[34]

Indeed, one could easily argue that it is Peckinpah's Garrett whose longings, yearnings, and desires are in question. His Garrett is too sensitive to impose himself on Ida as Wurlitzer's Garrett does, and of course Peckinpah deleted this boorishness in revising the scene; but Peckinpah's Garrett is precisely a man whose longings and desires have found no suitable outlet except the world Ida and her home embody so fully and yet so futilely. Unlike Wurlitzer's Garrett, a man of very limited sensitivity, Peckinpah's Garrett understands that the life he has put together in Lincoln is not worth living, just as his remarks to Billy in the jailhouse scene prove that he is aware of the morally questionable foundations of his new position. We see this when Garrett says of the escaped Billy, "And he's in old Mexico, I hope. Where we should be, if I had any sense," lines Peckinpah had Wurlitzer add (in a slightly different formulation) to the November shooting script. And we see it again when Peckinpah has Garrett reply to Ida, "I'm sorry," a response Wurlitzer's Garrett could never have uttered, just as he could never have realized that he and his wife ("we") would be better off in a place like Mexico rather than entrapped in the false conventions and dubious political dealings of their life in New Mexico.

The real question is why Garrett cannot act on his insights, why he has locked himself into a course of action so inhospitable to his/their best interests. As in all great tragedies, the answer to this sort of question is difficult and perhaps beyond rational categories. One possible answer may emerge if we ask why Peckinpah "identifies" with Garrett, as Wurlitzer suggests. Peckinpah surely saw his own history in the story of a man caught in compromising career choices, but we think the stronger basis for identification is personal rather than professional. In 1975, two years after completing *Pat Garrett and Billy the Kid*, Peckinpah told Jon Tuska that he could not live comfortably with his own better impulses: "I would love to be married and live in a split-level house. I love all that shit, but I don't do it. I get in too many problems. I drink too much and I get in too many fights" (quoted in Weddle 1994, 451). In the end, Garrett is the creation of a man who married five times. Garrett's problems in accepting Ida recall Pike Bishop's problems in accepting Aurora. Once again we are reminded of Macbeth, another man who knows he has made a disastrous choice and yet cannot bring himself to do anything about it.

One might rephrase the question and ask why the rather unlikable Garrett is a tragic character. He was not such a character for Wurlitzer, who tells us that he came to be moved by "Garrett's decision to sell out in order to survive, to live rather than die, to abandon obsolete descriptions of courage and freedom for a more complicated if more corrupt sense of order" (1973, v). This is the Garrett who speaks of "staying alive," who finds the values of his outlaw past "obsolete" and can only turn to the respectable (if corrupt) alternative embodied in his new position in Lincoln. Wurlitzer is "moved" by this figure but did not make tragic claims for him until confronted by Peckinpah's reconceived version of the character. Seydor's view of Garrett as a tragic figure derives from Wurlitzer's character in some ways, but Seydor stresses Garrett's awareness that his past life was not so much "obsolete" as "impoverished, restricted, and limited" (1997, 285). Garrett's word for this life is "stale," as when he asks Billy if he doesn't get "stale" lounging about Old Fort Sumner with the boys, shooting off the heads of chickens for sport and occasionally rustling a few head of Chisum's cattle. Seydor's Garrett, unlike Wurlitzer's, is aware that he must abandon this kind of life not only to survive, but to discover something more sustaining. For Seydor, Garrett's tragedy is that "now that he is ready to become a responsible citizen, all that he has made himself fit for is to become a legal gunman, sheriffing for wealthy landowners and speculators" (1997, 285).

Seydor's notions are to be preferred to Stephen Tatum's view that Garrett represents "that part of the self which accepts the burdens of maturity and social responsibility" (198), for Seydor, like Garrett himself, understands that there is nothing mature or socially responsible about Garrett's new role in Lincoln. Unlike Garrett, however, Seydor cannot see Ida herself and the life she represents as a genuine option to the stale repetitions of his outlaw past and the corrupting conveniences of social life in Lincoln. For Seydor, Ida is a failed stratagem: "It is clear that this marriage is a loveless one; that Garrett married because it is more or less expected of him in his new lifestyle" (1997, 284). No doubt the marriage started as such a ploy, but Ida and the home she offers Garrett are not "loveless," and Garrett himself says that they should be in Mexico if he had any sense. Here Garrett acknowledges the option of leaving both his past and the world of Lincoln behind, with Ida beside him, in an uncharted quest into the unknowns of Mexico, Peckinpah's favorite place in all the world.[35] Ironically, the film deals repeatedly with the question of whether Billy should go to Mexico, where he would no longer be the famous Billy the Kid, but it is Garrett for whom this third option is both real and seemingly impossible to realize or even pursue. Garrett's tragedy is that he cannot embrace the uncertainties of this option, as if his recent decision to become sheriff of Lincoln County and build the false life it offers and requires is as irrevocable as Macbeth's decision to murder Duncan.

The first section of *Pat Garrett and Billy the Kid*, from the new opening scenes to Garrett's haunting confrontation with Ida, defines the protagonist's condition and tragic state as richly as Shakespeare captured these things in the first act of *Macbeth*. We shall see that the parallel continues, for in each work the long, painful consequences of the protagonist's tragic mistake are detailed over the rest of the action. From this point to the end, Ida Garrett disappears, never to be mentioned by Garrett or anyone else, as if Garrett has indeed put her behind him as a rejected alternative,[36] while we watch with something like the horror which attends Macbeth's "progress" the grim steps of Garrett's descent into the senseless hell he has elected for himself. Garrett's murder of Billy the Kid climaxes this awful journey, but the decisive and fatal step has come much earlier, before the film begins and then again when Garrett effectively rejects Ida, when, that is, Garrett cannot act on what he knows to be "sense" and commits himself to the dreary course Peckinpah will trace relentlessly in the scenes which follow.

II

... death is not the ultimate tragic experience.

— Emily R. Wilson (5)

There is the interim before the acting of a dreadful thing, but there is also the interim after, as Oedipus and Macbeth discover, as does King Lear.

— Adrian Poole (2005, 105)

It's like a Greek tragedy; I'm bound in the inexorable whorl, the clash of the triangle. There's nothing I can do.

— Rick Bass (29)

The narrative progression after Garrett leaves Ida recalls the final three and a half acts of *Macbeth*, as the protagonist in each case marches toward his own doom with greater and greater emphasis on his moral decline. Prior to the respective conclusions, in which Macbeth dies in battle and Garrett kills Billy, the most obvious difference is the narrative pace, for *Macbeth* proceeds with enormous energy, as "the physical and spiritual terror rises in swift crescendos" (Harbage 20), while the movement in *Pat Garrett and Billy the Kid* is at best languorous, primarily because Garrett procrastinates so as to give Billy every chance to leave the territory. This marked difference in effect should remind us of other differences between the two works, for *Macbeth* is a play which dramatizes its hero's fall from early achievement and renown, whereas *Pat Garrett and Billy the Kid* is a film in which the protagonist's fall has occurred before the action commences. The early scenes in *Macbeth* testify to Macbeth's great reputation, as a Captain refers to him as "noble Macbeth" (I.ii.67), Ross calls him "a peerless kinsman" (I.iv.58), and Duncan himself says, "we love him highly" (I.vi.29), while the early scenes in Peckinpah's film portray a man who has already fallen, ironically by rising to his new position as sheriff, and who is treated with contempt even in the first scenes.[37] These differences noted, however, the progressive decline after Garrett leaves Ida is perhaps the strongest parallel with Shakespeare's great tragedy.

Peckinpah begins to chart this decline with Garrett's visit with Governor Wallace in Santa Fe. The scene itself is very close to Wurlitzer's original version, but Peckinpah alters its effect by changing a few key details and reversing the order of events. In Wurlitzer's script, we first see Garrett after he leaves Lincoln when he enters the town of Pecos, home to Sheriff Baker and his wife/deputy (Katy Jurado), and the scene in Santa Fe follows the shootings in Pecos. Peckinpah wisely reverses the order of these two scenes, for the impression left by the scene in Santa Fe would be very different, and much less effective, if it followed the devastating events in Pecos (devastating for Garrett himself as well as for the audience). The scene in Santa Fe is the proper beginning of Garrett's descent, for here he remains a character of some moral strength and even appeal, qualities which will begin to fade in Pecos and will progressively decline as the story continues.

Peckinpah cuts Wurlitzer's prelude to the scene with Governor Wallace, a nasty fight in a bar in which Garrett beats up a local tough (Wurlitzer 1973, 44–45), and moves the encounter with Wallace and two representatives of the Santa Fe Ring from a railroad car (Wurlitzer 1973, 45) to the governor's palace. Both decisions allow Garrett to appear in more dignified surroundings as he deals with his masters in the unpleasant business of eliminating Billy the Kid. Even in Peckinpah's version, however, the scene places Garrett in the compromising company of those who effectively dictate Garrett's options as Lincoln's principal lawman. Though Wallace first waxes eloquent about the "fabulous melancholy" of rainy New Mexico evenings, a speech taken almost verbatim from Wurlitzer (1973, 46), he soon shifts to other speeches in which all present are reminded that their primary concern must be protection of investors who are loath to tolerate the uncertainties associated with Billy the Kid. Representing these investors, Lewellyn Howland (Jack Dodson) and Norris (John Chandler) quickly seem to outrank the governor so far as giving orders to Garrett is concerned.

Garrett's response to Howland and Norris is central in this scene. In Wurlitzer's original scenario Howland insults Garrett all too bluntly by referring to him "as a man who is half outlaw himself and still smart enough to be on the take from Chisum" (1973, 46–47). By the November shooting script, no doubt at Peckinpah's insistence, this speech is rather subtler but perhaps no less offensive, with Garrett said to be "a man who is half outlaw himself and still smart enough to be elected Sheriff by Chisum and the rest of the big ranchers" (1972, 45).[38] Norris follows up this assertion of Garrett's dependence on the wealthy who control things by offering him $500 of a $1000 reward for bringing in the Kid. Garrett's reply in the film is memorably defiant: "Well, I aim to bring the Kid in, but until I do, better take that $500 and shove it up your ass and set fire to it." Peckinpah reinforces this expression of independence on Garrett's part by having Wallace remark, "Commendable notion, Sheriff," as he and Garrett withdraw from Howland and Norris. This comment does not appear in Wurlitzer's original or revised script and seems intended to congratulate Garrett on his principled contempt for the crude manipulators who in fact dictate the context in which Wallace and Garrett function in their public roles. With this conclusion, the scene in Santa Fe definitely belongs in the first position among the post–Ida episodes, for Garrett will never again seem so admirable or in charge of things.

We next see Garrett as he rides past the ruins of an old Spanish mission into Pecos, a stagnant, flea-bitten river town not unlike the small towns Huck and Jim witness as they drift down the Mississippi River on their raft in *Adventures of Huckleberry Finn.* At a cockfight being held in the middle of the main street, Garrett discovers a scrofulous good-for-nothing named Gate (Tom Bush) who is living with Black Harris (L. Q. Jones), one of Billy's gang, out by the Pecos River. Garrett has come to see if Black and those with him have a "sign" on Billy's whereabouts. This may seem the beginning of Garrett's serious efforts to pursue the Kid, but in fact it represents the first of his procrastinations, for if Garrett were really set on tracking down Billy he would first explore Old Fort Sumner. Garrett herds Gate to the house/jailhouse of Sheriff Cullen Baker, a former associate he hopes to enlist for his trip out to Black Harris' place. Patently going through the motions of seeking Billy, Garrett rather clearly does not anticipate the deadly consequences of his first foray into the field.

As others have noted, Sheriff Baker is one of the great characters in *Pat Garrett and Billy the Kid.* Garrett finds Baker working on a boat he is building behind his house, an activity Wurlitzer invented but allowed Baker to make no comment on in the original script. Peckinpah has Baker explain that he hopes to sail off down the river one day and "drift out of this damned territory," a pipedream which anticipates the family Garrett later encounters drifting downstream on a raft and a carpenter at Old Fort Sumner named Will, played by Peckinpah himself, who is building a child's coffin in which he plans to bury his few material possessions before leaving the territory. The desire to escape from the meager material conditions of the present is apparently widespread, and Garrett's identification with this desire is registered by one of Peckinpah's key additions in the first scene with Baker. As Garrett slowly follows Baker into his house, Peckinpah has Garrett stare for some time at the unfinished boat, a moment Peckinpah insisted on retaining in the film despite the difficulty of cutting it into the evolving scene (Seydor 1997, 283). The ensuing conversation with Sheriff Baker suggests that Baker should remind Garrett of his own former integrity as well as his desire to escape from the territory.

When he first finds Baker, Garrett explains that he wants to visit Black Harris and asks for Baker's help. Baker replies that he has reached a point in life where he won't do anything unless there's a piece of gold attached. Garrett pauses, perhaps surprised by his old friend's attitude, then finds a gold coin and flips it to Baker. Once inside the house, Garrett tells Baker and his wife he is ready whenever they are. Baker agrees with his wife's reservations about the undertaking, but he nonetheless pulls out Garrett's gold coin and flips it back to him. The honorable Cullen Baker goes with Garrett because it is his job, perhaps in part because an old friend asks him to go. Baker's gesture here is one of Peckinpah's contributions to the scene, for in Wurlitzer's script Garrett pays Mrs. Baker when Garrett and Baker enter the house (1973, 32), then pays her more coins when Baker expresses his deep concerns about the mission (1973, 33), and none of these coins is returned. Seydor notes that Peckinpah's treatment of Baker's subsequent death "completely transformed what is in the original script" (1997, 262), but Peckinpah transforms the earlier scenes with Baker and his wife almost as decisively. He begins with Baker's stirring speech against serving the town of Lincoln and those who are running it, a speech from Wurlitzer's original script we have already cited (1973, 32). But Peckinpah's alterations make all the difference in what then transpires before Garrett and the Bakers leave to engage Black Harris. The business with Baker's boat, first Baker's speech about drifting out of the territory and then Garrett's longing stare at the boat, provides a haunting quality to the episode, and Peckinpah's reconception of Sheriff Baker as captured in his return of Garrett's gold piece and his obviously loving relationship with his wife transforms Baker into one of the film's most admirable characters.

Peckinpah's handling of the scene at Black Harris' cabin is as impressive as anything he was ever to do in film. Wurlitzer's version begins with Garrett riding with the Bakers in their buckboard to the cabin, where he and Baker argue with Harris before Baker initiates the gunfight: "Let's take 'em" (1973, 39). Peckinpah has Garrett ride his horse some distance behind the Bakers and not even reach the cabin before the shooting has begun, for the Bakers come in shooting without the preliminary conversation of Wurlitzer's script, a tactic not unlike the one Garrett employs in the shooting of Charlie Bowdre at Stinking Springs and in the shooting of Billy at the end of the film. By placing Garrett behind and away from the first action, Peckinpah distances Garrett from the violence as if he did not expect it and wanted to avoid it. Once Garrett arrives on the scene the battle is an unavoidable reality, and Garrett ends up killing Black Harris (who is shot by Mrs. Baker in Wurlitzer's script [1973, 36]). The dialogue between Garrett and Black is much as Wurlitzer conceived it except that Black now refers to the fact he and Garrett first rode into Lincoln County together many years ago, "about 15 years," as Garrett confirms. Peckinpah had Wurlitzer add a version of this exchange to the November shooting script, no doubt to stress that Black is not just one of Billy's many men, but someone with whom Garrett has a long and presumably friendly history. It is very much to Peckinpah's point that Garrett and not Mrs. Baker kills Black, whose death seems to immobilize Garrett, who stares at the dying Black as long as he earlier stared at Baker's boat.

The stricken look on Garrett's face as he stares at Black is matched by his expression as he turns to watch Baker, who, mortally wounded in the gunfight, has walked slowly from the cabin to the bank of the Pecos River. There he sits down while clutching his wounded gut and shares long looks with his wife, who has followed him on this final trek to a river he will never use to sail out of the territory. Katy Jurado is magnificent in these final moments of her life with Baker. She kneels some distance away from her husband, weeping profusely but letting him "go it alone," as Steve Judd wanted to do at the end of *Ride the High Country.* This is one of the most beautiful and supremely elegiac moments in all of Peckinpah's films, enhanced all the more by the restoration of the lyrics to Bob Dylan's "Knockin' on Heaven's Door" to the 2005 soundtrack. Peckinpah surely intends the starkest of contrasts between the closeness of Sheriff Baker and his beloved wife and partner, and the impossible distance Garrett has built between himself and his estranged wife Ida. Peckinpah strengthens this contrast by making Mrs. Baker Hispanic, as she is not in Wurlitzer's script. Like Garrett, we last see Baker poised in the frame between two weary-looking cottonwood trees growing by the waterside, another painful analogue to Steve Judd's experience in the high country just before he is betrayed by his trusted friend Gil Westrum. Garrett's prolonged stare at the Bakers suggests that he realizes his expedition to Pecos has resulted in the needless deaths of two old friends, in Baker's case the embodiment of a personal integrity to which Garrett can no longer aspire.

Jan Aghed has testified to watching Peckinpah improvise the scene of Baker's death at the end of shooting on the Pecos episode (65), an interesting account which should remind us that in Wurlitzer's original script Baker lies dying near the cabin as the scene ends with none of the rich additions which follow Black's death. Nearly everything which distinguishes this great scene derives from Peckinpah: the fact that Garrett and Black Harris rode into Lincoln County together 15 years ago; Garrett's stunned expression as he watches Black die at Garrett's hands; Baker's long walk to the river bank and the overwhelmingly touching communion between husband and wife as Baker dies; and finally Garrett's long, mournful gaze at the Bakers as he witnesses the devastation he has brought to Pecos. From this point to the end of the film, Garrett's manner reflects his grim awareness of the tragic part he has chosen for himself. Indeed, Garrett's emerging state recalls Emily R. Wilson's concept of tragic "overliving," which she applies to a range of tragic characters, including Macbeth and King Lear, who seem to have outlived their historical moment and who come to see their life "as a living death," as Wilson in fact remarks of Macbeth (132).

Like Macbeth, however, who refuses to kill himself even when he has no chance of military success, Garrett persists in a life which is "all aftermath" (Wilson 132). In the theatrical release and in Seydor's 2005 Special Edition of *Pat Garrett and Billy the Kid*, we next see Garrett as he rests under a tree while a raft drifts by carrying a large family downstream. We will address this famous scene in our concluding section. The raft scene is followed by Garrett's encounter with John W. Poe as Garrett makes his way to visit with John Chisum. Poe discovers Garrett on the trail as Garrett huddles near a fire he has built against the darkness of night. Poe reminds Garrett that he was present during Garrett's meeting with Governor Wallace, then announces Wallace has made him a deputy. Garrett obviously dislikes Poe even before Poe asserts that he answers only to Wallace, Howland, and Norris, an insult to Garrett's authority added by Peckinpah. Though "Garrett sees in Poe everything he loathes about himself and the decisions he has recently made," as Seydor shrewdly points out (1997, 279), Garrett offers him coffee and accepts his company, effectively accepting his status as Garrett's deputy. This is the beginning of the end for Garrett, the point from which his evasions of direct action against Billy can no longer be sustained. Though Poe will later complain that Garrett does not seem focused on capturing the Kid, Garrett's acceptance of Poe and the authority of those who sent him signals Garrett's capitulation to his "duty" to pursue Billy.

The next day we see Garrett and Poe riding together through Chisum's beautiful streams and fields, as if they are now a "team." Poe rides a large white horse, an ironic symbol of the "rightness" of the lawful authorities he and Garrett represent.[39] Earlier, Poe begins to philosophize as their pace slows to a walk: "Country's gotta make a choice. Time's over for drifters and outlaws and those who got no backbone." Garrett's response may seem decisive, but it points to the fatal contradictions in his present position: "I'm goin' to tell you this once. I don't wanna have to say it again. The country's gettin' old, and I aim to get old with it. Now, the Kid don't want it that way. He might be the better man for it, I ain't judgin'. But I don't want you explainin' nothing to me, and I don't want you talkin' about the Kid and nobody else in this goddamn territory." Though Garrett's apparent loyalties are, like Poe's, with those organized against the Kid, his protective language about Billy suggests what Len Engel aptly describes as "the tragic consequences resulting from an intellect that decides to move in one direction and a heart that resists and moves in another" ("'Who Are You?' 'That's a Good Question': Shifting Identities in Sam Peckinpah's *Pat Garrett and Billy the Kid*," 208). This scene helps prepare for and explain Garrett's explosive response toward Poe when his "deputy" moves to cut off Billy's trigger finger after Garrett has killed the Kid. In its internal contradictions, it also prepares for Garrett's difficult encounter with Chisum, another of his "masters," in the scene which immediately follows.

The scene with Chisum is yet another example of Peckinpah's transformative powers. Wurlitzer's Chisum is a rather nasty figure who first appears in the earlier scene in which Billy's friend Silva (Jorge Russek) is surrounded by Chisum and his men. Wurlitzer has Chisum himself shoot Silva, whose dead body is then propped atop his equally dead horse (1973, 40).

Peckinpah excludes Chisum from the scene with Silva and projects a very different kind of man in the conversation with Garrett and Poe. When Garrett asks Chisum if he has any knowledge of Billy's whereabouts, Chisum rather affectionately, if sardonically, describes the Kid's "location" as anywhere and everywhere: "Billy the Kid is in Tascosa, Billy the Kid is in Tombstone, Billy the Kid is in Mexico, Tularosa, Socorro, White Oaks, *and* Billy the Kid is at my table right at this moment, eating tacos and green chili peppers with my niece, just like old times." Peckinpah adds the reference to Chisum's niece and "old times," playing on common lore concerning Billy and Sallie Chisum to evoke a time when Billy was accepted into Chisum's home, unlike Poe, who is told to eat in the bunkhouse behind the large barn.

The effect here is to humanize Chisum, who in fact resembles Garrett in a number of ways. Each wants to catch the Kid, but each seems to know that with the Kid's death a way of life in the old West will also die — wild, erotic, untamed and free, like the unbroken horse one of Chisum's cowboys is unsuccessfully trying to ride as Garrett and Poe come upon Chisum at his corral. This is a loss both Garrett and Chisum will deeply regret, even though Chisum is among those trying to rid the territory of Billy and Garrett is his agent. Appropriately, Peckinpah's Chisum sits on a fence while he talks to Garrett and Poe, two paired and pleasant plumes of smoke from his ranch house rising over his shoulder as he speaks. This is Chisum's home and that means something to him. When Garrett and Poe depart, we see Chisum still sitting alone on his fence, caught like Garrett between an older world, a way of life with genuine appeal, and the big money powers from the Santa Fe Ring who represent a much greater threat to his world than anything Billy the Kid can do to him. Peckinpah's Chisum understands something of this, as we sense when he says goodbye to Poe: "Interesting meeting you, Mr. Poe. Perhaps we'll meet again sometime." If Poe is Garrett's future executioner, he is also Chisum's, and the older man seems incipiently conscious of just how "interesting" Poe is likely to prove.

Peckinpah significantly alters Garrett's role in this encounter as well. He follows Wurlitzer in having Garrett first challenge Chisum's condemnation of Billy, "He says you owe him $500 in back wages," but his Garrett pulls back from this confrontational stance almost at once. Wurlitzer's Garrett is almost as defiantly insulting to Chisum as he was to Howland and Norris in Santa Fe. "You have to kill him," Wurlitzer's Chisum insists. "He'll be killed," Wurlitzer's Garrett replies. "But not for you" (1973, 60). Wurlitzer then has Chisum dismiss Billy as "too short" and someone who "never killed a man dead center in his life" (1973, 60), to which Garrett responds, "He'd sure as hell put one through the center of you" (1973, 61). Peckinpah deletes these rowdy exchanges as untrue to his conception of both characters. In a moment Wurlitzer's Chisum puts Garrett in his place by reminding him of his debt to Chisum, "Glad to be of service, Garrett. But don't overuse it," a subtle putdown Peckinpah retains in the film (1973, 61). Peckinpah also retains the key passage in this scene, Garrett's softly spoken remark to Chisum, "I appreciate the loan" (1973, 62), an admission of Garrett's financial ties to Chisum. But Peckinpah cuts the rest of this conversation, in which Chisum says, "Heard you got some good bottom land north of Roswell," and Garrett replies, "Good enough. Far enough from you" (1973, 62). In both Wurlitzer and the film, Chisum then asks, "Are you going to get him?" Wurlitzer's Garrett replies in the surly spirit of the entire conversation: "Yeah. Most likely. Leastways before he gets you" (1973, 62). Peckinpah's Garrett says nothing to Chisum's question and turns to leave such questions and his hopelessly compromised position with Chisum behind him.

Garrett's silence and his earlier acknowledgment of Chisum's loan speak volumes about the guilt Peckinpah's Garrett feels in this scene, which effectively contrasts with the bluster Garrett permitted himself in Santa Fe and which Wurlitzer reinvented here, as if Garrett's harrowing experience in Pecos had not changed him at all. The anger Wurlitzer's Garrett expresses repeatedly to Chisum is repressed in Peckinpah's film, in part because Peckinpah's Chisum is much less abrasive and insulting, in part because Peckinpah's Garrett is once again ashamed of his position, perhaps as much so as he was with his wife. This repressed anger, at himself but also at those who create the situations he finds so intolerable, will emerge unforgettably in the next sequence involving Garrett at Lemuel's trading post/bar.

Bliss argues that the scene at Lemuel's is one of the best examples of the meaningful "parallelism" Peckinpah achieves by alternating scenes which focus first on the Kid, then on Garrett (1993, 244). The relevant scene involving Billy is also at a trading post and is climaxed by Billy's shooting of Garrett's new deputy, Alamosa Bill, much as the scene at Lemuel's is brought to a violent end when Garrett shoots Holly. Peckinpah highlights this comparison by altering the sequence of events in Wurlitzer's script. In Wurlitzer, the scene with Billy at the Horrells (1973, 67–71) precedes Garrett's stay at Lemuel's (1973, 74–82),[40] and the two episodes are separated by the scene in which Billy discovers the mortally wounded Paco (Emilio Fernandez) as Billy rides toward Mexico (1973, 71–74). Peckinpah rearranges events so that we first see Garrett and Poe arrive at Lemuel's, where they share a drink before Garrett sends Poe out on the trail by himself, then switch to Billy's arrival at the Horrells and the subsequent duel with Alamosa Bill, and finally return to Lemuel's for the unexpected arrival of three of Billy's men, Holly, Beaver (Donnie Fritts), and Alias (Bob Dylan). The scene with the dying Paco is delayed until this three-part sequence at the two trading posts is complete. Bliss thinks the parallel scenes contrast Garrett's sadistic cruelty toward Holly, Beaver, Alias, and Lemuel with Billy's self-protective violence against Alamosa Bill (1993, 244–45), but it seems fairer to say that each scene records its protagonist's deft manipulation of Western conventions to achieve control over others.

This is not to deny the extraordinary unpleasantness of Garrett's performance at Lemuel's. Like Billy at the Horrells' trading post, Garrett encounters unexpected problems at Lemuel's, but Garrett's troubles are very much of his own making. The real contrast here is with the fight at Black Harris' cabin, a scene Garrett enters after the shooting has already started and over which he can exercise no real control. At Lemuel's, by contrast, Garrett is totally in control and fully responsible for the several results: the violence against Beaver, the humiliation of Lemuel, the shooting of Holly, and the sardonic remark at the end to Alias (added by Peckinpah during production) in which Garrett directs Alias to tell Billy they have had a little drink together. The sequence of insults to Garrett, effective reminders of the impossible situation he has created for himself, comes to a shattering climax in which Garrett fights back, inflicting violent and unusually ugly retaliation on people who are only nominally his enemies.

The insults at Lemuel's begin with Poe's unsubtle suggestion that Garrett's seven-week "quest" to find Billy has left Garrett all but lifeless: "Are you gettin' tired, Garrett? Looks like you're only good for another two weeks."[41] These lines were added to the November shooting script (1972, 66), replacing Poe's remark in Wurlitzer's original script that Poe himself is "only good fer another two weeks" (1973, 76), a change obviously intended to revive the stream of insults directed at Garrett. Subsequently, Lemuel insults Garrett at least three times, when he refers to "all that law" inside Garrett busting to get out, when he tells Garrett that he's seeing "the bad-news side of things" while looking "right-dab" at Garrett himself, and when he tells Billy's men that the belligerent Garrett is "gettin' his bark back on like he thinks it'll make him young again, like the Kid." The most piercing of Lemuel's remarks is an indirect insult as well, as Lemuel deplores Garrett's pursuit of Billy as unworthy of a man once exceptionally close to his prey: "You used to be just like a daddy to that boy." The insults at Lemuel's climax when Holly, forced to drink continuously from a whiskey bottle, first lashes out at Garrett's erratic pursuit of the Kid ("Are you afraid to take it to him, or what?"), then seals his own fate by saying, "Don't take it personal, Pat, but ever since you and the Kid been together, you been just a little short of supplies."[42] Significantly, this line first read, both in Wurlitzer's original script (1973, 81) and in the November shooting script (1972, 72), "Don't take it personal, Pat, but you'n him been a little short of supplies ever since you been knowin' each other." Peckinpah alters the line so that the insult is directed at Garrett alone, as is the case in all the earlier scenes in which Garrett's companions point up his failures and evasions.

Whatever one thinks of Billy's conduct at the Horrells, there can be little doubt that we see Garrett at his moral nadir at Lemuel's. But it is misleading to suggest that in this scene "Garrett takes pleasure in killing," as Bliss asserts (1993, 245), for even someone as hostile to Garrett as Brad Stevens sees that the Garrett of this scene "clearly takes no pleasure at all in his actions" (270). Once again we think the relevant comparison is to the Macbeth who succeeds to the Scottish crown after murdering Duncan. Throughout the rest of his play Macbeth commits one horrific act after another, most memorably the assassinations of Banquo and Macduff's wife and children,[43] but he derives no satisfaction, let alone pleasure, from his deeds and ends up reflecting, "I am in blood / Stepp'd in so far that, should I wade no more, / Returning were as tedious as go o'er" (III.iv.136–38). He goes on to remark, "I have supped full with horrors" (V.v.13), and to acknowledge that he has lived long enough in one of the great dramatic speeches in all of English literature, quoted above as an epigraph to this chapter (V.iii.22–28). Macbeth commits his great crimes under the falsely-won privileges of kingly power, while Garrett acts always within his legal rights as an elected sheriff, but both men know all too well that their deeds are shameful exercises of the amoral power they have achieved by rejecting everything good or admirable in their characters. Macbeth's soliloquies make this clear throughout Shakespeare's play, whereas Garrett's guilty awareness fully emerges only with his actions after he kills Billy.

We have referred to Garrett's performance at Lemuel's trading post as his moral nadir, but others have said much the same thing about his interlude with the prostitutes of Roswell, his destination after leaving Lemuel's. Ostensibly Garrett comes to Roswell to find out Billy's whereabouts and to enlist its sheriff, Kip McKinney (Richard Jaeckel), in the hunt for Billy. In truth, however, Garrett seems to desire a respite from the rigors of the trail, especially the debacles at Pecos and Lemuel's, but also the humiliations at Santa Fe, on the trail with Poe, and at Chisum's ranch. His circuitous route toward Billy almost complete, Garrett seems bent on a form of personal relaxation at Roberta's brothel/bar before undertaking what he now appears to accept as inevitable: his engagement with the Kid. We are meant to see that Garrett knows Roberta's well, for in the preview version of *Pat Garrett and Billy the Kid* Roberta's barkeep, Rupert (Walter Kelley), reminds Garrett that the last time he was there he needed "four [prostitutes] to get it up and five to get it down," a line suggested by Wurlitzer's "Last time you had three or four up there" (1973, 98) and added by Peckinpah during production.[44]

Garrett's familiarity with Roberta's is one of the many elements in the film enriched by the restoration of Garrett's scene with Ida. As we soon see when he begins to entertain no fewer than five prostitutes,[45] Garrett is used to turning from the irresolvable tensions of his marriage to the comforts of anonymous, irresponsible sexuality. First, however, Garrett must deal with Billy's favorite whore, Ruthie Lee. Wurlitzer's Ruthie Lee is "very young, not more than sixteen" (1973, 98), and sassily insulting in a manner even Peckinpah had to tone down, even as he recreated her, as played by Rutanya Alda, as a mature woman in her late twenties or early thirties. Asked how she's been, Wurlitzer's Ruthie Lee replies, "Younger and more alive than you" (1973, 98), and in the same spirit she goes on to say, "Why don't you pack it in, Pat? You're gettin' too old to follow Kid around" (1973, 99). Wurlitzer's Ruthie Lee is first struck by Garrett because she insults him (1973, 99), not, as in the film, because she refuses to give up information about Billy. Wurlitzer's Ruthie Lee then insists she will not betray Billy until slapped again, so Garrett eventually hits her four times and hits her hard enough to draw blood (1973, 99). Peckinpah's Ruthie Lee offers none of the insults in Wurlitzer and endures three not-so-vicious slaps before telling Garrett that Billy is at Old Fort Sumner. There is something distinctly theatrical about her "resistance" to Garrett's interrogation, and Garrett's slaps, though unpleasant, seem to participate in the staged theatrics of the scene, as if the whole business were foreplay instead of serious inquiry. This is a far cry from the genuine tragic "theater" we describe in Garrett's first and only encounter in the film with his wife Ida. This impression of an artificially staged conflict with Ruthie Lee is reinforced when Garrett gets his answer (one he surely anticipated) and four other prostitutes come in to join Ruthie Lee and Garrett.

The staged or fantasy element in this scene escalates all too quickly for most of Peckinpah's critics. Wurlitzer provided only two prostitutes and had Garrett say of the "party" to come, a "party" we do not witness, "It's goin' to be real quick" (1973, 100). Peckinpah ups the number of whores to five and captures the playful first stages of an orgy which is going to be anything but "quick," patiently recorded here in 75 seconds of screen time. Fulwood finds the scene "gratuitous" (157, n.7), Bliss thinks it "degenerates into absurdity" (1993, 218), Kitses laments "Peckinpah's fantasies of sexual excess" (2004, 239), and Seydor offers a series of critical put-downs: "downright preposterous" (1997, 265), "ridiculously overdone" (1997, 271), "ludicrous" (1997, 304). Seydor notes that virtually everyone on the set tried to dissuade Peckinpah from including so many whores if not the scene itself, but Peckinpah "refused to listen" (1997, 266).

We think that Peckinpah was right to reject the advice of his critics, those on the set and those to come. The prostitute scene brilliantly contrasts Garrett on liberty with the tense, nervous, apologetic Garrett of the scene with Ida. Earlier, at Governor Wallace's, we see Garrett stare at the breasts of a waitress, but here he is free to indulge himself in a childish form of free play which is virtually liminal in the context of his all-too-constrained social relationships. Here, for the only time in the film, Garrett smiles broadly and indulges himself in careless play, the sort of activity which should remind us of how painfully unplayful his life has become because of his own mistakes and self-imposed constrictions.[46] Indeed, Peckinpah emphasizes the temporary escapism of the scene by following it immediately with Garrett's slow descent from the second floor of Roberta's, now fully clothed in his inevitable black suit, his working clothes, as formal and somber as the public Garrett himself. From this point to the end of the film, Garrett will remain in character, finally—and tragically—committed to his role as Billy's executioner.

With Poe and Kip McKinney, Garrett rides toward Old Fort Sumner to complete the circular movement begun when he visited Billy at the start of the film. As others have noted, *Pat Garrett and Billy the Kid* is filled with circular structures. The film begins with Garrett's death in the prologue and concludes with this death reprised in the epilogue; the theatrical version begins and ends with Garrett and Billy at Old Fort Sumner; Old Fort Sumner is itself a circular structure in Peckinpah's film, though it was in fact squarish (Utley 120); Garrett instructs his new deputy, Alamosa Bill, to travel a two-week circle in pursuit of the Kid; Chisum's men form an ominous circle around Silva before they shoot him for rustling Chisum's cattle; Garrett enters Pete Maxwell's place at the end through a white picket fence very like the one he opens to enter his own house in Lincoln, and his movements in Maxwell's house are distinctly reminiscent of his cautious search for Ida; and the film is littered with wagon wheels, Western embodiments of the medieval and Renaissance concept of the Wheel of Fortune, so central to Shakespearean tragedy: at Paco's death scene, where he is impaled on such a wheel; at Will the coffinmaker's, where Garrett stands beside a broken wagon wheel which dominates the center of the film frame; and at the end of the film, with the crucial freeze frame in sepia of the mortally wounded Garrett falling off the wagon, about to disappear right by the conspicuous wheel, his dislodged hat floating in frozen space like the lady lover's slipper in Fragonard's "The Swing." The many circular structures and repetitions reinforce the sense of entrapment Garrett experiences throughout and which he has brought upon himself.

As Seydor rightly concludes, "the whole last sequence is beautifully sustained and among Peckinpah's finest achievements" (1997, 301). Echoing Seydor, Maximilian Le Cain calls the moments surrounding Billy's death "one of the most eerily beautiful pieces of filmmaking in the history of the cinema" (6). Once again Peckinpah realizes the full potential of his materials by changing the sequence in Wurlitzer's original screenplay and the somewhat revised November shooting script. Wurlitzer's original script includes many of the key elements, most obviously Garrett's shooting of Billy, but it is filled with features Peckinpah had to pare away in order to focus on Garrett's search for the Kid and Billy's final tryst with his girlfriend Maria. Wurlitzer devotes a good deal of screen time to Poe and McKinney arguing (1973, 105–106, 111–12, 114–15, 116–17), to Billy blustering in a saloon scene (1973, 107–110) and then targeting Chisum for retribution (1973, 112–14), to Billy talking with McKinney (1973, 119–21), to Billy visiting with Maria's family (1973, 121–23), and to Billy quarreling with Maria (1973, 112–14, 123–25). All of these things are distracting, and the scenes in which Billy and Maria quarrel are completely at odds with Peckinpah's final scenes.

By November Peckinpah had begun to recast the original script with several important changes Wurlitzer later rejected in his published screenplay. The November shooting script still includes the several scenes in which Poe and McKinney quarrel (1972, 90–91, 93–95, 97) and Billy talks with McKinney (1972, 99, 104, 105), but it eliminates Billy ranting in the saloon and targeting Chisum, the scene in which Pete Maxwell (Paul Fix) complains and Maria goes to help (Wurlitzer 1973, 125), and, most crucial, Billy and Maria quarreling. The November script now includes scenes in which Billy waits for and meets Maria (1972, 96), Billy and Maria ask Pete Maxwell if they can use one of his rooms (1972, 96),[47] Billy and Maria undress in this room (1972, 97), Billy and Maria lie on a bed, having made love (1972, 98), and Billy goes for food (1972, 111) rather than to an outhouse (Wurlitzer 1973, 125). The November script does not include the elaborate treatment of Billy and Maria making love, obviously added by Peckinpah during production, but it does embody the crucial shift toward Peckinpah's radically revised conception of Billy's relationship with Maria. It cuts Wurlitzer's scenes in which Billy walks through a "white gate" (1973, 123) and a "white fence" (1973, 125) to reach Pete Maxwell's, perhaps in anticipation of the scene added by Peckinpah in which Garrett (again) walks through a white picket fence. And it adds the important moment when Poe starts to cut off one of Billy's fingers after Garrett has killed the Kid (1972, 113–14). Here Garrett actually shoots Poe in the shoulder (1972, 115), whereas in the film he hits him with his gun and kicks him away. Like Wurlitzer's original screenplay, the November script includes no reference to the swing on Maxwell's porch and no explanation of where Garrett spends the night before riding out of Old Fort Sumner in the morning.

The November shooting script also follows Wurlitzer in having Garrett and his assistants ride into Old Fort Sumner, a ride we do not witness. One of Peckinpah's most important decisions during production was to have the three men walk up to the fort and then walk through it as they search for Billy while heading for Pete Maxwell's place. This allows Peckinpah to focus on Garrett's movements as Wurlitzer failed to do in any of his scripts. In lieu of the several scenes cut by November and the scenes in which Poe and McKinney quarrel and Billy talks with McKinney cut by Peckinpah during production, Peckinpah follows Garrett and his men as they walk through the dark, fog-ridden streets of Old Fort Sumner, with distinct emphasis on Garrett's trek. More phantom than man, Garrett "moves like a ghost" with "Tarquin's ravishing strides" toward his quarry (*Macbeth* I.ii.55–56). As he glides between the fort's crumbling walls, he casts a large, misshapen shadow against these walls, resembling a monstrous creature out of a German Expressionist film of the 1920s. At one extraordinary moment, Garrett passes by a burning fire and rounds a corner where his shadow looms large and menacing against a wall, while a second shadow reflects against that wall several yards away. The two shadows suggest once again Garrett's tragic doubleness, shadowed it would seem by the Kid's imminent death as well as his own. The second shadow may really be Kip McKinney's, but as we encounter the scene it looks like Garrett's. Garrett is so split and doubled against himself, he appears to be pursued by both shadows, his own and the Kid's. Anyone familiar with the epic march of the Wild Bunch to the loggia in Agua Verde in which the Bunch round a corner, moving forward with the smoke of a burning fire behind them, will note the striking but ironic similarity, ironic because the Wild Bunch march heroically toward certain death to rescue their comrade in the bright of day, while Pat Garrett is on a murderous mission to kill his friend in the dark of night.

Garrett's stalking of Billy is only one of the features Peckinpah added to the final sequence. The next key addition is Garrett entering Pete Maxwell's through a white picket fence, "weathered and warped from many years of neglect," as Weddle notes (1994, 479), but an inevitable reminder of the white picket fence Garrett passes through to get to his own house in Lincoln. Peckinpah may have picked up on the picket fence at Pete Maxwell's noted by historians such as Utley (192), then proceeded to create such a fence for Garrett's home. Alternatively, he may have encountered the "white gate" and "white fence" in Wurlitzer's original treatment of Maxwell's, then hit upon the rich possibilities in providing a white picket fence for Garrett in Lincoln. As Weddle says, Garrett again pauses before the second picket fence, then "swings it open with the same deliberate motion he'd used when entering his wife's house" (1994, 479). We have previously quoted from Weddle's acute characterization of Garrett's picket fence and towering Victorian house in Lincoln (1994, 478–479). Among Peckinpah's critics, Weddle is most alert to the importance of the scene with Ida and these physical details which accompany it. This is suggested, consciously or unconsciously, by Weddle's referring to the house in Lincoln as Ida's and not Garrett's. Garrett's reluctance to enter Maxwell's house is all too like his reluctance to confront Ida, and Peckinpah's depiction of Billy and Maria forces us to see Garrett confronting, however reluctantly, an enviable domestic scene he cannot hope to emulate. Garrett's awareness of his failure in this regard is vividly suggested by Peckinpah's next addition. Peckinpah has Garrett walk up to Maxwell's porch, where he hears Billy and Maria making love in a nearby room. Remarkably enough, Garrett hesitates, then sits down in a swing on the porch to wait until Billy and Maria are finished. It is as if Garrett, slowly swinging back and forth, honors the kind of relationship he himself cannot have even as he prepares to end it by killing Billy.

Peckinpah's presentation of Billy and Maria, here and throughout the film, is a major addition to the script, one we will discuss more fully when we turn to the Kid. Here we would agree with Stevens that Billy's relationship with Maria is meant to contrast with Garrett's relationship with Ida, for Billy and Maria's affair seems "based on tenderness, affection and a mutually shared sexuality, enjoyed for its own sake, as an expression of love" (276). This contrast reinforces that between the Bakers and the Garretts, and we should recall Peckinpah's important decision to make Mrs. Baker Hispanic, for all three couples in the film involve an Anglo man and an Hispanic woman of similar ages, ranging from the relatively youthful Billy and Maria to the more senior Bakers. Garrett and Ida stand between the other two couples in age and contrast with both in their marital troubles, so obviously traceable to Garrett's inability to turn to the life so richly embodied in Ida and the home she has fashioned.

Peckinpah's next and perhaps most crucial addition occurs during the audaciously Eisensteinian montage sequence (34 shots, approximately 63 seconds) when Garrett finally kills

Death in doorway. Billy the Kid (Kris Kristofferson) is shot to death by Sheriff Pat Garrett (James Coburn) in Pete Maxwell's (Paul Fix's) bedroom.

the Kid. The scene begins with the Kid out on the porch seeking food from the cooler after making love with Maria. He sees Poe and Kip McKinney crouching darkly in a corner of the porch. "Who's that?" he calls out, and Peckinpah cuts not to the two men but to Pat Garrett entering Pete Maxwell's bedroom. Again the Kid, sticking his knife into the cooler, famously asks in Spanish, "Quién es?" and once again Peckinpah cuts not to Poe and McKinney but to Garrett. It is clear that these *Hamlet*-like questions are meant for Pat Garrett, whose whole identity, like Hamlet's, is radically put into question throughout the film. This is underscored by Pete Maxwell's earlier question to the stranger who has entered his room, "Who the *Hell* are you?" as Garrett moves to a chair beside Pete's bed. The whole scene represents a painful symbolic foreshadowing of the death of the old West.

Once a killer, the Kid now appears to give in mildly, without volition, to his fate while he holds his gun to the side, arms out in a crucifixional pose, and innocently flashes his "Mona Lisa–like smile" (Tatum 160) toward his friend *and* assassin, Pat Garrett, who shoots him dead. As if to underscore the realization that his whole being is at stake in this powerful scene, Garrett fires at his own image in a mirror seconds after he shoots the Kid, himself a willing victim in this tragic clash between Eros and Thanatos. As Stevens suggests, this moment represents Garrett's "recognition of, and revulsion at, the dark side of his personality" (273), a dark side hauntingly foreshadowed by Peckinpah's depiction of Garrett in sable silhouette as he stands in Maxwell's doorway, then sits in darkness, death-like and motionless, facing the camera, beside Pete Maxwell's bed, awaiting the Kid. Garrett shoots not only his image in the mirror but that of Maxwell's large oaken bed, prominent in the frame, Garrett's self-revulsion and contempt for life — we recall the Garretts' barren bed — so great he destroys them both in one booming, reverberating blast, echoing through all space and time.

Interestingly, even here the tormented Garrett is doubly doubled. The Garrett who gazes in shock at himself in the mirror seems appalled, mouth agape, eyes wide open in horror, but the Garrett who in a second cinematic shot pulls the trigger and shatters the glass seems an emotionless, cold-blooded killer. The warring Pat Garretts and their wrenching contradictions remain to the end, felt here in the broken images of the fragmented, doubled "Garretts" we and Garrett himself see in the mirror's "mocking, Dorian Gray–like distortion" (Seydor 1997, 276). We would also note that even as Garrett seeks his own suicidal self-destruction and exposes his "tortured conscience" (Prince 1998, 142), his "guilt, self-doubt, and self-contempt" (Seydor 1997, 297), a large black bullet hole appears in the mirror, as Garrett, photographed from behind, almost willfully walks before the shattered glass, his heart mirrored in that terrible void. Garrett shooting his heart out in the mirror suggests a dark and infinite abyss in this tortured man and ties that abyss, and his own personal damnation, to the slain Kid. This is why, in the midst of the mirror-shooting montage, Peckinpah shock-cuts abruptly from the staring Garrett to three separate shots of the slain Kid eventually lying in perfect repose on the stone porch, the St. Christopher's medal Maria gave him earlier now prominently displayed in the second and third shots as he lies silent after falling to the floor, his head bouncing in the first shot. We are perhaps to imagine that even in death the legendary Kid will travel far, no doubt around the world, most certainly to the city of light and art, "Paris, France," where Billy is to be found according to Black Harris in the preview version of his death scene. Meanwhile, the trapped and traumatized Pat Garrett will never shake off the fate he has made for himself, and the narrow grave which awaits him 28 years later in the bleak New Mexico desert.

The scene in which Garrett shoots Billy reinforces this sense of an imprisoned Garrett by its use of triangular images which complement the film's circles mentioned earlier. The imagery of destabilizing, fateful triangles—confirming that Garrett is now doomed no matter what he chooses to do— begins (and ends) with Garrett trapped inside a triangle of three assassins in the prologue/epilogue, shifts to more metaphorical forms in the film's major relationships (Garrett/Ida/Billy; Garrett/Billy/Maria; Garrett/Billy/Poe), and recurs through the scene of Billy's death. Here the Kid enters the film frame and passes twice through the dinner triangle, hanging over Pete Maxwell's porch and swaying lightly in the late night breeze, as he walks from the bedroom to get something to eat from Pete's cooler after making love with Maria. When Billy is shot, Poe lunges to see what has happened and knocks this triangle sideways, so that it careens violently back and forth, in strong contrast to the rigidly controlled Garrett who initially sways softly on the swing, held up by its triangular ropes, which he tries to hold steady and still when he first arrives on the verandah. At this point Poe effectively replaces Billy in the tragic scenario Garrett has created. The next morning, as the bruised, resentful Poe prepares to leave Old Fort Sumner, the knife Billy stuck in the cooler before drawing his gun on Poe and Kip McKinney is still ominously present, framed next to Poe's shoulder. The dagger-like knife seems to come alive and take on its own Macbethian meanings, assimilating itself into Poe's menacing identity as Garrett's future assassin. As he walks past the silent Garrett sitting on the swing, Poe casts a deep shadow over him, an omen of Garrett's own death years later. In the background Poe's shadow leaves Garrett's darkened body and visually seems to pierce the back of Garrett's head while advancing along the wall behind Garrett as Poe descends the stairs and leaves. Poe's "walking shadow" (*Macbeth* V.v. 25) figuratively penetrates Garrett's mind, again conjuring the notion of the guilty man's descent into his own personal hell. As the logical conclusion to the decisions he has made, Garrett is truly "dead inside" and will carry death with him from this point forward.

Peckinpah continues to rework Wurlitzer's materials even after Garrett shoots the Kid. He eliminates the several women who come crying and shrieking to Billy's fallen body (Wurlitzer 1973, 129), a scene suggested by popular lore as well as the episode in Neider in which many women help dress the Kid for burial (198), preferring to reserve this moment for Maria alone. He has Garrett retire to the swing on Maxwell's porch where he will spend the night, a ruined man going back and forth, lost in melancholy, thinking about Billy. It is interesting that for years Peckinpah kept this swing as a memento of the filming of *Pat Garrett and Billy the Kid* (Simmons 200). MCM unwittingly honored the importance of the swing by using a publicity still not found in any released version (see Neale 18) in which we see a well-lit Pat Garrett standing on the porch over the slain body of the Kid, a large triangular, rope-like shadow projected on the adobe wall next to him, outside Pete Maxwell's bedroom. During production Peckinpah placed the swing with those triangular support ropes on Maxwell's porch and used it in ways he obviously thought important: to situate Garrett as he waits for Billy and Maria to finish making love, to provide Garrett a place to spend the night and reflect on what he has done before leaving the scene of his crime in the morning, to offer in its ropes yet another triangular image encasing Garrett. All of these usages play against the enduring romantic association of swings with young lovers. Whether or not Peckinpah knew Fragonard's comically erotic "The Swing," with its detached lady's slipper reminding us of solitary, loveless Garrett's falling hat as he dies at the end of the epilogue, Peckinpah's swing proved one of his film's most memorable artifacts. The one real addition here, before Garrett returns to the swing, is Poe's taking out his knife, which recalls the Kid's sticking his knife in the cooler, and attempting to cut off Billy's trigger finger, surely an image of castration, followed by Garrett's emphatic cry, "No-o-o-o-o!" before he strikes Poe over the head with his gun, then kicks him. We think this moment is tied to Garrett's shooting of the mirror, the display of Garrett's tortured conscience, as his fury at someone about to deface Billy is clearly a form of displaced anger at the man who has actually killed the Kid.

Garrett's ties to Shakespeare's Macbeth are at their strongest here, or perhaps we should say A. C. Bradley's Macbeth, for it is Bradley who famously saw Macbeth as "convulsed by conscience," a man whose later speeches register "the protest of his deepest self" against himself (280). Macbeth's self-judgments help to explain why we continue to care about the man even as he steps farther and farther into blood: "But after all we have seen and heard of this great and terrible man, it is difficult to share with equanimity in the summary judgment which Malcolm passes on him, 'this dead butcher'" (Poole 1987, 47). In his own way, even as he lashes out at men such as Holly and Poe, Garrett provides his own judgment on himself, as well as ample proof of Emily R. Wilson's argument that "death is not the ultimate tragic experience" (5) and Adrian Poole's contention that with genuine tragedy "the difference is permanent, the damage irreversible" (1987, 14). So it is for the "victor" at the end of *Pat Garrett and Billy the Kid*, even as he rides off to live another 28 years before suffering the same fate he inflicts on Billy the Kid.[48]

III

BERNARDO: "Who's there?"

—*Hamlet* I.i.1

PAT GARRETT: "Who're you?
ALIAS: "That's a good question."

BILLY THE KID: "Who's that? ... Quién es?"

PETE MAXWELL TO PAT GARRETT: "Who the *Hell* are you?"

BILLY THE KID TO PETE MAXWELL: "Hey Pete, who's that out there?"
—*Pat Garrett and Billy the Kid*

To this point we have said little about Billy the Kid's role in the tragedy of Pat Garrett. We remarked early in this chapter that Billy's primary function is to contrast with Garrett, and we have noted a few specific contrasts, such as Billy's relationship with Maria and Garrett's with his wife Ida, but the overall contrast between Billy and Garrett is complicated by the difficulty in defining Billy's essential nature. Indeed, critical reactions to Peckinpah's Billy the Kid could not be more diverse. Kitses and Seydor disagree about many aspects of *Pat Garrett and Billy the Kid*, but they agree that Billy is distinctly unheroic. For Kitses, "Billy is as compromised as Garrett, as trapped in a righteous narcissism, a saviour without a cause" (2004, 225), whereas Seydor finds Billy "a likable—even charming—sociopath" (1997, 289) who is "obtuse and unregenerate to the end" (1997, 297), so obtuse that he really believes Garrett might just want to have a drink with him at the end of the film (1997, 292). Yet Bliss speaks of Billy's "indomitable spirit" (1993, 246), Stevens sees Billy as representing "friendship, love, self-respect and generosity" (270), and Tatum describes Billy as "a sacrificial victim who is closely allied with nature" (125). Peckinpah's critics have responded to his Billy as if he were a bizarre composite of earlier Billys such as Howard Hughes' romantic "outlaw" (*The Outlaw*, 1941) and Stan Dragoti's almost laughably revisionist punk (*Dirty Little Billy*, 1973). We believe that Billy's friends and foes have exaggerated his strengths and flaws, that his admittedly diverse features are not so incompatible as they have been made to seem, and that in any case these features are intended to contrast with Garrett's rather than to form a complex but unified "character" in their own right.

Billy's detractors love to cite Peckinpah's comment about the historical William Bonney: "Billy the Kid was no hero. He was a gunfighter, a real killer" (William Murray 73). Billy is certainly depicted as a real killer in *Pat Garrett and Billy the Kid*. Though Robert Utley finds evidence that the historical Billy killed four men (203) and participated in at least five other killings (204), relatively modest numbers for a man of Billy's reputation, Peckinpah's Billy either kills or participates in the killing of 16 men in the course of a film which covers only the last few months of Billy's life. In all versions of the script, from Wurlitzer's original screenplay to the finished film, Billy tells J. W. Bell about executing Bell's friend Carlyle: "I shot him three times in the back of the head. I blowed his head off" (Wurlitzer 1973, 7; November shooting script 1972, 17).[49] Despite Bliss' ardent defense of Billy for turning on the count of three during his 10-step "duel" with Alamosa Bill (1993, 245), there is something equally chilling about the Kid's execution of the less-devious Alamosa, who turns on the count of eight, and Billy's violation of the Western dueling code is Peckinpah's addition, for in the different scripts Alamosa turns on the count of nine but Billy waits until the count of 10 and kills Alamosa after Garrett's unlikely deputy shoots and misses (Wurlitzer 1973, 70; November shooting script 1972, 60–61). Moreover, the depiction of Billy's unsavory gang, captured so well by Kitses and Seydor, is entirely Peckinpah's addition, for in Wurlitzer's original script Billy returns to Old Fort Sumner after escaping from the Lincoln jailhouse to be told by Luke (Harry Dean Stanton) that the old gang have more or less disbanded and most of the men at the fort are "new" (1973, 23). One does not have to agree with Kitses and Seydor about the "obtuse" Billy the Kid to appreciate that much of Peckinpah's portrait is decidedly unsentimental.[50]

Unlike Peckinpah, however, Kitses and Seydor seem not to see the problem in depicting Billy as virtually without value. This problem is especially acute in Seydor's reading, for Seydor shares our view that Pat Garrett is a tragic figure and yet he mercilessly denigrates Billy to the point it is hard to appreciate the poignancy of Garrett's betrayal of the Kid. If "[v]irtually nothing Billy does is heroic, noble, or honorable," as Seydor claims (1997, 289), why should we care so very much that Garrett must track down the Kid in order to secure his new life? If Garrett sees no value in the outlaw past he shares with Billy, as Seydor alleges (1997, 287), why should he feel any reservations, let alone guilt, for rejecting his past and betraying the men with whom he shared it (Billy, Black Harris, Holly, and, in effect, Sheriff Baker)? When Billy remarks early in the film, "We did have some times, didn't we?" Garrett nods and smiles in agreement, and the film's tragic logic requires that he mean it, for only then do we understand the *loss* Garrett experiences in trying to change his life so dramatically. It is therefore imperative that Billy be depicted as more than a sociopath or psychopath — however "charming" — and in fact as a charismatic figure of flawed but quite real substance. This does not mean that he must represent "friendship, love, self-respect and generosity," in Stevens' grand formulation, but Peckinpah's Billy must sometimes be capable of these feelings if we are to appreciate Garrett's dilemma in his pursuit of the Kid.

Peckinpah's task in characterizing Billy again recalls *Macbeth*, for Shakespeare's source, Holinshed's *Chronicles*, depicts Macbeth's victim as a flawed king against whom Macbeth had many grievances, a Duncan Shakespeare completely transforms in order to emphasize Macbeth's guilt for an unforgivable betrayal (see Honigmann 138). Here Peckinpah does not need to rehabilitate Billy so thoroughly, but he too must establish the worth of the man his protagonist assassinates. Toward this end Peckinpah deleted a number of scenes in Wurlitzer in which Billy comes across as crude if not coarse: what Seydor aptly labels "a digressive frontier roof-raising party" (1997, 262) in which Billy wears a dress to a baile and ends up stripping several men naked and sending them off to make their way (Wurlitzer 1973, 48–55)[51]; a lengthy scene in which Billy and Maria lie naked in a corral until interrupted by a man named Tom Ketchum, who recalls the good old days when Billy cut the throats of puppies for the pleasure of doing so and whom Billy urinates on for presuming to a "friendship" Billy cannot even remember (Wurlitzer 1973, 62–66)[52]; and a long, genuinely weird scene in which Billy, ostensibly riding toward Mexico, stops at an empty cabin for the night only to awake to the presence of a comatose or otherwise mysteriously silent man whose relevance to the film's story remains unexplained as Billy rides on (Wurlitzer 1973, 93–96). These cuts tend to reduce Billy's role in the film and therefore highlight Garrett's centrality, but they also protect Billy from the burden of Wurlitzer's more eccentric moments in building his character.

Even more important in reconstructing Billy as a figure with whom we can sympathize are the many scenes Peckinpah retained but significantly altered to Billy's advantage. The shooting of J. W. Bell is a good example. In Wurlitzer, after telling Bell how he brutally killed his friend Carlyle, Billy says, "I'm going to kill you, Bell," and he immediately starts firing his gun, first missing, then shooting Bell in the back (1973, 7). By the November shooting script Peckinpah had changed the scene so that Billy says, "I don't want to kill you, Bell," and he only shoots when Bell turns to run (1972, 17). Finally, in the film itself, Peckinpah has Billy say, "I don't want to kill you, Bell," then implore Bell to cooperate by adding, "Don't. Don't do it, please."[53] The shooting of Bell is still an extremely unpleasant moment, all too typical of the life Billy has chosen, but Peckinpah's version of the incident is much more sympathetic to Billy than Wurlitzer's. Similarly, Peckinpah alters the scene in which Billy sleeps with one of the female campfollowers at Old Fort Sumner by eliminating the premature ejaculation Billy experiences at the end of the scene (Wurlitzer 1973, 24; November shooting script 1972, 29). One of the most thoroughly altered sequences is the so-called turkey chase which concludes with the shooting of Silva. In Wurlitzer, Billy and Alias *shoot* at the turkeys they come upon (1973, 39), whereas in the film Peckinpah has them rope the turkeys in a scene which might even be said to offer up a wonderful slice of Americana.[54] Peckinpah's comical version of the turkey chase is dramatically interrupted by the shooting of Silva. In Wurlitzer, Billy and Alias are unable to respond and finally return to the sorry spectacle of Silva lying atop his dead horse (1973, 46). In the November shooting script, Peckinpah has Billy and Alias fire upon Chisum's men and kill one (1972, 42C), and in the film Billy kills at least three and possibly four of Chisum's men in retaliation for the killing of Silva.

There are many other examples of Peckinpah's efforts to present a more sympathetic Kid, for virtually every scene is altered in ways large and small to achieve this end. We have previously cited the cuts Peckinpah made in the concluding sequence to eliminate Billy's bellicose defiance of Chisum, whom he mistakenly fears more than Garrett ("Garrett ain't the problem" [Wurlitzer 1973, 113]), and to replace Billy's bickering with Maria with the extraordinarily tender lovemaking between Billy and Peckinpah's completely-revised version of Maria. A recurring change is the film's insistence on Billy's widespread popularity, as evidenced in the sympathies of Billy's men, Ida, Paco, the Horrells, Lemuel, Ruthie Lee, Sheriff McKinney, Pete Maxwell, Maria, and even the men who pursue Billy, Chisum and Pat Garrett himself. This is virtually the same list of characters who insult Garrett, and the remarkable diversity among Billy's supporters suggests that Billy cannot be dismissed as an obtuse sociopath. Finally, Wurlitzer projected a Billy the Kid overly fond of his own reputation, a man who says over Silva's body, "I ain't forgettin', and I ain't about to be forgot neither" (1973, 41), and who rejects going to Mexico because he would no longer be the famous Billy the Kid: "In Mexico I'd be another drunken gringo whorin' and shittin' out hot chili peppers and gettin' old" (1973, 63). Peckinpah downplays Billy's vanity, first by deleting Billy's speech over Silva, then by assigning Billy's speech about Mexico to Luke: "Hell, in Old Mex he'd be nothin' but another gringo shittin' out chili peppers and waiting for ... nothin'."[55] In the film Billy does not reject what Luke says, but at least he is not the boastful, vainglorious 21-year-old Wurlitzer created. Indeed, one of the reasons Peckinpah makes Billy appear to be 30 (and Garrett at least 40) is that in this version of the Billy the Kid saga Garrett first betrays and then kills a man with whom he has been friendly for many years. Kris Kristofferson was in fact 36 and James Coburn was 44 when *Pat Garrett and Billy the Kid* was made, though Kristofferson "looks rather closer to 30, and can easily pass for late twenties," as Seydor points out (1997, 281).

This is not to say that Seydor is altogether wrong when he sees Garrett as "alienated from the world he used to inhabit" (1997, 287), the world Billy continues to inhabit and even to exemplify to the moment of his death. Peckinpah himself added the lines in which Garrett rejects the "stale" life Billy persists in living. But Peckinpah also added the lines in which Garrett acknowledges the good "times" he and Billy shared in a past which was not simply "grosser, dirtier, more violent and shabby" than the present, as Seydor argues (1997, 287). Indeed, it is appropriate that Peckinpah should present a Billy the Kid who represents the worst but also the best of Garrett's past and present, for in a tragic action Garrett's rejection of Billy and what he embodies must be tempting and yet excruciatingly painful, and in this particular tragic action Garrett betrays and ultimately kills the best part of himself.

Given the logic of *Pat Garrett and Billy the Kid*, it was perhaps inevitable that Peckinpah would go beyond his efforts to establish Billy's virtues as well as his faults to suggest hints of transcendence in this "real killer." Peckinpah rejected the mode of transcendence suggested in Wurlitzer's script, however, for Wurlitzer saw Billy as a man acutely aware of his present and future status as a figure of myth. Early in his script, as Billy escapes from Lincoln, Wurlitzer writes, "His whole being, if not his consciousness, is deeply aware, as the crowd is deeply aware, that he inhabits a myth, the myth of Billy the Kid" (1973, 10). For Wurlitzer, Billy's "awareness" of his mythical status leads to a crucial decision: "What became interesting was Billy's decision not to flee, to accept the consequences of his own myth, no matter how unreal, even though it meant his death" (1973, vi). In conversations with Jan Aghed, Wurlitzer reiterated the notion that Billy makes an "existential choice" to remain true to his mythical persona: "In other words, he chose to be Billy the Kid" (Aghed 67). By the November shooting script, Peckinpah had Wurlitzer delete the commentary in which we are told of Billy's deep awareness that he inhabits a myth, and Peckinpah's film eliminates any suggestion that Billy makes an intellectual choice, existential or otherwise, to accept the consequences of his own myth. As we have seen, Peckinpah reassigns the one surviving speech alluding to Billy's reputation from Billy to Luke, and he alters the scenes after Billy leaves for Mexico to provide a more concrete reason for Billy's return to Old Fort Sumner than a suicidal commitment to his own reputation.[56]

The hints of transcendence to which we refer are not attributed to a self-conscious Billy but recur throughout the film as subtle suggestions of Billy's inherent superiority. Several of Wurlitzer's allusions to Billy's reputation are retained. The first is a song Billy makes up while preparing to leave Lincoln in which he playfully asserts that he has been "everywhere" and proceeds to list these many sites, various rivers, towns, and women ("your mama"), all confined to the American Southwest (Wurlitzer 1973, 10; November shooting script 1972, 20). This possibly self-mocking song anticipates Chisum's witty speech about Billy's having been seen everywhere, including Chisum's own table where Billy supposedly dines with Chisum's niece (Wurlitzer 1973, 61; November shooting script 1972, 52). The most intriguing of Wurlitzer's allusions comes when Garrett shoots Black Harris. Black has told Garrett he knows where the Kid is, and with his dying breath he gives up the secret: "Paris, France" (Wurlitzer 1973, 36; November shooting script 1972, 41). These several allusions refer to the legendary Billy the Kid who became famous after his death on July 14, 1881. More important for the moment are the numerous suggestions that Billy, unlike his old friend Pat Garrett, is a character supremely at one with nature.

The notion that Billy should be identified with nature and even such mythological figures as Dionysus is common to other cinematic versions of the Kid, such as Gore Vidal's teleplay *The Death of Billy the Kid* (1955) (see Tatum 124–25) and Arthur Penn's *The Left-Handed Gun* (1958), with its Vidal screenplay. Bliss notes the several scenes in which Peckinpah's Billy is closely associated with wild horses which provide "a commentary on the Kid's unruly spirit, which seems impossible to tame" (1993, 237). Bliss' first example is especially apt. As the Kid leaves an outhouse accompanied by J. W. Bell, suddenly, in a nearby corral, horses rise in seemingly unmotivated panic and begin neighing and running wildly around the corral, kicking up bright clouds of dirt. This scene is shot in shimmering Aegean light (not unlike the transcendent light which bathes the redeemed Deke Thornton [Robert Ryan] and his horse at the end of *The Wild Bunch*) and seems to suggest that the Kid's mere presence — he gazes at the horses momentarily — rouses their passions. This scene is followed by another striking suggestion of the Kid's closeness to elemental nature. As Billy rides out of Lincoln, the camera tracking his exalted departure in a crane shot, Peckinpah suddenly cuts to a closeup of what appears to be a blacksmith's forge and bellows, its frame-filling, billowing flames rising high within the forge, before following in a long shot the Kid's exit from Lincoln. This sequence adds the element of fire to the fenced-in containment or earth we experience with the horses and the decidedly feminine pond or water we will soon experience with Billy as he makes his way back to Old Fort Sumner.

The scene with Billy at the pond is the most exquisite of the film's transcendent moments and reminds us once again of Kathleen Murphy's obituary on Peckinpah in which she stresses his quasi-religious obsession with water's life-giving and redemptive powers (1985, 74). As darkness falls, the dying sunlight captures the Kid's mirrored reflection in the water, while his corporeal identity appears to vanish into the descending night. In the vastly superior 2005 version of the scene,[57] the Kid, riding among trees, is borne to the waterside through a long dissolve which seems to melt his identity with that of the water. One striking lap dissolve shows the Kid, a beautiful orange-pink sunset behind him, riding behind a black tree he virtually dissolves into and emerges from as if it shares some part of his primordial being, while within that same montage we see the Kid, now doubled in the long dissolve, halt near the pond. This remarkable series of poetic dissolves culminates in the arresting image of the Kid pausing on horseback before the mirroring pond while his horse drinks, two waterside trees beside Billy and his horse reflected in the water. Even as the chill desert evening arrives, Billy rather curiously removes his poncho, as if to open himself even more nakedly to nature and to gaze more intently at his own image in the water. The scene and others like it seem overtly and Ovidianly narcissistic (see Neale 17), as if the Kid were conscious of the archaic spell he casts over the still water. As the Kid pauses beside the pristine pool, we observe his image, and that of the trees, reflected in the pool in a truly transcendent moment. Now almost entirely invisible, the Kid as a corporeal figure disappears into the enfolding darkness and a mythic nature-god, perhaps water-loving Dionysus himself, seems to emerge in the water's reflection.

For Jim Kitses the figure of the Kid in the water is "an inverted Ford icon" (2004, 245) which stands in ironic, even sardonic contrast with the unabashedly patriotic images of John Ford's troopers in films such as *Fort Apache* (1948) and *Rio Grande* (1950). In Kitses' reading, the Kid's "pause" invites us "to understand that this is our reflection, too, America in the dark and dead in the water, asking us to turn the cowboy over in our mind, and to discover that, as always, Peckinpah is exposing the negative of the myth and its classical iconography" (2004, 245). Kitses seems to have confused the extravagantly beautiful imagery of the Kid and the trees reflected in the water with the scene in the mountains in *Ride the High Country* in which Steve Judd shaves in front of a gloomy, stagnant lake, "in the dark and dead" with its stripped fallen timbers and two trees still standing on either side of Steve as if to indicate imminent betrayal, perhaps Christ nailed to the cross. In *Pat Garrett and Billy the Kid*, we see before us not an anguished image of the "fabulous melancholy" (Kitses 2004, 229) which suffuses the dying of the old West symbolized by Pat Garrett in this bleakest of Peckinpah's films, but rather a sudden, all too brief nature epiphany, a moment of artistic incandescence alike in kind if not in degree to the Wild Bunch's legendary departure from Angel's village in *The Wild Bunch*. Even as the Kid slowly rides out through the water, passing from the frame, Peckinpah strikingly holds onto that ecstatic vision of the water, the reflected trees, and the dying diurnal light, as if to remind us just how much of Billy's primordial identity he takes from that pool, and how the two identities, water and Kid, are for one brief moment united.

Peckinpah is obviously aware that Billy's otherworldly moments, rather like Wordsworthian spots of time, are transitory and inevitably give way to modes of being a good deal less exalted. The apparently passionate horses Billy walks past, for example, reappear in episodes far less positive. As he prepares to leave Lincoln, Billy has a stable worker bring the best of his horses, but the horse throws Billy to the ground as if unaware of the Kid's magical powers. This comical moment is followed by another scene in which anxious, neighing horses seemingly respond to Billy, this time only moments before Billy and his men kill four so-called bounty hunters who have come for Billy at Old Fort Sumner, a scene which graphically acknowledges the violence which frequently accompanies Billy's "unruly spirit" and of course pervades every stage of the film.[58] Similarly, Peckinpah breaks the spell established with Billy at the pond by having Billy ride on from this perfect frame to one in which he passes through barbed wire fencing presumably marking the boundaries of Chisum's huge ranch, a scene reminding us of Billy's complaint to J. W. Bell that the major ranchers are trying to "fence in" the territory's natural richness and anticipating the later moment in which Garrett and Poe pass through similar barbed wire on their way to Chisum's ranch. Billy's descent from the exalted moment at the pond continues as he passes through the barbed wire to arrive back at Old Fort Sumner, where he reclaims his favorite campfollower from Luke and begins to make love with her in the presence of all his men and their own female companions. Thus Peckinpah acknowledges the all too historical Billy who is thrown to the ground by a "passionate" horse, driven to deadly violence by his enemies, fenced in by the territory's principal business interests, and crudely promiscuous.

This decidedly mortal Billy the Kid is of course the one Garrett tracks down and kills. But the hints of transcendence we have identified are not cancelled by evidence of Billy's failings and ultimate vulnerability, for Billy remains the only character in the film capable of these exalted moments, no doubt the source of his immense appeal to virtually every character in the film. Billy's appeal is not always mysterious or transcendent, however, and here too Billy contrasts with Garrett. We refer to Billy's capacities for friendship and love, on display at many points in the film but especially in his relationships with Alias and Maria.

It may seem odd to refer to Alias as Billy's friend, for the enigmatic Alias (surprisingly, his name is taken from an historical character who was an actual friend of Billy the Kid) is usually seen as a scribal figure introduced into the film to chart or observe Billy's legend. Peckinpah once said that he thought of Alias as "the writer who portrays the legend" (Huberman and Holt 19), and Kris Kristofferson compared him to the Fool in *King Lear*, "an observer through it all" (Simmons 173).[59] Peckinpah directed Wurlitzer to expand Alias' original, quite limited role (Weddle 1994, 467), and the November shooting script includes new material in which Alias kills the fourth bounty hunter with his knife (1972, 33), gives the departing Paco a new knife (1972, 50) and proceeds to talk with Billy about living in Mexico (1972, 50A/B), talks again with Billy as the Kid leaves Old Fort Sumner for Mexico (1972, 55–56), rides into a sheepherders' camp as Billy is about to ride away after the death of Paco (1972, 90C),[60] and converses with Billy at Old Fort Sumner the night Billy is killed (1972, 99, 100/104, 105). During production Peckinpah added Alias to the scenes in Lincoln in which Billy escapes and Garrett returns to begin organizing his efforts to recapture the Kid. Here Alias is depicted as a newspaper reporter for the *Lincoln Bulletin* who is obviously taken by the charismatic Billy the Kid and gives up his life in Lincoln to become one of Billy's men. Alias' admiration for Billy and his disdain for Garrett fit nicely into the film's insistence on Billy's popularity and Garrett's emerging role as an object of contempt, but it is hard to see why Peckinpah thought of Alias as a writer, or why Seydor sees Alias as representing "the chronicler or storyteller" (1997, 288), for after he leaves Lincoln, handing over his reporter's pad and pencil as he departs, Alias chronicles nothing and tells no stories (unless we take him to be the "author" of Bob Dylan's recurring songs about Billy the Kid). For the body of the film, Alias functions as Billy's friend rather than as the Kid's chronicler.[61]

Peckinpah worked throughout production to enhance Billy's friendship with Alias. By November he had Wurlitzer add the detail of Alias assisting Billy in the fight with the bounty hunters, and in production he added the concluding dialogue in which Billy affectionately jokes with Alias about his odd name. As Stevens notes, the turkey chase which follows is designed as "an affirmation of friendship with Alias" (272). Initially, in Wurlitzer's original screenplay, Billy and Alias shoot at the turkeys in a thoroughly unpleasant episode; subsequently, in the November shooting script, Billy and Alias rope the turkeys but exchange no comments while doing so; finally, in the film itself, Billy invites Alias to join him in pursuing the turkeys and the two exchange a number of playful remarks while capturing their turkeys, including Alias' mock-insult to Billy, "I could have roped four or five if it wasn't for you." Shortly thereafter, Peckinpah expands the dialogue between Billy and Alias after the departure of Paco. Billy is thinking of leaving New Mexico for Old Mexico and remarks, "Mexico might not be bad for a couple of months," to which Alias responds, "Depends on who you are."[62] In the next scene, as Billy prepares to leave for Mexico, Alias approaches and says, "Mexico won't be so bad for a few months," to which Billy replies, "I guess that depends who you are." The mirrored, chiasmus-like reversal of dialogue in these scenes suggests that "Billy is able to relate to Alias as an equal," as Stevens claims (273), and reinforces the playful camaraderie hinted at in the aftermath of the killings at Old Fort Sumner and lavishly displayed throughout the turkey chase. Subsequently, it is Alias who drinks with Billy at Old Fort Sumner and warns Billy as a friend that Garrett is coming to get him. Improbably enough, Peckinpah develops Billy's friendship with Alias more persuasively than any of his other relationships except that with Maria.

Billy's friendship with Alias is clearly intended as a contrast to Garrett's relationship with Poe, a man Garrett travels with but despises (see Stevens 273). Indeed, we are forcefully reminded that Garrett is depicted as having no close relationships. Nonetheless, we should not romanticize Billy's friendship with Alias or any of his other personal connections. Though Billy is liked by almost everyone in the film and is especially engaging with the Horrells (including the small boy he lifts and hugs), none of his relationships is characterized as deep or profound. Even the admirable tenderness of Billy's relationship with Maria does not cancel realities such as Billy's promiscuity and the fact there is no hint that Billy's affair with Maria is anything but a temporary dalliance. Billy's friendship with Alias has greater promise, but as Barry W. Sarchett notes, Alias remains largely "detached" and cannot really "help" Billy except when he kills the bounty hunter (178). Much as he admires Billy, as friend or as artistic subject, Alias is as impotent as Billy's other admirers, even his gang, against the dark forces Garrett represents and tragically comes to embody.

We have previously noted the many changes Peckinpah initiated to establish Billy's relationship with Maria as an overwhelming contrast to Garrett's unhappy marriage with Ida. Interestingly, this process involved reducing Maria's role as Peckinpah found it in Wurlitzer's original screenplay. In Wurlitzer, Maria is a relatively major character who appears in no fewer than 12 scenes and is often central in these scenes, all of which involve her tempestuous relationship with Billy. Wurlitzer's Maria is loud and profane (1973, 25), often whining and quarreling with Billy, who strikes her on one occasion (1973, 38), even as she strikes him (1973, 63). She is aggressively independent, a homeowner who lives with her family and repeatedly counsels Billy to leave before he is killed. At the end of the script, on the night Billy is killed, she is completely estranged from Billy, who has returned to Old Fort Sumner and again rejected her advice to leave (1973, 114, 124). Peckinpah dramatically reduces Maria's appearances in the film, so much so that Kitses claims she is "barely recognisable as Billy's girl after cuts" (2004, 237).[63] This seems a strange conclusion, for Peckinpah creates a character who is nothing but "Billy's girl," shorn of her house and family, her aggressive efforts to send Billy away, her willingness to quarrel and even fight with Billy. The woman who emerges from this reconstruction is in fact an entirely different character, altogether Peckinpah's creation.

Peckinpah's Maria recalls the prostitute with whom Pike Bishop sleeps at the end of *The Wild Bunch*, for Maria is also a striking, impressive figure who virtually never speaks in the film. (The prostitute never speaks; Maria has one line in which she tells Billy she will get him something to eat after they make love at the end.) Maria is not a prostitute, however, a point Peckinpah wanted to make by showing her standing — like Mrs. Garrett, with whom she is clearly to be compared — next to a frame-dominating string of blazing red *ristras* and cooking in the cantina as she gazes warily into the bar area where Garrett and Billy, himself framed by an inviting fireplace fire and a string of *ristras*, go to have their drink together at the beginning of the film.[64] Later, Maria brings breakfast plates to Billy and Luke as Billy and his men meet the bounty hunters at the corral, and Billy watches Maria as she returns to the kitchen, smiling at Billy before she disappears into the building. Billy again stares at Maria after Paco leaves and Billy and Alias finish their conversation about going to Mexico. In the next scene, as Billy prepares to ride out from Old Fort Sumner, Maria comes forward, tears in her eyes, to give Billy the richly significant St. Christopher's medal he will still be wearing the night Garrett kills him. In these brief moments, Peckinpah establishes Maria as a complete contrast to the campfollowers/prostitutes with whom Billy and his men sleep, as well as the prostitutes who entertain Garrett in Roswell. Very attractive but shy, seen almost always at a distance, Maria provides only food and the cherished medal until the film's final sequence.

As we have previously suggested, Maria participates at the end in the most sympathetically-depicted lovemaking in all of Peckinpah's films. Whereas the crucial scene with Pike Bishop and the young prostitute begins after they have made love, here Peckinpah patiently represents every stage of the final tryst, from the moment Billy and Maria meet at Pete Maxwell's house, to the scene in which Billy asks Pete if they can use one of his bedrooms (Maria dressed in white, like Mrs. Garrett, and poignantly wearing the same blouse and skirt she wears in the earlier cantina scene), to the unhurried scene in which they undress, then get into the ominously cold bed Pete has provided. Under the approving gaze of Gilbert Stuart's most famous painting of George Washington, they are warmed soon by a brilliantly hued patchwork Mexican quilt, its bright geometric reds, yellows, golds, and greens, mixed with delicate patterns of leaves and flowers, indicative of the Kid's connection to nature and his genuine passion for Maria. The several stages of their lovemaking are climaxed not so much by the orgasm they share, the Kid quietly intoning a sacramental and ultimately sacrificial "Jesus, Jesus," but their gestures after they finish, as they share last kisses while each tenderly touches the other's cheek and their arms symbolically cross. Billy and Maria display sincere affection and, to quote Stevens again, "a mutually shared sexuality, enjoyed for its own sake, as an expression of love" (276). Peckinpah's Maria, unlike Wurlitzer's, participates in this activity with none of the qualifications we would have to make in describing Billy's interactions with women elsewhere in the film. Maria becomes the occasion for demonstrating the best of Billy, the kind of man he is capable of being, ironically realized in the last moments of his life.

It may be objected that Maria has been reduced to a love object, always devoted and available, all too schematically unlike the hectoring Maria of Wurlitzer's script. To the extent it is valid, this criticism should be directed at Billy rather than Peckinpah, for Maria is precisely the sort of woman the narcissistic, "unbridled" Billy would be attracted to. Nor is Maria fairly characterized as a vacuous fantasy figure, for at the end she displays heartfelt grief when she alone comes rushing to Billy's fallen figure after the shooting and remains huddled in despair the next morning as Garrett prepares to make his exit from Old Fort Sumner. In the film's final moments Maria is allowed to display something like the wrenching grief we witnessed earlier with Mrs. Baker as, kneeling and weeping, she helplessly watches her husband die beside the Pecos River, much as the earlier shot in which we see Maria cooking at the cantina reminds us of Ida preparing her Sunday dinner for the ungrateful Pat Garrett. Indeed, Maria, Mrs. Baker, and Ida Garrett, significantly different in so many ways, constitute the film's remarkable depiction of three Hispanic women whose dignified humanity stands out in a world marked by masculine violence in every imaginable form. Younger than Ida and Mrs. Baker, Maria is less developed and perhaps less complex, but her genuine love for Billy, embodied in her gift of the St. Christopher's medal, her moving gesture of placing her hand on Billy's face as they kiss one last time after making love, and her uninhibited grief over Billy's body, elevates her to something like the lofty position of the older women among the film's more sympathetic characters.

Moreover, Maria participates in the film's concluding—and to some extent ironic—

suggestions of Billy's martyrdom. Peckinpah places the grieving Maria on the floor beneath the dead Billy's feet as he lies on a table which held the food-laden fiesta at the beginning of the film, as if his body has become a kind of Holy Host. Maria's presence beneath Billy's body is like that of her namesake, the Blessed Virgin Mary, who stood beneath the cross and then later beside the dead Christ as his recumbent body was prepared for entrance into the tomb chamber. While there are no nail holes in the Kid's feet, the searingly human image of those feet is remarkably similar to Andrea Mantegna's famous fifteenth-century painting "Lamentation over the Dead Christ" (1470–75), in which Christ's feet are graphically depicted while his aged, weeping mother stands over him as he lies on a slab of marble. Peckinpah's handling of Billy and Maria in these final scenes should remind us of Billy's transformation after he returns to Old Fort Sumner following Paco's death. Though he tells his men they will resist the forces of Chisum and Governor Wallace, Billy engages in no retaliatory actions and kills no one from this point to the end of the film. Resembling Christ at Gethsemane, Billy seems resigned to his fate and projects a maturity we also observe in his last encounter with Maria. The Christ-like suggestions which mark his final moments should not be taken too literally, but they do climax Billy's most sympathetic incarnation as the legendary Billy the Kid and therefore underline once more the horrific nature of Pat Garrett's mission.

Alias and Maria, Billy's friend and his lover, respectively, provide concrete evidence of Billy's capacity for human connections, his brutal existence and sometimes savage conduct notwithstanding. They are important figures in the film's pervasive contrast between Billy and Pat Garrett, for Garrett's Alias is a man he loathes and is eventually assassinated by and his Maria is an even more commanding companion he cannot embrace for reasons he knows make no "sense." Though we largely see Alias and Maria in their relations with Billy, they occasionally provide more direct insights into Garrett himself. Maria's loving gesture in placing her hand on Billy's face starkly contrasts with Garrett's empty, grasping hand captured in the freeze frame as Garrett falls from his buggy at the end of the epilogue, and this contrast should remind us of Ida's central complaint to Garrett: "You don't touch me. You are dead inside." Garrett cannot respond to Ida's obvious appeal, her heartfelt desire to *touch* as Billy and Maria touch. As Ida suggests, Garrett is dead to such gestures and the human possibilities embodied in the film by the Horrells, the Bakers, Billy and Maria, and Ida herself. And Alias helps focus attention on Garrett's acute problems in establishing his new identity in a scene Peckinpah added during production. After finishing his shave in the Lincoln saloon/barbershop, Garrett looks around and sees Alias for the first time. "Who're you?" Garrett asks. "That's a good question," Alias replies, a response befitting his curious non-name. Though he is no scribe, the philosophical Alias suggests here the difficulty but also the importance of knowing who one is, much as he will later advise Billy that he must understand who *he* is to decide whether he should go to Mexico or remain in Old Fort Sumner. Strangely, Garrett says nothing in response to an answer which is really a question implicitly thrown back at him. We can perhaps surmise that Garrett's failure to pursue Alias' identity tells us how evasive Garrett is about his own.

Alias is a free spirit who highlights by contrast the socially constrained Pat Garrett. In both Wurlitzer (1973, 26) and the November shooting script (1972, 31), Beaver names the young man Alias, but in the film Peckinpah has Alias name himself and insist on the name when challenged. Unlike Garrett, who knows he and Ida would be better off in Mexico but cannot bring himself to leave his accustomed world, Alias is prepared to redefine himself and his surroundings at will, as when he tells Billy, "I could live anywhere. Could leave anywhere too," lines Peckinpah added during production. As Sarchett notes, Alias wears a differently-colored hat with each appearance (178), as if playfully asserting the freedom and indeterminacy implicit in his name. Stevens thinks that Billy shares Alias' independence, that "Billy and Alias are totally self-defining, answering to no-one" (274), but it seems more accurate to say that Billy always asserts his freedom from the social and economic forces which weigh on Garrett but only sometimes achieves this rather rarefied state, as when stopping by the pond or chasing turkeys with Alias. In the end Billy, like Pat Garrett, cannot go off to Mexico, let alone "live anywhere." Billy contrasts with Garrett in many ways, but he too must deal with the questions of identity implicit in his famous question to Poe and Kip McKinney, "Quién es?" This question—"Who is it?" or, more broadly, "Who is there?"—lies at the heart of all great tragic actions and is explicitly announced in the first words of *Hamlet*, perhaps the most famous of tragedies. While the question is historically related to the Kid,[65] it is more directly associated in the film with Garrett, who, were he to look more deeply into the mirror of himself, would realize that the real crisis he faces is that of his own fractured identity.[66]

We should recall that Garrett does look into mirrors in this film. At the end, of course, he shoots a mirror with the image of himself and stares at the fragmented reflections of the several "Pat Garretts." Earlier, just before his shave and subsequent conversation with Alias, whose image first appears in the barber's mirror, Garrett walks toward that same filthy, lather-specked mirror and enters its frame within the film's frame. This creates a *mise-en-abyme* effect, wherein a smaller, mirrored visual image is imprinted on or contained within the larger visual image of the entire film frame, and serves as a kind of doubling commentary or interpretation, "a means by which a work turns back upon itself" as a "reflexion" within the larger action we are witnessing (Dallenbach 8). These striking effects should remind us of what distinguishes the conflicted Garrett from Billy in a more positive sense. While Billy is capable of transcendent moments within the natural world and human relationships Garrett will never attain, Garrett is aware of his own shortcomings as Billy seems never to be. Indeed, whether or not Garrett is "convulsed by conscience," Bradley's wonderful description of Macbeth, he is painfully aware of his failures and limitations, and acutely aware that for the most part they are self-inflicted. Garrett even feels the appeal of a natural world with which he can never be at one, as we first sense in a brief scene in which Garrett, riding toward Santa Fe and Governor Wallace, stops for the night and stares out over a picturesque valley as enthralling as anything Billy experiences.[67] Then again there is the famous frontier raft interlude, so reminiscent of George Caleb Bingham's eerily serene masterpiece *Fur Traders Descending the Missouri* (1845), a scene in which Garrett sits under a familiarly bifurcated tree beside a river, gazing in the early evening at the slow-moving water and perhaps witnessing the passing of a youthful world, a pastoral, elegiac experience of which Billy is incapable. The older, sadder, and decidedly more melancholy Pat Garrett has much more to regret than his younger friend, but it is precisely his self-awareness which qualifies him for a tragic part in Peckinpah's unprecedented version of the Billy the Kid story.

Garrett's self-awareness is nonetheless a problematic feature of Peckinpah's film, his often expressionless, enigmatic face reminding us of King Duncan's comment on the traitorous Thane of Cawdor, "There's no art / To find the mind's construction in the face" (*Macbeth* I.iv.12–13). As Len Engel remarks, Pat Garrett, the failed friend and husband, "seems not very satisfied with the new identity he has carved out for himself" and too often masks that identity beneath an impassive expression. But there are moments when "[Garrett's] face tells another story; it reveals his unhappiness and self-disgust" ("'Who Are You?' 'That's a Good Question': Shifting Identities in Sam Peckinpah's *Pat Garrett and Billy the Kid*," 203). Earlier, we contrasted Garrett with Pike Bishop because Garrett fails to acknowledge his mistakes and perpetuates them to the end of the film. For Garrett, we suggested, there is no redemptive self-knowledge, no "larger wisdom" required of the tragic protagonist by critics such as Robert Heilman. Yet Garrett's recognition of his guilt, often subtle and repressed, recurs throughout the film. Perhaps it is best to see Garrett's *anagnorisis* as occurring throughout the action, as early as his confrontation with Ida and as late as the moment he shoots at his reflection in a mirror, even as we acknowledge that Garrett's recognition is an incomplete form of Aristotle's famous concept, for Garrett represses the guilt he experiences periodically and continues on his wretched course of action as though, like Macbeth, he cannot allow his self-awareness to call into question the life to which he is committed. This means that Garrett is a unique figure among Peckinpah's tragic protagonists, much as Macbeth is unique among Shakespeare's. If one requires "personal dignity" on the part of one's tragic hero, as Arthur Miller does (6–7), or if one believes the tragic protagonist must meet his or her fate "with courage and dignity," as Peckinpah himself argued in his M.A. thesis (12), then of course Garrett cannot reside in the tragic pantheon and Macbeth himself is arguably unwelcome. But if one is willing to entertain as tragic the story of a man struggling to recast his life but making terrible choices as he does so and saddled more and more inalterably with the disastrous consequences of these choices, then Peckinpah's *Pat Garrett and Billy the Kid* falls firmly within the tragic tradition.

We would emphasize that this film is indeed Peckinpah's in every meaningful sense. If Peckinpah transformed *The Wild Bunch* by altering 50 percent of the dialogue, as Seydor estimates (1999, 76 n.20), and adding such characters or features as Crazy Lee (Bo Hopkins), the flashbacks, the scene in Angel's village (1999, 55), Don José (Chano Urueta) (1999, 57), the exit from Angel's village (1999, 58), and the display of Pancho Villa's forces (1999, 59), we would argue that he did even more to redesign *Pat Garrett and Billy the Kid*, as we see most clearly in the frame story, the early scenes which introduce Garrett and Billy the Kid, Garrett's confrontation with a reconceived Ida, the redefined Bakers, the revised raft scene, the recast Chisum, Billy and Maria, the prostitute scene, and the entire final sequence at Old Fort Sumner. Perhaps nothing points to Peckinpah's achievement here more than his handling of the film's major Hispanic women, for whereas Kitses argues that "[l]oyalty to women is not an issue" in the film (2004, 233), we think that Peckinpah brilliantly establishes that loyalty or disloyalty toward Ida, Mrs. Baker, and Maria is one of the touchstones by which his male characters are to be judged in a film which offers Peckinpah's most impressive treatment of women even as it embodies his greatest tragic action after *The Wild Bunch*.

IV

We would like to conclude this chapter by updating Paul Seydor's 1997 review of the several versions of *Pat Garrett and Billy the Kid* (298–306). Seydor suggests there are "three basic versions of *Pat Garrett*" (1997, 209), the so-called preview version Peckinpah assembled in early 1973 before being dismissed by James Aubrey, then president of MGM, the much shorter theatrical version released later that year by MGM, and the Turner Entertainment version first shown in 1988. In fact, however, the Turner is the first of the two preview versions, the one which did not include the crucial scene with Garrett and Ida, whereas the second preview version did include the scene with Ida even as it differed from the first preview in several other respects.[68] Prior to 2005, then, the three major versions of the film were the first preview (subsequently distributed by Turner), the second preview (never distributed), and the theatrical version released by MGM in 1973. Seydor's authoritative assessment, that of Peckinpah's foremost critic and a professional film editor, effectively presents the rationale for a fourth version of the film, Seydor's 2005 Special Edition, which restores all but two of the longer scenes deleted in the theatrical version but otherwise retains the more finely-cut theatrical version of scenes common to the preview and theatrical versions. Seydor's 2005 Special Edition does not pretend to represent the director's "final cut," for such a cut was never prepared in the first place, but rather to offer an augmented version of the theatrical release, one which restores the major scenes the theatrical editors would have retained if allowed to substitute a slightly longer version of Peckinpah's film. We believe that Seydor succeeds admirably in presenting the best version we now have of Peckinpah's second-best film.

The preview version of *Pat Garrett and Billy the Kid* was only made available in 1988, but it is the first of the major versions. Peckinpah and his editors prepared this 124-minute version of the film to be shown at the two previews Peckinpah's contract authorized before the studio could exercise control over the version to be released.[69] Seydor laments that the preview version "was never fine cut at all": "you cannot fine cut a feature film and you absolutely cannot fine cut a Peckinpah film, with its massive coverage and multiplicity of choices, in a month" (1997, 298). Of course, Peckinpah planned to fine cut his film over a period of many months after the previews, but he was never allowed to do so. Despite his reservations about the editing of the preview version, Seydor cites this version as "[t]he first, longest and best" of the versions prior to his own 2005 Special Edition (1997, 299), presumably because of the crucial scenes subsequently cut for the theatrical release: the frame story, the scene with Ida, the scene with Chisum, the scene with the five prostitutes at Roswell. Whatever Peckinpah thought of the theatrical version's more advanced editing, he was appalled at cuts which deleted altogether crucial characters such as Ida and Chisum, and Seydor agrees that, whatever its limitations, the preview version is truer to the story Peckinpah was trying to tell. Seydor restores most of the cut scenes in his 2005 Special Edition, though he does not restore the epilogue, for reasons we will discuss in a moment, and he leaves out as well the three-minute scene at Tuckerman's Hotel in which Poe beats up a miner to extract information about Billy's whereabouts and the much shorter scene in which Rupert curses Garrett for the mess he leaves at Roberta's. Seydor objects to the scene at Tuckerman's Hotel as "the only scene with neither of the title characters present" (1997, 271), but in fact the excised scene with Rupert is open to the same objection.

It is hard to defend the theatrical version of *Pat Garrett and Billy the Kid*, for the excised scenes with Ida and Chisum are absolutely crucial, the missing frame story and prostitute scene are, in our view, almost as important, and there is something horrifying about the story Garner Simmons tells of the studio wanting to restore "balance" to the script by cutting scenes involving Garrett in order to bolster Billy's role (183). Nor can it be mere coincidence that the theatrical version deletes numerous obscenities or off-color remarks, whether spoken by Ollinger, Gate, Lemuel, Rupert, or Peckinpah himself in his role as Will the coffinmaker. Nonetheless, we think Peckinpah's editors—Roger Spottiswoode and Bob Wolfe—deserve great credit for what they salvaged in the difficult negotiations which produced the theatrical version. (Garth Craven, the film's second editor, did not participate in the theatrical editing.) James Aubrey wanted the film reduced to 96 minutes but agreed to add 10 minutes in negotiation with Peckinpah's people, who worked on what did become a 106-minute release for two weeks, not the six months Peckinpah typically devoted to postproduction or the full year he gave to editing *The Wild Bunch* (Weddle 1994, 481).[70] Working with three studio editors, Spottiswoode and Wolfe managed to improve the film in many ways, fine cutting all the scenes, altering the sequence of events at a number of points to achieve greater coherence and maximum emotional effect, and saving the famous raft scene which Aubrey expressly forbade Peckinpah even to shoot (Seydor 1997, 261). In discussing Seydor's decision to edit an augmented theatrical version, we will have more to say about the ordering of several narrative sequences and the decision to move the raft scene from its late position in the preview version, two examples of the excellent work done by Peckinpah's editors.

If Seydor's "epilogue" to his 1997 chapter on *Pat Garrett and Billy the Kid* provides the essential rationale for his 2005 Special Edition, Seydor offers more of his thinking on the subject in the commentary to the DVD version of this edition. Seydor explains that he has used the theatrical version of scenes common to the preview and theatrical versions because it benefits from the additional hard work put in by Peckinpah's editors, the very people with whom Peckinpah would have continued to work in preparing the theatrical release. Seydor deviates from the theatrical version only when there is extremely good reason to do so, as when restoring the key scenes cut for the theatrical release, the prologue and the scenes involving Ida and Chisum, or replacing the hideous version of Paco's death imposed on the theatrical release by Gordon Carroll and others (see Seydor 1997, 271–72), or reluctantly including the prostitute scene from the preview version because everyone with whom Seydor spoke agreed that Peckinpah was inalterably set on retaining this scene. A key decision guiding Seydor's editorial practice was to avoid what he calls "internal editing," that is, combining elements from the preview and theatrical versions. He acknowledges doing a bit of such editing in splicing together the restored prologue and the shooting of the chickens in the first scene at Old Fort Sumner, a scene reduced by some 40 seconds. Otherwise, Seydor has not altered a scene chosen for inclusion in his Special Edition, though he acknowledges making very slight adjustments in the transitions from one scene to the next in this newly-constituted version of the film.

This means, in effect, that Seydor limited himself to one version of a scene or the other, declining to exercise his own judgment by combining elements from the two available scenes. The resulting version of the film represents the sequence of scenes Peckinpah wanted, or would have wanted upon further deliberation, arranged more cogently than is sometimes the case in the preview version, and edited more thoroughly than was often the case when Peckinpah left the project. Seydor offers this version as an augmented theatrical release rather than his own creation, a claim apparently confirmed by the inclusion of the prostitute scene despite Seydor's contempt for it. Before passing judgment on the 2005 Special Edition, we should look more closely at its strengths and a few of its weaknesses or inconsistencies.

One of the unrecognized strengths of the theatrical version (and the 2005 Special Edition which follows the theatrical version) is the altered sequence of events. Most discussions focus on the deleted scenes, but the editors of the theatrical version corrected a number of sequential problems in the preview version, problems which derive from the order of events in Wurlitzer's original screenplay and which Peckinpah had yet to address in light of his alterations in preproduction and production. The first prominent example is the sequence previously discussed, from Billy riding on the trail after escaping from Lincoln, to the magnificent scene at the pond, to Billy making his way through barbed wire as he goes back to Old Fort Sumner, and finally Billy's boorish behavior once he arrives at the fort. In the preview version, these scenes do not follow each other but rather are alternated with other material involving Garrett, the typical to-and-fro pattern between Billy's scenes and Garrett's scenes in Wurlitzer. The editors of the theatrical version had the good sense to bring the several Billy scenes together, thus maximizing the effect of what we have called Billy's descent from the transcendent moment at the pond, to the harsh realities suggested by the barbed wire, to Billy's all too untranscendent conduct at Old Fort Sumner.

A second important improvement in the narrative sequence comes much later. In the preview version, which again follows Wurlitzer, Garrett arrives in Roswell before Billy's return to Old Fort Sumner after Paco's death. Much of the Roswell material therefore precedes Billy's return: Garrett's conversation with Rupert and the prostitute scene. Poe's squeamish report to Garrett as the sheriff lies in bed with four of the prostitutes and Garrett's conversation with Kip McKinney follow Billy's return, but they occur the day after Garrett arrives in Roswell and Garrett, Poe, and McKinney immediately head toward Old Fort Sumner, so there is no more than two or three days for Billy to return to Old Fort Sumner, announce his intention to make a stand against Garrett, Chisum, and "the goddamned governor," take some target practice the next day, have a drink with Alias, and meet with Maria that night for their final tryst. The theatrical editors realized that Peckinpah wanted a very different effect here, one nicely captured in Seydor's account of Billy's return: "When Billy returns from his aborted flight to Mexico, Eno [Luke Askew], speaking for the whole gang, tells him, 'You just give the word, there's enough of us left'; and Billy replies, 'Nobody's running us off.' Our first impulse is to think, yes, now he will assume the burden of consciousness and act. Instead, he becomes more desultory and dilatory. He target shoots some tin cans as Alias and some kids applaud; and in one extended moment that seems to be about nothing but that perfectly captures the essence of his lethargic ambivalence, he has a drink with Alias as the gang looks on, just waiting, waiting, waiting" (1997, 290). To protect the plausibility of the effect Seydor describes so well, the theatrical editors altered the sequence of events so that Billy arrives back at Old Fort Sumner *before* Garrett reaches Roswell, thus permitting us to imagine that Billy's "desultory and dilatory" actions (or inaction) occur over a period of many days and not just one or two.

The placement of the raft scene is one of the most interesting features in each version of *Pat Garrett and Billy the Kid.* In the preview version, once again following Wurlitzer's original screenplay (1973, 86–88) and the November shooting script (1972, 79–80), the raft scene comes relatively late, after the shooting of Holly and the scene at Tuckerman's Hotel. As originally written, this scene is not incongruously placed, for Wurlitzer has Garrett camped by a small river, as in the film, but he has Garrett take off his clothes and wade into the river, then hastily retreat as he hears gunshots which prove to come from a raft which passes Garrett's position. A large family occupies the raft, led by "a huge red-bearded man" who is shooting at empty whiskey bottles tossed into the river ahead of the raft. Here Garrett tries to talk with the man, who continues to fire unsuccessfully at the latest bottle. Finally Garrett fires at the bottle, the man on the raft fires at Garrett, Garrett fires at the man ("His bullet strikes the side of the raft"), and only then do Garrett and the man watch each other until "the raft floats around a bend and out of sight." This version of the scene is all too consistent with the violent Pat Garrett on display throughout the scene at Lemuel's, but the scene Peckinpah shot is radically different, for Garrett does not wade into the river or retreat at the sound of shots, he sportively fires at the man's bottle in much the same spirit he shot at the chickens Billy and his men are trying to hit in the film's first scene, and when the man on the raft shoots at Garrett, Garrett raises his rifle to respond but does not do so, so both the man on the raft and Garrett hold their positions for a moment and then lower their guns as the raft passes on.

Peckinpah's raft scene is disastrously out of position in the preview version, for the playfulness and restraint Garrett shows here are completely at odds with the later Garrett who shoots Holly and will soon execute the Kid. Presumably recognizing the problem, the theatrical editors moved the scene forward to a position just after Billy leaves Old Fort Sumner for Mexico. This is a more defensible placement, for the raft scene now precedes the shooting of Holly. In the commentary to his 2005 Special Edition, Seydor argues that the raft scene should come earlier rather than later because it deals with Garrett's "character" but does not advance the action as all the later scenes are designed to do. Seydor does see that the raft scene must come after Sheriff Baker's death at Pecos, as it is a thematic echo of Baker's half-finished boat and dream of drifting out of the territory. Interestingly, Seydor moves the raft scene even closer to the Pecos episode than the theatrical editors did, for in the 2005 Special Edition the raft scene follows the death of Silva and precedes the scenes in which Billy says goodbye to the departing Paco and then leaves himself for Mexico. Seydor says that this departure from the theatrical ordering was inadvertent, but we must say that the "error" here is a splendid improvement, for the scene is now even closer to the Baker material and is introduced by a beautiful descending crane shot from the death of Silva to a magnificent stand of sun-spangled trees (reminiscent of the Kid by the pond), their shadows reflecting brilliantly in the river, with Garrett sitting calmly by a tree, a camp fire just behind him, gazing at the evening scene of the river. Indeed, Seydor says that this shot seemed so "right" to him, so consistent with Peckinpah's usual practice, he was surprised to learn that he and not Peckinpah had hit upon a positioning of the raft scene Peckinpah might well have arrived at if given the time to finish editing the film.[71]

The theatrical version offers a more coherent and affecting order of events, then, and Seydor's 2005 Special Edition benefits from following the theatrical sequence. Seydor's decision to adopt the theatrical version of common scenes is more debatable. The scenes in the theatrical version are almost always shorter than their counterparts in the preview version. Seydor argues that this is consistent with Peckinpah's common practice, which was to start with a great deal of footage and gradually reduce a scene to its most effective length (1997, 301). For Seydor, the theatrical version represents two weeks of additional editing in Peckinpah's style, even if Peckinpah was not present,[72] and one proof of its superiority is that it is significantly shorter even if one does not count the missing scenes. Indeed, whole scenes represent less than half of the deleted footage in the theatrical version. The excised scenes add up to almost 12 minutes of film time (including the scene with Ida), but the theatrical version adds two scenes not in the preview version, the new credits sequence (100 seconds) and the scene between Garrett and Ruthie Lee (80 seconds).[73] This means that almost 10 minutes of cuts were made from scenes left in the film but slightly or not so slightly reduced; many of the cuts were only a few seconds, but several scenes, such as Garrett and Billy in the cantina or Garrett encountering Will the coffinmaker, lost around a minute. It seems to be Seydor's position that the theatrical editors made a virtue of necessity, for as they worked toward the dictated length of 106 minutes they shortened virtually every surviving scene and therefore achieved the fine cut Seydor prefers in almost all scenes selected for his Special Edition.

We say that Seydor's preference for the shorter version of the common scenes is debatable because many viewers and critics, including David Weddle, prefer the preview version as a whole and many of its somewhat longer scenes. As Weddle explains in the commentary to the 2005 Special Edition, he and others prefer the more episodic qualities of the preview version, precisely the apparent digressions and colorful language pared away by the theatrical editors. Seydor acknowledges that "[o]ver the years the long version has acquired something of the same mystique as the European version of [*The Wild Bunch*]," but he believes this preference is "undeserved" for reasons he marshals very effectively (1997, 298). Nonetheless, Seydor's principal example of the theatrical version's superiority is the opening scene with Garrett and Billy in the cantina (1997, 300–301), yet Michael Bliss presents a strong case for the superiority of the preview version of this scene (1993, 229) and we ourselves think there are good arguments on both sides, as we will explain toward the end of this chapter.

Our own reservations about Seydor's Special Edition do not involve advancing the preview version over the theatrical version except in the obvious case of restoring most of the lifted scenes. We think Seydor has rightly retained the theatrical order of events while reinstating the crucial excised scenes. We agree with his decision not to restore the scene at Tuckerman's Hotel, as we share Seydor's confidence that Peckinpah would eventually have come to the same conclusion. Moreover, we agree that most of the common scenes are better in their theatrical version. We therefore think that the length of Seydor's Special Edition—115 minutes—is about right, falling almost precisely halfway between the 106 minutes of the theatrical version and the 124 minutes of the preview version. Our reservations involve occasional inconsistencies in Seydor's application of his editorial principles and our belief that Seydor's reluctance to indulge in "internal editing," though understandable, occasionally deprives him of opportunities to improve the film by combining elements from the preview and theatrical versions.

The inconsistencies in Seydor's editorial practice are few and should not be exaggerated. We think there are only three other scenes and one shot from the preview version which deserve to be included in a work such as Seydor's. The shot is of Maria cooking in the cantina Garrett and Billy retire to in the opening scene at Old Fort Sumner.[74] As we argued earlier, the preview version effectively establishes that Maria is not a prostitute and introduces her in the film prior to her first appearance in the theatrical version at the corral in Old Fort Sumner. This early shot occurs only in the preview version of the film and Seydor is committed to the theatrical version of common scenes, but he makes an exception elsewhere by including the preview shot of Garrett's great white house immediately after Billy tosses the destroyed shotgun he has used to shoot Ollinger at the deputy's dead body, the trajectory of the broken shotgun aimed not only at Ollinger but at the Garrett house. We think the shot of Maria cooking is at least as deserving of inclusion. A moment only slightly longer than this shot also deserves to be restored: the previously-mentioned scene which depicts Garrett gazing out over a magnificent mountain valley, then looking pensively, almost sadly, at his watch as he camps for the night on his way to Governor Wallace's mansion in Santa Fe. Without this brief interlude from the preview version, itself a conscious foreshadowing of the "fabulous melancholy" Governor Wallace associates with "rainy New Mexico evenings," we are left with only the opening seconds of the raft scene to suggest Garrett's attraction to the natural world; with this scene, Peckinpah is able to suggest and then reinforce Garrett's response to nature, limited as it may be and subordinated to the time-bound exigencies of his life-altering decision to pursue a different career and therefore a different life. That Governor Wallace's aide chides the time-obsessed Garrett, "You're late, Pat!" when he arrives at the mansion the following rainy evening indicates once again the fateful dialectic of evasion and pursuit which holds Garrett in its tragic grasp. Sooner or later Garrett must kill the Kid and destroy himself in the process.

The two major scenes from the preview version which deserve inclusion are the gunfight at Black Harris' cabin and the epilogue. Whatever one thinks of these scenes, it is well-known that Peckinpah wanted to use a version of the former which did not include Bob Dylan's lyrics to "Knockin' on Heaven's Door" and to conclude with the epilogue which completes the frame story. If Seydor includes the prostitute scene because he knows Peckinpah was adamant about retaining it, it seems that he should also have retained the preview version of Baker's death and the epilogue. We would grant that Peckinpah's views on the prostitute scene are better known and perhaps approach 100 percent certainty, but everything we know about the other two scenes suggests he was unlikely to change his mind about either no matter how many months he was given to fine cut the film.[75] Ironically, we agree with Seydor's major point for retaining Dylan's lyrics, for we also find the scene more affecting with the lyrics. But Jerry Fielding was absolutely opposed to the use of this song "where a guy is dying and the emotion speaks for itself" (Simmons 186), and in the commentary to the 2005 Special Edition Seydor acknowledges that Peckinpah supported Fielding, presumably the reason the preview version assembled by Peckinpah does not include Dylan's lyrics. It is easy to imagine Peckinpah reversing himself on the inclusion of the scene at Tuckerman's Hotel, but it is hard to imagine Peckinpah changing his mind about something Fielding felt so strongly about. Here both versions of the scene are very affecting, so Seydor's decision to go with what he found in the theatrical version does not harm the film and may even enhance its effect, but this decision does not seem consistent with the inclusion of the prostitute scene. We would also note that substituting the preview version of the scene at Black Harris' cabin would restore Black's final words, "Paris, France," which we have already cited as a significant moment in the film's depiction of Billy's legendary status. Black's final words achieve even greater resonance if we relate the martyred Kid's growing mythical stature to the St. Christopher's medal Maria placed around his neck as he headed for Mexico. When Garrett shoots him and the Kid falls to the floor, we behold in closeup the shining medal lying in full view around the Kid's neck, followed by a shot of the traumatized Pat Garrett. It seems that St. Christopher, the "patron saint of all travelers," will be sending the legendary Kid out into the world on his timeless journey long after Pat Garrett is dead and largely forgotten by history.

Seydor's decision to drop the epilogue is a more serious matter. We have no evidence that Peckinpah was of two minds about the epilogue except that he shot an alternative ending in which the frame freezes on Garrett riding away and a boy who has thrown rocks at Garrett and is now about to disappear from the right side of the frame. This ending rolls the credits over the image of Garrett disappearing into the desert, as Seydor put it in 1997 (302), and does not reprise the execution of Garrett in 1909. Seydor chose to use this alternative because he does not like the epilogue, which he attacks in the commentary to the 2005 Special Edition as flawed by its "direct repetitions" of the prologue. Even if one does not want to honor Peckinpah's commitment to the frame story, we disagree with the notion that the epilogue offers nothing but "repetitions" of the prologue. We also think that Peckinpah's original final scene merges perfectly with the epilogue, as Peckinpah films Garrett's departure from Old Fort Sumner in a signature long dissolve, the longest in the film, so that one of the domestic buildings, with its porch and hanging planter (and tellingly triangular ropes which support it), seems to enter the barren desert of 1909 and the place where Garrett is slain. This lingering, melancholy dissolve heightens the sense of Garrett's final departure from the human world, from the Kid, and even from Mrs. Garrett in the earlier scene at their house. This is the world Garrett will never know again.

The epilogue itself presents a somewhat different depiction of the shooting of Garrett which heightens our awareness of the now silent Garrett trapped in a triangular vise by his three assassins. It also establishes a much more direct connection between the Kid and Poe—whom we do not know in the prologue—through a brilliant flash cut in which we witness Poe aiming his gun and preparing to shoot Garrett just before Peckinpah dramatically cuts to the Kid 28 years earlier as he seemingly puts the final, fatal bullet into his old friend. We have seen the Kid do the same thing in the prologue montage, but that is quite different from his identity fusing with Poe's. Peckinpah edits the epilogue so that the Kid and Poe become the same person, a Freudian "substitution" of the Kid for Poe which acts as a subliminal, subjective representation of Garrett's guilt for killing the Kid and his unconscious wish to die at the hands of his old friend. The epilogue also offers a thematically significant focus on the wagon wheel which dominates the frame at the end, as Stevens notes (269), and the richly suggestive images of Garrett's hat at the bottom of the freeze frame completely divorced from Garrett and his disembodied right hand reaching up to something or someone it can no longer grasp. All things considered, the epilogue is a memorable addition to Wurlitzer's original script and its deletion is to be regretted.

The freeze frame of Garrett's hat perhaps requires further comment, for Seydor thinks the image is gratuitous if not frivolous. In fact, however, hats figure prominently throughout the film. Garrett wears a dark hat at all times, as if it is part of the respectable façade he adopts with his new position in Lincoln, and the permanent separation of Garrett from his hat at the end is quite telling. Garrett's one hat through the main action contrasts significantly with Alias' many colorful hats, a new one for every scene in which he appears, or the hat Garrett forces Alias to pull down over Lemuel's eyes before Garrett shoots Holly, or the metaphorical hat Sheriff Baker invokes when he says of Pecos, "This town's got no hat size no how." Garrett's conservative black hat *could* be the kind Baker has in mind, but Baker makes it clear he doesn't respect Garrett's new role and almost certainly doesn't think much of Garrett's hat, either, which has insufficient "size" to stick to Garrett as he falls past the Wheel of Fortune at the end.[76] For once, we think Seydor has not given sufficient weight to his own belief that Peckinpah's visual details almost always carry serious implications for character or theme.

Our suggestions for a bit more "internal editing" will be even more conservative, for we appreciate Seydor's position that once one begins to combine elements from the preview and theatrical versions the possible revisions are endless. Nonetheless, Seydor has exercised his good judgment in selecting which scenes to include, and we think a similar editorial judgment should at least occasionally permit internal editing which is to the film's advantage. We have two proposals to make, the first involving Seydor's principal example, Garrett's encounter with Billy in the cantina. In the theatrical version, this scene ends with Holly's question to Billy, "Why don't you kill him [Garrett]?" and Billy's reply, "Why? He's my friend." Seydor thinks the theatrical editors were right to delete the material which follows in the preview version: J. W. Bell's speech to the gang about "staying alive," Bell's careful exit from the cantina (unlike Garrett, he walks backward so as to avoid turning his back on Billy's men), Black Harris' remark, "Well, he sure ain't your friend no more," and Billy's response to Black, "I reckon."[77] We agree that in a broad sense all of the Bell material is expendable, though we think Bell's backward walk is amusing and believe that all of the amiable Bell's appearances contribute to his characterization and to the film as a whole, alleviating at times its relentless bleakness, until Bell is himself shot in the back by the Kid. But we also share Michael Bliss' conviction that Billy's reply to Black Harris alters our understanding of Billy, who "has accepted the fact that his friendship with Garrett is over" (1993, 229). Seydor responds by saying "we still have almost two hours in which the story will unfold, letting us decide for ourselves whether Garrett remains Billy's friend" (1997, 301), but this does not speak to Bliss' point, which is that the Billy of the preview version is under no illusions about the implications of Garrett's decision to become sheriff, while the Billy of the theatrical version seems stubbornly to resist these implications by asserting that Garrett is (still) his friend. The preview Billy is simply less "obtuse" than Seydor judges him to be all through the film.

It is interesting to discover that in the November shooting script Peckinpah's first version of this scene does not end on Billy's assertion that Garrett is his friend, but rather goes on to include a version of Black's comment and Billy's assent ("I reckon") that Garrett is no longer his friend (1972, 6). During production Peckinpah added the material involving J. W. Bell which accounts for most of the footage deleted by the theatrical editors. We would like to see the scene assembled as Peckinpah first wrote it, without the Bell material but concluding with Black's remark about Garrett and Billy's assent. We think this "new" version of the scene would be only a few seconds longer than the theatrical version and more faithful to Peckinpah's conception of Billy throughout the film.

Our second proposal involves the late scene in which Garrett talks with Will the coffinmaker. The theatrical version of this scene is very brief (30 seconds), as Will acknowledges Garrett, refuses Garrett's offer of a drink, contemptuously says, "So you've finally got it all figured out," and finally tells Garrett, "Go on, get it over with." The preview version is almost three times as long and includes a much expanded *mise-en-scène* as well as a motley collection of good and bad materials: several key shots of Will's surreal carpenter's shop, which includes a canted cross, rather like something out of a fogbound nocturnal graveyard in a Universal horror film of the 1930s; Garrett positioned suggestively next to a bifurcated tree which reminds us of the tree Billy passes through before arriving at the pond, or the tree Garrett crouches behind in the raft scene; Garrett standing beside the significantly broken wagon wheel which dominates the center of the film frame, like the symbolic Wheel of Fortune at the end of the epilogue; a slender diagonal rope which splits the frame as if to imply a kind of ontological separation between Garrett and Will/Sam Peckinpah; Will standing inside a canted triangular window frame, Peckinpah's acknowledgment of the tragic triangles which encase his protagonist and perhaps himself as well; Will staring at the coffin he is building and saying to Garrett, "You know what I'm gonna do? Put everything I own right here, and I'm gonna bury it in the ground. Then I'm gonna leave the territory," perhaps to head for Mexico as Garrett tells Ida they should do and Peckinpah actually did; and Will in a moment of execrable excess ranting at Garrett ("When you gonna learn you can't trust anybody, not even yourself, Garrett? You two-bit, chickenshit, badge-wearing sonofabitch!").

The theatrical editors chose not to discriminate the good from the bad in this remarkable scene, finally settling for the 30-second encounter Seydor has retained in his 2005 Special Edition. We think this scene cries out for further editing, to avoid the unhelpful brevity of the theatrical version and the embarrassing invective which mars the preview version. The *mise-en-scène* should be retained, with its carpenter's shop and cross, its bifurcated tree and wagon wheel, its rope and canted window frame. Will's speech about filling the child's (or k/Kid's) coffin with everything he owns and burying it before leaving the territory *must* be retained for its tantalizing hints of the Billy the Kid legend buried once and for all, as well as for its thematic ties to Sheriff Baker's unfinished boat and the drifting raft, a series of three variations on the theme of the desire to escape the territory which is not really a series without Will's speech. But the crude diatribe against Garrett should remain among the appropriately deleted excesses of the preview version. At something like 60 seconds rather than 30 or 90, this scene could be an extraordinary if somewhat self-conscious reminder of the tragic step Garrett is about to take, having figured out, in Will's cryptic assertion, that there can be no resolution to Garrett's dilemma except the brutal act Garrett must himself perform.[78]

We believe that the inclusion of the brief theatrical version of the scene with Will the coffinmaker is almost as unfortunate as omitting the epilogue. In addition to the losses just cited, the excised footage eliminates the eerie, fog-ridden suggestion, reinforced by Will's bizarre carpenter's shop and cross, that Garrett encounters here a supernatural figure rather like the spirit of Hamlet's father, a character famously thought to have been played by another Will, William Shakespeare. Sarchett suggests that Will resembles the comic Gravedigger in *Hamlet* (180), but the enigmatic ghost of Hamlet's father lectures Hamlet in a manner rather like Will's hectoring stance toward Garrett (and who is to say that Garrett himself doesn't ironically become more ghost than man after he kills the Kid?). Read in this way, the scene with Will may seem essentially unrealistic, but no more so than the scene with Billy at the pond and Garrett's several shadows as he walks through Old Fort Sumner, or the "miraculous" exit from Angel's village and Pike's late scene with the young prostitute in *The Wild Bunch*. Moreover, we should recall that Peckinpah is responsible for all the stranger details here, including the name of Will for Wurlitzer's nameless carpenter (1973, 121), for Peckinpah added the carpenter's shop and cross, the tree and wagon wheel, the fact that Will is making a child's coffin rather than a trunk and plans to bury this coffin rather than tie the trunk to a stage (Wurlitzer 1973, 121), and the tirade Will directs at Garrett. To accept the brief theatrical version of this scene, Peckinpah would have had to sanction not only the severe reduction of his own role, as Seydor notes, but the virtual elimination of a scene he expanded and transformed from its origins in Wurlitzer's original screenplay. We know that Peckinpah was capable of eliminating his own handiwork, but it seems far more likely that he would have reduced the scene along the lines we have suggested but retained its essential features.

We remarked at the beginning of this chapter that we would evaluate the major versions of *Pat Garrett and Billy the Kid* by how well they embody the film's tragic action, so we would like to close by offering our views on this subject. Seydor's Special Edition of 2005 is superior to its predecessors for the reasons previously cited: its adoption of the more finely-cut scenes from the theatrical version; its restoration of the more essential scenes cut from the preview version; its use of the superior order of events followed in the theatrical version; its magnificent technical advances in color and sound. It is impossible to overestimate the importance of the inclusion of Garrett's scene with Ida for the first time in an accessible edition, for we think most viewers will share David Thomson's view that "the long, bitter scene between Garrett and his wife" radically "changes my sense of the film (yet again)," a change which leads Thomson to conclude that *Pat Garrett and Billy the Kid* is "one of the great American films" (2002, 672). It should therefore surprise no one that we think Seydor's Special Edition maximizes the tragic potential of Peckinpah's story. The preview version includes all the scenes crucial to Pat Garrett's tragedy, but its greater attention to the minor characters and their eccentricities, obscene and otherwise, distracts us from Garrett's more central tragic trajectory. The theatrical version cuts away the preview version's excesses but eliminates a number of the scenes essential to Garrett's tragedy while effectively placing greater emphasis on Billy the Kid. Seydor's Special Edition restores the scenes crucial to Garrett's story while avoiding the distractions of the preview version. Our minor reservations notwithstanding, we think it offers something very like the film Peckinpah himself would have arrived at if allowed to see the project to completion.

Chapter Six

Bring Me the Head of Alfredo Garcia: The Revenger's Tragedy

> For what shall it profit a man, if he gain the whole world, and lose his own soul?
>
> —Mark 8: 36[1]

> I did *Alfredo Garcia*, and I did it exactly the way I wanted to. Good or bad, like it or not, that was my film.
>
> —Sam Peckinpah as quoted in Simmons (208)

> I think I can feel Sam Peckinpah's heart beating and head pounding in every frame in "Bring Me the Head of Alfredo Garcia"...
>
> —Roger Ebert (1)

> Fifty or a hundred years from now people will be looking back on [*Bring Me the Head of Alfredo Garcia*] the way we look back on Faulkner today.... People will look back on us and wonder how we failed to understand *Alfredo Garcia*.
>
> —Paul Seydor as quoted in Weddle (1994, 498)

We remarked earlier Peckinpah's distaste for the conventional Western, an aversion so deep he went so far as to deny he himself made Westerns: "I have never made a 'Western.' I have made a lot of films about men on horseback" (quoted in Schrader 25). Jim Kitses has rightly rejected this notion and those who would accept it,[2] arguing persuasively that "Peckinpah's indebtedness to the collective tradition of the Western is everywhere apparent" (2004, 246). While we agree with Kitses, we think he has not quite understood Peckinpah's point. Paul Schrader prefaces Peckinpah's claim to have never made a "Western" by saying Peckinpah "doesn't mind being labeled a 'Western director'" (25), a qualification which suggests that Peckinpah meant to distinguish *his* Western films from the conventional fare embodied in literally thousands of unremarkable Westerns. So Kitses is right to see Peckinpah as deeply indebted to the tradition of the Western, but Peckinpah (and critics such as Paul Seydor) are also right to see his Westerns as anything but conventional or formulaic.

This should help us understand Peckinpah's apparent rejection of the revenge Western, the most popular Western subgenre and therefore, for Peckinpah, indistinguishable from the conventional Western he disdained. For Peckinpah, we would suggest, the conventional "Western" was all too often a story of revenge. This association helps explain why Peckinpah denigrated several of the greatest revenge Westerns, John Ford's *The Searchers* (1956) and Budd Boetticher's Ranown Cycle (see Simmons 194, and Seydor 1997, 355), and never referred to Anthony Mann's Westerns in his many interviews. Peckinpah must have found these films all too reminiscent of the standard revenge Western, a film in which the hero, apparently dedicated to violent retaliation against enemies who have wronged him or his loved ones, at the last minute undergoes a conversion experience and forgoes revenge, usually for the love of a good woman. Peckinpah seems to have regarded the revenge Western as a classic example of the genre known as melodrama, a form in which disaster is anticipated throughout until it is averted at the conclusion, usually quite implausibly.

Peckinpah's reservations about the typical Western, especially the revenge Western, no doubt involved the form's many unrealistic features. But in some ways it was a more serious problem that the genre seemed to deny the opportunity to develop tragic plots. As we saw in reviewing even the best Westerns, Western directors have almost invariably turned away from the tragic possibilities inherent in their stories. Sheldon Sacks' theoretical distinctions may help us to set this historical trend in a formal context. Sacks notes that comic and tragic actions differ most significantly in creating diametrically opposed expectations about the fates of their principal characters, comic actions leading us to expect the best and tragic actions the worst for these characters (20–21). Sacks posits a third and rather popular option among represented actions, a form in which "the final stabilization of relationships may result either happily or unhappily for the characters with whom we are most in sympathy." These "serious actions," as Sacks calls them (22), differ from comic or tragic actions by developing their materials so as to permit a favorable *or* unfavorable outcome, either of which would be perceived as acceptably realistic. One of Sacks' favorite examples was *Great Expectations*, a novel which appeared at different times with quite different endings, one in which Pip ends up married with Estella and one in which Pip and Estella are estranged. Sacks noted that while he favored the "darker" ending, he thought Dickens had constructed his novel so that either conclusion was consistent with the narrative pattern and therefore acceptable. Almost all of the Western films discussed in Chapter One are "serious actions," as they neither anticipate a happy conclusion nor assure us that their protagonists are doomed. The best of these films offer bittersweet endings in which the hero survives but is embittered by what he has learned (as in *High Noon* [1952]), or separated from what he has come to love (as in *Shane* [1953]). Indeed, the best examples of this mixed form appealed even to Peckinpah, who praised *High Noon* and especially *Shane* as among the best Western films.

These excellent balancing acts are all too rare, however, and in any case Peckinpah could hardly fail to notice that Western directors, great and not so great, almost always opted for the happier conclusion, whether bittersweet (as in *High Noon* and *Shane*, or, if Peckinpah had noticed, Ford's *The Searchers* [1956]) or decidedly upbeat (as in the many Westerns of Anthony Mann and Budd Boetticher). One can search the entire roster of "serious" Westerns and come up with almost no examples of such films ending unhappily; our own search uncovered only Martin Ritt's *Hombre* (1967) and Robert Altman's *McCabe and Mrs. Miller* (1973). As we argue more extensively in Chapter One, the search for tragic Westerns (other than Peckinpah's) is almost as futile, perhaps identifying a handful of films: King Vidor's *Duel in the Sun* (1946), Mann's *Devil's Doorway* (1950), Henry King's *The Gunfighter* (1950), Arthur Penn's *The Left-Handed Gun* (1958), David Miller's *Lonely Are the Brave* (1962), and Sydney Pollack's *Jeremiah Johnson* (1972). Peckinpah wanted his work to be seen as entirely divorced from the conventional or standard Western, but he also came to see that his own films would have to depart from the practice of even the best Western directors if he was to embody his tragic vision in a tragic form.

Peckinpah's career suggests that he also felt the need to avoid the revenge Western if he was to achieve tragic effects. This explains why he resisted the conclusion to his first film, *The Deadly Companions* (1961), which ends with the protagonist renouncing vengeance in a manner Peckinpah found implausible but was forced to accept by his producer. It also suggests why

Peckinpah first altered the original script of his third feature film, *Major Dundee* (1965), to move in the direction of Melville's *Moby-Dick*, arguably the greatest revenge tragedy after *Hamlet*, but finally elected to dramatize instead the heroic vindication of his protagonist, as if he could not bring himself to develop the standard revenge formula in a tragic mode. Earlier, in *Ride the High Country* (1962), and thereafter, in *The Wild Bunch* (1969) and *Pat Garrett and Billy the Kid* (1973), Peckinpah developed very different tragic Westerns in which the revenge motif is discarded as part of the conventional formula he was determined to avoid. Indeed, *Pat Garrett and Billy the Kid* might be read as an anti-revenge Western, as the film traces its protagonist's fitful but ultimately "successful" efforts to track down a former friend rather than someone who has done him wrong.

When Peckinpah finally decided to make a revenge tragedy, then, he elected to combine the trappings of a modern Western with the dramatic practice of Elizabethan and Jacobean tragedy. In *Bring Me the Head of Alfredo Garcia* (1974), Peckinpah departs from his background in Westerns in at least two conspicuous ways even as he retains a number of Western features: (1) he makes his story contemporary, as noted in one of his early comments in the script: "Because it's today, baby, not 1880, and like it or not, exactly this kind of bullshit still exists" (6)[3]; (2) he structures his story as a revenge tragedy in the manner of Shakespeare and his contemporaries.[4] It seems to have taken several years for Peckinpah to hit upon the appropriate form for *Bring Me the Head of Alfredo Garcia*, for the idea Frank Kowalski first presented to him in 1969 included the basic premise of a wealthy tyrant promising a large bounty for the head of the man who has impregnated his youthful daughter but no real sense of what form this story would take. Kowalski stipulated that the film's protagonist would come to know that the soon-to-be father is already dead, but his "germ" for the film apparently left the nature of the narrative to follow undetermined (Simmons 187).

Gradually, over the next three years, Peckinpah came to imagine this bizarre tale as a modern revenge tragedy or "tragedy of blood" in the manner of Thomas Kyd's *The Spanish Tragedy* (ca. 1587), Shakespeare's *Hamlet* (1599–1601), and Thomas Middleton's *The Revenger's Tragedy* (1606–7),[5] plays he almost certainly knew from his drama studies at Fresno State College and the University of Southern California drama department (indeed, *Hamlet* was Peckinpah's favorite Shakespearean play). He eventually completed a script with Gordon Dawson which incorporates most of the relevant features of the major Elizabethan and Jacobean revenge tragedies. Some would question Peckinpah's commitment to this form because his script allows the protagonist, Bennie (Warren Oates), to escape at the end with his million-dollar haul intact, whereas the death of the revenger is "a virtually unbreakable rule in English Renaissance revenge plays" (Maus xxi). But Peckinpah seems always to have conceived of Bennie's fate as disastrous, his physical survival and new wealth notwithstanding, for the script concludes: "AND THE CAR CARRIES [Bennie] OFF DOWN THE HIGHWAY WITH ALL OF THE MARBLES BUT ONE — The only one that really mattered" (126). The "marble" which matters is Bennie's lover Elita (Isela Vega), now dead because of Bennie's sordid quest to turn Alfredo Garcia's head into a fresh start in life. Peckinpah eventually came to see there was no way Bennie could survive at the end and that he probably did not want to survive, so Peckinpah changed the script during production to conclude with Bennie's death (Simmons 205).

We think that *Bring Me the Head of Alfredo Garcia* is among the most disparaged of Peckinpah's films precisely because viewers and critics have misjudged its form. Though relatively realistic for a revenge tragedy, *Bring Me the Head of Alfredo Garcia* is formally and emotionally extreme, a highly stylized work in the manner of its English precursors. Its protagonist is an unimposing drifter, one of Northrop Frye's relatively inarticulate "low mimetic" heroes from the bottom rungs of the tragic ladder (1957, 39), whose claims on our attention and sympathy only emerge within the formal confines of a revenge action which is ultimately tragic. As we review the film's dramatic progression, we will therefore devote a good deal of space to the parallels with Elizabethan and Jacobean revenge tragedy which provide coherence and meaning to a film often derided as incoherent and meaningless. Like several previous critics, we will also pay proper attention to *Bring Me the Head of Alfredo Garcia* as a love story, Peckinpah's most impressive venture into this field, but always as the love story is crucial to the realization of this particular — and unique — tragic form in Peckinpah's canon. If Peckinpah made this film "exactly the way I wanted to," as he has said, it is incumbent upon us, his critics, to clarify what in fact he did, with special attention to the many ways Peckinpah the director improved upon the work of Peckinpah the scenarist to realize his most powerful film after *The Wild Bunch* and *Pat Garrett and Billy the Kid.*

I

> Sam Peckinpah is like a rough and powerful painter — the most powerful painter in motion pictures today.
>
> — Emilio Fernandez as quoted in Simmons (202)

> [*Bring Me the Head of Alfredo Garcia*] is about two things: it is about a love story, and it is about vengeance, a dish, as Machiavelli said, that is best served cold.
>
> — Sam Peckinpah as quoted in Bryson (144)

Bring Me the Head of Alfredo Garcia begins with a kind of prologue to the tragic action which follows, a prologue in which Peckinpah's painterly skills are even more in evidence than in the earlier examples we have discussed. Curiously, the film does not begin with the protagonist or his commitment to revenge, for Bennie's first appearance in the film is delayed for 10 minutes and his vengeful mission does not take shape until the last one-third of the film, in the aftermath of Elita's death. Most classical revenge tragedies begin immediately with the revenger's anger or assigned task, as with Vindice's first speeches in *The Revenger's Tragedy* or Hamlet's meeting with the ghost of his father at the beginning of *Hamlet.*[6] Peckinpah begins instead with another act of revenge, that of El Jefe (Emilio Fernandez), who cries for the head of Alfredo Garcia, the young man who has impregnated El Jefe's daughter Theresa (Janine Maldonado).[7]

First, however, the film opens with perhaps the most beautiful and yet disorienting scene in all of Peckinpah. We are introduced to a mother duck and two young ducklings moving slowly along a still, serenely lovely lake, watched from the bank by a young girl dressed in a flowing shift, a "simple yet ceremonial white" (Murphy and Jameson 44). In accordance with the nature of tragedy, particularly revenge tragedy, *Bring Me the Head of Alfredo Garcia* is obsessed with time and the nature of time, so it is fitting that the film begins with a sumptuous, paradisal scene we cannot place in time. When are the events we witness taking place? The eighteenth century, the nineteenth century of most filmed Westerns, or the twentieth century, as proves to be the case? The ambiguous historical moment of the film underscores Peckinpah's obsessive theme of conflicting spatio-temporal realms, the old and the new sparring with each other, and it is appropriate that for the first and last time in a Peckinpah film all events take place in Mexico, for Peckinpah the site in which these conflicting realms are most conspicuously in evidence.[8] As Paul Seydor has said, Mexico represents for Peckinpah a different time and place, the Old West of the past brought back to life: "Sam was always kind of obsessed with the presence of the past in the present. The distant past, the present past, and how it all kind of exists as one.... [In films such as *Bring Me the Head of Alfredo Garcia*] you kind of see history visualized as space."[9] The opening scene initiates a disruptive pattern of radically contrasting moods and tempos which will persist throughout the film, as its idyllic beauty, promising a kind of time out of time, a sacramental state of bliss, almost immediately proves to be an illusion, shattered by the violent savagery Peckinpah also associated with Mexico.

Peckinpah's handling of this first scene is extraordinary as he moves back and forth from the ducks and lake to El Jefe's pregnant daughter. The ducks move gracefully from screen right to left across the captivating water, one of those "momentarily Thoreauvian ponds" which in Peckinpah represent baptismal possibilities for new life (Murphy 1985, 74). By the slant of the sun it seems to be mid-afternoon, moving through slow dissolves to late afternoon, as the sunlight casts a luminous glow on Theresa, who is seen in medium closeup from the water, then filmed from behind, the lake and the water birds fully in view, and then again photographed at some distance from the water, as if from the water's point of view. This assertion is not entirely metaphorical, for the young girl's closeness to the water and her watery womb are crucial to our understanding of the film. Gaston Bachelard, who associates lakes with milk and birth in his *Water and Dreams* (1942), quotes the poet Paul Claudel's meditation on a walk beside a silent lake: "'...while you were wandering, something here was already looking on. The lake is a large tranquil eye. The lake takes all of the light and makes a world out of it. Through it, the world is already contemplated, already represented'" (28). For Peckinpah, the lake is like his own chosen "divinity," the movie camera. The lake "sees" and "represents," much as a camera sees and represents. This is borne out in another remarkable dissolve in which the girl is seen in a long shot from the water, then, as the shot begins to dissolve, her body is juxtaposed and seems to merge with two ducks swimming off to her left. Within the dissolve, and even more startling in freeze frame, she looks like a mermaid floating among the ducks and ducklings. Theresa, who can't be older than 16 or 17, is very pregnant, her legs and body lying against a fallen log, her bare feet moving rhythmically back and forth in the water (we think of Steve Judd [Joel McCrea] sacramentally soothing his weary feet in a California foothills stream in *Ride the High Country*). A rectangle of light, seemingly emanating from her body, analogous to a halo or penumbra of light surrounding a medieval painting of the Virgin Mary, extends out into the lake.

Remarkably, there are no ducks or lake in the Dawson/Peckinpah script for *Bring Me the Head of Alfredo Garcia*, so Peckinpah built up the entire scene during production, much as he devised the luminous pond scene in *Pat Garrett and Billy the Kid*. Moreover, just as the pond scene with Billy the Kid (Kris Kristofferson) is followed immediately by images and behavior which qualify if not deflate the film's most positive images concerning the Kid, so the lake scene in *Bring Me the Head of Alfredo Garcia* is undermined almost at once in two ways. First, the spectacular natural imagery is seriously qualified despite the serene and spiritual beauty of the pregnant young woman by the lake. In another of those mesmerizingly slow metaphorical dissolves which define and complicate his films, Peckinpah, at the very moment he dissolves from the mother duck and ducklings moving right to left across the screen, crosses their paths in a similar dissolve with another white duck moving left to right, as the camera continues to pan, in a separate shot, from right to left. What makes this moment so disturbing is that Peckinpah dissolves from the first shot to the second just as the camera is directly focused, fixed in the lower middle of the frame, on an ugly drainpipe, no doubt emanating from the stables and hacienda we have not yet seen. The polluting drainpipe, a human creation, completely violates the tranquil, pastoral beauty of the lake scene. We know that Peckinpah holds bodies of water sacred, in films as diverse as *Ride the High Country*, *Pat Garrett and Billy the Kid*, and *The Getaway* (1972), so for him to position the drainpipe so prominently is clearly to foreshadow troubles to come. As the very slow dissolve between the two shots unfolds, the drainpipe, really the previous shot where the camera stops panning, is fixed and unmoving, yet it appears to be gliding, serpent-like, into the next shot straight toward Theresa's legs, where it literally dissolves just as it arrives at her bare legs, right below her pregnant belly. The drainpipe, circular and ominous, a void-like hole half-filled now with murky dark water, seems to sully if not pollute this innocent moment by the lakeside. The moment is brief but menacing, especially disruptive when viewed in slow motion.

The lake scene's brief glimpse of paradise is broken a second time by the urgent calling of a servant girl to Theresa, informing her that her father wants her "ahorita" ("now") back at the hacienda. This second girl is very nervous, for she fears the worst for Theresa and doesn't want her to go. Almost immediately, in Peckinpah's signature overlapping sound, the loud ring of spurs heralds the arrival of two of El Jefe's henchmen who wear six-guns and are dressed like cowboys, as if we are still in the nineteenth century, the familiar world of the classic Western. These men accompany Theresa, who arises to the wonderfully serendipitous sight and sound of a duck off in the distance suddenly ascending into the air, its white wings spread out as if it were an aquatic angel, then sinking softly back into the water, suggesting that nature is helpless to shelter the frightened Theresa. She and the servant girl then join the two henchmen in their trek to El Jefe's hacienda, the four of them abreast, the men on the outside, the two girls on the inside. The two men are photographed from the hips down, emphasizing the equine power of their bodies, divorced from any personal or even humanizing element. As Peckinpah notes in the script, "The procession has a feeling of a death march — the only sound — spurred boots, bare feet and her slippers" (3). Throughout the film Peckinpah continually breaks his composition by showing parts— not wholes— of his characters' bodies, thus reinforcing the decapitation metaphor explicit in the film's title and suggesting a radical, modernist fragmentation of self, body and soul seemingly in pieces and controlled by faceless and impersonal forces.

These dark implications are reinforced in a brief episode just before Theresa is taken to her father. As she rises to go with her father's men, we witness a horseman pass by, followed by another vaquero pulling a newly-broken young horse by a rope, his rifle resting in its holster against a red horse blanket. Peckinpah cuts from the tethered horse, which barely enters the frame, to Theresa rising from the ground, no longer protected by the majestic, sword-like agave plants which surround her. The figurative connection between the young girl, completely under the control of her father, and the tethered horse with a rope around its neck, rather like a noose, is brilliantly established through the split-second editing of the scene, the quick cut from the tethered horse to the imminently "tethered," ultimately tortured young girl. (We would also note that Alfredo Garcia is later referred to as a "stud.")

As Theresa makes her way from the lake to her father's hacienda, we hear El Jefe in voice-over reading from an old Latin Bible, the Vulgate of St. Jerome, then see the man seated at his impressive antique desk in what has been called a chapel but which is more aptly described as a great room or hall without a gold altarpiece twenty feet square and other religious artifacts to be found in a private chapel next to El Jefe's great room, "the room for a man who likes to play God," as Peckinpah once said (quoted in Simmons 202).[10] Theresa's march to her father clearly echoes the more famous— and glorious— "death march" of the Wild Bunch to the central loggia as they confront General Mapache (the same Emilio Fernandez) who holds their tethered comrade Angel (Jaime Sanchez). It is a dramatically riveting scene, with aural and visual crosscutting between El Jefe reading and the march to his hall. As Theresa and the others climb the steps to the central hall and enter, we hear the sound of the giant wooden door slam shut, closing off the great room from the outside world. The sunlit lake, the ducks, the sheltering trees and agave plants now seem far away, the world inside the hall coldly formal and foreboding. El Jefe reads lines taken primarily from St. Jerome's Latin translation of Psalm

143, though some of his words are in Spanish. The reading is difficult to decipher, but words like *victoria* and *prosperidad*, which precede the quotation from Psalm 143, indicate the lines were not chosen for their Christian humility and meekness. Garner Simmons' account seems to suggest Peckinpah randomly chose the passage El Jefe reads (203), but the reading turns out to be highly relevant to the film. The psalm describes how a boy, David, confronts a giant, Goliath, and vanquishes him with "five smooth stones" before cutting off his head, an account which invokes decapitation and anticipates the David and Goliath–like confrontation between the nondescript Bennie and the seemingly omnipotent El Jefe. Moreover, when El Jefe breaks from Psalm 143 he offers a final blessing on the martyrdom of San Andreas Apostole, or St. Andrew the Apostle, brother of Peter and devout follower of the martyred John the Baptist, the most famous of beheaded saints.[11]

After the reading from the Vulgate, the scene in El Jefe's great room proceeds much as it appears in the shooting script. First, however, Peckinpah's camera pauses to take in a number of what look like ancestral portraits Peckinpah authorized on one of the walls (Simmons 202). The pause is longest on a large, apparently seventeenth-century portrait of a muscular Spanish nobleman and soldier-knight, his right hand on his hip, his left hand resting on the hilt of his sword, his ominously black helmet resting beside him, just as El Jefe uses the word *victoria* ("victory"), followed by *prosperidad* ("prosperity"), in verbal conjunction with the classic portrait of an heroic warrior. Then, in a startling move, Peckinpah pans rapidly to a second portrait which is nothing like the traditional Renaissance painting of the heroic knight, probably a conquistador. This second painting is a smaller canvas couched in shadowed darkness at the right side of the film frame, situated near two family portraits which also shared the frame in the first fixed shot of the Spanish nobleman. The second painting is not readily decipherable, but Peckinpah's formally disruptive whip pan, followed by the camera freezing on the painting, tells us that he wants to establish the analogy, no doubt ironic, between the triumphant portrait of a Spanish knight and the genuinely eccentric, even grotesque figure we now see before us. It is the portrait of a man dressed in a red cloak, his eyes shadowed in deep black, his hair long and black, with an angled triangular red hat. The subject resembles a cardinal of the church, though his cap is three-cornered and pointed at the top, like a Peruvian ceremonial cap. He is seated as if trapped in an ornate chair, his back half-turned away from us and his head cocked sideways as he gazes rather furtively, even fearfully, out at the viewer. The subject's head does not seem quite connected to his neck at the right place, a prescient omen for a film about decapitation. His cardinal's cloak, if that is what it is, is broken by dark folds, with a black oblong next to his left arm.

This painting seems to exist in broken, fragmented pieces, completely unlike that of the conquistador. It has some of the characteristics of post–Renaissance Mannerist paintings, works of art in which classical forms are stylized or grotesquely exaggerated into canted, tortured angles which militate against the classical, balanced perfection of the idealized forms embodied in High Renaissance art, typified by Raphael or Leonardo da Vinci. Mannerism derives its etymological meaning from the Latin *manus* or hand and focuses on "invention," that is, "a self-conscious stylization involving complexity, caprice, bizarre fantasy ... elegance, preciosity, and polish" (De la Croix and Tansey 631). Its principles seem very like those of *Bring Me the Head of Alfredo Garcia*, a film in which El Jefe utters the word *manus* as he reads from the Bible and hands are a recurring metaphor. Because of the way in which the cleric seems imprisoned in his imposing chair, however, another possibility presents itself. This may be a painting in the Christ at the Column tradition made famous by Caravaggio, Bramante, and Velázquez, among others, in which Jesus is depicted as tethered or anchored with ropes or chains to a sturdy column or stone structure, not unlike the clerical figure's ponderous chair, the night before he makes his agonizing journey to Golgotha bearing the heavy wooden cross.

If one steps back to study this portrait further, the most shocking revelation occurs. Seemingly embedded in the painting is the back and body of a nude woman, including her buttocks. This trick of the eye, a doubling of male and female anatomies, is a startling juxtaposition of the putatively sacred and profane, as well as a nod to many Ecce Homo paintings which depict Christ as both male and female, suffering for *all* of humanity. Stepping back even farther, one sees two reddish-white shapes seemingly poised in a twisted, arthritic fashion. Are they the manacled hands of some kind of Inquisition-style torture ritual? Is the cardinal really being tortured? We are reminded of "Portrait of a Cardinal" (ca. 1600), a famous painting by an artist who often worked in the Mannerist mode, El Greco, in which an archbishop, a Grand Inquisitor, gazes through dark, circular glasses (analogous to the dark circles surrounding the cardinal's eyes) at something to the right of the picture, one hand resting in feminine calm over the armrest, the other strangely clenched and gnarled, as if he is holding something in what one art critic calls "the compulsive gesture of the left hand."[12]

The woman embedded in the cardinal's garb seems especially relevant to Peckinpah's film, for if she herself is an object of torture, she anticipates Theresa's imminent ordeal with her father and later the nude, Pietà-like figure of Elita, Bennie's girlfriend, as she attempts to cleanse herself in a shower. Peckinpah seems to know exactly what he is about in placing this rich, troubling portrait in juxtaposition with the knight, a figure of absolute power and prominence, then cutting to the ghostly white face of yet another woman, Theresa's "magnificent, hieratic" mother (Murphy and Jameson 44), who is seated among a group of black-clad women who stand out amongst a large audience awaiting Theresa's arrival. This woman (identified as Carmen in the script) sits in a chair resembling the one in the second painting, her hands tensely clutching the chair's arms while another whitened hand, like that of El Greco's Grand Inquisitor, emerges in the film frame behind her. The feeling generated by the mother's face and the dark figures which surround her is pensive, fearful, ultimately terrified. El Jefe's great hall, stripped of all religious symbols except the Bible from which he reads, is really an "insulated mausoleum of old honors and customs" (Murphy and Jameson 44), part of a culture which clings to a long dead past and its ruthless, patriarchal ways. The mother is surrounded by a priest and two nuns in red who wait tensely. An old woman, perhaps Theresa's grandmother, stares off to the side fatalistically. As Theresa arrives, Peckinpah cuts to her mother in closeup, the woman's face filled with murderous rage against her husband, as if she knows what is about to occur.

El Jefe continues to read from the Latin Bible as Theresa and those who accompany her enter the great room of a man identified in the script as the "absolute ruler of a ranch larger than the state of Rhode Island" (4), whose power is boundless within his world and enforced by the gun (one of his bodyguards holds a rifle pointing forward and up as Theresa enters). Soon the daughter stands before her father, who begins to smoke a cigar as he finishes his lesson. El Jefe looks up at Theresa and asks in a seemingly kind voice, "Quién es el padre?" (a clear echo of Billy the Kid's crucial "Quién es?" at the end of *Pat Garrett and Billy the Kid*). Theresa stands in resolute silence, her "rounded, gravid form" (Murphy 1999, 2) an imposing challenge to her imperious father. El Jefe asks again, and she raises her chin even more defiantly. She is a powerful man's daughter, a figure of considerable strength, of moral and physical courage. But at El Jefe's subtle command his henchmen tear open her dress, exposing her breasts. Still she resists, refusing to cover herself, removing her arms from her torn dress and lifting her head proudly. She is proud of her pregnancy, her womanhood, and the man she loves. The scene is strangely sexual, with powerful Oedipal undertones, but the real point is that El Jefe, an absolute monarch, wants to control every aspect of his daughter's existence.

El Jefe will not again ask kindly who the father is. He gestures again to the two men who take Theresa's arms, bend her over, and begin to break her right arm. Angrily he cries out one more time, "Quién es el padre?" but still she resists. Peckinpah cuts to the mother, who has risen from her chair and cries out, "Noooooo!" just as the arm is about to break. The bone does crack, but Peckinpah, who "visibly winced, his eyes filling with tears" as the arm was broken (Simmons 204), eventually took the advice of Garth Craven, who had shot background aerial footage of the vegetation surrounding the hacienda, to shift to a long outside shot as the sound of the breaking bone is heard, thus placing this atrocity in the context of a nature so welcoming to Theresa as she lay beside the serene lake, like a nymph of pastoral myth.[13] Here, however, we see centered at the lower foreground of the frame, before the hacienda, the shape of a dead tree, its bent and twisted branches extending upward like a shattered hand, a Golgotha image traditionally related to the central "tree" on Calvary. At this point Theresa cries out the name of Alfredo Garcia as the father of her child.

In this extraordinary scene, so like *King Lear* in the struggle of wills between a brutal and all-powerful father who nonetheless appears to care about his daughter and a daughter whose feelings about her father are not clear, Theresa's public rebellion before her mother (who clearly hates her husband), her grandmother (who grimly accepts what happens because she has no doubt seen it before), and the other assembled guests represents an unacceptable assault on El Jefe's authority. He will not allow her to shame him before all of these people (even as he shames her). Doubtless he has been asking her to name the father for some time, and the others present may have witnessed such interrogations before. But once El Jefe finally learns who the father is and looks at his daughter's locket, a head shot of Alfredo Garcia brutally pulled off Theresa's neck by El Jefe's chief assistant, he suddenly becomes a more human figure deeply affected by the information he has tortured his daughter to obtain. "He was like a son to me," El Jefe says in English, a strangely convincing utterance Peckinpah added during production.

We now approach the essential elements of both Shakespearean and Greek tragedy. A father is willing to sacrifice his daughter's love and a "son's" life to retain his honor and power. This is horrifying, and Peckinpah makes us feel its Aeschylean magnitude, especially in the vengeful, Clytemnestra-like gaze his wife gives El Jefe after Theresa's arm is broken. Playing the role of the all-powerful generalissimo (he is wearing some kind of military uniform), El Jefe interprets Alfredo's act as a betrayal of Alfredo's friendship and loyalty toward him, and this leads to the shockingly severe sentence he pronounces on the young man when he offers a million dollars to the man who can "Bring me the head of Alfredo Garcia." As his anger builds, El Jefe snarls again in Spanish, "Traigala me," language so guttural and full of rage it seems to capture onomatopoetically the sudden transition to a twentieth-century world of roaring automobiles, motorcycles, and eventually airplanes as El Jefe's men are galvanized in mad pursuit of the fortune Alfredo Garcia's head represents.

The shots of El Jefe's men spilling out of his hacienda and filling the countryside in search of Alfredo Garcia conclude what we have called Peckinpah's prologue to the tragic tale to follow. With the rich additions Peckinpah provided during production, these opening 10 minutes constitute perhaps the most effective beginning to any of Peckinpah's films, rivaled only by the elaborate gunfight at the start of *The Wild Bunch* and the incisive depiction of Doc McCoy's (Steve McQueen's) life in prison in the opening scenes of *The Getaway*. At this point the action moves to Mexico City, where El Jefe's men have reason to believe they will find Alfredo. The most important of El Jefe's representatives are shown arriving at the luxurious Camino Real Hotel: Max (Helmut Dantine), the man who yanked Theresa's locket from her neck; Max's accountant Frank (Don Levy); Sappensly (Robert Webber) and Quill (Gig Young), two suave hoods who seem to have more than a passing interest in each other; and two Mexican bounty hunters, Chalo (Chalo Gonzalez) and Cueto (Jorge Russek), whose rumpled appearance contrasts with the elegant Sappensly and Quill but who will prove no less deadly. The most interesting moment in this scene involves Sappensly, whom we first see sitting beside an eight-year-old blonde girl holding a red carnation in an old horseless carriage next to the hotel's entrance. Peckinpah, famous for creating the lines, "We all dream of being a child again, even the worst of us. Perhaps the worst of us most of all" (*The Wild Bunch*), adopts here Robert Webber's suggestion that a little blonde girl should be the origin of his character (Simmons 199). As we soon learn, Sappensly is a cold-blooded contract killer, but his feelings for Quill, who is truly disturbed, probably psychotic, are loving and protective, as we will see in the scene in the Tlaquepaque bar where the killers meet Bennie and even more dramatically in the late scene in which Sappensly and Quill are killed. No matter how despicable a character is, and there is obviously something perverse about a hired killer cozying up to a little girl, all of Peckinpah's characters, even El Jefe, have moments of genuine humanity.

Peckinpah then provides a series of shots in which El Jefe's men canvas the hotels, bars, ranches, and haciendas of Mexico City looking for their prey. As Sappensly and Quill converse with a waitress in the dining room/bar of the Prado Hotel (formerly the Alameda Hotel), across the street from the Alameda Park, Mexico City's most famous public park, Quill shows the woman a photo of Alfredo Garcia that she does not recognize. We note that Sappensly and Quill take the chance to order drinks and Quill's martini glass contains a large magnified olive which disturbingly resembles a dead eye. Directly behind the two hired killers is a beautiful fountain, its waters bubbling up over a goblet-shaped fountainhead, always a positive sign in Peckinpah and especially in a film which begins with his most prolonged panegyric to water. Behind the fountain, ignored by Sappensly and Quill, is the great Diego Rivera's "A Dream of a Sunday Afternoon in Alameda Park" (1947–48), a superb mural of Mexico's past, present, and imagined future, with imagery of both hope and oppression running throughout the painting. Just over Sappensly's shoulder in the frame is a disturbing figure wearing a white death mask, a Calavera Catrina or "death beau." "Calavera" means skull (from Calvary, or Skull Hill, where Christ was crucified) and is doubtless meant to parallel the quest for the head, or skull, of Alfredo Garcia.

Calaveras are associated with the Dia de Los Muertos or "Day of the Dead" (All Souls'/ Saints' Day), two days following Halloween when the spirits of the dead walk the earth. We should recall that Bennie carries on a "spirited" conversation with the head, soon to be skull, of Alfredo throughout the last third of the film and constantly hears Elita's voice in his head after she is murdered. The Calavera Catrina is depicted with bright white feathers coming out of her head and a pale white leafy boa around her shoulders, its two ends a rattlesnake's head and tail. Not coincidentally, the Calavera is holding hands with the boy-like self-portrait of Diego Rivera, an indication that Sappensly and Quill, seemingly insuperable, will soon encounter death as well. This ghastly figure, its blank, empty eyes not unlike those of the tortured cardinal in El Jefe's mausoleum-like great room, is coupled with the painting's depiction of Rivera's third wife, the dark-eyed and dominating Frida Kahlo, herself a well-known Mexican artist, who stands just to Sappensly's left and holds in her hand a yin/yang ball, the ancient Chinese symbol of the positive balance of masculine and feminine forces in nature and in human existence. Together these two figures suggest how precariously *imbalanced* the lives of Sappensly and Quill really are.[14] This whole scene, from the fountain to the Rivera mural, is a compact treatise on the tragic theme of blindness and insight, one of Peckinpah's richest additions during production.[15]

We finally meet Peckinpah's protagonist after 10 minutes of film time, the longest such delay in his canon. Bennie, a rather lowly tourist-bar piano player, is played by Warren Oates, a longtime member of Peckinpah's traveling troop of actors (*Ride the High Country*, *Major Dundee*, *The Wild Bunch*). Although he starred in several films during his career, Oates was basically a character actor rather than an A-line star. Short and not particularly attractive, a killed-off "loser" in many of his films, he was the perfect antihero for this eccentric tragedy. Bennie works in the Tlaquepaque bar Sappensly and Quill walk into one day in search of information about Alfredo Garcia. Inside the saloon Bennie is serenading a gaggle of aging tourists who are about to leave the Tlaquepaque, in Bennie's cynical formulation, to take "your wooden hearts out and find the soul of Mexico." Bennie and his group are singing "Guantanamera," a song made popular in the late 1960s by the Sandpipers but composed originally by the great Cuban poet Jose Martí. This is what the tourists want to hear, not an indigenous Mexican song. Ironically, the mariachi music heard outside in the streets is quintessentially Mexican, and Tlaquepaque is an actual city in the province of Jalisco, famous for its mariachi bands. We sense at once that Bennie is solely in the business of making money and that the Martí song means nothing to him. Bennie is surrounded by tourist-trap photos and signs used merely for decoration, including weathered photos of Emiliano Zapata and Pancho Villa, and he has the words "Viva Zapata!" sewn into the arm of his leather jacket. It may be that Bennie plays "Guantanamera" halfheartedly (if that) with only his left hand, as if his right hand is truly his *right* hand, because he knows his existence in this setting is spurious. As it happens, imminent tragedy walks in the door with Sappensly and Quill, and eventually Bennie's existence will be deepened and his consciousness expanded to the dimensions of a tragic protagonist as this "common" man undergoes a terrible but illuminating transformation.

As Sappensly and Quill walk into the bar, Sappensly places his hand affectionately, protectively, over Quill's shoulder, while the mariachi music plays happily in the background and a red car passes by the camera, akin to the red car which came streaming out of El Jefe's hacienda as the engine of revenge was starting up and, more significantly, the battered red Impala convertible Bennie and Elita will drive in pursuit of Alfredo's infamous head. After the tourists leave, Sappensly and Quill continue to fill Bennie's tip jar, another circular empty space like the drainage pipe in El Jefe's lake, as they ask their questions about Alfredo Garcia. Two prostitutes approach and Sappensly hits the one who places her hand on his groin with his elbow, cracking her jaw (making much the same sound we heard when Theresa's arm was broken) and knocking her out. Shocking as this act is, we sense that Sappensly is really protecting his friend Quill, who is the object of the other prostitute's attentions and who might have done something even worse. Oddly enough, Bennie says nothing after the prostitute is struck and moves from the final notes of "Guantanamera" to a song which does mean something to him, one he plays with both hands, a classic 1940s melancholy love song, "I'll Remember April." When the urbane Quill asks, perhaps disingenuously, for the song's title ("What's that?"), Bennie mistakenly remembers the title as "I Remember April," thus placing its time in the past rather than in the future. Functioning marginally and unhappily from day to day, incapable of deep passion or feeling for anything or anyone (even his presumed "amor," Elita), Bennie thinks he has no real possibilities, so it is not difficult to see how he can only imagine himself happy in the past, or in an imaginary future (as when he will possess Alfredo's head), but takes no pleasure in the present moment, not even the love he comes to feel for Elita but will not wholly acknowledge — or accept as life-changing — until it is too late.

Unhappy in his present life, embarrassed when he tells Sappensly and Quill he has been in the Tlaquepaque for six years, Bennie is a rootless émigré who seems to live on memories of a long-distant past, when he used to play the piano in a high-toned club, "The Black Cat in TJ [Tijuana]," a "classy place" where Paulette Goddard walked in one night. But Sappensly and Quill don't care about The Black Cat or sentimental old songs. They care about catching and killing a "stud" named Alfredo Garcia and collecting a huge bounty for it. As Quill mentions Alfredo's name, we hear the sound of a car crashing in the distance, a crackup which many critics have seen as indicating subliminally the death of Alfredo Garcia (who has already died in a car crash), but which is also the tragic harbinger of another crackup, both physical and psychological, in which Bennie dies in a bullet-riddled car at the end of the film. Ultimately, Sappensly and Quill care only about each other. Bennie should catch on to how dangerous they are when he asks Quill his name. When the literate Quill cleverly responds, "Dobbs. Fred C. Dobbs," then requests slyly that Bennie play the now trite "Guantanamera" again, Bennie should know — but doesn't — that the doomed American prospector Fred C. Dobbs (Humphrey Bogart), in search of his own golden fleece in a favorite Peckinpah film, John Huston's *The Treasure of the Sierra Madre* (1947), is another prototypical "loser" like Bennie. As Mark Crispin Miller notes, it is Bennie, not Quill, who is the true subject of the Fred C. Dobbs allusion (9). Warren Oates in fact resembles Bogart, a little man kicked around by life who wants to escape his poverty, his sense of hopelessness, and who ends up dead from his quest to find a "way out."

Bennie and the other workers at his bar have denied any knowledge of Alfredo Garcia, but once Sappensly and Quill leave it becomes apparent they do know the young man. Bennie learns from one of the employees that "Al" was recently in town and that the person who would know about his visit is Elita, Bennie's own amor. This information leads Bennie to Elita's workplace, where he finds her serenading a small audience of one guest (or client) and several tuxedo-clad musicians in what seems a club like the one in Tijuana Bennie celebrated with Sappensly and Quill but which is probably an upscale brothel. As we first meet Elita her back is to the camera, much like Theresa as we first encounter her gazing at the lake's blue waters. The song Elita sings, and her friendly relations with her musicians, convey a strong sense of warm naturalness as she proffers what Kathleen Murphy and Richard T. Jameson nicely characterize as "a gift of love" (46). In a typical Peckinpah transvaluation of values, the brothel is suffused with Elita's capacity for love, both sensual and spiritual, for as the film as a whole makes clear, Elita unites the yin and yang polarities we first see in Frida Kahlo's hand in Diego Rivera's Alameda Garden mural. With Elita poised at the side of the frame, the room is dominated — and her song is complemented — by a very large bouquet of Renoiresque flowers, for this too is a "classy place" and Elita is close in spirit to Paulette Goddard, the true-hearted, waif-like companion of Charlie Chaplin's hero as they exit hand in hand at the end of *Modern Times* (1936). All of this seems lost on Bennie, however, who arrives enraged and vengeful toward both Elita and Alfredo Garcia for seeing each other behind his back. For the first but not the last time in this film, we are forced to consider Bennie's resemblance to El Jefe.

Angry and disheveled, Bennie confronts Elita and even threatens to strike her. Elita explains that she was indeed with Alfredo, a former lover who had come "to say goodbye," a "complicated" transaction which took the three days and nights she begged off from Bennie with a cold. That Alfredo comes to say goodbye suggests he knows he is sought by El Jefe's men and that his time is short, but Bennie's response is oblivious to such considerations: "If I get my hands on him, I'll kill him." Elsewhere Peckinpah designates hands, especially Elita's hands, as agents of love, but Bennie's hands promise nothing but future violence even as they perform such violence here, for as Gabrielle Murray notes, "Benny roughly grabs [Elita's] arm and drags her from the room, brutishly confronting her about her indiscretion" (115). Bennie may not be serious about killing Alfredo, but later he will say much the same thing to Paco (Kris Kristofferson), the biker who threatens to rape Elita, "I'm gonna kill you, you gringo sonofabitch," and soon thereafter he does kill Paco. With Paco and his biker friend John (Donnie Fritts), as well as the many men he kills later, Bennie reacts to violence against himself and Elita, but here "what smoulders inside him is jealousy of the dead man [Alfredo Garcia]" (Mark Crispin Miller 10). Bennie learns from Elita that Alfredo is indeed already dead, the victim of an accident after he drunkenly left Elita to return to his home in Saltillo, where, as Elita says, "his car refused the road and the rocks took him." Elita's moving, even poetic account should remind Bennie that Elita gave love and emotional comfort to a doomed man, much as she will try to do later for Bennie himself, but Bennie's only response is to mutter "Jesus Christ!" (to which the deeply religious Elita replies with a heartfelt "Amen") and quickly depart for the Camino Real Hotel, where El Jefe's people await word of Alfredo's whereabouts. As he leaves, Bennie is not thinking about Elita and her love for him, but only of the money he may be able to get from his knowledge of what has happened to Alfredo. Bennie is the true prostitute here, not Elita, and his kiss with Elita as he departs is a liar's kiss.

As Bennie enters the Camino Real Hotel to meet with Sappensly and Quill, the camera focuses on a mirrored image of the hotel's front desk which looks like an Antonioni-esque version of a surrealist painting. A couple in the mirror is talking outside the box-like structure of the desk, a hood is standing by the desk, another man dressed in a dark suit and sunglasses (like Bennie's) stands in the shadowy background, the clerk's bright red jacket recalls and anticipates the film's many uses of the color red, and no one seems to be communicating with anyone. Bennie enters the frame from the right, moving through the hotel's actual foyer and into the framed mirror image on the wall. As we have seen, Peckinpah uses mirrors in his films to convey a sense of distance between his characters and their deepest natures, a sort of analytical frame within a frame to take a closer look at who they think they are (their self-framings) and who they really are (Peckinpah's double framing of them). This occurs most memorably in *The Wild Bunch*, when Pike Bishop (William Holden) enters a woman's room after shooting Mapache, and in *Pat Garrett and Billy the Kid*, first in the saloon scene with Alias (Bob Dylan) just before Garrett (James Coburn) goes to see his wife Ida (Aurora Clavel) for the first and last time in the film, and again in Pete Maxwell's (Paul Fix's) bedroom when Garrett, having killed Billy the Kid, gazes in horror at his own image in a mirror before blowing it into shattered fragments. At this stage in *Bring Me the Head of Alfredo Garcia*, Bennie, wearing his ubiquitous dark glasses, sees nothing. He walks out of the larger frame, moving across the lounge area and into the disorienting mirrored space of the check-in desk, where we witness painted on the wall above him the dark silhouette of a human figure, a sort of anticipatory doubling of Bennie's own descent into darkness. Just before this we see Bennie as cinematically decapitated, the strange and disturbing image of his moving, seemingly disembodied head at the bottom of the frame, rather like the anamorphic skull which skitters menacingly across the bottom of the frame in Hans Holbein's seventeenth-century *memento mori* painting, "The Ambassadors." If Peckinpah is a rough and powerful painter, as Emilio Fernandez remarks above, the evidence is to be found everywhere in his films, even in his transitional scenes.

The surreal effect only intensifies as Bennie, accompanied by one of Max's hoods, arrives at an extraordinarily tacky penthouse in the hotel, with the strangest mix of globular and geodesic lampshades (usually circular, fake suns and moons) and garish red art mixed with the reproduction of a Picasso pen and ink of a bullfighter and a bull. The vapid sounds of Muzak in the background seem virtually inevitable. Max and his assistant Frank interrogate Bennie about what he knows of Alfredo Garcia, while Sappensly and Quill eye him whimsically. While being called a "loser" by Frank, Bennie manages to negotiate \$10,000 for bringing Alfredo's head to El Jefe's men, significantly more than the \$1,000 Quill originally offered and the \$5,000 Max first proposes, but a relatively paltry sum in relation to the El Jefe offer Bennie knows nothing about. In response to Frank's insult, Bennie replies, "Nobody loses all of the time," but Bennie's chances do not appear too good. Bennie lives for the quick fix, the tourist dollars, the "big" money Quill puts in his tip jar. When Max asks, "You're interested in money, aren't you, money you can spend?" we know all we need to know about Bennie's sense of impermanence, his immersion in chronological time, his plans for an ephemeral future he invokes by telling Elita the $10,000 will enable them both to escape from their current situations. Bennie seems not to comprehend he is about to make a pact with the devil. Bennie asks for a $5,000 advance, but Sappensly gives him only $200 and a warning that after four days they will be pursuing him as well as Alfredo. This does not seem to bother Bennie, as he knows Alfredo is already dead. He walks out of this sordid penthouse smiling to himself at his good fortune and proceeds to buy a machete for the grim task ahead of him. In reality he has sealed the fates of himself and Elita, as well as many others who will perish in their wake.

Bennie returns to the apartment he shares with Elita, who awakens him later that night in a playful, loving mood despite his treatment of her earlier. In the morning she continues to be sportively affectionate, though his ill temper continues as he snaps a towel at her bottom (recalling the nude woman embedded in the portrait of the cleric), orders her out of bed, and asks whether Alfredo gave her "good head" (a peculiar, even nasty query which fits all too well with the film's many references to physical heads). Finally, Bennie and Elita pack up for a journey to visit Alfredo's grave, the real purpose of which Bennie keeps from Elita. As they make their way to their run-down convertible, they pass through the heavily populated enclave or *barrio* in which they live. In his original conception of the story, Frank Kowalski said that Bennie lives "in some shithole apartment" (quoted in Weddle 1994, 493), but Gabrielle Murray captures the very different impression Peckinpah's *barrio* creates: "Although the enclave where they live appears impoverished, it is full of color, conversation, children playing, and festive music" (114). As Murray notes, there is such a strong sense of community that Chalo and Cueto, the bounty hunters Max has no doubt sent to shadow Bennie, find themselves participating in the *barrio*'s activities, Chalo eating and Cueto buying colored ice for the children (116), much as the Gorches (Ben Johnson, Warren Oates) play cat's cradle with a young senorita from Angel's village in *The Wild Bunch*. Significantly, there is nothing about the *barrio* in the Dawson/Peckinpah script, so Peckinpah created this scene during production, presumably to flesh out the communal setting in which Elita seems entirely at home and Bennie (impenetrable sunglasses and all) seems an alien intruder. We should recall Peckinpah's previously-quoted praise for the Mexicans: "In Mexico they don't worry so goddamn much about saving the human race or about the wheeling and dealing that's poisoning us. In Mexico they don't forget to kiss each other and water the flowers" (William Murray 192). At this point there can be no question who is wheeling and dealing and who is kissing and watering the flowers in Bennie and Elita's "family."

Almost miraculously, however, Elita begins to have a transformative effect on Bennie as they make their way out of Mexico City. Elita plays her guitar as they drive through the countryside and sings a new song, "Bennie's Song," named in honor of her lover. Bennie joins in as they seem to leave the tensions and intractable conditions of their life in the city behind them. Bennie has a gun he learned to use in the army; here he first fires in the air, then fires at turkeys congregated beside the highway, though he reassures Elita, "Hell, I wasn't tryin' to hit 'em, you know." Bennie's mood seems almost festive in Elita's presence, as we come more and more to appreciate that Elita is "the film's heart," as Murphy and Jameson put it (46), that she is "the center of potential, the source in the film of all that Peckinpah holds dear" (Mark Crispin Miller 10). This impression is strongly reinforced when Bennie and Elita stop to share a picnic lunch amidst a beautiful rolling green field and bright green trees. This is a crucial moment in the film, one which almost marks a turning point toward something more positive and enduring for Bennie and Elita. As Elita lies in Bennie's arms, in a series of shots somewhat jagged in composition, but not clumsy and amateurish as Pauline Kael would have us believe (71), the camera indicates just how fragile and tenuous, how ultimately breakable, their love is. Here again Elita's sense of temporality is distinguished from Bennie's sense of time as always ongoing, strictly chronological and quantifiable, "time as the future passing through the present and so becoming the past" (Reardon 1), or, in a well-known phrase, time as "one damn thing after another" (Kermode 1968, 46). For Elita, who is first seen sitting, singing, *composing*, as if trying to capture felt life in a different medium, time means something radically different. It embodies a quest for what the ancient Greeks and the Christian church call *kairos*, a kind of permanent or spiritual time which is the *right* time, or time out of time, a form of being or "presence" which is closely aligned with her emotions as she attempts to create through her love a vision of paradise, embodied here as a roadside epiphany equivalent to the paradoxically all-too-brief timeless moment of Theresa by the lake.

The idea of the perfect moment of time in space, a biblical and Greek concept, corresponds with our earlier Nietzschean reading of that moment of bliss Mr. Thompson (Jason Robards) and Mr. Helton (Per Oscarsson) share in Peckinpah's *Noon Wine* (1966), the sacred moment of the perfect noon. Elita lives this principle in her everyday life, but Bennie unwittingly takes it away from her. Even here, as they sit beneath a tree, restless Bennie talks about all the different places he would like to go once he has money, but Elita, who seems to have traveled throughout Mexico, doesn't care where they go as long as they are together. Wherever she is, the world converges into a seamless oneness. But Bennie, who has "never been any place I'd want to go back to," propels himself into an impossible future he conjures out of taking Alfredo's head; he is driven to find "the golden fleece," the rather modest fortune he believes will free them both from their tawdry occupations. "This *time* I'm moving up" (our emphasis), Bennie says, tactfully concealing from Elita the means he will employ to achieve this end. Elita replies, "Ah, moving up. The most important, at least to me, is that we're together, Bennie. We're together." Elita is not trying to get anywhere, nor is she driven by the desire for money, place, or prominence in society. The whole world is happening for her in the now, as past, present, and future fuse into the moveable feast which is her life. When Bennie tells her that Alfredo would want them to be happy with the money, Elita's response is important: "It's good knowing what you want, Bennie. It so happens I don't know what I want. You see, we women have so many different ways." Elita is saying that money, money they can "spend," in Max's formulation, may have some importance, but it is not her goal in life. Many things can give her pleasure and define a life, and she has discovered a number of them on this trip: their singing, their drinking, their picnic under a whitewashed tree.

Another "way" for Elita would be marriage, something Bennie has never discussed with her. As the scene beneath the tree concludes, Elita asks Bennie if he has ever considered marrying her. He responds, "Yes, I have." She begins weeping and asks why he has never asked her. His weak response, "I don't know, but I do now," leads her to say, "Ask me again. Ask me." Bennie replies, "Will you marry me?" As she weeps and he looks at her, the camera cuts to a long shot of the two of them beneath the tree. It is an immensely poignant moment, perhaps the most intimate moment between a man and woman in all of Peckinpah's films, capturing as it does "the painful awkwardness of these two desperate losers playing at hopefulness and decency" (Mark Crispin Miller 11). The camera movements establish a greater and greater stabilization of the scene, for its composition seems less broken up as Bennie and Elita move closer and closer to each other in their joint love and her tears/his tears unite them. But it is not quite right to say, "It is in this scene that Benny tells [Elita] that he loves her" (Mark Crispin Miller 11), for as Gabrielle Murray points out, "it is not until the shower scene that Benny tells Elita he loves her" (150, n.25). Bennie promises Elita that he will marry her in a church on Sunday, as she requests, but he does not declare that he loves her, nor does he seem prepared to give up his brutal, even gruesome quest for Alfredo's head. Moving as this scene undoubtedly is, its true value is that it captures for the first time Bennie's irreconcilable commitments to Elita and his quest for the golden fleece. In this crucial sense it is a pivotal moment in the tragic action.

Moreover, the picnic scene is marred by tragic omens. Chalo and Cueto are following Bennie and Elita into the Mexican countryside, and just before the hoodlums come upon the picnic, their car pulls out of a dusty place beside the road, kicks up huge clouds of dust, then heads off down the road after Bennie and Elita. The screen then turns from green to gray and a beautiful plot of trees in the distance becomes ghostly pale, white and gray, as the scene dissolves into the picnic setting where Bennie and Elita sit under the tree by the road. The ghostly trees and the dust from the car seem like emissaries from the world of the dead come to destroy this brief idyll, especially as dust throughout the film is associated with a dry season, the very antithesis of vibrant springtime (the film takes place in April), more like autumn, the season of death and tragedy. As Chalo and Cueto drive past the two lovers, gazing at them as they sit, we realize there is apparently no escaping time and Bennie's desire to cut off Alfredo's head to win his grisly reward. Eventually, it is Chalo and Cueto who will kill Elita and beat Bennie nearly to death in the graveyard where Alfredo is buried. In retrospect, the picnic scene will seem a beautiful but fanciful dream.

The picnic scene is perhaps the best example of Peckinpah's ability to transform the materials of his script during production. In the script, Bennie and Elita stop at a "roadside rest" and sit together on a stone bench (33), not under a tree amidst the green field and the intensely green trees. Elita has already asked Bennie if he will marry her *before* they begin the picnic (31), so of course the subsequent scene does not lead up to her question as to why Bennie has never asked her to marry him and references to the marriage are hardly solemn, let alone poignant. "And we marry someday in the church?" Elita asks. "Yeah — in the church we marry someday," Bennie replies. "Bullshit, Bennie!" Elita responds, then goes on to ask if they can name their first baby Alfredo (35). The Elita of Peckinpah's film is playful but not so obtuse as she is made to seem in the script, and Bennie, for all his crudeness, is hardly so callous as to acknowledge at this point his intention to sever Alfredo's head, as he in fact does in the script (37). In the film, Bennie only reveals his awful intention well after the picnic scene, as Bennie and Elita flee after Bennie shoots the bikers Paco and John. Peckinpah seems to have reconstructed the picnic scene before production began, for the first takes place Bennie and Elita under the tree, there are no comic references to the impending marriage, and the scene was designed to climax with Elita's query as to why Bennie has never asked her to marry him and Bennie's awkward reply that he doesn't know why (Simmons 197). Kris Kristofferson has explained that the additional dialogue in which Elita urges Bennie to ask her now was improvised by the remarkable Isela Vega as the scene was first shot, with Warren Oates' reply improvised in response (Simmons 197). Peckinpah not only retained this footage as the deeply-affecting conclusion to the scene, he also took the hint of Isela Vega's transformed version of Elita to change the subsequent encounter between Elita and Paco from a rape scene to one in which, in Kristofferson's words, "He took all the macho outa it" (quoted in Simmons 198).

The so-called rape scene follows the picnic and destroys any illusions that their impending marriage will turn things around for Bennie and Elita. Bennie's car blows a tire, so he and Elita stop for the night in open countryside. As evening arrives they are visited by Paco and John, two bikers who look like refugees from *Easy Rider*. In the script Paco picks up Elita's guitar and sings an unnamed song "beautifully" (41), no doubt an opportunity for the musical Kristofferson to perform, but in the film it is Elita who sings the love song "Cielito Lindo" ("Beautiful Heavens"), entirely appropriate for the peaceful night beneath the stars Bennie and Elita have planned but painfully ironic given the bikers' intentions. In the script Paco holds a gun on Bennie while John takes Elita back "beneath the nearby trees" (42), but in the film John holds the gun and Paco leads Elita back among the surrounding grasses and volcanic rocks (recalling the rocks which "took" Alfredo). As they begin to leave, Bennie snarls at Paco, "I'm gonna kill you, you gringo sonofabitch," but Elita cautions him: "No, you won't, Bennie. I've been here before and you don't know the way." Earlier, Bennie has told Max and his men that in pursuit of Alfredo's head he will "go all the way or pass," but his way is not Elita's. Earlier as well, when Bennie obsessively declares his goal of getting the $10,000, Elita replies, "we women have so many different ways." Elita's "way" may seem to refer to her experience as a prostitute, but more generally she seems to mean by "way" or "ways" that no single life has any one direction, that one must partake in life by being present to it as it unfolds. As Murphy and Jameson remark, "The way, in this case, is oddly ceremonial" (47), ceremonial in the religious sense of enacting an ancient ritual of redemption, even salvation, as Elita eventually offers Paco something he has probably never known before, love which is freely given. The confrontation between Elita and Paco which follows is a difficult one, perhaps as controversial as anything in Peckinpah, but we think an adequate reading should emphasize what Elita means by her "way" or "ways."

Elita's reference to "the way" is very close to the spirit of Taoism, something the director of *Straw Dogs* (1971) knew very well. It was Peckinpah himself who changed the title of Gordon M. Williams' source novel *The Siege of Trencher's Farm* (1969) to *Straw Dogs*, based on a quotation attributed to the Chinese philosopher Lao-tse: "Heaven and earth are ruthless and treat the myriad creatures as straw dogs; the sage is ruthless and treats the people like straw dogs" (Simmons 124–25). Straw dogs are sacrificial "creatures" burned in order to appease the sages of Taoism, who see themselves as opposed to obsessive directionalism and who define the "way" of Tao (which means "Way") (Chan 136). Taoism also means "the One" as well as that which is "natural, eternal, spontaneous, nameless, and indescribable. It is at once the beginning of all things and the way in which all things pursue their course." It seeks "to regard the fundamental as the essence, to regard things as coarse, to regard accumulation as deficiency, and to dwell quietly alone with the spiritual and the intelligent" (Chan 137). Taoism is a philosophy of nature and revolves around the idea of "'taking no action that is contrary to Nature'—in other words, letting Nature take its own course" (Chan 136).

We don't mean to suggest that Elita is a Taoist. A devout Christian, she would doubtless be far more familiar with Jesus' well-known words in John 14: 6: "I am the *way*, the truth, and the life; no man cometh unto the Father, but by me" (our emphasis). Nevertheless, the repeated use of the word "way" at crucial moments in this film (almost all added during production) suggests that Peckinpah is manipulating the word in a complex fashion.[16] He places the events of Bennie's initial undoing at the Camino Real Hotel, and while "camino" usually means "road," another meaning is "way." We should perhaps recall that the famous Mexican highway from the nineteenth century, "El Camino Real," the Royal Road or Royal Way, led up into California near the Pacific coast, not too far from Peckinpah's inland childhood home of Fresno, which Bennie mildly derides later in the film. In the final scene of *Straw Dogs*, after a protracted siege of savage violence, Henry Niles (David Warner) tells David Sumner (Dustin Hoffman), the formerly willful and intellectually arrogant husband of an equally troubling wife, Amy (Susan George), "I don't know my way home," and the chastened and humbled David replies, "That's okay. I don't either." The sense we derive from this scene is that David, moving in his automobile through darkness and a thick, sea-borne mist, now knows how liberating it is *not* to know and to let the forces of nature, of the world and human feeling, move through him and guide him to a dramatically different conception of "home." Elita doesn't know what she wants, unlike Bennie, but she does know the "way" to proceed, as David Sumner is beginning to learn as well, with an openness to alternatives Elita celebrates ("we women have so many different ways") and Peckinpah captures in his portrait of Elita throughout the film but never so provocatively as in Elita's confrontation with Paco.

In the Dawson/Peckinpah script we do not see Elita with her potential rapist (John instead of Paco) until Bennie breaks free and rushes to discover a screaming Elita in the grasp of her attacker, who has "a fistfull [*sic*] of her hair" in one hand and a knife in the other (44). In the film Peckinpah follows Elita and Paco as he leads her into ancient high grasses to rape her. Paco has a large knife and begins to cut up her sweater, exposing her breasts, obviously expecting her to submit meekly. Instead, as Gabrielle Murray remarks (119), she emulates the proud, resistant Theresa by slapping Paco twice, in essence putting him in his place.[17] Paco is surprised and slaps her back, but then, seemingly chagrined and defeated by her superior will, he retreats deeper into the waving grasses and dark volcanic rocks, where he sits and holds a delicate blade of grass. Elita goes to him in what can be perceived as a strategic concession to Paco, "forcing a sexual encounter on her own terms to prevent Paco from taking out his frustration on Bennie" (Simmons 198), but Elita's advances also seem an act of grace, of forgiveness, as if she would liberate him from his own crude and rapacious nature, his ultra-machismo. She goes to Paco and says, "Please don't... Please."[18] He touches the strands of her hair ever so gently, while she offers her love as she did to Alfredo and Bennie. There is nothing acquisitive or controlling about it. Paco responds to her gesture as befits someone who wears on his jacket a cross and the ancient symbol of the yin and yang, the same symbol held as a ball in Frida Kahlo's hand in Diego Rivera's Alameda Park mural. While many "hippies" of the 1960s and 1970s adorned their clothes with this symbol, it takes on deeper meaning here as Elita's form of "free love" perhaps introduces Paco to a sense of himself he did not know existed. As the association with Frida Kahlo suggests, Elita knows her way "home" because she embodies the concept and takes it with her wherever she goes.

Ironically, even though Bennie loves Elita, this scene ends any chance that he will be able to turn away from the direction in which he is headed. Bennie escapes from John, grabs his own gun, and runs off to rescue Elita from Paco. Unlike the Bennie of the script, who catches John in the act of raping and apparently preparing to kill Elita, the Bennie of Peckinpah's film comes upon Elita and Paco preparing to make love, lying together and kissing amidst the ancient grasses and stones. "Hey, you're dead," Bennie calls out just before he shoots Paco twice, then shoots the trailing John, killing them both. The best critics of *Bring Me the Head of Alfredo Garcia* have absolved Peckinpah of the apparent artistic crime of creating "a peculiar sense of complicity between rapist and victim" (Murphy and Jameson 46), recognizing that "*this* rape is eerily transmuted into an act of love—'love' being understood here as the distillation of human relatedness, of corporeal and spiritual connection" (Murphy and Jameson 46), that "[t]he rape has transformed into a scene of erotic fecundity and shared sensuality" (Gabrielle Murray 119) or what we have called an act of loving grace. Oddly, however, none of Peckinpah's critics save Garner Simmons has noted Bennie's great crime at this point.[19] Simmons remarks that "in killing Paco and his partner, Bennie is not rescuing Elita but *himself*" (198), a point we would take even further. Peckinpah's best critics seem to respond to Bennie's actions at this point in the film as if they were watching the Bennie of the script who acts to protect Elita and avenge the violence against her, a Bennie Elita is said to "worship" in the aftermath of her rescue and whom she explicitly defends: "You did what you had to do" (45). In the script Bennie's defense of Elita even seems to mark moral growth, for we are told, "He's beginning to change" (45). Elita's reaction in the film is far less enthusiastic, as she assures Bennie she will not be a problem with the authorities: "You did all right. I will tell the police." We think Elita is being very kind here and that Bennie's vengeful act against Paco should be seen as realizing his hateful threat against Alfredo. Indeed, we think the climax to the scene with the bikers is the film's tragic turning point.

Peckinpah's better critics would not agree with our identification of the film's turning point, tragic or otherwise. Murphy and Jameson tell of Peckinpah asking an admirer, "Where does the film turn around?" (47). They do not record Peckinpah's answer to his own question, but they immediately identify the moment Bennie is struck by a shovel at Alfredo's gravesite as the obvious answer (47–48). Earlier, Mark Crispin Miller argues that Elita's death "is the film's turning-point, its structural center and moral climax" (12), and later Gabrielle Murray confirms that "Elita's death is the film's turning point" (109). Moreover, the commentators on the 2005 DVD edition of *Bring Me the Head of Alfredo Garcia* (Nick Redman, Paul Seydor, David Weddle, and Garner Simmons), who offer the best "reading" of this vastly undervalued film even though the form is not that of print, say almost nothing about Bennie's guilt in murdering Paco and John, not unlike Murphy and Jameson, who offer no judgment on the killings one way or another, and Gabrielle Murray, who also declines to evaluate the killings.

We would respectfully ask these acute readers of Peckinpah's film why Peckinpah questioned the admirer about when his film turned around if the answer is so "obvious" as Murphy and Jameson assert and the other critics either confirm or imply by their silence, as if there could be no question that Bennie's execution of Paco and John is just retribution for their evil deeds. We would even ask why this scene is in the film at all, as it has nothing directly to do with Bennie's decision to pursue Alfredo's head or his nightmarish dealings with El Jefe's men and ultimately El Jefe himself. In answer to our own question, we would argue that here Bennie releases all the rage he feels against a world which has rendered him powerless. His reaction against the humiliation imposed on him (far more than on Elita) fully warrants Miller's argument that in shooting the bikers Bennie "repeats the patriarch's inhuman mistake" (12), a linkage with El Jefe Bennie himself will assert at the end of the film. The shootings are a true and absolutely relevant turning point, for subsequently there can be no turning back from the grim course Bennie has undertaken. We think Gabrielle Murray is wrong, then, to argue that "when [Bennie] first kills one of El Jefe's agents, he becomes a murderer" (109). Bennie may not have intended to hit the turkeys at which he fires his gun, but when he uses the skills he learned in the army to satisfy his rage at Paco and John, there should be no question he acts deliberately and murderously (leaving aside the degree of legal guilt). There is ample justification for Peckinpah to all but eliminate Elita's praise for Bennie in the script and to not simply qualify the suggestion that Bennie is "changing" for the better but instead to imply strongly that Bennie has thrown away any chance of achieving a new self through marriage with Elita.

As we noted earlier, Peckinpah reserves until this moment, as Bennie and Elita flee the scene of his crimes, to have Bennie finally tell Elita that he must bring back Alfredo's head if he is to be paid his $10,000. The Bennie who has just shot Paco and John is not about to turn away from what has become a sordid quest for the means to remake his life — with or without Elita. Elita is shocked to hear what Bennie has in mind because for her his plan to "desecrate" Alfredo's grave is nothing less than a sin. She pleads with Bennie to turn around, go home, and begin their life together all over again. But Bennie, who has always confused "pesetas" with "amor," who lusts after "pan, bread, dinero," as he lectures Elita (of all people) about the nature of reality, will not stop until he has Alfredo's head, even if it will be "all over" with Elita if he does this. When Bennie coarsely tells Elita that "Alfredo is the saint of our money, and I'm going to borrow a piece of him," he seems not to realize that he uses the same word Paco employs when he says he intends to "borrow" Elita in order to rape her. Little wonder the landscape becomes more and more parched and barren, nothing like the green fields at the beginning of their journey, as Bennie and Elita approach Alfredo's hometown, far from the pregnant Theresa sitting by the lake or the two lovers who shared a picnic beneath a tree.

Before Bennie and Elita reach Alfredo's gravesite, Peckinpah offers a crucial scene in which they spend the night in an inelegant hotel. No scene derived from the original script is more thoroughly transformed. In the script Bennie and Elita make love as if in celebration of Bennie's heroic rescue of Elita. Elita emerges from the bathroom, "lovely, wet, naked and infinitely desirable." "I am clean now, mi Vida," she says to "her man" (50). "Reina ... you were always clean," Bennie replies. They sink onto the bed to make "gentle love," like "two children finding themselves" (51). By contrast, there is nothing celebratory about the scene in Peckinpah's film. We first watch Bennie reloading his gun before a mirror while sitting on their bed, much as he will do later when he returns to their apartment in Mexico City. Alerted to the sounds of a running shower, Bennie makes his way to the shower stall and opens the curtain to discover Elita sitting down and crying while the water flows over her naked body. She looks like a nude, fallen Madonna or Pietà-like figure who is trying to cleanse herself of all that has happened that day. The scene may seem to evolve very positively, for Bennie creeps into Elita's arms while the water is still pouring and here, for the first time, he says, "I love you," and the two of them embrace. Indeed, the emotions which emanate from Elita's entire body seem to make their way into Bennie's face, which registers a physical pain and suffering we would associate with the ambiguous melding together of the tortured clerical figure and the erotically charged naked woman in the crucial Christ at the Column painting which adorns the wall in El Jefe's great hall. This apparent transformation in Bennie, climaxed by his declaration of love for Elita and the reunion they share, might even suggest that we witness here a positive turning point which goes beyond the pleasantries and merrymaking of their exit from Mexico City.

It would be too harsh to deny the more hopeful components of this scene, for here we experience what Miller aptly calls Bennie's "residual humanity" (9) and Elita's suffering confirms the depth which underlies her considerable charms. But we cannot forget that Elita's tears, hardly cathartic, are for the devastating discoveries she has made this day. That Bennie reaffirms his pursuit of Alfredo's head despite her protests and her assurance they cannot continue together if he does this is probably the worst news from this horrific day, for whether or not Bennie loves her, and his declaration in the shower seems absolutely authentic, his love for her and hers for him do not alter his determination to go on with his unacceptable quest. Indeed, even as the shower scene appears to anticipate a new start, Bennie's plans in the morning will be unchanged, for he cannot grasp what is irreconcilable about his desires for Elita and the money which will finance their new life together. There is also the weighty matter of what Bennie has done this day, terrible deeds which lie behind Elita's tears almost as much as Bennie's unwillingness to turn back with her. It is common for the protagonists of Elizabethan or Jacobean revenge tragedies to commit grave crimes in pursuit of their cherished revenge, as we see most famously in what Michael Neill calls Hamlet's ruthlessness (2005, 346), conspicuously on display in the stabbing of Polonius, the entrapment of his old friends Rosencrantz and Guildenstern, and his notorious indifference to the consequences of these acts, but even more glaringly in Hieronimo's murder of the innocent Duke of Castile at the end of *The Spanish Tragedy*, among other examples of the deadly collateral damage which characterizes almost all revenge tragedies. What sets Bennie apart from his predecessors is that he commits his vile acts *before* he begins his quest for revenge after Elita is murdered. Bennie's rage and sense of victimization have emerged so clearly this day, Elita can do nothing but cry for both of them and what she can only see as their hopeless relationship. Gabrielle Murray believes that with the shower scene we can imagine Bennie and Elita turning back (121), but Bennie is resolute in his warped quest and all too literally the killings have begun.

The next day, as they near Alfredo's village, Bennie reasserts his odd position that taking Alfredo's head is in *their* best interest. In a small village along the road Elita stops at a kindly carpenter's shop — the religious symbolism here is quite evident — to ask the direction to

Alfredo's place, then pretends to learn nothing: "I guess we came all the *way* for nothing, huh?" (our emphasis). Bennie's response is like an ultimatum: "Let me tell you something, baby. I coulda died in Mexico City, or TJ, and never known what the hell it was all about. I got a chance. Gonna take it. And we're not going to miss it. Now get in [the car] and sit down and take me to him [Alfredo]." By the time they arrive at Alfredo's village, which is very poor, Bennie and Elita are barely speaking. As they pause before a funeral party, trumpets blaring and drums beating as it bears a child's coffin into the graveyard, the sense of something ending is overwhelming. Elita walks away from Bennie, purchases flowers from an old woman, and enters the graveyard. We hear the sounds of the Garcia family praying around Alfredo's grave as Elita approaches, followed by Bennie, who shows no feeling for the grieving family and no reverence for the dead — a tragic irony which will soon overwhelm him — while he continues to smoke and wear his opaque dark glasses as he nears the grave. Elita kneels beside the grave and offers her condolences to the family, telling them she was a friend of Alfredo's. But the grandmother wants nothing to do with Elita, whose profession she seems to divine, and asks her to leave.[20] Angry as always, Bennie tells the Garcias that he and Elita have traveled a long way "to pay our respects" to Alfredo, one of the most hypocritical speeches in the history of film, and they are sent to a crude local bar where they can get a room for the night.

When Bennie and Elita enter the bar, they watch a man step into the open "mijitorio" in order to urinate. We are reminded of Quill's misogynistic response when asked what would be appropriate if he wants to buy drinks for the "ladies," the two prostitutes who have approached Sappensly and Quill: "Burro piss?" Quill's reply seems to be echoed in this awful place. While the final third of *Bring Me the Head of Alfredo Garcia* generates an overwhelming sense of descent, of going deeper and deeper into perdition, Elita's humiliation, suffering, and guilt make these final moments of her life almost intolerable. The meager room to which they are directed is filmed in an overhead shot, with a large crucifixion-style beam across the ceiling and a magazine painting of the illuminated Virgin Mary over the bed. Murphy and Jameson describe the room as "an underground chamber" (47), and it does give the sense of being buried alive, anticipating the grave toward which Bennie and Elita are moving. In the room Bennie can hardly bear to look at Elita, who sits silently staring at the back of his guilty head. He rationalizes their immediate situation, saying this room is a "palace" compared to being "drunk in Fresno, California." In his insistence on materializing all values, he makes one more attempt to convince Elita that his plan is just: "Do you think he'd give a damn if his head could buy you what you've always been looking for ... a way out?" Bennie has never known and never will know the "way" to understand Elita or what she is looking for, until, of course, it is too late. Elita asks if they can go to a church she has seen in town, doubtless to pray, but Bennie only says, "Yeah ... later." This echoes what Pat Garrett says to his wife Ida, "We'll deal with this when it's over." By then, however, it will be too late and there will be nothing to deal with. Garrett's betrayal of Ida and Bennie's betrayal of Elita underscore the common theme of damned masculinity in each film, in which women are treated as unworthy of making their own judgments. Here a tear falls from Elita's eye as she waits to leave this hideous room. She will not speak again.

When they go to the graveyard that night, Bennie knocks over a heart-shaped wreath and bouquets of flowers placed on Alfredo's grave. Elita retrieves her bouquet and carries it away. Then, her face half-masked in shadow, her hands folded as if in prayer, tears falling down her face, she kneels near the grave and watches Bennie when she is not looking down. Several times Bennie halts in his digging and looks over at Elita as she looks back, a silent witness to the desecration of Alfredo's grave, the destruction of their love. Elita then rises and retreats farther away as he prepares to sever Alfredo's head with his machete. Unseen by Bennie and framed by the same green "blade-like agave leaves" (Murphy and Jameson 48) which sheltered Theresa by the lake, she finally walks slowly away, toward the graveyard entrance. Jerry Fielding's subtle score supplies a tinkling, shimmering music as Bennie, digging away, approaches the buried "treasure," the "golden fleece," he so desperately desires. Suddenly, as he reaches the coffin and opens the grave, the day-for-night photography changes and out of the purely gray/black background a shovel comes driving toward Bennie's head and the picture goes black for approximately five seconds.

Peckinpah could have chosen to film the attack on Bennie with a relatively realistic depiction of Chalo and Cueto's actions, but he did not do so.[21] The alteration of the color composition to black and white, or rather black and gray, seems to suggest that what happens here, presented expressionistically, comes not just from two of El Jefe's henchmen but from a different zone of reality, from within Bennie's subconscious mind, the blow striking him inwardly even before it strikes him from without, implicating him all too personally in Elita's death, for the attack on Bennie surely suggests that Elita is already dead. The rest of the film will deal with Bennie's vengeful pursuit of those who have killed his lover, a search which inevitably leads to himself.

II

> Most tragic protagonists are responsible for how they suffer.... Recognition of their role in the making of what affects them is a large part of what makes their catastrophes tragic. A revenger's position is different. His predicament is imposed on him, and to know this is part of his plight.
>
> —John Kerrigan (12)

> Hope of revenge shall hide our inward woe.
>
> —*Troilus and Cressida* V.x.31

> Poor Tom, that eats the swimming frog, the toad, the tadpole, the wall-newt, and the water; that in the *fury of his heart*, when the foul fiend rages, eats cow-dung for sallets; swallows the old rat and the ditch-dog; drinks the *green mantle* of the standing pool... [our emphases].
>
> —Edgar, in *King Lear* III.iv.132–37

> He who seeks revenge should remember to dig two graves.
>
> —Chinese proverb

With the death of Elita, *Bring Me the Head of Alfredo Garcia* becomes a full-fledged revenge tragedy. This is not to underestimate the film's earlier acts of revenge, El Jefe's call for Alfredo's head and Bennie's shooting of Paco and John, crucial stages in the film's tragic structure. Indeed, many Elizabethan and Jacobean revenge tragedies include several revenge subplots in addition to the protagonist's quest for revenge, topped by the half dozen or so revenge conspiracies in *The Revenger's Tragedy.* Michael Neill suggests that multiple revenge plots characterize the genre in the sixteenth and seventeenth centuries, for "what is striking about Elizabethan and Jacobean revenge plays is the way in which their heroes and villains openly embrace an ethos of excess." This "fondness for excess," as Neill calls it (2005, 342), is surely one of the strongest links between *Bring Me the Head of Alfredo Garcia* and its dramatic predecessors, for Peckinpah's film will eventually depict more than 20 killings as Bennie completes the catastrophic sequence of events initiated by El Jefe's ugly order. To understand the meaning of what happens in the film after Elita's murder, we need to appreciate the genre Peckinpah is developing and his significant departures from its conventions.

Katharine Eisaman Maus offers a concise definition of how revenge tragedies work: "Revenge tragedies feature someone who prosecutes a crime in a private capacity, taking matters into his own hands because the institutions by which criminals are made to pay for their offences are either systematically defective or unable to cope with some particularly difficult situation" (ix). Often, as in *The Spanish Tragedy*, *Hamlet*, and *The Revenger's Tragedy*, the criminals cannot be brought to legal justice because they rule the country in question or stand very near to the ruler. Thus the need for the revenger to take matters into his own hands and the almost universal tendency for the dramatist to present his protagonist's actions as necessary and morally defensible. Robert Ornstein thinks that in only three plays—*Antonio's Revenge*, George Chapman's *The Revenge of Bussy D'Ambois* (1610–11), and Cyril Tourneur's *The Atheist's Tragedy* (1610)—"do major playwrights question the rightness of revenge" (23). Elizabethan and Jacobean revenge tragedies therefore reflect the common view, from the ancient Greeks forward, that revenge satisfies the need for justice in an imperfect world. In his *Rhetoric*, Aristotle asserts that "[t]o take vengeance on one's enemies is nobler than to come to terms with them; for to retaliate is just (*dikaion*), and that which is just is noble" (quoted in Kerrigan 22). In his *Nicomachean Ethics*, Aristotle makes much the same argument: "men demand that they shall be able to requite evil with evil—if they cannot, they feel they are in the position of slaves" (quoted in Kerrigan 51). This second Aristotelian argument anticipates the famous biblical injunction: "thou shalt give life for life, Eye for eye, tooth for tooth, hand for hand, Burning for burning, wound for wound, stripe for stripe" (Exodus 21: 23–25). Subsequently, what Neill terms "the traditional code of chivalric honor" (2005, 329) evolved to justify personal acts of revenge, and Fredson Bowers has plausibly argued that this aristocratic code underlies Elizabethan revenge tragedy (7).

Harry Keyishian proposes that Shakespeare himself recognized "the potentially redemptive functions of revenge" (2), though Shakespeare is a vast subject and plays such as *The Winter's Tale* and *The Tempest* suggest he held very different opinions on other occasions. The key to this view of the subject appears to be that the protagonist in revenge tragedies is a victim who has no responsibility for his situation, as Keyishian argues while citing Helen Gardner (6). John Kerrigan formulates this point of view in the epigraph to this section cited above, in which he suggests the protagonists of most tragic actions are centrally involved, even culpable, in their "catastrophes," while the revenger's "predicament" is imposed on him. As Maus articulates this position, "The protagonist must confront a dreadful situation not of his own making" (x); indeed, from "the protagonist's point of view he is simply the random victim of appalling misfortune" (xi). One might well ask how this random victim becomes a tragic protagonist—why a revenge tragedy is tragic. The answer seems to lie in what the initially innocent protagonist/victim comes to do. As Neill points out, the protagonist almost always ends up implicated in "excessive" savagery which compromises his goal of restoring order (2005, 343). Hamlet's excesses have confounded spectators and critics for more than 400 years, and other famous revengers far surpass Hamlet in their barbaric responses to barbarism. "Vindice and Hieronimo," Maus notes, "repay their enemies with compound interest, gleefully embellishing their victims' death and involving innocent bystanders in the final bloodbath" (xi). The fondness for excess we remarked in the creators of revenge tragedy produces protagonists whose "visions of restored equilibrium" almost always fail (Maus x) and who may finally seem as "corrupt" as their opponents (Kerrigan's judgment on Vindice [7]). At the very least, the protagonist of revenge tragedy almost always ends up a compromised and very complicated figure, one whose complexities make for genuinely tragic actions which invariably end with his own death among many others.

We think that *Bring Me the Head of Alfredo Garcia* rather clearly qualifies as a revenge tragedy. The ethos of excess embodied in its 20 plus killings is a defining characteristic, but there are many others. Bennie must pursue his own course of retribution because there are no legal outlets available in his world and apparently none in the world of the film. El Jefe effectively functions as the evil ruler who must be confronted in so many Elizabethan and Jacobean revenge tragedies. The justice embodied in Bennie's attacks on El Jefe's men and finally El Jefe himself is essentially traditional, and the deaths of six members of the Garcia family constitute the grim collateral damage noted by almost all critics of this form. Neill remarks that the revenger "typically cherishes" a memento of what he has lost, "a picture, a blood-soaked kerchief, a cadaver, or a skull" (2005, 247) (Hieronimo has two such mementos, a bloody handkerchief and his son's cadaver), and no one who has seen *Bring Me the Head of Alfredo Garcia* will forget Bennie's incessant "conversations" with Alfredo's skull throughout the final stages of the action, a skull which recalls Hamlet's Yorick because in both cases the head is not that of the protagonist's loved one. Details such as this one justify David Weddle's characterization of the film as "bizarrely stylized" (1994, 495), the sort of judgment people have been passing on Elizabethan and Jacobean revenge tragedies for four centuries. Its various dramatic features aside, *Bring Me the Head of Alfredo Garcia feels* like a revenge tragedy for anyone who has seen the plays in this tradition aside from *Hamlet*.

Yet Peckinpah's version of this early modern genre also differs from its dramatic forbears in a number of ways. As a modern film *Bring Me the Head of Alfredo Garcia* ranges broadly through different physical environments and cultures, and does so with a realistic attention to details, often significant details, none of the relevant plays (not even *Hamlet*) aspires to achieve. Far more significant, however, is the manner in which his protagonist and therefore the tragic action are handled. If the typical protagonist of Elizabethan and Jacobean revenge tragedy is a victim of injustice, at least until he tries to rectify what has been done to him, Bennie is an entirely different kind of figure, someone who is primarily responsible for the massive injustice which is Elita's death. Chalo and Cueto may literally kill Elita, and El Jefe surely sets the tragedy in motion, but it is Bennie and no one else who brings Elita into the perverse situation which leads to her murder. This means that Bennie resembles the traditional tragic protagonist described by Kerrigan rather than the protagonist of revenge tragedy Kerrigan sees as imposed upon by others. We hope to elucidate the difference this makes as Peckinpah brings his tragic action to conclusion amidst the mayhem so characteristic of the dramatic tradition he has reconfigured to suit the story he wants to tell. We especially wish to establish that, contrary to even the best criticism on this film, the principal subject of the film's final stages is Bennie's guilt.

After the screen goes black for several seconds, we return to the shallow grave where we last saw Bennie struck by the shovel. Time has passed, it appears to be early morning, and no one is in sight. Suddenly an arm comes lurching from the earth — we originally see it underground —framed by two crossed agave plants. The arm is Bennie's and he is alive. Next to him, also buried in the soil of Alfredo's grave, is Elita, though all we see of her is a solitary hand, as if it were reaching toward him from the land of the dead. Bennie initially thinks Elita is alive, but as he pulls the rest of her body to the surface of the grave he discovers she is dead. He tries to revive her, embraces her dead body, and finally is angered by her being dead. "Stay with him!" he shouts as he throws her body on Alfredo's carcass, as if she were death's paramour and Alfredo her newly-found lover, a moment made all the more grim, even Poe-esque, by the fact we now see that Alfredo's head is missing. Even as he behaves so irrationally, Bennie cries in heartfelt grief, offering one of the best examples of Miller's thesis that the key to Peckinpah's films is the marriage of Eros and Thanatos. Bernard K. Dukore suggests that Bennie "rises from the grave, symbolically reborn" (50), but rebirth hardly seems the right word for the intense grief and anger Bennie feels while rising from his premature burial.

Murphy and Jameson characterize the events which follow as "a ferocious dying fall dur-

In a graveyard, between two crosses, Bennie (Warren Oates) vows revenge for the slain Elita (Isela Vega), who is lying in the ground before him *in Bring Me the Head of Alfredo Garcia.*

ing which Benny retraces the journey he (and the film) has made" (48), a wonderful, even uncanny way of describing Bennie's progression/regression from this point to the film's conclusion. Unlike revenge protagonists of the dramatic tradition, Bennie begins at once to avenge Elita's death. In *The Revenger's Tragedy*, Vindice waits no fewer than nine years to avenge his lover's murder, in *The Spanish Tragedy* and most famously *Hamlet*, the protagonist vacillates for extended periods of time about when he should retaliate, but Bennie's response is almost instantaneous. Leaving Elita behind, Bennie drives to a watering trough covered in a "green mantle" of slime and attempts to cleanse himself from a tap which as we first see it barely drips, a bitter contrast to the luxurious lake by which the pregnant Theresa takes in the sun. Three members of the Garcia family appear and Bennie, tormented by guilt over Elita's death, tells them to stop looking at him with their "goddamn fucking eyes." This aversion to being observed is repeated after Bennie learns from the Garcias that two men recently seen in the village have just left. Bennie vows to pursue and kill these men, whom he takes to be the hoods who passed them at the picnic, then rails again at the Garcias as they separate, "Damn your eyes." Even as the maddened Bennie pursues Chalo and Cueto, then those who sent them, the guilt manifested grows more and more conspicuous despite the revenge Bennie imposes on others. Bennie cannot bear to be stared at, but later he will be unable to look at himself as well.

Bennie catches up to Chalo and Cueto fairly quickly, for ironically it is now their turn to suffer a flat tire. The expert marksman yet again, Bennie manages to kill both hoodlums and take possession of Alfredo's head sitting in their car. He even pumps two extra shots into Cueto's expired body, an act he knows to be beyond the pale: "Why?" he asks aloud. "Because it feels so goddamn good." This moment epitomizes "the hollow splendor of revenge" Miller sees in Bennie's vengeful quest (2), the insatiable and lawless "wild justice" Sir Francis Bacon lamented in an early seventeenth-century treatise on the subject (Bushnell 66). The savagery here is followed by the bizarre whimsy of Bennie talking to the skull he has seized, recalling Hamlet's philosophizing over poor Yorick's skull and Vindice walking onto the stage at the beginning of *The Revenger's Tragedy* "holding a skull" which proves to be that of his dead mistress and to which he speaks as if it were still alive.[22] Very much like Vindice, Bennie begins a "conversation" with the head of Alfredo as he drives on. He calls the head "Al," offers him/it a drink when he pours tequila over the head, and says, "Sorry, Al. Sorry" when the head falls to the floor. He even confides in "Al": "Three days and three nights, huh? I hope you enjoyed her. I did." This sort of reference to Elita may seem offensive and a strong signal that Bennie is sinking deeper and deeper into madness, not unlike Fred C. Dobbs' later fate in *The Treasure of the Sierra Madre.* In fact, however, Bennie's commentary on Elita runs throughout his dialogue with himself for the rest of the film and constitutes the best available evidence that Bennie realizes, belatedly, the immense value of what he has lost in Elita, indeed, the value of what he has thrown away.

When Bennie stops in a rural village to eat breakfast and drink a "cerveza" on his way back to Mexico City, Peckinpah creates a scene of highly suggestive symbolic importance. As Bennie arrives, we hear church bells ringing down from a mountainside and see the cathedral from which they originate. Simultaneously, in a striking crane and pan shot descending from the church, we see a boy, standing still on the hillside beneath the church, who watches Bennie's car approach and comes running down to see who it is. The associated imagery of the child, the church, and the church bells, familiar to us from church bells scenes in *Straw Dogs* and *Pat Garrett and Billy the Kid*, keys the moment to Bennie's spiritual, one might even say religious, crisis, and anticipates the strange relationship between the dead Alfredo's head and the baby to whom Theresa has just given birth. It is here that Bennie mutters to "Al," "Three days and three nights, huh? I hope you enjoyed her. I did." Peckinpah rarely uses the biblically charged number of three without purpose. We have come to see that Elita is a deeply religious person who wants to marry Bennie "in a church" and who attempts, unsuccessfully, to stop Bennie from "desecrating" Alfredo's grave. She spent three last days with Alfredo because she understood this doomed man's need for solace. In her own fashion she was attempting to "save" him, as she also does with Bennie and Paco. For all of them it is to no avail, however: Alfredo dies when he drives off the road into some rocks; Paco dies among rocks when Bennie shoots him; and Bennie will complete the pattern at El Jefe's ranch, when his stone-like "wooden heart" cracks in a blaze of gunfire beneath a dusty tree.

With all three men Elita offers her transformative love, body and soul, to those most in need. Bennie, who genuinely loves Elita, cannot reciprocate because he is blinded by his pursuit of the money he will obtain with Alfredo's head and now the fury he feels for her death. As Bennie violently stabs at an ice block to put ice around Alfredo's putrefying head, his intense anger surfaces in his stabbing motions. Soon the little boy asks if he can wipe off the dusty windows of Bennie's car, and as he does so, he sees scores of flies buzzing around the wrapped-up head. "Señor," he says to Bennie, "muchas moscas," perhaps an allusion to Jean-Paul Sartre's *The Flies*, a re-telling of Aeschylus' great family tragedy of patricide and matricide, the *Agamemnon.* But Bennie puts the boy off when he tells him what is in the bag: "Cat. Dead cat. Used to belong to a friend of mine." The gruesome association of a dead cat with Alfredo's head, with Elita as its owner, should nevertheless remind us of Bennie's happier past, those brief moments years ago when he played piano at "The Black Cat in TJ," a "classy place" where Paulette Goddard walked in one night. Now his past is dead, and his "friend" Elita (whose "classy" name means "Elite") is gone because of what he did. This is one of those moments in the film when Bennie draws close to madness, his grief and guilt enraging him as he chops away at the block of ice almost as if it were his own head, an act of Dantean self-torment. Still he drives on, as if the (always self-reflexive) revenge he seeks will somehow allay the overwhelming realization that, like Pat Garrett, he has killed the one thing in his life he truly loved.

After Bennie leaves Alfredo's village, seven members of the Garcia family, led by their ancient grandmother (Tamara Garina), pile into an old car even more dilapidated than Bennie's in search of Alfredo's missing head. Moments like this remind us that revenge tragedy has always had a strong "affinity with comedy or farce," as Maus puts it (xxi), whether manifested in conversations with skulls or the sheer number of characters absorbed into its convoluted plots and eventually killed off. The Garcias come upon Chalo and Cueto, search for Alfredo's head, and then drive on in pursuit of Bennie. After they capture Bennie in a remote section of the highway, Peckinpah alters the script to very good effect. In the script, one of the Garcia men lectures Bennie on the impropriety of what he is doing and Bennie replies that he will bring the head back when he is done (95), a wildly implausible idea Bennie has already used on Elita to get her to go along with his plan to steal the head (65). Grandmother Moreno then negotiates with Bennie as to how much he will pay her family for Alfredo's head (97), a negotiation she takes up with Sappensly and Quill after they arrive (100). Peckinpah deletes Bennie's improbable offer to bring back the head as an insult to Elita's intelligence and an evasion of the sacrilege Bennie must know he is committing here. He also deletes the grandmother's unseemly negotiations about the price for Alfredo's head as compromising the moral (and religious) principle which motivates the Garcias. In the film it is only Bennie who pathetically holds out the possibility that the Garcias can be bought off, thrusting the few bills he has on him at the grandmother and throwing the money at the Garcias when they are unresponsive to his offer, money which is whipped away by the wind, surely a reference to the gold Fred C. Dobbs loses to Gold Hat (Alfonso Bedoya) in *The Treasure of the Sierra Madre*. Bennie does acknowledge, reluctantly, that he has stolen the head for money and was prepared to sever Alfredo's head ("I didn't do it, but I would have"), but his breezy comment, "That's the way it goes," reminds us that Bennie's "way" is very different from Elita's.

Bennie's refusal to give up Alfredo's head to the Garcias, reminiscent of his intransigence with Elita, creates a standoff which is finally broken by the arrival of Sappensly and Quill, who pretend to be lost tourists. When Bennie tells Sappensly indirectly that the head is here but will have to be taken, Sappensly signals to Quill that they need to take action against the Garcias. The pathological Quill takes out a machine gun hidden inside his trench coat and proceeds, with Sappensly's help, to mow down the Garcias with the exception of their eldest member, probably Alfredo's grandfather (Chano Urueta), only to be shot himself by a younger family member hidden over a small hill. Before noticing that Quill is wounded, Sappensly helps kill the young man who shot Quill and turns nonchalantly to Bennie to ask who these people were. "Just a family," Bennie replies, an ironic utterance which registers his dawning awareness of the inhuman mission he has undertaken and the moral monsters with whom he is now associated. He is therefore prepared when Sappensly tries to kill him after calling out to Quill, "You okay, Johnny? Johnny?" (Quill's name in the script is the florid "Jon Quill"). When Sappensly turns on Bennie with his gun, Bennie shoots him first. Strangely, Sappensly does not fight back. Instead, like a doomed lover, he moves toward Quill, calling softly, "Hey, Johnny," before he is shot a second time by Bennie, who now knows Sappensly and Quill had no intention of paying him. It is here we should realize what Robert Webber meant when he told Peckinpah his character should be associated with an innocent young girl. As we first saw in Bennie's bar, Sappensly has always protected the crazy Quill. Whether or not they are lovers, they are clearly bound together and defined by their own private ethic. Sappensly's "Hey, Johnny" is the dying lament of a brutal killer for hire who is nonetheless capable of deep feeling and who elects to give up his fight with Bennie now that "Johnny" is dead. This is Peckinpah at his best, adding the relevant materials during production while honoring a favorite Renoir quote from *The Rules of the Game* (1939), "The terrible thing about life is that everyone has his reasons."

The massacre of the Garcias is followed by what is in many ways the most important scene in the film. This may seem far from obvious, for the scene in question, in which we see Bennie return to his apartment in Mexico City, includes no real "action" following the 10 deaths on the highway back to Mexico City and preceding the many deaths depicted in the film's two climactic scenes. Nonetheless, no scene is more crucial to our understanding of Bennie's character. We see Bennie move from a dark street to the dark room he has shared with Elita, all the while carrying the head of Alfredo in a sack. Once he enters their room he puts the head in a basket, gets a bottle of tequila, looks at himself in a mirror but can't stand doing so and puts his dark glasses back on, cuts ice to put on Alfredo's head, places the sack in the shower and turns on the water, goes to the bed with his tequila in hand, reloads his gun as he did before going to Alfredo's gravesite, leans back on the bed and listens to Elita's singing in his head, talks to her picture near the bed about "Al" taking a shower, begins to laugh and then cry, drinks from his bottle, cries again, and gets up to walk back toward the shower.

Bennie's relations with Alfredo are almost as crucial as those with Elita in this "uneventful" scene. As Bennie prepares the shower for Alfredo's head, he says, "A friend of ours tried to take a shower in there," a familiar remark which reflects the sympathy Bennie has come to feel for Alfredo amidst the mad chaos of their trek together. Earlier, Bennie has all but apologized to Alfredo for wishing him dead: "It wasn't your fault, I know that. We're going to find out, you and me." As in this second shower scene, Bennie speaks to Alfredo as a comrade who also loved Elita, someone who also wants to know who gave the deadly order which led to Elita's death. Gone is the vicious jealousy Bennie felt toward Alfredo, no doubt an important factor in his willingness to treat Alfredo's carcass as a commodity. Bennie's "dialogue" with Alfredo's head will continue in this more generous spirit to the end of the film. The bizarre friendship forged here recalls Bennie's ironic remark to Sappensly about the Garcias, "Just a family," another sign that Bennie is beginning to understand the human implications of the tragic events unfolding.

Even more significant are the several signals in the scene which point to Bennie's grief and guilt concerning Elita. The moment when Bennie takes off his glasses and tries to look at himself in the mirror but cannot do so is yet another wonderful use of mirrors in Peckinpah's films. The guilt expressed here shares the stage with Bennie's profound grief as he leans back on their bed and hears in his head Elita's rich laughter as she speaks and sings, sounds he has been hearing ever since her death. As the Bennie and Elita love theme fills the room, Bennie begins to laugh and cry, providing what David Weddle describes as "an extended look at grief," one which exhibits "all the colors of grief," and Paul Seydor perceives as visual evidence of Bennie's "guilt." Weddle and Seydor make these acute comments in the commentary to the 2005 DVD edition of *Bring Me the Head of Alfredo Garcia*, a discussion which highlights Bennie's guilt as none of the published critiques has done. Bennie's pain here should recall his agonized look in the first shower scene in which he tells Elita for the first time that he loves her. This earlier expression of emotion did not stop Bennie from pursuing his "golden fleece," and the emotions revealed as Bennie looks into the mirror and listens on the bed to Elita speaking, laughing, and singing will not stop him from pursuing vengeance against El Jefe's men and ultimately El Jefe. Nonetheless, these poignant moments in the apartment speak to the growth of consciousness Bennie is experiencing as he searches with "Al" ("you and me") for vengeance against those who have cut short Elita's rich life. What remains is for Bennie to acknowledge his own central role in this disaster, a formulation reserved for the film's climactic scene.

The next day Bennie takes his basket to Max at the Camino Real Hotel, along with a resplendent bouquet of flowers, always associated with Elita, but also with Theresa and the flowering spring trees by the lake. Bennie encounters Max having his feet washed and manicured by "two Magdalens" (Murphy and Jameson 48), two of the prostitutes he acquired from Sappensly and Quill when they first arrived at the hotel. This crude parody of the biblical foot washing contrasts with Theresa bathing her feet in the lake's warm waters, the late afternoon sun casting a golden glow on her feet in the water. Water's cathartic power to cleanse, heal, and even purify is again profaned and polluted, as we shall see yet again in the baptism scene with El Jefe's grandson when Bennie finally arrives at his compound. As Bennie apparently prepares to exchange Alfredo's head for his $10,000, he asks Max and Frank, "How much is it worth?" As Frank cautions him to settle for what he was promised, Bennie handles the basket and makes one of his most poignant speeches: "This belonged to a very special lady. Once upon a time she filled it up with food and we went on a picnic. We turned off a dirt road and we ate the food she prepared with her hands, very special hands. And that's why I'd like to know why you don't *take* it [he takes the head out of the basket and bangs it on their table] and tell me what the head of Alfredo Garcia is worth, and to who, comprendo?" Bennie then takes his gun out of the basket and begins shooting, first Frank, then Max, and eventually two of their men.

In the midst of the gunfight, Bennie walks past a mirror in the suite and watches with the self-loathing felt by Pike Bishop and Pat Garrett as his own image is shattered by one of Max's men. Bennie then emerges next to the mirror and shoots the man who thought he was shooting Bennie but was only shooting into the mirror. This doubling of Bennie's image is characteristic of the tragic films, but this time it is not Bennie who shoots his own image but the hood. It makes no difference, for Peckinpah wants to establish the similarity between Bennie and Max's gunmen, even as Bennie realizes what he has done and that the head of a man or the life of a woman isn't worth any sum of money in the world. This recalls Max's final words, when he reaches into his pocket, pulls out El Jefe's card, and says, "This is the man who will pay..." just as he is killed by Bennie. Max wants to avoid being shot and is about to tell Bennie that El Jefe will pay him a million dollars for the head of Alfredo Garcia. But it doesn't matter anymore to the furious, grieving Bennie, who takes the card from Max's hand after killing the others. As Seydor says in the commentary to the 2005 DVD, "What profit a man to gain the whole world if he sell his soul?" Bennie knows the truth of this biblical wisdom, for his revenge against El Jefe's men seems to provide no satisfaction whatsoever, let alone make Bennie feel "so goddamn good."

Having tenderly replaced Alfredo's head, Bennie leaves the suite with Elita's basket, the $10,000 he has been paid, Theresa's locket with Alfredo's smiling photo (taken from Max's suit jacket), and El Jefe's card. Next we see an airplane leaving Mexico City, presumably reversing the course we saw earlier when El Jefe's men came to the capital. Bennie rents a car and drives out to El Jefe's heavily guarded compound, richly verdant in springtime with beautiful horses— avatars of the late Alfredo Garcia — running wild beyond a fence. Bennie must know that if he kills El Jefe, he will not survive. Though he has managed to prevail against smaller numbers, Bennie is now entering a situation in which the odds are as desperate as they were for the Wild Bunch when they challenged Mapache. Even generic expectations are against Bennie, for though "good usually triumphs and evil is destroyed at the close of Jacobean tragedy," as Ornstein observes (44), the "triumph" to which Ornstein points never includes the physical survival of the revenging protagonist, who dies in part because, as Ornstein also sees, "we are made to feel how vulnerable are the walls—the political, religious, legal, and familial institutions—which seek to check or contain the uncivilized fury of civilized man" (44). The social walls in Peckinpah's world are virtually nonexistent rather than vulnerable, and Bennie's "uncivilized fury" has proven to be as intense as El Jefe's. The sheer logic of his situation points to his demise, whether we count those massed against him or consider Bennie's expanding awareness of his own complicity in the film's tragic events. After killing El Jefe Bennie will say to Alfredo's head, "C'mon, Al ... we're goin' home." For Peckinpah's tragic heroes, as for Shakespeare's, "home" is death, as we think Bennie now understands.[23]

As Bennie enters El Jefe's hacienda, the guitar music with which the film began starts up again, recalling the slow movement from the freeze-frame black and white of the ducks to the color and motion of the lake turning blue and the appearance of Theresa. The film is circling back to its beginnings, as in almost all revenge tragedies. Indeed, one of the bleak absurdities in *Bring Me the Head of Alfredo Garcia* is its almost compulsive repetitions. As Murphy and Jameson note, Bennie repeats in reverse the quest for Alfredo's head with which the film began. He embodies the *reductio ad absurdum* of all revenge tragedies, what René Girard calls unending "reciprocal violence" (52–53), in that he repeats the murderous acts which initiate and then litter such works. The film begins with El Jefe's call for revenge and will end with Bennie's revenge against El Jefe. This is not to say El Jefe and Bennie are one and the same, only that Bennie's murderous acts, even in a "good" cause, produce extraordinary havoc and destruction. We will see Bennie heroically restore Theresa's baby to its mother, promise to return Alfredo to his "home" in a graveyard, and effectively return to Elita, even if in death, actions which mark his spiritual growth in this terrible story. But Peckinpah himself has reminded us of the enormous cost of this growth: "This is the story of a man caught up in the brutality of the world around him, who loses all sense of morality with one act of violence begetting another, until there is no return to respectability, only retribution. The lasting theme of the film is that such acts only end in disaster for those involved" (quoted in Prince 1998, 265, n.93).[24] As we shall see, these acts end in Bennie's tragic illumination as well, but at nothing less than the cost Peckinpah formulates here.

In this final scene, however, the lilting pastoral theme suggests the possibility of change. A baptismal ceremony is taking place for El Jefe's new grandson, a ceremony which offers the promise of spiritual purification and eternal life in God. A celebration of the boy's christening begins when the priest announces the service "finito"; the guitar music continues, fireworks commence, and adults throw coins to little children, who are everywhere. Unhappily, though, as Miller points out (7), the ceremony reminds us of the ending of Francis Ford Coppola's *The Godfather* (1972), in which Michael Corleone (Al Pacino), playing godfather to the baby of his sister Connie (Talia Shire) and his brother-in-law Carlo (Gianni Russo), systematically slays the heads of the Four Families and prepares to kill Carlo right after the christening ends. Peckinpah cuts between Bennie carrying Alfredo's head, which itself has been doused with water, tequila, and dry ice, and the holy water poured on the baby's head while he is held by one of the maids to Theresa, whose wan, expressionless face masks her grief over Alfredo's death and her baby's fate in this environment. Meanwhile, the black-hooded mother who cried out when Theresa's arm was broken stands off to the side, again dressed in black with a black spiderweb veil, her dark malevolence toward El Jefe not masked at all. It may be said she awaits her own vengeance against this destroyer of all which is living. Indeed, she will take her revenge moments later when, standing in the doorway to the great room and smiling silently to herself, she watches mourners and nuns gather in prayer around the "throne" of El Jefe, who has fittingly died in his magisterial chair. *Sic semper tyrannus.* A tyrant is dead, but the wife does not grieve, nor does she join the hypocritical mourners, among them Theresa's grandmother.

When Bennie enters the great room, his movements ironically echoing the Wild Bunch's march to the loggia in Agua Verde, El Jefe says that he has been "expecting" him, which may mean he knows what has happened in Mexico City or simply that, given human nature, he has "expected" someone to claim his massive reward. Now a proud grandfather at his grandson's christening, he offers Bennie a drink, but Bennie responds, "I got nothing to celebrate." Whereas in the script El Jefe is unwilling to pay for the head he no longer cares about in the presence of a male child (119), Peckinpah has El Jefe casually agree to pay the million dollars for what Bennie calls "the merchandise which you bought." El Jefe shoves the money at Bennie and says, "Take it and go. I have everything I want. I have my grandson. So go, and don't forget to take *that* [the head] and throw it to the pigs." This is said before Theresa, who stands with Alfredo's baby in her arms. Bennie then mutters a nearly inaudible "No" before indicting all the guilty parties in this sordid tale: "Sixteen people are dead because of him ... and you ... and me. And one of them was a damned good friend of mine." This is perhaps the film's most important speech, embodying as it does Bennie's recognition that he is as guilty as El Jefe (and far more so than Alfredo). This tragic self-knowledge is incomplete, as all such moments tend to be, for Bennie seems not to be counting Paco and John, who are not victims of El Jefe's vendetta but whose deaths should haunt Bennie's conscience as much as any except Elita's.[25] Nonetheless, Bennie's insight here is a considerable achievement given where he started in this disastrous sequence of events. At this point Bennie becomes a traditional tragic protagonist, *hamartia* and all. We would argue that Peckinpah's ability to transform the typical protagonist of a revenge tragedy into a tragic protagonist more affecting than Pat Garrett and almost as affecting as Pike Bishop defines his remarkable success in this film.

Inevitably, however, the revenge Bennie has sought must continue even though he has come to understand the futility of his mission. He draws his gun out of the sack holding Alfredo's head and, echoing Theresa's mother, says "No!" four more times as he shoots El Jefe's henchmen in the great room, perhaps six more casualties, leaving one servant standing still with his arms raised, rather like the old man at the slaughter of the Garcias.

Then Bennie says something which reverberates through the whole film: "The first time I saw him, he was dead." Of course, on a literal level he is talking about Alfredo, his companion of late. But he might well be talking self-reflexively about himself and the "first time" he saw himself clearly, his dark glasses removed, the one true and loving thing in his life, Elita, taken from him because of his own rapaciousness. Bennie told his tourist patrons to leave the Tlaquepaque and "take your wooden hearts out and find the soul of Mexico," but it was he who sold his "heart" or soul for money when he made his deal with El Jefe's men, he who broke his own heart when he broke Elita's even before she was killed by Chalo and Cueto. Bennie is already dead when he understands that he has rejected Elita, with whom we associate the film's true music, its sense of place in both city and country, the woman of redemptive flowers and baptismal showers, of life's true flow. The same Elita who is no doubt cast out of the Garcia gravesite and thrown by some lonely roadside to be devoured by wild animals.

Remarkably, Bennie seems to be approaching the religious state Elita occupied when she pleaded with Bennie in her presciently broken English to "make a round" and return to their home in Mexico City after the two bikers were killed. The phrase "make a round" implies not simply changing direction but rather turning one's life around, beginning to imagine that life in new ways. In this sense Elita evoked, no doubt unconsciously, the Greek and Christian concept of *metanoia* (analogous to Aristotle's *perepeteia* or "reversal"), which literally means to "turn around" but figuratively implies a genuine "change of *heart*" (our emphasis), a form of repentance the theologian John Davidson has defined as a mystical process: "Mystically [*metanoia*] signifies a redirection of the attention from the world towards God" (468–69). At least in part its origin is in Matthew 3: 2, where John the Baptist implores the people to turn their lives around: "Repent ye: for the kingdom of heaven is at hand." In her life and especially her death, Elita has brought Bennie to the brink of such "repentance."

When Theresa commands Bennie to kill her father ("Kill him!"), the Aeschylean elements

In El Jefe's (Emilio Fernandez's) great hall, with Alfredo Garcia's head in the bag beside him, Bennie (Warren Oates) draws his gun and utters his final, apocalyptic "No!"

in this remarkable film reach their climax. Bennie utters one final low guttural "No!" like a voice from the dead, then does as she commands, thus completing his own now pointless quest and freeing Theresa's son from a life of crime and brutality. She then instructs Bennie to leave fast. Before he goes Bennie gives Theresa the locket with Alfredo's picture, wraps his hands in hers (as though they were Elita's "very special hands"), and says to her, "You take care of the boy. I'll take care of the father." These are Bennie's last words before he drives out of the compound, busts through the central gate, and is met with a storm of bullets. His car comes to a stop in a cloud of dust along the roadside, appropriately amidst the enfolding agave plants we associate with both Theresa and Elita. We now know why Peckinpah had "Viva Zapata!" sewn onto Bennie's jacket (and the name "Samuel" partially visible on the jacket as well), for Bennie's end resembles that of the great Mexican revolutionary in Elia Kazan's 1952 film starring Marlon Brando, who is trapped in an open arena-like space and slain by his betrayers, riddled by hundreds of bullets. Unlike Zapata, of course, Bennie has betrayed himself as well as Elita, but the tragic knowledge he finally acquires and the *cathartic* knowledge we as viewers achieve link him to Peckinpah's most tragic figures. Peckinpah allows us inside of Bennie's car during his final death throes. Here there is nothing like the erotic, balletic deaths of Bonnie and Clyde, deaths often compared to Bennie's. Instead, we see Bennie shot through the glass rear window, then slumped over the wheel of his car, Alfredo's head and El Jefe's money beside him, though the money meant nothing to him as he left the hacienda and he only picked it up as an ironic afterthought. In saving the mother and child from a terrible future, and in promising to restore Alfredo to his "home," Benny has completed his journey from "grave to grail" (Murphy 1999, 1) and can now achieve some kind of final rest.

The extraordinary closeup of a machine gun pumping bullets from its bore, coughing flames and smoke, provides a fitting conclusion to this film's long meditation on violence and the betrayals of the human heart. As the gun continues to fire, it gradually devolves into slow motion and the sound is more and more muffled, as if it comes to us from a great distance or a time long ago. Finally, we are left with nothing but a freeze frame of the bore alone, its familiar void-like dark hole the single focus of what seems the film's last shot. Then the frame is swallowed in grave-like blackness (akin to the ominous dark screen we see at the beginning of the film) before the iconic words, "Directed by Sam Peckinpah," emerge beside it as low-key, mournful music accompanies what appears to be the film's end. But the director has several more surprises in store for his audience. In a moderately rapid dissolve the image of the gun bore is superimposed on Theresa as, in freeze frame, she again receives her baby from El Jefe in the scene we have recently witnessed. Peckinpah seems to be commenting on the dread legacy of violence this baby will inherit, much as he does with the little boy who wanders the grounds among the bodies after the shootout in the great room and ends up next to the praying grandmother and the dead El Jefe. Then Peckinpah offers a pair of reprised freeze-frame images which conclude the film: first, Theresa seen from behind looking out at the luminous lake; second, Sappensly gazing into the bag which contains Alfredo's head. Michael Bliss suggests that Theresa and Sappensly see much the same thing: "beauty becoming horror, and horror becoming beauty, with the ultimate realization that the two concepts are, in the end, identical" (1993, 262). We ourselves think that Peckinpah always draws a firm line between beauty and horror, here and elsewhere in his films, but these concluding images acknowledge that all too often beauty gives way to horror, the tragic truth which informs *Bring Me the Head of Alfredo Garcia* even as the film dramatizes Bennie's growth in consciousness about his own complicity in life's many horrors.

We would like to close with two observations about the originality of *Bring Me the Head of Alfredo Garcia* as a revenge tragedy. The first is that making the protagonist deeply complicit in the injustice he seeks to avenge is virtually unique among tragedies of this kind. A play Peckinpah probably knew, Shakespeare's *Titus Andronicus* (1589–93), may seem comparable, for Titus' decision to sacrifice the son of Tamora, the vanquished queen of his enemies, inspires her own campaign of revenge which costs Titus two of his sons and his cherished daughter Lavinia. Yet the parallel with Peckinpah's film is inexact, for Titus goes mad and suffers greatly but never acknowledges his own role in the cruel events which destroy his family. As Gustav Cross suggests, "Titus is no King Lear: his sufferings do not bring increased self-knowledge or greater understanding of the human condition. He is incapable of recognizing that his misfortunes stem from that stern inflexibility manifested at the beginning of the play when he rejects Tamora's pleadings" (16–17). The most compelling revenge protagonists, Hamlet and Captain Ahab, say, are more than capable of recognizing their own difficulties in their pursuit of justice, but like all revenge protagonists, they begin blameless, righteously so, and only become compromised as they struggle to implement the appropriate vengeance. As we have argued, Bennie is fully implicated in his film's evils from the first, no less so than Pike Bishop or Pat Garrett, more traditional tragic protagonists. In this crucial respect, *Bring Me the Head of Alfredo Garcia* is a work of great originality, much as Peckinpah suggested in his public comments on the film.

The other original feature of Peckinpah's modern revenge tragedy is the role performed by Elita. The originality here is one of degree rather than kind, for of course nearly all revenge tragedies offer female characters who suffer because of their male companions, including the protagonist. Hamlet's Ophelia is a major example, and even Ahab has his more or less abandoned wife and family. But no traditional revenge tragedy offers a character like Elita, one whose qualities make her the work's center of value. Indeed, Elita, especially as played by Isela Vega, emerges as the most impressive female character in all of Peckinpah's films and indispensable to any adequate reading of this seemingly hyper-masculine work in a hyper-masculine form. The closest parallel is to be found in a play usually denied revenge tragedy status, John Webster's *The Duchess of Malfi* (ca. 1614), in which the avenger, Bosola, is not the play's protagonist even though he finally kills the Duchess' evil brother Ferdinand, who has conspired with his brother the Cardinal to first imprison and then execute the Duchess. Like Bennie, Bosola participates in the plot which ends up taking the heroine's life and is therefore as guilty as the evil brothers, as he himself comes to acknowledge. One could argue *Bring Me the Head of Alfredo Garcia* plays like a recasting of Webster's great tragedy in which the avenger is also the protagonist from the beginning. The real parallel here is that between Elita and the Duchess, however, for each in her own way is the spiritual center of her work, the abused and ultimately murdered embodiment of what her creator values most. As long ago as 1975 Mark Crispin Miller remarked that in *Bring Me the Head of Alfredo Garcia* Peckinpah "cherishes the things we call life-affirming" (3), a seemingly strange judgment on one of the most violent films of its own or any period. We think Miller was paying the right kind of attention and especially to Elita, as luminous a character as Webster's much more famous Duchess.

Conclusion

> For if the dance of comedy enacts "the whirligig of time" in which all things turn and return as though governed by the seasonal patterns of rotation and renewal, the processional endings of tragedy answer to the alternative sense of time as an ineluctable linear process. [The] whole action of a tragedy move[s] from its opening spectacle of blackness to its concluding ritual of death.
>
> —Michael Neill (1997, 283–84)

> Peckinpah was born into the essential truth that there is no greater sadness than the passage of time...
>
> —Benjamin Kerstein (8)

The epigraphs offered above speak to what we have called "the poetics of loss" and the obsession with time which inform all of Peckinpah's tragic Westerns. Those pursuing a thematic approach to these films could do far worse than to highlight this subject, for all of the films reflect this concern and some of them deal with it as their principal intellectual/emotional content. One thinks of Steve Judd (Joel McCrea) in *Ride the High Country* (1962), an aging ex-lawman whose majestic death evokes the romantic longing for a West which "used to be" (a phrase echoed several times in *The Wild Bunch* [1969], most notably when Pike Bishop [William Holden] exhorts his men to perform as a cohesive unit, "just like it used to be"). One remembers Pike telling the rest of the Wild Bunch that their storied outlaw days "are closin' fast," words we have chosen for the epigraph of this book. One thinks especially of Pat Garrett's (James Coburn's) film-long effort to resist the fearful changes of time by joining forces with the most powerful political and economic figures of his period. All of these efforts to forestall or reshape the passage of time fail, of course, and this failure is the dramatic subject in each of these great Western films, tragedies all. We see similar attempts to redefine or even reverse the vicissitudes of life in the other tragic Westerns, *Noon Wine* (1966) and *Bring Me the Head of Alfredo Garcia* (1974), films in which the respective protagonists, Mr. Thompson (Jason Robards) and Bennie (Warren Oates), literally or effectively commit suicide, acknowledging their own guilty roles in their films' catastrophes but also the futility of their efforts to reshape the "permanent" and "irreversible" damage Adrian Poole rightly sees as fundamental to all true tragedies (1987, 14). There can be no escaping the trap of time for these doomed protagonists, for as William Storm notes, "what truly underlies tragedy's reflection of temporality is the condition of the tragic itself, the basic disjuncture of past and future within which being—that is to say, the tragic self—is made to exist" (87). No past or future event can eradicate the authentically *timeless* instant of the tragic deed. Try as they might, none of Peckinpah's tragic figures can escape the awful burden of the thing done which cannot be undone.

Our own study has touched on this central thematic concern, as well as other topics and ideas relevant to Peckinpah's tragic Westerns, but our primary interest has been formal rather than thematic, as we have sought to establish that five of Peckinpah's films are tragic actions of remarkably varied kinds. We would like to conclude by summarizing our findings and offering final thoughts on Peckinpavean tragedy, whether it can be conveniently defined and what kind of achievement it represents. First, however, we want to comment on Peckinpah's *other* films, the 10 non-tragic films we have occasionally cited but effectively pushed to the side in our focus on the tragic films. We wish to generalize about the non-tragic films in order to better define what characterizes the five films we have analyzed at such length.

I

We will not be studying Peckinpah's 10 non-tragic films in any depth or detail, but we do want to point up some of the things they have in common as a group. They should not be categorized as "comedies" or "histories," the famous formal alternatives to Shakespeare's "tragedies" in the First Folio of 1623. Indeed, none of these 10 films strikes us as a straightforward comedy, though *Convoy* (1978) comes very close and all of these films offer conclusions which avert the tragic possibilities which have arisen and all conclude happily or very close to happily. None is a failed tragedy (though *Straw Dogs* [1971] is a possible exception, as we have already acknowledged and will consider again in a moment); indeed, they all seem to us "serious actions" as defined by Sheldon Sacks in his *Fiction and the Shape of Belief* (1964).

As we noted in Chapter Six, Sacks defines a "serious" action as one in which the characters and events are handled so as to anticipate neither a happy (or comic) nor disastrous (or tragic) conclusion. Such an action eventually concludes one way or the other, or in some mixed fashion, but the author (or filmmaker) does not insist on the likely outcome until he or she devises the actual finale, presumably resolving the problems or (as Sacks would have it) the instabilities introduced earlier. The form in question resembles life as it is often characterized, with its ups and down, and achieves closure which is neither inevitable nor thoroughly happy or unhappy, though it often veers decisively toward one or the other of these poles. We noted in Chapter One and Chapter Six that Western film directors have often opted for a relatively happy outcome. Our earlier discussions contrast the practice of almost all other Western directors with Peckinpah's in his five tragic films, but it is only fair to acknowledge that the majority of Peckinpah's films (10, in fact) make many of the same choices and should also be recognized as serious actions which avert tragic conclusions.

The non-tragic films fall along a formal spectrum which runs from near-comedies to near-tragedies. Somewhat loosely defined, the near-comedies are *The Ballad of Cable Hogue* (1970), *Junior Bonner* (1972), and *Convoy*. The boisterous *Convoy*, Peckinpah's "highest-grossing picture" (Weddle 1994, 518), recalls Burt Reynolds' *Smokey and the Bandit* films and similarly skirts or falls into (depending on one's taste in these matters) a broadly defined comic genre which includes much action adventure, much raw humor, and a healthy avoidance of the consequences one might expect in a more realistic treatment of the material. It is hard to take *Convoy* very seriously, though Peckinpah's handling of the road sequences is predictably superior.[1] *The Ballad of Cable Hogue* resembles *Convoy* in its more extreme comical moments, especially Peckinpah's notorious (and unrepeated) use of fast-motion sequences in rendering Cable Hogue's (Jason Robards') romance with Hildy (Stella Stevens), the film's golden-hearted prostitute. *The Ballad of Cable Hogue* is a more serious film, however, one Michael Bliss even defines as a tragedy (1993, 128), no doubt because its protagonist dies at the end. Cable's accidental death does move the film from its more comic features to something like midpoint between comic and tragic boundaries, but it is also a good reminder that tragic form is not really defined by its hero's death. Far more important is the sense of impending doom which pervades tragedies and structures our responses throughout the tragic action. In *The Ballad of Cable Hogue*, by contrast, Cable avoids such doom repeatedly, establishing himself as one of Peckinpah's preeminent survivors, and even flourishes with his joint discoveries of life-sustaining water and love, until he is overtaken by the virtually comic auto accident which brings his completely satisfying life (and the film which records that life) to a mellow if not quite comic conclusion.

By far the most artistically successful of Peckinpah's near-comedies, *Junior Bonner* is one of the hardest of his films to pigeonhole generically. On the one hand, it is Peckinpah's least violent film, the principal example of what Paul Seydor and others call his "gentle" films, for here there are no deaths, no shootings, and almost no physical violence except the beating Junior takes in trying to ride the biggest bull in a rodeo and the comic "fight" Junior and others conduct at the end of a dance (an event, fight and all, surely meant to remind us of the more elegant dances which recur throughout John Ford's Westerns).[2] On the other hand, the problems Junior faces with the surviving members of his family—his estranged parents, Ace (Robert Preston) and Ellie (Ida Lupino), and his wealthy brother Curly (Joe Don Baker)—are sufficiently intractable to call into question our suggestion that this film is anything like a comedy. In the course of the action we observe Junior's cordial but somewhat circumspect reunion with his mother, now living by herself, his much warmer reengagement with his father, whose rodeo past has inspired Junior's own choice of careers, and his contentious, ongoing quarrel with his brother, whose foreclosure on their father's house inspires the one genuinely violent moment in the film when Junior knocks Curly through a sheet of glass. None of these relationships is significantly improved, let along resolved, so the film never comes close to achieving a comic resolution, and Junior's concluding gesture of financing his father's latest pipedream, gold digging in Australia, bespeaks his good heart and love for his father, but also leaves us wondering why he doesn't first repay the money he owes his mother.[3] As Peckinpah achieves wonderfully mixed effects such as this one, *Junior Bonner* comes to embody a realistic grasp of life's perennial difficulties and a rare wisdom —whatever label we attach to it.

At what we have termed midpoint between comic and tragic bounds fall three "action" films, *The Deadly Companions* (1961), *The Getaway* (1972), and *The Killer Elite* (1975). With varying success, all three films develop violent plots in which we are encouraged to believe the protagonists will somehow survive and more or less achieve their goals. We say "more or less" because in *The Deadly Companions* and *The Killer Elite* the protagonist succeeds in ways not quite expected by him but probably no surprise to the audience. In *The Deadly Companions* Yellowleg (Brian Keith) pursues vengeance against the man who scalped him during the Civil War only to renounce such violence at the end and turn instead to the new love interest (Maureen O'Hara) conveniently provided by a script Peckinpah wanted to recast but was forbidden to alter. As previously discussed, Peckinpah's "solution" to this implausible resolution was to have Yellowleg gun down a relatively innocent character before engaging Turkey (Chill Wills), the man who scalped him. It isn't clear how this would have turned out if Peckinpah's producer had not intervened, but it should be clear *The Deadly Companions* would have become something quite different from a commonplace revenge Western which almost always ends happily, with the protagonist turning to a new life and typically a new love. Not coincidentally, perhaps, *The Killer Elite* is another film in which Peckinpah was ordered to stick to a script in which his protagonist, Mike Locken (James Caan), sails away at the conclusion having successfully completed his comeback mission as a private agent/bodyguard. Peckinpah toyed with revising this predictable ending as well, by resurrecting one of Locken's friends who has been killed during the climactic shootout and placing him on the boat with Locken as he sails away at the end (see Simmons 220). The hard truth is that there is nothing Peckinpah could have done at the last minute to camouflage the fact he was not allowed to make these two films his own.

Like *The Deadly Companions* and *The Killer Elite*, *The Getaway* is a violent "action" film which ends happily, so happily Mark Crispin Miller believes the ending "is a tongue-in-cheek happiness" designed to "startle" an audience used to films in which young couples outside the law are shot down in the end (5). In this case, however, Peckinpah had almost complete control over the project,[4] including supervision of Walter Hill's adaptation of the extremely dark source novel, Jim Thompson's *The Getaway* (1958), a script which fully anticipates the "happy" conclusion to which Miller (and others) have objected.[5] The film begins grimly enough with Peckinpah's powerful presentation of Doc McCoy's (Steve McQueen's) dreadful routine in prison, but the film turns around once Doc is able to secure a parole from a powerful and corrupt member of the parole board to whom Doc sends his wife Carol (Ali MacGraw) to negotiate his freedom in exchange for his organization of a bank robbery. Not exactly a comedy (unless we see it as a dark version of what Stanley Cavell calls a comedy of remarriage), *The Getaway* becomes Peckinpah's most artfully crafted success story, beginning with the wonderful sequence in which the reunited Doc and Carol leap fully clothed into a small river in a park, then go home to the most delicately handled and touching love scene in Peckinpah's films (even more so than Billy the Kid's [Kris Kristofferson's] tryst with Maria [Rita Coolidge] at the end of *Pat Garrett and Billy the Kid* [1973]), then continuing with the elaborate details of the bank robbery, Doc's recovery of the bank money Carol has allowed someone to steal, Doc's several evasions of the police when Doc and Carol are apparently trapped, and finally concluding with the events at the El Paso hotel when Doc twice declines to kill someone who has tried to kill him, conclusively establishing what the film has suggested all along: that Doc is a thief but not a killer, a professional who happens to rob banks.

Peckinpah may be seen as romanticizing the criminal, a common complaint about his other films, especially *The Wild Bunch*, but he hopes to win us over with his careful attention to the details of Doc's life, rendered here so meticulously as to provide what Paul Seydor designates the "surface pleasures" Peckinpah was able to extract from the conventional materials with which he was working.[6] Like Peckinpah's more famous criminals, Pike Bishop and Pat Garrett, Doc becomes a compelling human study, deeply flawed but essentially decent, a professional we never see committing the mistakes or worse which underlie Pike's and Garrett's tragic fates. Doc's least attractive feature, the irrational jealousy he feels about Carol's sleeping with Jack Benyon (Ben Johnson), the man who arranges Doc's parole, is gradually transformed as Doc and Carol work together to survive and Doc comes to see that everything Carol has done (including shooting Benyon rather than himself) has been done for him. This leads to one of the oddest reunion scenes in all film, this one enacted not in an apartment bed but in the middle of a huge trash dump, where Doc and Carol "remarry" though they have no time for sexual celebration. Their reunion precedes their joint efforts to survive the attack on the El Paso hotel and authenticates the encomium on marriage delivered by the old man (Slim Pickens) who drives them across the border into Mexico, an "escape" Peckinpah's tragic heroes cannot negotiate but Doc and Carol have come to *deserve* at the end of this most satisfying of Peckinpah's non-tragic films.[7]

Four of Peckinpah's non-tragic films can be described as near-tragedies, though only *Straw Dogs* comes truly close to the tragic border. We have previously discussed Peckinpah's early efforts to shape *Major Dundee* (1965) into a *Moby-Dick*–like tragic action tracing Dundee's (Charlton Heston's) obsessive quest to track down the Apache war-party which has massacred one of Dundee's companies. The first half of this film amply documents Dundee's faults as a leader and the massive obstacles to achieving his military goals, thus preparing the way for an Ahab-like debacle as he pursues the Apaches from New Mexico to Mexico. *Major Dundee* became a near-tragedy or even a failed tragedy when Peckinpah reversed course and decided to portray Dundee as a military hero, someone able to work through his mistakes to a triumphant (if costly) military success. As we argue in Chapter Three, Dundee's comeback is hastily contrived in the film's final minutes and constitutes one of Peckinpah's least persuasive conclusions. *Cross of Iron* (1977), Peckinpah's other military film, and *The Osterman Weekend* (1983), his heroic attempt to legitimize Robert Ludlum's source novel, are much more credible and successful films, but neither realizes the tragic possibilities of its material. Indeed, Peckinpah seems to have resolutely avoided developing his German officers in *Cross of Iron* as tragic figures, preferring to present them as victims of the brutalities of war (in this case World War II) which level all significant traces of humanity in this, perhaps Peckinpah's most depressing film. *The Osterman Weekend* is a much livelier depiction of technology's pervasive role in modern life, but the victims of those who deploy their technological "toys" for sinister purposes never rise to anything like heroic status and remain Ludlum-like ciphers or unwitting dupes, despite Peckinpah's best efforts with a script he was again required to film unchanged.

Straw Dogs is much the best of the near-tragedies, a film which rivals the five tragic Westerns in its intense depiction of men and women in crisis. For Peckinpah, as we suggested in Chapter One, *Straw Dogs* is so much like his tragic films it is itself a tragic action. William Murray, Peckinpah's *Playboy* interviewer, characterized the film's protagonist, David Sumner (Dustin Hoffman), as an "intellectual [a college professor] who's running away from himself and refuses to take a stand on anything," someone who finally takes such a stand in defending a man threatened by a group of local toughs and who "becomes a man through this resort to violence," a murderous "mayhem" he finds enjoyable (68). Peckinpah completely rejected this reading, pointing out that David is sickened by the violence he discovers in himself, a violence he has effectively created by refusing to deal with the thugs who taunt him throughout the film. At this point Peckinpah announces his "belief" in *catharsis*, which he seems to understand as the experience of his audience rather than his characters. For the audience if not for David, the remarkably violent finale to *Straw Dogs* inspires "a purging of the emotions through pity and fear" (William Murray 68). Peckinpah does not directly say that *Straw Dogs* is tragic, but he seems to think it is and therefore invokes the Aristotelian concepts of pity and fear. Yet Peckinpah himself praises David for having "guts enough and sense enough to stand up and do what he had to do" despite his sickening discovery of the violence in himself (William Murray 68). This is to say that David grows because of his dreadful experience and is free to confront the future with a new sense of himself and his world, as we argued in Chapter Six. Where is the permanent and irreversible damage in all of this? We think Peckinpah's "reading" of his own film is exactly right, but we would respectfully reject his use of tragic terminology.

We would argue that Peckinpah's artistic task in *Straw Dogs* was to render convincingly David's harrowing siege while persuading us that he survives the experience psychologically as well as physically, then finds that he "can't go home again," that is, he can't go back to the life he has lived because he is a different man (see William Murray 68). Earlier, we cited Gerald Mast's masterful analysis of how Howard Hawks structured *Red River* (1948) so that, *pace* those who dislike the ending, we accept the fact that Tom Dunson (John Wayne) and Matthew Garth (Montgomery Clift) can *never* kill one another at the conclusion (or at any other time). We believe that a detailed analysis of *Straw Dogs* would demonstrate that Peckinpah has similarly prepared us for the non-tragic conclusion to his film even as he establishes there is nothing inevitable about this outcome, the essential component of Sheldon Sacks' "serious" action. Indeed, all of Peckinpah's non-tragic films would yield valuable insights from such an analysis, for Peckinpah often (if not always) structured these films so as to justify the non-tragic resolutions which contrast dramatically with the resolutions to the tragic films. Though it is tempting to argue that Peckinpah's tragic films (like Shakespeare's tragic plays) represent his "real" feelings about life, excellent films such as *Junior Bonner*, *The Getaway*, and *Straw Dogs* (like Shakespeare's better histories, comedies, and romances) should remind us that Peckinpah's tragedies are not great because they are tragedies but because they are splendidly-made tragedies.

II

Like our earlier review of famous Western films thought to be tragic, this brief overview of Peckinpah's non-tragic films should suggest that his tragedies constitute a distinctive group despite their differences. In their different ways, each of the tragic Westerns tells the story of a man who suffers permanent and irreversible damage (usually death) because of the conditions he confronts and/or the decisions he makes. Unlike the protagonists of virtually every other major Western film, as well as his own non-tragic films, Peckinpah's tragic heroes cannot escape the fateful consequences of their dramatic situations. They differ significantly in the extent to which they are responsible for these situations, but they share the tragic fate anticipated throughout the action of each film and richly realized in each film's conclusion. Our individual chapters have traced the diverse particulars which underlie Peckinpah's several embodiments of this common tragic narrative. Rather than reprise our findings in these earlier chapters, we would like to conclude by highlighting several features common to all the tragic films: the characterization of the protagonist as an active agent in his tragedy rather than a victim; the increasingly crucial development of Peckinpah's female characters; and Peckinpah's central role in revising these films as well as directing them.

We have stressed the differences among Peckinpah's five tragic protagonists, the great range between Steve Judd and Pat Garrett, but it is crucial to Peckinpah's version of tragedy that none of his protagonists is a victim of forces beyond his control. Steve Judd may seem a partial exception, for his demise does not derive from a moral "flaw" or even an unwitting "mistake," and he certainly suffers from modern America's indifference or even hostility toward Steve's classic virtues of personal integrity, loyalty, and professionalism. ("Modern" here is early twentieth century, but Peckinpah obviously sees the film's crisis as continuing through the century.) But *Ride the High Country* firmly establishes Steve Judd as someone who chooses to be the person he is rather than adapt to the mercenary standards of a new era, so he is ultimately responsible for his own fate even though there is nothing "mistaken" about his exemplary conduct. This makes possible the unique form of Christian tragedy embodied in *Ride the High Country*. By contrast, the protagonist of *Noon Wine*, Mr. Thompson, is the first of Peckinpah's more typical tragic figures, all of whom bring about their own catastrophes by committing grave mistakes which derive from their own decisions rather than their circumstances. Unlike the protagonists to come, Pike Bishop and Pat Garrett, Mr. Thompson is unaware of his weaknesses, the vanity and self-indulgence which underlie his dependence on his hired hand Mr. Helton (Per Oscarsson), and therefore he fails to understand why he might resort to violence against Homer T. Hatch (Theodore Bikel) in order to protect Helton — and himself. Even at the end, as Mr. Thompson prepares to kill himself, he continues to blame Hatch for their fatal quarrel, as if he were a mere victim, but the act of suicide tells a very different tale about the guilt he feels and its irreversible challenge to his self-conception as a "good" man.

The later tragic protagonists, Pike Bishop, Pat Garrett, and Bennie, are crucial to the guilt-ridden forms of tragedy Peckinpah began to develop with *Noon Wine* and brought to rich and varied fruition in *The Wild Bunch*, *Pat Garrett and Billy the Kid*, and *Bring Me the Head of Alfredo Garcia*. Pike Bishop is the most compelling of these guilty figures, a man whose demise does not derive from a single mistake but rather a series of occasions where he fails to live up to his Steve Judd–like standards (always allowing for the differences implicit in Steve's history as a lawman and Pike's as an outlaw). Pike's decision to lead his band of four men against a virtual army to retrieve his comrade Angel (Jaime Sanchez) is in response to his feelings for Angel but also his many previous failures to protect those for whom he is responsible, most especially the love of his life, Aurora (Aurora Clavel), whose death haunts him more than any of the compromises involving his gang members. Pike's guilt is essential to the film's coherence, for his suicidal decision makes no sense unless he understands that because he is so intensely conscious of his previous failures he faces a classical Hobson's Choice at the end: to betray his self-conception yet again by walking away from Angel's predicament, or to end his life while trying to embody his convictions.[8] As we argue in Chapters Four and Five, Pike Bishop is Peckinpah's most traditional hero insofar as he faces his grave dilemma because of his own mistakes and ultimately his commitment to the values he must die defending.

Peckinpah's final two tragic protagonists, Pat Garrett and Bennie, represent remarkable variations on the tragic structure which informs *The Wild Bunch*. Like Pike Bishop, Pat Garrett is aware of his crucial mistakes as his film opens and must deal with similar but even more lacerating emotions as the action continues and his errors multiply. We have compared Garrett to Shakespeare's Macbeth, a much more famous example of a protagonist who commits a terrible mistake he cannot undo and in fact repeats again and again as he protects the title achieved through his initial mistake. Garrett's mistake is not literally irreversible, of course, for commitment to the corporate elite of New Mexico is obviously different from murdering one's kinsman and king. Moreover, Garrett knows what he should do to reverse his chosen course in becoming sheriff of Lincoln County, as he makes clear in the crucial scene with his wife Ida (Aurora Clavell). Yet he cannot bring himself to honor his own insights and change his life once again, as if his "crime" is as inalterable as Macbeth's. Peckinpah relentlessly traces the devastating effects on Garrett of pursuing his task of hunting down and killing Billy the Kid, a former friend he may still value more than anyone else in his life. His "success" in assassinating the Kid marks his utter self-destruction, as he seems to understand when he shoots his own image in a mirror moments after killing Billy. This is why it is not only historically accurate but artistically acceptable that Garrett should be Peckinpah's one tragic protagonist to survive the immediate action, for none of the protagonists suffers a darker, more damaging fate than Garrett, who is "dead inside," as his wife tells him, and who insures there will be no spiritual revival by completing his deadly, suicidal mission.

Bennie, the protagonist of Peckinpah's last tragedy, *Bring Me the Head of Alfredo Garcia*, is another variation on the pattern embodied in *The Wild Bunch*, for unlike Pike Bishop or Pat Garrett he is not aware of the self-inflicted disaster he commits early in his film. In this regard he resembles Mr. Thompson, though his error in pursuing Alfredo Garcia's head for $10,000 (the same amount the Wild Bunch receives from General Mapache [Emilio Fernandez]) involves greed rather than fear that his comfortable world is about to be taken away from him. Bennie's tragic decision is even more incriminating than Mr. Thompson's, for he pursues his sordid quest after he declares his love for Elita (Isela Vega), who makes it clear she cannot continue with Bennie if he desecrates Alfredo Garcia's grave in his quest for money. Whereas Mr. Thompson's fatal mistake occurs in a brief moment (however long the build-up to his violent act), Bennie persists in his grotesque search over several days and commits a series of horrific acts while doing so, much as Pat Garrett repeats his terrible error again and again with each deadly stage in his hunt for the Kid. If Bennie recalls Mr. Thompson early in the action, he comes to resemble Pike Bishop and Pat Garrett once Elita is murdered and he begins his quest for revenge, for every step along the way, incredibly violent and increasingly pointless, gives rise to the great guilt he now feels for his own complicity in the scheme which leads to Elita's murder. Bennie's final attack on El Jefe (Emilio Fernandez) resembles Pike's action against Mapache, and Bennie's guilt and grief strongly recall Pike's final emotions, but Bennie's violence at the end is less redemptive and less meaningful than the cathartic destruction of Mapache's army. Nonetheless, it is to Bennie's—and Peckinpah's—credit that Bennie and the film in which he appears invite comparison with Peckinpah's most compelling character and greatest film.

The extent to which Peckinpah's tragic protagonists are responsible for their own fates sets Peckinpah's tragedies apart from most forms of modern tragedy. Less unique but troubling to many is Peckinpah's focus in all of his films on male protagonists. It is interesting, however, that Peckinpah's development of his female characters expands over time as they become increasingly crucial to the action of each film. In *Ride the High Country*, Elsa Knudsen (Mariette Hartley), the one female character of note, is important to the events depicted but relatively undeveloped as an independent character. As Paul Seydor remarks, Peckinpah's Mrs. Thompson (Olivia de Havilland) represents a breakthrough of sorts as a character of major importance to the story and greater complexity than the women in previous Peckinpah films (1977, 133), qualities Peckinpah largely added to Katherine Anne Porter's story, as we note in Chapter Three. In the last three tragedies, women become even more crucial to the tragic action even in relatively small parts, such as those of Pike Bishop's lover Aurora and Ida Garrett, Mrs. Baker (Katy Jurado), and Maria, the three Hispanic women we have emphasized in our reading of *Pat Garrett and Billy the Kid*. The climax to this trend is Peckinpah's Elita in *Bring Me the Head of Alfredo Garcia*, a film in which Elita is no less important than the male protagonist and substantially more attractive as a character. Indeed, Isela Vega's performance is essential to the film's tragic impact, for Elita's death must be heartfelt by the audience as well as by Bennie if Bennie's loss is to have the effect Peckinpah desired. We have told the story of Peckinpah picking up on the compelling strength of Vega's performance and adjusting his film to accommodate the wiser, more captivating Elita who adds so much to the project's effect. With this final film, it can be said that the tragic films as a group offer one of the most affecting presentations of women not only in Peckinpah (for many women, small praise indeed) but in recent American filmmaking.

We obviously believe Peckinpah's tragic films comprise a very great achievement, not only the one body of tragic works among Western directors but, with the exception of Orson Welles' six tragedies,[9] the most distinguished collection of such films in all of American cinema. This may seem a grandiose claim, but very few of the greatest directors have turned to the tragic mode more than once or twice. Whether or not one agrees with this assessment, we think it is important to see how extensively Peckinpah participated in shaping these films as writer as well as director. Whether recasting 80 percent of the dialogue in *Ride the High Country*, as Seydor estimates (1997, 43), adapting *Noon Wine* by himself, revising *The Wild Bunch* in the manner Seydor has charted so brilliantly, redesigning *Pat Garrett and Billy the Kid* both in preproduction and production, or writing *Bring Me the Head of Alfredo Garcia* (with Gordon Dawson) and then taking the film to new heights during production, Peckinpah has put his writerly mark on his tragic films as very few directors have ever done. Our efforts to document his transformative efforts with these films have been directed at demonstrating the very conscious artistry which underlies his better films, preeminently the Westerns addressed in this study. Notwithstanding the problems he confronted throughout his difficult life and those he brought to the set on even his greatest films, Peckinpah's commitment to his tragic art was ultimately sufficient to produce five of the great tragic films in the history of American cinema.

Notes

Chapter One

1. It may seem a bit strange to group *Noon Wine* with Peckinpah's feature films, but we think this television production is one of Peckinpah's finest works as well as clearly relevant to a study of his tragic films. In Chapter Three we will have much more to say about the place of *Noon Wine*, a film very few people have seen, in Peckinpah's career.

2. As Tom McAlindon notes (1), Kenneth Muir first suggested that we abandon our efforts to define Shakespearean tragedy and confine our attention to Shakespearean tragedies (12).

3. Kitses derives his information from Joseph McBride (435–37), who provides other examples of how Ford's studios and producers, especially Darryl F. Zanuck, recut or even reshot scenes from a number of films. See also Spittles 12, 19, 95. The extent to which Anthony Mann's films were affected by studio intervention will figure in the discussion of Mann to follow. Peckinpah's problems with his studios and producers are legendary, of course, and will figure in almost every chapter of this study.

4. To put it mildly, not everyone would agree with this view of York's pursuit of Geronimo. As mentioned, Westbrook sees nothing but American imperialism at work here. Kitses takes much the same view: "Yet what is the purpose of the campaign York is leading against Geronimo as the film ends? Nothing in the film can account for further action against the Apache, given their sympathetic depiction" (2004, 69). In *The Material Ghost*, Gilberto Perez, who echoes Robert Warshow in titling his chapter on Westerns and gangster films "American Tragedy," is more compassionate toward York, but he goes so far as to see him as "an agent of imperialist aggression" (250) whose "fall" in the course of the film makes *Fort Apache* an American tragedy: "Ford sorrowfully takes the view that York acts as he must under the circumstances. One may want to take issue with this view. But one cannot feel superior to it. Righteousness will not do in the face of this political tragedy" (251). Even as he acknowledges the Ibsenian "life lie" which York tells in order to uphold the tradition and honor of "the Regiment," Ford seems personally to hold a more understanding, far less "sorrowful" view of York and even his praise for Thursday. Echoing the conclusion to *The Man Who Shot Liberty Valance* ("When the legend becomes fact, print the legend"), Ford told Peter Bogdanovich that "if printing a falsehood will help the morale of the Cavalry or the nation — then print the legend" (Bogdanovich 34). One can reject this view, of course, much as one can reject Ford's use of Geronimo's bloodthirsty reputation (previously encountered in *Stagecoach*). It should be apparent, however, that Ford did not intend *Fort Apache* as a tragedy.

5. Our reading of *The Searchers* may be understood as a response to Martin W. Winkler's "Tragic Features in John Ford's *The Searchers*." Winkler goes beyond identifying "tragic features" in Ford's film to argue that *The Searchers* is a tragic action which focuses on Ethan Edwards' descent into madness and his exclusion from the emerging Western community when he is "refused entry into the land of home and family, peace and civilization" (201). We would note that Ethan is not "refused entry" to the Jorgensen home but rather wisely chooses to remain apart from the scene of Debbie's reunion with her family. We would also wonder by what logic Ethan's lifting up Debbie rather than killing her "is the best proof of the film's tragic nature" (200)? Winkler adduces a few Greek examples of tragic actions which end happily, but he offers no modern examples of this extremely doubtful practice except to cite Robert Warshow's equally doubtful claim that even when serious Westerns end happily they really depict their hero's "defeat." More significantly, perhaps, we would also note that Winkler avoids any mention of Ethan's genuinely humane moments in tracing his supposed descent into madness and ignores such telling decisions as Ethan's agreement to submit to a legal inquiry into the shooting of the dry-gulching Jerem Futterman (Peter Mamoskos) and his two henchmen and Ethan's allowing Marty to enter Scar's camp before the military's raid so as to give Debbie a chance to survive the attack. Winkler's essay seems to us a very selective account of Ford's most complicated and greatest film.

6. For an extremely interesting discussion of *Devil's Doorway* as a complex version of a "pro–Indian" type of Western, see Richard Slotkin, *Gunfighter Nation* (1992) 366–74.

7. "All" of these films follow this pattern if one assumes, as we assume, that Will Lockhart and Barbara Waggoman (Cathy O'Donnell) are certain to be reunited in the near future. Lockhart's decision to ride off at the end (though he tells Barbara where he can be found in Laramie) recalls Wyatt Earp's departure from Clementine Carter at the end of *My Darling Clementine*, but Mann's film is less ambiguous about the eventual outcome.

8. After making *High Noon*, Zinnemann went on to direct *From Here to Eternity* (1953), *Oklahoma!* (1955), *The Sundowners* (1960), and *The Day of the Jackal* (1973), among other films.

9. Phillip Drummond makes the same point about the lack of complexity in Kane's character (76).

10. Edward Countryman and Evonne von Heussen-Countryman reach more positive conclusions about *Shane* by reading the film in the rich context of Stevens' other films, especially those he directed just before and after *Shane*. Much as we admire their analysis, easily the most extensive discussion to date, we think that the film's limitations emerge if one considers its place within the Western film genre.

11. Toward the end of his career, his leverage much diminished, Peckinpah again worked under the stipulation that he could not alter the script he had been given, first with *The Killer Elite* (1975) and then *The Osterman Weekend* (Weddle 1994, 498, 536). As Peckinpah's greatest strength as a scenarist was in rewriting the scripts of others, this recurring prohibition is one of the many ironies in Peckinpah's career.

12. Like almost everyone writing on *The Deadly Companions*, we say that Peckinpah "chose to go outside the script" in having Yellowleg and not Turkey (Chill Wills) shoot Billy. In fact, however, Peckinpah may well have restored what was in the original script by A. S. Fleischman, whose screenplay was the basis for his novel *The Deadly Companions* (1960) in which Yellowleg shoots Billy before going after Turkey (Dukore 206, n.14; 207, n.28). By the time Peckinpah shot this scene, the film's producer, Charles FitzSimons (Maureen O'Hara's brother), had recast Fleischman's script so as to make it clear that Billy is killed by Turkey and not Yellowleg. Technically, then, Peckinpah went outside the *revised* script when he had Yellowleg shoot Billy. FitzSimons subsequently recut Peckinpah's scene to suggest that Billy is shot by Turkey, the ex–Confederate soldier Yellowleg has been pursuing ever since Turkey scalped him during the Civil War. This is the version included in the released film. Kitses (2004, 207) and others ridicule FitzSimons' decision, but we agree with Seydor that FitzSimons' response to Peckinpah's scene is "not without some reason": "How can you have a man shoot another against whom he bears no grudge and then turn around and be unable to kill a man he's hated for years?" (Seydor 1997, 36). To justify the manner in which Yellowleg kills Billy, Peckinpah would have had to revise the entire film.

13. Our account of Peckinpah's early life derives largely from David Weddle's excellent critical biography. Weddle's grasp of his subject's art as well as his life equals that of the best biographers of twentieth-century American filmmakers.

14. Or was Peckinpah married six times to four women? Weddle says that in the late 1970s Peckinpah took up with Marcy Blueher, an Albuquerque widow, "and made her the fourth Mrs. Peckinpah," though he drove her away within a few months (1994, 527). Were Peckinpah and Marcy Blueher legally married? Most accounts continue to credit Peckinpah with five marriages, and Weddle himself refers in his index to Marie Selland, Begonia Palacios, and Joie Gould as Peckinpah's first, second, and third wife, respectively, but does not identify Marcy Blueher as Peckinpah's fourth wife.

15. We elaborate here an idea memorably expressed by Kathleen Murphy in her obituary for Peckinpah: "Peckinpah found baptisms where he could, in tacky hotel showers, in the free flow of wine and tequila, in momentarily Thoreauvian ponds, and always in the blood of his much fallen and fragmented heroes" (1985, 74).

16. We take this image for Peckinpah's life from James Coburn's commentary on Peckinpah in the film documentary *Sam Peckinpah's West*.

17. We do not want to gloss over the problem of Peckinpah intending to create the responses of pity and fear in *Straw Dogs*. If *Straw Dogs* is a tragedy, then we should have a different title and another chapter. We do not think the film is tragic, but it is possible that Peckinpah thought it was, much as Ford apparently felt about *The Searchers*. Both *Straw Dogs* and *The Searchers* deal with men who survive great ordeals and, more to the point, seem to learn from their experiences, even if Ethan Edwards, unlike David Sumner, cannot really change who he is. The knowledge they achieve may be bitter, but the process by which they obtain it — the action of each film — is anything but "irreversible" and should not be characterized as tragic.

18. We know little of what Peckinpah thought about Mann or Leone. So far as we can tell, Peckinpah had nothing to say about Eastwood's films. Interestingly, Seydor tells us that Peckinpah disliked Budd Boetticher's films (1977, 355), which he perhaps saw as low-budget, second feature B-Westerns, all quite similar to each other (especially the three celebrated "Ranown" Westerns of Boetticher, Randolph Scott, screenwriter Burt Kennedy, and producer Harry Joe Brown). That these late 1950s and early 1960s classics are now considered a unique contribution to the development of the Western may indicate a certain bias on Peckinpah's part, but that bias was shared by most of his Hollywood peers. One wonders if Randolph Scott, the iconic star of these remarkable films, ever talked to Peckinpah about Boetticher during the filming of *Ride the High Country*. In any case, our theory concerning how Peckinpah responded to the Western tradition largely derives from the Westerns discussed earlier in this chapter.

Chapter Two

1. All biblical quotations are to the authorized King James version of *The Holy Bible* as reproduced in *The Scofield Reference Bible* (New York: Oxford University Press, 1909). This is the version of the Bible Peckinpah very likely grew up reading in an age without "modernized" alternatives.

2. For accounts of Peckinpah's role in shaping *Ride the High Country*, see Simmons 41–54, Weddle 1994, 197–218, and Seydor 1997, 43–60. Weddle notes that Peckinpah did not supervise the musical score, which he did not like (1994, 217–18). The music was incorporated by the film's producer, Richard E. Lyons (Simmons 52).

3. We have previously suggested that the "tragic flaw" argument is not really Aristotelian if Gerald Else and others are correct in translating Aristotle's *hamartia* as a "mistake" rather than a moral "flaw." Our claim at this point therefore refers to the argument commonly identified with Aristotle's *Poetics*. We will return to this issue at the end of this chapter.

4. Frye's useful definition enables us to situate *Ride the High Country* within the somewhat hybrid ranks of works of literature and film which are both Christian and tragic. For many critics and theologians, however, Christian tragedy represents a contradiction in terms. For a well-reasoned refutation of the subgenre "Christian tragedy," sees D. D. Raphael, *The Paradox of Tragedy* 37–67. For a spirited defense of the same idea, see Nathan Scott, Jr., "Foreword," *The Tragic Vision and Christian Faith* ix-xix.

5. This is a polite way of saying we will be talking

about Peckinpah's use of water in every chapter, especially those dealing with *Noon Wine*, *The Wild Bunch*, and *Bring Me the Head of Alfredo Garcia*. We believe that our own apparent obsession with the subject mirrors Peckinpah's.

6. That Peckinpah, and not a costumer, deliberately chose the common red bandanna may seem farfetched to some readers, but he was as color-conscious as an artist, and obsessed with loading complex meanings into the smallest details: "[Lucien] Ballard reflects that Peckinpah's attention to the ambience of his films is an integral part of his technique. He remarked that, for example, while making *Ride the High Country* Peckinpah selected virtually every piece of clothing the actors were to wear, a practice he carried over through each of his projects" (Reisner and Kane 25).

7. Seydor points out just how prophetic are the new lyrics the Hammond brothers invent to celebrate Billy's marriage to Elsa, especially the line "For to tie the knot that binds them 'til they die" (1997, 49). But it is equally interesting to look at the actual lyrics of "When the Roll Is Called Up Yonder," as they seem decidedly inappropriate for a wedding, since they focus almost solely on the afterlife. That the Hammonds, inveterate children of darkness, should sing of "that bright and shining morning/When the dead Christ shall rise/When the morn shall break eternal bright and fair/And the saved of the earth shall gather/Over to the other shore," indicates how deeply Peckinpah's irony cuts into their choice of hymns.

8. The final script and earlier drafts of *Ride the High Country* are in the Peckinpah Collection at the Margaret Herrick Library, Academy of Motion Picture Arts and Sciences, Beverly Hills, California.

9. Those viewers who first watched *Ride the High Country* on television or videotape will be familiar with a rather tacky and excessive golden border, a Leo the Lionesque frame within a frame, which MGM seems to have added to its pan and scan video release to further dramatize Steve Judd's death. Peckinpah had nothing to do with this gilded and gaudy addition, and doubtless would have been outraged by it. Nevertheless, for a reading of that golden border within the context of the whole film, see John L. Simons' "The Double Vision of Tragedy in Sam Peckinpah's *Ride the High Country.*"

10. Joel McCrea/Steve Judd's "glorification was explicit, unsubtle and shattering," writes Paul Schrader (quoted in Weddle 1994, 214). Although we disagree with Schrader's reading of the final scene as "unsubtle," we too find Steve's "glorification" to be emotionally "shattering." Even Randolph Scott, the stony, stoical hero of so many Budd Boetticher Westerns, "had tears streaming down ... his face," reported Mariette Hartley (Weddle 1994, 214). This was to be Scott's last film, and his farewell to the Western, a genre to which he had contributed so much.

11. For more on the distinctive tragic form of *A Farewell to Arms*, see Robert Merrill, "Tragic Form in *A Farewell to Arms*."

Chapter Three

1. It appears that Peckinpah wanted — and expected — to release a three-hour version of *Major Dundee*. Seydor quotes Peckinpah's claim that 55 minutes were "removed or never included" in the version Columbia first released (1997, 72), which would get us very close to 180 minutes for Peckinpah's "intended" version. But it is also clear that Peckinpah tried to work with Bresler and the other editors to achieve a somewhat shorter final cut. Weddle refers to a version 161 minutes long (though he notes Peckinpah wanted to restore an additional 10 minutes to this version) (1994, 250), Simmons suggests the film was 154 minutes long when Peckinpah left the project (71), and Marshall Fine claims the last cut Peckinpah worked on was 150 minutes long (99). We have little doubt that all of these numbers — and versions — existed at one time or another, as Peckinpah and the other editors worked and reworked the film, mostly in the direction of shortening it.

2. It is possible that Peckinpah saw the Bresler cut at a preview at the Egyptian Theater on Hollywood Boulevard described by Weddle (1994, 252), then later saw the even shorter version released by Columbia. Those who knew Peckinpah agree he would have responded more or less the same way to both versions.

3. Of the three scenes restored in the extended version, the first depicts Major Dundee and his men recapturing the Confederate prisoners who have escaped from the major's fort, but it does not include the conversation in which Sergeant Gomez tells Dundee that Gomez was captured by Apaches as a child and later fought with them against his native Mexicans; the second greatly expands (by more than five minutes) Peckinpah's treatment of Dundee's tortured, drunken stay at Durango, but it does not include "a long montage of [Dundee's] memories of all that has happened" (Kitses 2004, 211); and the third, which ends with the revelation of Riago's mutilated body, is much as Kitses describes it. Of the five other scenes Kitses cites, several were apparently only partially shot, including the opening sequence in which Dundee's B troop arrives at the Rostes ranch and participates in a Halloween party, the massacre which ensues when Sierra Charriba and his Apache warriors attack the ranch, and the knife-fight between Sam Potts and Gomez during the fiesta at the Mexican village. Kitses says the opening scenes were never shot (2004, 211), but Simmons describes Peckinpah's extraordinary efforts to fit these scenes into his very difficult shooting schedule (70). Seydor remarks in the commentary to the 2005 Sony edition that these efforts did produce footage but not enough good footage to be used even if Columbia had been willing.

4. The Riago scene provides a mildly amusing academic story. In 1969, Kitses describes the discovery of Riago's "mutilated corpse" as the last of eight scenes deleted from the three-hour version Peckinpah preferred (140). In 1980, in the first edition of *Peckinpah: The Western Films*, Seydor summarizes Kitses' account of the cuts but remarks that Kitses makes "one mistake," as the Riago scene is "in the film" (53, n.14). Subsequently, in 1993, Bliss writes a footnote in which he describes Kitses' account of the cuts made in *Major Dundee* and cites Seydor's correction of Kitses' "error" about the Riago scene (315, n.1). In 1997, in the second edition of his book, Seydor deletes the earlier note in which he identified Kitses' mistake, perhaps because he was no longer sure Kitses was wrong. Finally, in 2004, in his second edition of *Horizons West*, Kitses asserts that "a fragment" of the scene involving Riago's death is in "most prints of the film" (246, n.4), a claim which silently acknowledges Seydor's original "correction."

The irony here is that the scene in question *was* deleted from the version Columbia released, although it may not have been deleted from all prints of the film, and the Peckinpah scholars who comment on *Major*

Dundee in the Sony extended version (Seydor among them) speculate that Seydor may have seen the scene in question in one of those prints. This seems very likely, for in the filmography of his 1997 edition Seydor lists the running time for *Major Dundee* as 134 minutes (394), which suggests that he has always worked from the Bresler cut. It is well known that when Warner Brothers removed several scenes from *The Wild Bunch* after the film first opened these cuts were not made in all prints, so some viewers continued to see the film as Peckinpah intended it despite the "official" reduction in the film's text. These examples illustrate the endless problems in tracing the history of Peckinpah's films in their "final" form.

5. The Porter passage is from her 1956 essay "*Noon Wine*: The Sources." Peckinpah's copies of *Noon Wine* and "*Noon Wine*: The Sources" are in the Peckinpah Collection. We cite the essay as it appears in *The Collected Essays, and Occasional Writings of Katherine Anne Porter*; the passage quoted is on page 479.

6. Toward the end of Chapter One we discuss Peckinpah's several statements about *catharsis*. For other critical treatments of this subject, see Prince 1998, 108–12, and Gabrielle Murray 60–62.

7. Unless otherwise indicated, all page references are to Porter's *Noon Wine* in *The Collected Stories of Katherine Anne Porter*.

8. For an interesting review of the mysterious stranger motif in American fiction (including *Noon Wine*), see Roy R. Male's "The Story of the Mysterious Stranger in American Fiction."

9. In Porter the period between Helton's arrival and that of Homer T. Hatch is nine years. Peckinpah shortens the gap to three years, no doubt to allow him to use the same young actors in the roles of Arthur and Herbert Thompson.

10. In Porter Helton dies in a prison cell after being captured earlier that day by a posse which is forced to subdue him physically. By having Helton die at the time he is captured, Peckinpah avoids having to report Helton's death off-stage or to include a second scene in the prison cell. Peckinpah also uses the fatal attack in a corral to develop his ironic characterization of Mr. McClellan (L. Q. Jones), the last neighbor visited by Mr. and Mrs. Thompson and the member of the posse who strikes the fatal blow against Helton. Unlike Porter's character, Peckinpah's McClellan is an active member of the posse who later speaks out hypocritically against Mr. Thompson the "murderer." It is very debatable whether this alteration of McClellan is an improvement on Porter.

11. We quote from Peckinpah's draft version of this speech because the draft (included in the Peckinpah Collection) establishes that Peckinpah always intended to have Mr. Thompson pause in speaking about the murder of Hatch just as he pauses when denying that he ever deliberately harmed his wife.

12. In Porter the "neat oblong patch" Mr. Thompson makes in blacking out the reference to his wife seems to allude to Mr. Hatch (Hatch/patch), whose death is again linked with his wife in Mr. Thompson's mind, as well as to Edgar Allan Poe's famous story "The Oblong Box," which tells of a grieving artist-husband who lashes himself to his dead wife's casket as both are borne out to sea in a violent storm. Indeed, Poe is generally relevant to the many plays on doubling throughout Porter's short novel, for no American writer works as many variations on the theme of the double, or *doppelgänger*, as Poe. For more on this connection, see Walsh.

Surprisingly, Poe figures throughout Peckinpah's tragic films. We have already had occasion to mention in *Ride the High Country* the Poe-like "premature burial" of Elsa Knudsen, the "Usheresque" tarn-like mountain lake with its fallen timbers and eerie night hawk cries, and the darkly ominous raven which sits on top of Henry Hammond's shoulder. In future chapters we will discover important Poe elements in *Pat Garrett and Billy the Kid*, with its use of the doubling motif and the crucial significance of Pat Garrett's assassin, John W. *Poe*, as well as in *Bring Me the Head of Alfredo Garcia*, perhaps the most overtly Poe-esque of Peckinpah's films, with its literal use of the "premature burial" motif and its evocative allusions to one of Poe's most terrifying tales, "The Black Cat." We have no evidence that Peckinpah was an avid reader of Edgar Allan Poe, a perennial favorite among young readers, but Poe certainly strikes us as a writer to whom the young, and even older, Peckinpah would have been drawn. Finally, while exploring the frontier raft scene in *Pat Garrett and Billy the Kid*, we have been amused by the intriguing controversy which has surrounded the identity of the strange black animal on the raft in George Caleb Bingham's mesmerizing *Fur Traders on the Lower Missouri* to which we allude in Chapter Five. To almost any viewer of the painting it appears to be a very Poe-esque large black cat, its image arrestingly doubled in the mirroring river, but it seems that Bingham himself thought he was painting a tethered black bear cub, which would certainly make more sense in a frontier painting with its poignant evocation of a threatened wilderness world. For both personal and aesthetic reasons we prefer to see it as a mysterious black cat.

13. Anyone who has seen Per Oscarsson's stunning performance in the 1966 film version of Norwegian novelist Knut Hamsun's *Hunger* (originally published in 1890) will recognize the striking similarities between Pontus, the slightly mad wandering artist/hero of Hamsun's novel, and Peckinpah's Mr. Helton in *Noon Wine*. Oscarsson's character, significantly unnamed in the film, is a writer of essays for local newspapers and magazines (in the novel he is a playwright) who is striving to make a living amidst the bourgeois, prosperous streets of Christiana (modern-day Oslo), but who ultimately seems to will his own starvation because, even though he has money for food, and has eaten earlier, he no longer wishes to eat. Spiritually starving and alienated from modern life like Kafka's hunger artist, a character with whom he has been compared, he cannot find the "food" he desires. He longs for an impossible world, much like the harmonica-playing Mr. Helton, who himself eats almost nothing although he too yearns for the wine of a paradise now past, only briefly present, then gone, in the sad-sweet tune he plays.

It seems apparent to us that Per Oscarsson created Olaf Helton as a close cousin of *Hunger*'s Pontus. Peckinpah, knowing genius when he saw it, allowed Oscarsson to develop this interpretation of Porter's character. Whether a Norwegian artist from the countryside or a wandering, alienated farm hand who is also an artist when he plays his melancholy song on his harmonica, Oscarsson completely *inhabits* his characters. We suspect that both Jason Robards and Olivia de Havilland were influenced by the strange otherworldly beauty and tragic terror of Oscarsson's haunted Mr. Helton. Had Peckinpah seen *Hunger*, a film released only a year before the making of *Noon Wine*? One would think that at least Daniel Melnick had seen it, or he would not have cast Oscarsson in the role of Helton. It is impossible to say whether *Hunger* directly influenced Peckinpah's adaptation, but Oscarsson's role in the earlier film seems to have made *Noon Wine* a richer, more profound work of art.

14. In one of her best performances as Catherine Sloper in William Wyler's outstanding adaptation of Henry James' *Washington Square, The Heiress* (1949), a film for which she won an Oscar, Olivia de Havilland demonstrates the ability to capture a complex, ambiguous — we would say tragic — doubleness when, like Mrs. Thompson, she evokes contradictory emotions within a single brief shot. At the end of *The Heiress*, Catherine demonstrates a passionate sense of regret at her rejection of her fortune-seeking former suitor, Morris Townsend (Montgomery Clift), whom she still loves, while almost simultaneously her face contracts into a hard, vengeful smile and she turns her back on him as he pounds away at her locked door. Famous for "eating actors alive," William Wyler was a ruthless and demanding director, and he drove de Havilland into what is arguably the finest performance of her career. Strikingly, Peckinpah did much the same thing with de Havilland in *Noon Wine*. "He really beat her up emotionally," reported Daniel Melnick, who watched Peckinpah mercilessly deride her, exposing her genuine vulnerability, even "while he kept the cameras running secretly." "[T]hat [final] moment of devastation and desolation was really the product of something Sam evoked for her in real life" (Fine 109). Peckinpah got the performance he wanted from de Havilland, but her Ellie Thompson was "too close to home" for the young director, whose tortured and contradictory feelings about his mother Fern surfaced for all to see in this uncompromising anatomy of a tragically broken marriage. Thus it was no surprise to those who knew the deeply riven Peckinpah family that *Noon Wine* was the one film her son made which Fern Peckinpah could not abide (Weddle 294; Seydor 1997, 134).

15. Robards was to become one of the more important recurring actors in Peckinpah's films, returning first as the title character in *The Ballad of Cable Hogue* and then as Governor Lew Wallace in *Pat Garrett and Billy the Kid*. His training as the foremost American tragic actor of his time is most relevant to his portrayal of Mr. Thompson, however, a part for which his experience with O'Neill's major plays amply prepared him.

Chapter Four

1. Of course, the original source for the gang's name is Butch Cassidy's train-robbing "Wild Bunch," or "Hole in the Wall Gang," famous for its flight into South America. But as the implicitly oxymoronic title of Peckinpah's first film, *The Deadly Companions*, indicates, he has a penchant for paradoxical pairs.

2. Paul Seydor, in his *Peckinpah: The Western Films — A Reconsideration*, makes a solid case against the criticism that "all the women are wholly unsympathetic" (159). For a contrary view at its most virulent, see Joan Mellen, *Big Bad Wolves: Masculinity in American Films*: "Viciousness is all in the Peckinpah Western, and male virility finds its purest expression in violence and in the blazing forth of primitive instinct." She concludes by calling *The Wild Bunch* "a homosexual *Love Story*" (272). Mellen is so blinded by her hatred of Peckinpah's films that she ignores their contradictions, implies that Peckinpah himself is never critical of his male characters, and assumes that he hates his female characters, which is patently untrue. An essay should be written, coolly and rationally, about women's reactions to *The Wild Bunch*. Brian Garfield, in *Western Films: A Complete Guide*, remarks, "I have met very few women who liked it, and can recall no female critics who approved of it" (348). While we know more women who have disliked rather than liked *The Wild Bunch*, we have met many who do like the film. Both Pauline Kael and Penelope Gilliat of *The New Yorker* have given the film high praise, Kathleen Murphy's obituary on Peckinpah is one of the most moving — and accurate — assessments of his career, and, more recently, Gabrielle Murray's *This Wounded Cinema, This Wounded Life: Violence and Utopia in the Films of Sam Peckinpah* offers an essentially sympathetic account of his films.

3. Peckinpah uncovers the disastrous equation between love (Eros) and death (Thanatos) in film after film, as Mark Crispin Miller demonstrates in his brilliant discussion of Peckinpah's most neglected masterpiece, *Bring Me the Head of Alfredo Garcia*.

4. Remarkably enough, Peckinpah agreed to delete the Aurora flashback before the film was first released and before the other cuts were made after its release. Seydor presents this concession as part of Peckinpah's negotiations with Warner Brothers: "As a conciliatory gesture Peckinpah agreed to remove one flashback [the two-minute sequence involving Aurora] from the domestic version only; in return the studio supported him and made *The Wild Bunch* its feature summer attraction" (1997, 139–40). Later, Peckinpah insisted that all of the deleted material should be restored, which only came to pass in 1995 with the re-release of the film. (We refer, of course, to the American version; the so-called European version included all relevant materials from the first.) No matter what practical considerations led Peckinpah to agree to the deletion in question, we think it remains the worst decision he ever made. Indeed, it is almost surreal in its implications. No episode in Peckinpah's frequent quarrels with his studios better points up the pressures he worked under throughout his career.

5. Seydor describes this shot as "surely the film's most beautiful single image" (1997, 164).

6. See Richard F. Hardin, "Ritual in Recent Criticism: The Elusive Sense of Community," for a helpful discussion of Turner's ideas on ritual and community.

7. Peckinpah emphasizes the antiseptic, anti-tragic nature of Starbuck, which was formerly Mexican and named San Rafael, as we can see from a pale, weathered storefront sign. In Melville's *Moby-Dick*, Starbuck is in every way the antithesis of the doomed tragic hero Ahab. As Newton Arvin has remarked, Starbuck is the very model of moderation, "and moderation is no cardinal virtue in Melville's calendar; Starbuck embodies that, and Starbuck hovers between a golden 'mediocritas' and plain mediocrity" (179). In his *Playboy* interview, Peckinpah, who lived in Mexico off and on for years, and who married the same Mexican woman, Begonia Palacios, no fewer than three times, implicitly describes what has been lost by turning a Mexican town, San Rafael, into an American town, Starbuck: "In Mexico they don't worry so goddamn much about saving the human race or about the wheeling and dealing that's poisoning us" (William Murray 192).

8. Peckinpah often alluded to his romanticism. As he says in his *Playboy* interview, "I love *outsiders* ... I'm nothing if not a romantic and I've got this weakness for losers on the grand scale, as well as a kind of sneaky af-

fection for all the misfits and drifters in the world" (William Murray 72).

9. Later versions of the Green-Peckinpah script are slightly different in their wording of this passage. The version quoted is dated 2/12/68 and appears in the script dated 2/7/68. All scripts of *The Wild Bunch* are to be found in the Peckinpah Collection.

10. Fish's prologue is entitled "Taking Sides." Since Fish writes, "While I was writing the chapters of this book, a scene from Sam Peckinpah's classic western *The Wild Bunch* was never far from my mind" (1), we assume the phrase "Taking Sides" is at least partly drawn from the film, specifically Pike's famous "When you side with a man you stay with him" speech. But that phrase, as both Pike and Peckinpah understand it, means exactly the opposite of what Fish intends. As we understand him, Fish would allow someone to "side" with someone else only if he or she is in complete agreement with the other person's moral character, as Fish indicates when he distinguishes "one side," the "man of principle," from the "other side," the "man who varies his obligations according to the moral worth of the persons he encounters; some people have a call on your integrity, others don't, and the important thing is to determine at every moment which is which" (1). At every moment? Does Fish really mean this? If he does, one suspects he has very few friends, for people, including good friends, constantly disagree about almost everything. To make this kind of severe criticism of other persons would mean that you are always judging them, which is no way for any relationship, or social unit, to endure. It would also mean, in Peckinpah's universe, that the Wild Bunch might never be a "bunch" at all, or would at least be a much smaller group, since the rather coarse and selfish Gorch brothers would hardly qualify for Bunch membership according to Fish's too rigid criterion. Pike's triumphant "side with a man" speech is meant to demonstrate leadership, to resolve, if ever so tenuously, differences within a very disparate group of men through a demonstration of superior will, and to humiliate the unruly Gorches into not shooting poor old Freddy Sykes because he let some horses fall down a sand dune.

11. In a related context dealing with tragedy, specifically *King Lear*, Stanley Cavell discusses the relationship between shame and guilt in Gloucester's relationship with his son Edgar:

> But if the failure to recognize others is a failure to let others recognize you, a fear of what is revealed to them, an avoidance of their eyes, then it is exactly shame which is the cause of his [the blind Gloucester's] withholding recognition.... For shame is the specific discomfort produced by the sense of being looked at, the avoidance of the sight of others is the reflex it produces. Guilt is different; there the reflex is to avoid discovery. As long as no one *knows* what you have done, you are safe; or your conscience will press you to confess it and accept punishment. Under shame, what must be covered up is not your deed, but yourself [277–78].

Although we as the audience know how Pike Bishop feels about his twin betrayals of Aurora and Deke, no one else is conscious of Pike's secret guilt over Aurora's death and Deke's capture. Dutch knows about the incident in which Aurora was killed and Pike's desire for revenge against her murdering husband, but he does not know about Pike's personal guilt over her death. On the other hand, Deke's shame at being forced to hunt down his friend and partner is the very public tool Pat Harrigan uses to bend Deke to his personal will. For a critique of Cavell's valuing of shame over guilt in Shakespearean tragedy, see Harry Berger, Jr., "Acknowledgments," *Making Trifles of Terrors: Redistributing Complicities in Shakespeare.*

12. Viewers familiar with the overarching symbol of regenerative water in Peckinpah's next film, *The Ballad of Cable Hogue*, as well as the river scene in *The Getaway* and the symbolism of maternity and water in the first shots of *Bring Me the Head of Alfredo Garcia*, will understand the importance the director assigns to virtually any manifestation of water.

13. In the scenes at Angel's village, the cat's cradle is also a sexual symbol because the cradle-like pattern is always transferred from one person's hands to those of another. In this film the exchange is always between males and females, and the motion of the exchange is overtly sexual.

14. Peckinpah uses the same device even more overtly *in Pat Garrett and Billy the Kid*, in which an even more self-loathing protagonist, Pat Garrett, shoots at his own image in a mirror right after he has killed Billy the Kid. In each case Peckinpah's protagonist responds to a personal, immediate necessity, performing an act of self-judgment which is among his film's most telling climactic moments.

15. Peckinpah thought of the woman here as named Yolanda and tried to include earlier footage which established that she is Mapache's mistress and shoots Pike as an act of revenge. Seydor explains that Peckinpah could never quite work this connection into the earlier scenes, so the finished film does not represent the woman until the late scene in which she shoots Pike (1997, 159).

16. Patrick McGee believes that Pike "unleash[es] [his] misogyny when he screams 'Bitch!' after being shot" (157); for McGee, Pike "strikes back brutally against all women for having betrayed his romantic fantasies" when he shoots the woman who has shot him (164). We must wonder what McGee's reaction would be in the same circumstances, though we would concede, as we have throughout this chapter, that Pike's feelings about women, like Sam Peckinpah's, are deeply conflicted. Still, it is clear that Pike loved Aurora, even as he was tragically late in arriving at their rendezvous, and that his tender feelings for the young mother and prostitute in Agua Verde demonstrate considerable *self*-loathing but no negative emotions toward the woman herself. Lastly, Pike, ambiguous about women to the end, deliberately aims his gun at the woman who subsequently shoots him, but instead of shooting her he turns and fires at the mirror and as we learn the soldier behind it. McGee fails to mention that it is Pike's initial *reluctance* to shoot the woman which leads to his death. Certainly Dutch and the Gorch brothers would have killed the woman first, as they demonstrate repeatedly in the Agua Verde melée.

17. We do not actually see the deaths of the bounty hunters. Apparently Peckinpah wanted to include this scene, but his producer, Phil Feldman, wisely persuaded him that "no more deaths could or should follow those of Pike and Dutch" (Seydor 1997, 144)

18. Seydor's reference to Don José and his men as "revolutionaries" is not inadvertent. In his latest discussion of *The Wild Bunch*, Seydor writes: "When Thornton joins up with Sykes' band of Indian revolutionaries and Peckinpah reprises the exit from Angel's village as the bunch are serenaded by the peasants, death really does lead to transfiguration, realism gives way to romance,

and our last image of these outlaws, in what is perhaps the single most self-reflexive moment of the film, is as heroes of an adventure that has already become the stuff of mythmaking and storytelling" (1999, 68). This passage appears in Seydor's "*The Wild Bunch*: The Screenplay," a masterful review of the evolution of the film's script from Roy Sickner's original idea to Walon Green's original script to the Green-Peckinpah screenplay, which Peckinpah continued to revise during production and postproduction.

19. In addition to the old B-Westerns with their reprised laughter, doffed cowboy hats, and rearing horses (one thinks of classic "oaters" featuring the famed "Trail Blazers," Ken Maynard, Bob Steele, and Hoot Gibson, among others), Peckinpah no doubt had in mind the classic samurai films of Akira Kurosawa, especially his generally acknowledged greatest film, *The Seven Samurai* (1954). Here too laughter is a tension-relieving palliative for these former samurai knights, now hungry, without shelter, and desperate to hold their lives together as they fight to save a small Japanese farming village from roving bands of outlaw gangs in sixteenth-century Japan. It is not difficult to imagine the connection between the ravaging of Angel's village by Mapache's army and the plight of Kurosawa's desperate peasants. Always the contrarian, Peckinpah told Ernest Callenbach that he had not put *The Seven Samurai* on his list of favorite films because it was merely "highly entertaining," not much more than a Japanese "oater," while at the same time he said, "I'd like to be able to make a Western like Kurosawa makes Westerns" (Callenbach 2008, 15).

20. The idea of reprising the exit from Angel's village only came to Peckinpah in the final weeks of editing the film (Seydor 1999, 69), apparently at the suggestion of Lou Lombardo (Seydor 1999, 78, n.34). Though we do not share the views of Seydor and others about the effect of this repetition, there is no question that the emotion generated is very powerful.

21. Critics other than Seydor and Prince have shared their general view of the conclusion. David Cook praises Seydor's reading of the ending (129); Bliss thinks that the Bunch "are reborn like the phoenix when they are reinvoked by the words and laughter of Thornton, Sykes, and the others" (1993, 104), and in a later discussion he sees the ending as marked by "resurrection accompanied by laughter" (1994, xxi); and Armando José Prats celebrates "Deke and the new Bunch's uncompromising fidelity to action" (51).

22. In his discussion of the film's conclusion (1998, 123–25), Prince notes that in an early cut Peckinpah ended with Deke sitting against the wall, thus eliminating the interplay between Deke and the new Wild Bunch and the reprised exit from Angel's village. Prince suggests that Peckinpah's producer, Phil Feldman, successfully argued that the conclusion as we know it should be retained. McGee understands Prince to be saying that Peckinpah "tried to remove" the present ending and in fact believed the conclusion with Deke sitting against the wall "would have been preferable" (166). Both critics seem to believe that Feldman forced Peckinpah to end the film in a way he did not "prefer." We think this is extremely unlikely. Peckinpah took advice from many parties, including his producers, but he also considered many possible versions of his films before settling on a final version (if indeed he was allowed to), and there is no evidence the present ending to *The Wild Bunch* was anything but Peckinpah's final choice.

Chapter Five

1. The film's prologue and epilogue do depict Garrett's death almost three decades after Garrett kills Billy the Kid, but the primary action occurs in 1881 and concludes with Garrett very much alive.

2. Kitses takes issue with Seydor's reading of Pat Garrett, but his real quarrel seems to be with Seydor's critical method: "Seydor constructs the films as a kind of dense visual literature, and treats their heroes as complex psychological characters rather than signs or types" (2004, 246, n.6). We would side with Seydor on this issue as well as his view that Pat Garrett is the film's tragic protagonist. If it is a "literary" approach to see Peckinpah's characters as more than "signs or types," we are happy to be included among those embracing this approach.

3. In addition to the analysis on page 284, Seydor offers passing reference to Ida on pages 265, 271, 273, and 299, respectively. He calls the scene "vital" and "remarkable" (1997, 265, 284), which makes it all the more difficult to see why the scene is analyzed so briefly. Once again, as in our chapter on *The Wild Bunch*, we seem to be quarreling primarily with Paul Seydor, Peckinpah's best critic and by far the best critic on *Pat Garrett and Billy the Kid*. The link here is that we think Seydor underestimates the importance of Pike Bishop's lover Aurora and Pat Garrett's wife Ida. In our view, each man's tragic situation involves his sexual relationships much more than Seydor seems to believe, though Seydor does see that Aurora and Ida Garrett are important characters in their respective films.

4. In the introduction to his published screenplay, Wurlitzer implies that the published script is not in fact the original screenplay, for he describes it as "a compromise between the first versions and the final shooting script" (1973, viii). Wurlitzer makes it clear that "the first versions" had already been altered before the screenplay was submitted to Peckinpah, so perhaps the script read by Peckinpah is technically not "the original screenplay." It is, however, almost certainly the script published in 1973, with almost no "additions" from the final shooting script. The November shooting script includes many changes either written or dictated by Peckinpah, and Wurlitzer deletes all of them in his published script, the point of which is to establish *his* story as opposed to that of Peckinpah's film.

5. Our copy of this script comes from Script City of Hollywood, California, and is somewhat misleadingly described on the title page as "From the following writer: Rudolph Wurlitzer." As it is dated November 3, 1972, and as shooting began on November 13, we take this to be the shooting script Peckinpah took with him to Mexico. The Script City script incorporates changes dated from December, 1972, to January, 1973; the latest change is dated January 16, 1973 (1972, 50–50A/B). There are other scripts in the Peckinpah Collection which incorporate slight changes after November 3, 1972; one includes changes to December 20, 1972 (#249), and another to January 31, 1973 (#759), very near the end of production. All of these scripts are dated November 3, 1972, however, with the changes added, so it is clear that the November 3 script served as the shooting script, with only minor changes or additions.

The version with changes to January 31, 1973, is labeled "Mr. Peckinpah's copy" and includes pencil emendations in Peckinpah's handwriting, always minor adjustments such as assigning Beaver's speeches to Eno. (In Wurlitzer, Eno is the half-breed, whereas Beaver is the half-breed in the film.) The only substantive difference between these "later" versions of the November 3 script and the Script City version is that the latter does not include the brief scene with Will the carpenter. The other November 3 versions do include this scene, which apparently was a candidate for excision because the version with changes to December 20 includes the following note: "Scene 377 [the scene with Will] has been left in. Only to be shot if time permits" (106). In these versions of the scene, Will and Garrett do not know each other and Will is making a trunk (not a child's coffin, as in the film) which he plans to take with him when he rides out of "this goddamn country" (106 in #249, 105 in #759). As we will see in the final section of this chapter, Peckinpah not only shot this scene but eventually expanded it beyond Wurlitzer's original version.

6. We have previously noted the excellence of Seydor's "*The Wild Bunch*: The Screenplay," an essay which details Peckinpah's role in refashioning Walon Green's original screenplay. Peckinpah was given credit as one of the co-scenarists for *The Wild Bunch*, whereas his role in reshaping *Pat Garrett and Billy the Kid* is uncredited. Nonetheless, we would argue that Peckinpah's role in revising *Pat Garrett and Billy the Kid* is no less crucial than it was in writing *The Wild Bunch*.

7. Two films from the 1950s do feature Garrett as protagonist, but neither involves Billy the Kid. In Paul Landres' *Last of the Desperados* (1955), Garrett (James Craig) tracks down four of Billy's gang. In Fred F. Sears' *Badman's Country* (1958), Garrett (George Montgomery) is allied with Wyatt Earp (Buster Crabbe), Bat Masterson (Gregory Walcott), and Buffalo Bill (Malcolm Atterbury) against Butch Cassidy (Neville Brand). Even a film called *I Shot Billy the Kid* (William Berke, 1950) offers a cast in which Donald Barry as Billy the Kid occupies the first position. For production details, see Garfield 209, 109, 200–201.

8. We must admit to some skepticism as to whether Wurlitzer was allowed to introduce new materials during production. Wurlitzer was on hand throughout the shooting, but, as he came to complain, all the changes were made by Peckinpah or ordered by Peckinpah.

9. Peckinpah's adaptation of Neider's novel was the basis, much altered, for Marlon Brando's *One-Eyed Jacks* (1960). Peckinpah found little of his work in Brando's film and disliked the product. For an interesting account of Peckinpah's work on this project, see Weddle 1994, 143–46.

10. This summary appears in a document labeled "Pat Garrett and Billy the Kid Story Conference Tape 1 9/8/72"; the quoted materials are on page 8. This document is housed in the Peckinpah Collection.

11. As many critics and historians have pointed out, Garrett was actually murdered in 1908.

12. The idea for the prologue came from Gordon Carroll, Peckinpah's producer, and we are told that Peckinpah "loved" the idea (Weddle 1994, 460).

13. Seydor says this scene "is attributed by Wurlitzer totally to Peckinpah" (1997, 263), yet a page earlier Seydor remarks that Peckinpah claimed to have written half the scene (1997, 262). Perhaps Wurlitzer attributed the scene "totally" to Peckinpah because Peckinpah insisted on the scene against Wurlitzer's wishes and forced Wurlitzer to contribute parts of the scene if not half of it.

14. As we have noted, Peckinpah "adjusted" many historical facts in his film. Wurlitzer also changed many things, most obviously in making Garrett a longtime sheriff when in fact he arrested Billy before he even became sheriff of Lincoln, and killed Billy barely six months after taking office. (When he arrested Billy in late 1880, Garrett was briefly serving as a deputy U.S. marshal prior to taking office as sheriff. See Utley 149.) In his prologue, Peckinpah rightly depicts Garrett as infuriated by the presence of sheep on his land, but Garrett's quarrel was with someone other than John Poe, who was in fact a friend of Garrett's even though he succeeded Garrett as sheriff of Lincoln County and who received Garrett's assistance in selecting his wife (Metz 131–32). All historians seem to agree that the Santa Fe Ring had nothing to do with Garrett's murder, if indeed there ever was such a group and if it participated in Billy's death.

15. In point of fact, Peckinpah's Billy *has* switched sides in the past, as he himself remarks to the Horrells and Alamosa Bill when he notes it was not so long ago that he wore a badge and Garrett was an outlaw, but the Billy of the first scene with Garrett — and thereafter — is beyond such temptations, as Garrett and the audience recognize from the first.

16. When he added the early scenes Peckinpah either wrote or commissioned, Wurlitzer did not notice that the "all these years" speech no longer made sense and left it in the November shooting script (1972, 70). In production Peckinpah altered the speech so that Lemuel refers to "all that law" busting to come out of Garrett, an odd way to refer to so short a stint as a lawman, but one in which Garrett's "years" of service have been deleted.

17. Peckinpah's Garrett is confronted with this choice more clearly than the historical Garrett, but the latter has been described as a man "elected to put Lincoln County's outlaws out of business" (Utley 198) and as "a law and order candidate" touted as someone who would get Billy the Kid (Metz 55, 57). The scene in which Garrett is challenged by the Santa Fe Ring's representatives is consistent with what we know of the real Garrett who became the candidate of such men as John Chisum after living little more than two years in New Mexico (see Metz 55–57).

18. Peckinpah is famous for accepting the better suggestions of his actors, especially those with whom he worked repeatedly. Garner Simmons provides a fascinating account of how R. G. Armstrong suggested or simply launched into a number of the "new" speeches Bob Ollinger makes in the jailhouse scene (especially in the longer version) (178–179), and Weddle describes James Coburn's "argument" with Peckinpah about having Garrett shoot at a mirror reflecting his own image immediately after killing the Kid, an action Coburn first suggested but which Peckinpah seems to have been preparing for throughout production (1994, 479).

19. Wurlitzer's November script has Garrett telling Billy, "The law is a way of thinkin' I'll live to get old and gray" (1972, 11), so presumably Peckinpah was thinking about Garrett's longer speech on this theme before shooting began. Indeed, the presence of this line taken from Neider suggests Peckinpah may have had more of a hand in drafting the original version of this scene than he later claimed. He almost surely contributed to it as Wurlitzer worked toward the script dated November 3, 1972.

20. Among others, Bliss agrees with Seydor's suggestion concerning the gun (1993, 329, n.17). There seems to be little historical support for this idea, however, which of course makes sense given the fact Garrett and Billy were not really close. Utley mentions rumors that a friend of Billy's left a gun in an outhouse, but he makes no reference to Garrett (263–64, n.15). Metz cites "re-

liable reports" that "a confidante" of Billy's left the gun, but he also makes no mention of Garrett (93).

21. We conclude that Peckinpah made this change because Wurlitzer dropped the presence of Ollinger's body in his published screenplay.

22. The fictional chronology here is difficult. We refer to Garrett's "mid-day meal" with Alamosa Bill, but this would suggest that Billy escaped that morning or that the people of Lincoln have left Ollinger's body in the street for more than a day. To put it mildly, we are not encouraged to put these events into anything but the roughest chronological order. Garrett has said to Billy that he will be gone two days collecting taxes, as if warning Billy how much time he has to escape. If Garrett in fact returns on the morning of the third day, and if Billy escaped earlier that morning, the time scheme is just barely possible. Ida will soon say she hasn't seen Garrett for "over a week," however, so either Garrett has been staying elsewhere in Lincoln before leaving to collect taxes or his two-day trip has expanded to at least seven days. Ida's remark about not seeing Garrett for over a week derives from Wurlitzer's original script (1973, 20), in which Garrett says nothing about a two-day trip to collect taxes, but Peckinpah retained Ida's lament as true to the marital situation explored in her scene with Garrett regardless of the chronological problem it poses.

23. Peckinpah's people were always aware of the similarity between *My Darling Clementine* and *Pat Garrett and Billy the Kid.* Producer Gordon Carroll, struck by the resemblance between Henry Fonda and James Coburn, remarked in an early story conference attended by Peckinpah that "[Coburn] looks sensational [with the moustache] ... and he walks— next to Fonda..." (Pat Garrett and Billy the Kid Story Conference Tape 1 9/8/72, p. 8).

24. We first see this Garrett home in the background as Billy enters an outhouse while talking with J. W. Bell. We see it again behind Garrett as he drives his buggy into Lincoln after Billy's escape. In the preview version of the film, we observe the house a third time after Billy throws the shattered shotgun he used to kill Ollinger at the deputy's dead body and, in the same direct line, Garrett's towering white house. Interestingly, this third shot of the house is not in the theatrical version of *Pat Garrett and Billy the Kid,* but Seydor includes it in his 2005 Special Edition of the film even though he uses the theatrical version as his editorial norm. All three shots of the house occur before we know the house is Garrett's, so the effect here is at best subliminal.

25. Seydor's remarks are part of the overvoice commentary on his 2005 Special Edition of *Pat Garrett and Billy the Kid.*

26. Again, Seydor speaks of Garrett's home as a "doll's house" in his commentary for the 2005 Special Edition of *Pat Garrett and Billy the Kid.*

27. It was common for Anglo officials to marry Hispanic women at this time in New Mexico. The real Pat Garrett and John W. Poe both married Hispanic women, and Garrett in fact married two such women, sisters named Gutierrez (Metz 40). Ida's counterpart was named Apolinaria and, as we shall see, was very unlike Peckinpah's Mrs. Garrett. We should note that Garrett's first of eight children with Apolinaria was named Ida (Metz 156, n.15).

28. In Wurlitzer's original screenplay, Ida says, "It's been a long two years" (1973, 20). By the November shooting script, she says, "It's been a long year" (1972, 26), as in the film. Just as Wurlitzer imagined a Pat Garrett who has been a sheriff for years, so he imagined a somewhat longer married life for Garrett and Ida. Peckinpah shortens the period to one year so that the marriage will be seen as part of Garrett's decision to pursue respectability.

29. In fact, as Paul Seydor reveals in a forthcoming essay on the making of his 2005 Special Edition of *Pat Garrett and Billy the Kid,* the scene with Ida was deleted (perhaps mistakenly) from the first preview version of Peckinpah's film, then restored in the second preview version. Seydor demonstrates that the 1988 Turner edition is the first preview version, so it did not include the scene with Ida. Roger Spottiswoode told the Turner people where they could find the relevant footage, but apparently nothing was done to restore this crucial scene (see Seydor 1997, 299).

30. The scene with Ida was used in the first TV network showing of the film, so it had seen the light of day before Seydor included it in his 2005 Special Edition of *Pat Garrett and Billy the Kid.*

31. Almost everyone except Weddle refers to the missing 16 minutes, but the editors who assembled the 1973 theatrical release cut slightly more than 18 minutes if the scene with Ida is counted, as it should be. The preview version was supposed to be 124 minutes long, the scene with Ida included, and the theatrical release was 106 minutes long.

32. Kitses actually refers to the scene with Ida and the later scene with Ruthie Lee as cuts which are "not crucial."

33. We should not romanticize this marriage, however. Garrett's biographer, Leon Metz, makes it clear that Garrett was repeatedly unfaithful to Apolinaria and often left her alone for long periods of time. As Metz writes of Apolinaria, "Obviously she was a very remarkable, tolerant, and understanding woman" (156).

34. Murray's stance on Peckinpah's treatment of women is much more nuanced than the positions of most of Peckinpah's critics, who seem to think Peckinpah, like Budd Boetticher, would have agreed with Robert Warshow that "in Western movies, men have the deeper wisdom and the women are children" (108).

35. We discuss Peckinpah's views about Mexico toward the end of Chapter One. It is interesting to contrast *Pat Garrett and Billy the Kid* with John Ford's *Stagecoach,* a film in which the hero and heroine happily escape to Mexico at the conclusion. As we suggest earlier, Peckinpah is preeminently a tragedian and Ford is not. (We should acknowledge, however, that Peckinpah himself, working in a non-tragic mode, allows Doc and Carol McCoy [Steve McQueen, Ali MacGraw] to escape to Mexico at the end of *The Getaway.*)

36. Ida's disappearance from the action after her scene with Garrett helps explain why MGM thought her role could be included among the cuts required for the 1973 theatrical release. After cutting a few early lines (e.g., Billy's caustic reference to Garrett as "an old married man"), the editors had only to eliminate the scene with Ida to all but excise her from the film.

37. The animus directed at Garrett from the first is Peckinpah's creation, for in Wurlitzer's original screenplay the people of Lincoln look upon Garrett with "distant respect" when he first enters the town and the script after Billy's escape (1973, 19).

38. In the film, this speech concludes a little differently: "and the other big ranchers."

39. Kitses notes the irony of Poe's white horse (2004, 239). Perhaps Peckinpah, always aware of the biblical dimensions of his films, intended a more foreboding allusion to the "pale horse" of death in the Book of the

Apocalypse. Poe is, after all, Garrett's eventual murderer.

40. The order of events in Wurlitzer and the November shooting script allows Holly to refer to the death of Alamosa Bill (Wurlitzer 1973, 78; November shooting script 1972, 69), whereas in the film there is no such reference and the shootings of Alamosa Bill and Holly seem to occur at about the same time.

41. In Wurlitzer's original script (1973, 75) and in the November shooting script (1972, 65), Poe "calculates" that Garrett has been away from Lincoln for at least six weeks. Peckinpah stretches the absence to seven weeks, as if emphasizing the desultory course of Garrett's "search."

42. Stevens takes Holly's remark about Garrett being "a little short of supplies" since meeting Billy to be sexual in nature, alluding to Garrett's impotence (275). In context, however, both in Wurlitzer and in the film, Holly seems to be referring to the disorienting effect each has on the other (Wurlitzer) or Billy has on Garrett (Peckinpah). There seems no good reason to read this effect as sexual, and, for what it's worth, Peckinpah denied that *Pat Garrett and Billy the Kid* is a love story about the principal characters (Aghed 66).

43. Macbeth himself does not kill any of these characters, of course, as Shakespeare tries to retain some sympathy for his protagonist even as Macbeth slides toward damnation, the loss of his "eternal jewel" (III.i.68), that is, his soul.

44. Weddle reports that James Aubrey, then president of MGM, disliked Walter Kelley and insisted on restricting his role as the studio negotiated with Peckinpah's editors on what would be retained for the theatrical release of *Pat Garrett and Billy the Kid*. Indeed, though it is usually asserted that Aubrey retained the raft scene in exchange for the frame story, prologue and epilogue, Weddle says the price for retaining the raft scene was most of Kelley's screen time, both as Garrett arrives at Roswell and after he has left (1994, 486–87). In the shorter, theatrical version, it is still apparent Garrett has been there before, but Rupert's obscene reference to the last visit is eliminated, as are many off-color elements in the preview version of the film.

45. Almost all critics refer to four prostitutes here, perhaps influenced by the fact there are four on Garrett's bed when Poe opens the door to report to Garrett. Earlier, however, four prostitutes huddle around Garrett while a fifth uses the bathtub in the room. Seydor is the one commentator on the scene who gets the number right (1997, 265).

46. Earlier, Garrett smiles during his interchange with Billy at the jailhouse, no doubt a reminder of his former relationship with the Kid. Garrett also smiles while manipulating Holly into pulling a knife on him, but this smile is contrived rather than genuine.

47. In Wurlitzer, Billy and Maria ask Pete Maxwell for the use of a room (1973, 124), but they do not undress or make love before Billy is killed.

48. Whatever their differences, Peckinpah's critics tend to agree that the ending to *Pat Garrett and Billy the Kid* is quite grim, even if they do not endorse Seydor's most emphatic claim: "Surely there is, in effect and implication, no bleaker, blacker, bitterer ending to any Western film" (1997, 285). Stevens alone rejects Seydor's reading as "simply unacceptable" (274), arguing that the young boy who throws rocks at Garrett, an apparent inversion of the scene at the end of *Shane*, conveys "a powerful sense of hope, of the ability for change and growth" (275). As no such "sense" applies to Garrett, the film's tragic protagonist, we would again side with Seydor's reading.

49. In the film these lines become "Shot him three times in the back; blew his goddamned head off."

50. Stevens would reject our final example here, for he believes that Billy's gang are "unambiguously affirmed" (272). The gang may not be as scurvy as Kitses and Seydor imply, but we think Stevens is alone in seeing Billy's men as the "unambiguous" center of value in this film.

51. The common lore about Billy wearing dresses resurfaces in Philip Kaufman's *The Great Northfield Minnesota Raid*, in which Robert Duvall's Billy the Kid makes his escape from the law in a dress he has taken off an old woman he and Frank James have just killed.

52. Peckinpah addressed the unpleasantness of this scene in two stages. In the November shooting script, he had Wurlitzer change the woman in the scene from Maria to Lupe, thus reinforcing our sense of Billy's promiscuity but protecting Maria from the scene's griminess, and he cut Tom Ketchum altogether (1972, 54). Subsequently, Peckinpah dropped the entire scene during production.

53. The first part of this speech, "Don't...," first appears in the November shooting script (1972, 17).

54. The turkey chase, replete with dance-like banjo music, is part of Billy's legend and is reported in Utley (45–46), though in Utley's version Billy is present but does not participate in the hunt. Peckinpah renders the buildup to the chase even more affecting by employing an extremely long lap dissolve from Garrett, looking more and more spectral and catatonic, staring off into dusty waste land space after he has turned away from both the dying Sheriff Baker and the expiring Black Harris, to a scene where his ghostly visage is superimposed over the Kid and his gang rustling Chisum's cattle out on the plains, just before the turkey chase begins. That the chase lasts so briefly and culminates in Silva's violent death at the hands of Chisum's cowboys indicates just how trapped Garrett is between a longed-for but vanishing past and an equally untenable future working for Chisum and the ruthless Santa Fe Ring, where his primary purpose is to kill the Kid.

55. Peckinpah again achieved his final effect in two stages. In the November shooting script, Billy repeats his rejection of going to Mexico (1972, 54), but Luke chimes in earlier with his own version of this theme (1972, 50). In the film itself, Luke's speech about Mexico simply replaces Billy's.

56. We refer to the much-criticized episode in which Chisum's men kill Paco. Billy happens upon the scene, shoots Chisum's three men, listens to Paco's dying words, and resolves to turn back to New Mexico. As Seydor notes in the commentary to his 2005 Special Edition of *Pat Garrett and Billy the Kid*, Billy then rides off in the general direction of Old Fort Sumner leaving Paco's daughter and her child to fend for themselves in a vast, unpopulated territory (see also Seydor 1997, 272). This is one revision which supports Seydor's claim that "sometimes Peckinpah's changes were not for the better" (1997, 265), for Wurlitzer included dialogue between Billy and Paco's daughter in which the latter assures Billy she will be able to reach her home in Old Mexico (1973, 74). (There is no child in Wurlitzer's original script.) We think that deleting this dialogue was a mistake, and that the scene is the worst in the film, a wholly failed attempt on Peckinpah's part to use the Kid's rather vague relationship with Paco to emulate the far subtler and more effective presence of distant gypsy wanderers in

Arthur Penn's *The Left-Handed Gun*, where the gypsies clearly symbolize the orphaned Kid's sense of rootlessness and homelessness throughout Penn's film. Peckinpah's scene does account for Billy's decision to go back to New Mexico, whereas in Wurlitzer's original version Billy does not decide to go back at this point and in fact is never shown resolving to return, but, as the commentators in the 2005 Special Edition agree, the film would probably be better off without the Paco episode altogether, perhaps replaced by a long shot in which Billy is shown riding toward Mexico, then halting and silently turning around to return to New Mexico. Leaving out Paco's death would isolate the earlier scene in which Paco leaves Old Fort Sumner, however, a scene Peckinpah added to the script.

Unlike Peckinpah's other critics, we would underscore the seminal importance of *The Left-Handed Gun* to the making of *Pat Garrett and Billy the Kid*. We would cite the following: the Paco scenes, so much more effectively and delicately presented in Penn's film; the stunning moment when Peckinpah's Billy passes by the blacksmith's flaming forge, a primordial Blakean image suggested, we believe, by Paul Newman's Kid describing himself at a blacksmith's satanic bellows as "coming alive," perversely and ironically reborn like the fiery resurrected paschal lamb (or "Pascua") in the Easter celebration depicted by Penn; Charlie Boudre's assassination of Sheriff Brady's Deputy Moon, depicted through a triangle on the streets of Lincoln before Penn's Kid rides out of town, the Kid himself photographed through that same portentous triangle; the play on Moon's name, as well as the shooting of the actual moon, seen reflected in a milky nocturnal pond by the Kid and his men, associating him, like Peckinpah's Billy the Kid before a similar pool of water, with the feminine world; Penn's Billy as crucified Christ symbol in the film's final scene, walking out of the house of the friends whom he has betrayed, Celsa and Ceval, arms out to the side, to meet his sacrificial death before Pat Garrett's blazing gun. Peckinpah's film would look very different without his genuinely felt *hommage* to Penn's brilliant and underrated "psychological Western."

57. The pond scene is almost identical in all versions of *Pat Garrett and Billy the Kid*, but the technical restoration of the scene in Seydor's Special Edition dramatically enhances its visual effects. Throughout our discussion of this scene we speak of Peckinpah's handling of its details even though Weddle informs us that the scene was shot by Gordon Dawson, Peckinpah's second-unit director and his future co-scenarist on *Bring Me the Head of Alfredo Garcia* (1994, 470). We can only assume that the scene was shot as Peckinpah wanted it, and that in any case Peckinpah approved its inclusion in the preview version of the film.

58. We refer to "four so-called bounty hunters" because virtually everyone writing on this scene calls them bounty hunters despite Billy's explicit remark that it is too early for bounty hunters and he must have known them sometime in the past.

59. Barry W. Sarchett identifies both of these quotations in his fine discussion of Alias (174).

60. This scene was cut from the film during production.

61. As Seydor notes, the "chronicler and storyteller" is "a convention in many Western stories" (1997, 288). Seydor cites Arthur Penn's *The Left-Handed Gun*, but he might also have mentioned Clint Eastwood's *Unforgiven*. Unlike *Pat Garrett and Billy the Kid*, these films depict actual writers.

62. In the November shooting script, we find a first version of this exchange, as Billy muses, "I guess Mexico ain't all that different for a few months," and Alias replies, "That depends on who you are" (1972, 50A/B). This exchange is neither repeated nor reversed in the following scene in which Billy leaves for Mexico.

63. Kitses seems to believe that Maria's role was reduced in postproduction ("cuts"), but there is no evidence that Peckinpah eliminated scenes involving Maria in preparing the preview version of the film or that the theatrical editors cut such scenes. Peckinpah "cut" Maria's role in preproduction and production, working to transform the character he found in Wurlitzer's original screenplay.

64. The shot of Maria cooking derives from a late scene in Wurlitzer in which Maria makes bread and tortillas (1973, 90) and effectively replaces a shot early in the November shooting script in which Maria serves drinks outside the cantina (1972, 3).

65. Utley (ix, 193) and Metz (117) report that Billy famously uttered this question just before his assassination. Neider has Hendry Jones ask "Quién es?" no fewer than four times just before his death (188–89). Wurlitzer included the query in his original screenplay (1973, 127), Peckinpah and Wurlitzer retained it in the November shooting script (1972, 102), and of course Peckinpah used it in the finished film.

66. For an excellent essay-length discussion of Garrett's divided identity, see Leonard Engel, "'Who Are You?' 'That's a Good Question': Shifting Identities in Sam Peckinpah's *Pat Garrett and Billy the Kid*."

67. This scene was deleted in the theatrical version of *Pat Garrett and Billy the Kid* and does not appear in Seydor's 2005 Special Edition.

68. Paul Seydor clarifies the differences between the first and second preview versions in his forthcoming essay "The Authentic Death and Contentious Afterlife of *Pat Garrett and Billy the Kid*: The Several Versions of Peckinpah's Last Western," which will appear in a volume of essays on Peckinpah edited by Michael Bliss and published by Southern Illinois University Press.

69. The 124-minute version became approximately 122 minutes with the deletion of the Ida scene in the first preview.

70. Seydor's forthcoming essay is very helpful in clarifying the events leading up to the theatrical release.

71. Seydor's remarks about the placement of the raft scene occurred in a telephone conversation with Robert Merrill.

72. Peckinpah was still at the studio while the theatrical release was being prepared, and Seydor believes that his editors may well have consulted with him about decisions such as the reduction of his own role as Will the coffinmaker. Indeed, Seydor thinks that Peckinpah's editors would never have all but eliminated Peckinpah's role without his approval. Weddle acknowledges that Peckinpah was nearby but is much more skeptical about the theory he was consulted, noting the many regrettable decisions Peckinpah's editors participated in whatever their personal feelings. We tend to agree with Weddle on this matter. Seydor's and Weddle's views are expressed in the commentary to the 2005 Special Edition.

73. Garrett's encounter with Ruthie Lee is not in the preview version, presumably because the scene with Poe at Tuckerman's Hotel already provides the information that Billy is at Old Fort Sumner. We believe that Peckinpah would have retained the meeting with Ruthie Lee, which works very well with the prostitute scene which follows, and deleted the scene at Tuckerman's Hotel,

which features neither Garrett nor Billy and is one of the weakest moments in either version. Here as elsewhere, Seydor makes the right decision in his 2005 Special Edition.

74. Maria actually appears very briefly at this point in the theatrical version. Photographed in deep space, she is almost subliminally present, partially framed (a painterly frame within a frame) in a doorway at the corner of a shot over the Kid's shoulder. As Maria works away, head down, she glances furtively at Billy and Garrett, who dominate the foreground, much as in the preview version she nervously looks outward in the full kitchen shot just seconds before we see her this second time. Both shots indicate the intense feelings and fears the now marginalized Maria has for the Kid. Very few viewers seem to have noticed that she is there in the second shot. Her appearance here only succeeds if we have originally seen her as a distinctive presence within the previous full frame, now omitted by Seydor because it is not in the theatrical version of the film. Seeing *both* Marias makes the second, briefer shot more powerful as, framed near the kitchen door, Maria gazes helplessly into what seems to be an altered or alien reality. This particular shot bears an uncanny resemblance to Diego Velázquez's great painting "Christ in the House of Mary and Martha" (1680), where an angry Martha is hard at work in her kitchen while through an opening in a wall we see Christ addressing a kneeling Mary in an adjacent room. The interplay between two planes of reality, the intensely realistic kitchen scene and the religious and mythic encounter between Christ and Mary, anticipates Peckinpah's Maria working away in the cantina kitchen while she looks on powerlessly as a legendary American event is unfolding.

75. In his forthcoming essay on the 2005 Special Edition of *Pat Garrett and Billy the Kid*, Paul Seydor takes a very different view on Peckinpah's commitment to deleting Dylan's lyrics and retaining the frame story. Seydor notes that when Peckinpah was considering Daniel Melnick's 1974 invitation to prepare a new edition of his film, Peckinpah indicated he was prepared to reconsider the use of Dylan's lyrics, among other changes. Moreover, Seydor adds that the prologue was Gordon Carroll's idea, not Peckinpah's, and was drafted only five weeks before production began. He points out that the idea for the epilogue only arose in postproduction and came not from Peckinpah but Roger Spottiswoode, who subsequently pieced together the epilogue from footage originally shot for the prologue (some of it used in the prologue, some not). Seydor offers good evidence that Peckinpah's editors were never happy with the prologue, let alone the epilogue, and Seydor's own technical objections to the prologue are extremely interesting. Nonetheless, we think that Peckinpah's reservations about the prologue, which he himself developed for the November shooting script, concerned the execution of the concept and not the concept itself. Peckinpah also embraced Spottiswoode's idea for the epilogue and included this conclusion in both preview versions of the film. We do not see the evidence for believing Peckinpah would have changed his mind about the frame story, prologue and epilogue, though we would reiterate our agreement with Seydor's view that the alternative ending in his 2005 Special Edition is very powerful and arguably superior to Peckinpah's conclusion at the time he left the film. We strongly recommend Seydor's essay, especially for the new light it provides on the two preview versions, "close but not identical," as Seydor puts it, as well as the fascinating information it offers on the making of the 2005 Special Edition.

76. In the prologue and epilogue Garrett is actually wearing a different hat, gray rather than black. The frame story is set in 1909, after all, 28 years after the film's main action. This detail may also be Peckinpah's way of acknowledging that Garrett has, according to his own stated desire, grown "rich, old, and *gray*" (our emphasis).

77. Curiously, Seydor omits Billy's response to Black Harris when itemizing the materials rightly cut by the theatrical editors (1997, 301). Seydor's rejection of Bliss' argument about this scene therefore avoids the primary point Bliss makes (see Seydor 1997, 384 n.33).

78. Simmons suggests that what Garrett has figured out is that Billy will not run (183). The natural extension of this insight is that Garrett must eliminate Billy himself.

Chapter Six

1. Paul Seydor notes the relevance of this biblical passage to *Bring Me the Head of Alfredo Garcia* in the commentary to the 2005 DVD edition of the film.

2. Kitses is especially unhappy with Paul Seydor: "Paul Seydor would have us believe that the genre was incidental to Peckinpah's success" (2004, 244). As Kitses himself notes, however, Seydor's 1997 "reconsideration" of his 1980 treatment of Peckinpah's Western films does greater justice to Peckinpah's reliance on Western conventions even as he transformed them.

3. Our copy of the script comes from Script City and is dated 7/8/72. No doubt Peckinpah's shooting script, its title page declares it to be a screenplay by Gordon Dawson and Sam Peckinpah. Throughout, however, as in the passage quoted here, one hears Peckinpah's voice quite clearly.

4. We have previously noted that Mark Crispin Miller (13) and Paul Seydor (1997, 35) identify *Bring Me the Head of Alfredo Garcia* as a revenge tragedy. Neither Miller nor Seydor goes on to relate Peckinpah's film to the relevant plays of Elizabethan and Jacobean England. We will also remark the echoes of ancient Greek tragedy, especially Aeschylus' *Oresteia*. Bernard F. Dukore has pointed us in this direction: "Not only is the theme of vengeance a stock-in-trade of westerns, it goes back in the drama past *Hamlet* at least as far as the *Oresteia* of Aeschylus—works the director no doubt knew" (154). Dukore also refers to the sixteenth and seventeenth centuries as "the period when revenge tragedies flourished in English drama" (180), thus joining Miller and Seydor in recognizing the literary tradition most relevant to *Bring Me the Head of Alfredo Garcia*.

5. Until fairly recently *The Revenger's Tragedy* was attributed to Cyril Tourneur, but most early modern scholars now agree the evidence points to Middleton as the play's author. For an authoritative review of this evidence, see R. A. Foakes xix–lxix.

6. As Katharine Eisaman Maus remarks of Elizabethan and Jacobean revenge tragedies, "Often an initial scene or speech retrospectively describes the original transgression" (ix). A few of these plays do resemble *Bring Me the Head of Alfredo Garcia* in beginning with an act of revenge different from the protagonist's but related to it. Well-known examples would be Kyd's *The Spanish Tragedy* and John Marston's *Antonio's Revenge* (ca. 1600).

7. Unlike many of the film's characters, Theresa is called by her name, "Señorita Theresa," by her servant Maria in the first moments of the film. There are numerous examples of characters whose names are never mentioned. These include Sappensly (Robert Webber), Quill (Gig Young), Max (Helmut Dantine), Frank (Don Levy), Cueto (Jorge Russek), and Grandmother Garcia (Tamara Garina). Several critics have noticed this feature of the film and proceeded to identify the relevant characters by the name of the actor playing the part. In fact, however, all of the fictional names derive from the Dawson/Peckinpah script. It is interesting to speculate whether Peckinpah intended to refer to Ernest Hemingway's great gangster story, "The Killers," by naming two of his characters "Al" and "Max." Among Peckinpah's films *Bring Me the Head of Alfredo Garcia* is certainly the most allusive.

8. Critics sometimes refer to El Jefe's ranch as situated outside Mexico. They get this idea from the shooting script, which begins by describing El Jefe's hacienda as located somewhere else ("It is not Mexico" [1]), and indicates at the end that Bennie has flown to Madrid, Spain, to confront El Jefe (112). Garner Simmons explains in the commentary to the 2005 DVD edition of *Bring Me the Head of Alfredo Garcia* that the Mexican board supervising films made in Mexico refused to authorize Peckinpah's project if the evil El Jefe's ranch was identified as in Mexico, so the relevant notations in the script were changed. We think it is absurd to suppose Alfredo leaves a ranch in Spain and travels to Mexico City before suffering his fatal accident. Virtually all viewers of the film will assume El Jefe's ranch is in Mexico, at a distance from Mexico City requiring the airplane travel we witness, and we think they are right to make this assumption.

9. Seydor offers these remarks in the commentary to the 2005 DVD edition of *Bring Me the Head of Alfredo Garcia.*

10. The information about El Jefe's great room and private chapel comes from Simmons, who was present during the filming of *Bring Me the Head of Alfredo Garcia* (201–202).

11. We would like to thank Professors Owen Cramer and Regula Evitt of Colorado College for identifying the Vulgate Bible used by El Jefe and translating much of the quoted material.

12. This information derives from the Web Gallery of Art, created by Emil Kren and Daniel Marx.

13. Simmons tells the story of Garth Craven's contribution in the commentary to the 2005 DVD edition of *Bring Me the Head of Alfredo Garcia.* At this point in the commentary Paul Seydor speculates that Theresa may suffer a broken finger rather than a broken arm, but the script stipulates that Theresa's arm breaks (5), critics such as Simmons (204) and Miller (7) refer to her broken arm, and at the end of the film she wears a sling on her arm, not her finger.

14. We would also note that Frida Kahlo's hand rests maternally, muse-like, on the shoulder of the boy-artist Rivera, a significant detail for a film in which hands figure prominently.

15. While writing this book we have been repeatedly amazed by the similarities between Peckinpah's imagery and *mise-en-scéne* and a number of famous paintings or images in western art. We have no proof that Peckinpah frequented museums, nor that he purchased or studied art books, nor even that he studied art history while in college or graduate school. (We do know that two of his daughters attended the prestigious California School of the Arts — or CalArts — and doubtless exposed their father to actual art.) Therefore, we have not made the case that Peckinpah deliberately alludes to these great paintings in his films, as, say, John Ford intentionally imitates Frederic Remington in *Stagecoach* and especially in Ford's Cavalry films. Indeed, we do not believe that Peckinpah knowingly or consciously borrowed visual motifs from significant works of art. It *is* our contention, however, that he was a visual artist of the highest caliber and absorbed the rich traditions of European — and American — art, as recent criticism confirms for a number of outstanding filmmakers, both European and American. In noting the similarities between Peckinpah's films and these great paintings, we hope to increase the reader's pleasure, both emotional and intellectual, in experiencing Peckinpah's extraordinary artistic sensibility. We also believe that Peckinpah did not suddenly discover at the age of 50 the power of Mexican art, so fully on display in the work of Diego Rivera and, by extension, his wife Frida Kahlo, in *Bring Me the Head of Alfredo Garcia.* The important use of these two famous painters, in addition to the unknown artists who painted the conquistador and the tortured cleric in El Jefe's great hall, suggests that Peckinpah, always more comfortable with his muse in Mexico, incorporated artistic images and works of art more self-consciously in his last great film. We would be remiss if we did not express our debt to art historian Rebecca Tucker, of the Colorado College Art Department, whose knowledge of Mexican and South American art has been invaluable to our interpretation of the cleric painting in particular and its possible relationship to the tradition of Christ at the Column, and to the connection between the kitchen scene with Mrs. Garrett in *Pat Garrett and Billy the Kid* and traditions of both western and Mexican art.

16. In a related vein Rebecca Bushnell adduces a somewhat different, decidedly un-religious meaning for *kairos* in its relationship to tragic time. Bushnell contrasts epic and tragedy: "Epic takes its time to play out a sequence of events when it embraces the sweep of history. Tragedy, in contrast, gains much of its power from its relentless focus on a critical moment in time, what in Greek is called a *kairos,* both a crisis and a test" (42). Adrian Poole underscores Bushnell's conception of tragic time: "*Kairos*: 'very now.' It is the sense of good timing needed by the conspirator, the artist, the killer" (2005, 103). For both tragic and religious thought the *kairotic* moment remains a defining concept for some kind of remarkable change, decidedly running counter to the flow of regular or chronological time.

17. Murphy and Jameson also note that Paco's stripping away of Elita's sweater is "a movement recalling the torture of El Jefe's daughter" (47).

18. These are very nearly the words Billy the Kid uses to implore J. W. Bell (Matt Clark) not to try to get away as Billy escapes from jail in *Pat Garrett and Billy the Kid.* In both instances, the words convey the speaker's sincerity.

19. As we will see in a moment, Miller does suggest that Bennie commits a "mistake" here which recalls El Jefe's at the beginning of the film (12).

20. The grandmother's contempt for Elita is better grounded in the script, for there we learn Alfredo has told the grandmother about Elita ("Unfortunately," the old woman says [60]). Somewhat curiously, the script refers to the family as the Morenos rather than the Garcias, for here one of Alfredo's middle names is Garcia and his last name is Moreno (56). Peckinpah dropped

this unnecessary complication in the film, but the credits still refer to Grandmother Moreno.

21. Peckinpah did in fact film the scene with Chalo and Cueto clearly in the frame, for such a still is included in Miller's 1975 article on *Bring Me the Head of Alfredo Garcia*. Peckinpah obviously chose not to use this particular shot.

22. Vindice is said to be "holding a skull" in the stage directions which precede the first lines of Middleton's play. See the edition edited by Katharine Eisaman Maus 95. Vindice's use of this skull is exhaustive, for he later employs it to poison his archenemy the Duke before stabbing the dying man (III.v.).

23. We think Weddle is right to say "Bennie had to die for his sins" (1994, 495), but the physical situation also militates against Bennie's survival.

24. Prince quotes from a letter of September 12, 1974, now housed in the Peckinpah Collection, folder #69.

25. Bennie's count here is interesting. We would opt for 15 deaths (not including Paco and John): Elita, Chalo and Cueto, six Garcias, Sappensly and Quill, and four of El Jefe's men at the Camino Real Hotel (Max, Frank, and two henchmen). Perhaps Bennie is counting Alfredo, who might well be seen as one of El Jefe's victims. Perhaps we are to think Bennie kills five men at the Camino Real, as there appear to be three men backing up Max and Frank, though we only see two of them shot by Bennie on screen. Perhaps 16 is simply a miscount. (In the script, Bennie speaks of "fourteen" people dead because of Alfredo, El Jefe, and himself [19].) In any event, Paco and John are not being counted here, or the number would have to be 17 or 18.

Conclusion

1. Not everyone agrees with even this limited praise. David Weddle thinks that the "logistics" necessary to do the film's chase sequences "overwhelmed" Peckinpah and notes that others (James Coburn, Walter Kelley, Katy Haber) had to direct a number of scenes in Peckinpah's absence (1994, 515).

2. For an excellent review of the dances in Ford's films, see Joseph W. Reed 114–26.

3. Those who note Junior's decision to finance his father instead of repaying his mother often suggest Peckinpah is unaware of the problem here. It is Peckinpah, however, who introduces the matter of Junior's debt to his mother and who does so in the context of Junior discovering Ellie's financial difficulties in living apart from her husband. Peckinpah does not reintroduce this material at the end of the film, but presumably he didn't think it was necessary to do so.

4. Steve McQueen, the film's producer as well as its star, did intervene on a few matters during postproduction, replacing Jerry Fielding's score and slightly re-editing his own action sequences. Though McQueen is quoted by Simmons as thinking "Sam wasn't happy with some of the changes" (167), Peckinpah has said that while he did regret the loss of Fielding's score, he understood McQueen's concern for the film and found the other changes acceptably minor (Aghed 68).

5. For information about the development of *The Getaway*, see Garner Simmons 154–68. In the commentary to the 2005 DVD edition of *The Getaway*, Simmons specifically notes that Peckinpah knew Jim Thompson's ultra-noir novel very well, so the changes in the ending (and elsewhere) were not made in ignorance of the source novel. See also Simmons 156.

6. Seydor makes this observation in the commentary to the 2005 DVD edition of *The Getaway*.

7. The trust Doc and Carol gradually achieve (or Doc achieves, for Carol is never untrusting or untrustworthy) seems to have been lost on David Thomson, one of the best living film critics, for Thomson writes, "Does anyone think the McCoys in *The Getaway* can trust each other for more than 20 seconds?" (2009, 35).

8. Once again we paraphrase Paul Seydor's definitive formulation of Pike's dark choices (1997, 169).

9. We share the view of many critics and film scholars that Welles' Falstaff film, *Chimes at Midnight* (1966), is a tragedy. This film, added to his versions of *Macbeth* (1948) and *Othello* (1952), plus *Citizen Kane* (1941), *The Magnificent Ambersons* (1942), and *Touch of Evil* (1958), rounds off a significant body of work in the tragic mode. There can be no doubt that Welles, smitten by Shakespeare from an early age, believed himself to be preeminently a tragedian. We do not believe that American filmmakers are hostile to the making of tragic actions, only that very few of them have made a significant number of tragedies. That four tragic films—*Citizen Kane*, *The Godfather* (1972), *The Godfather II* (1974), and *Chinatown* (1974) (though made by a Polish director, Roman Polanski)—are on many lists of the finest American films (we would of course add *The Wild Bunch*) would appear to confirm that American culture reveres its best tragic films.

Bibliography

Aghed, Jan. 1973. "*Pat Garrett and Billy the Kid.*" *Sight and Sound* 42 (Spring): 65–74.

Anderson, Lindsay. 1981. *About John Ford....* London: Plexus.

Arvin, Newton. 1950. *Herman Melville: A Critical Biography*. New York: Viking.

Auden, W. H. 1965. "The Christian Tragic Hero: Contrasting Captain Ahab's Doom and Its Classic Greek Prototype." In Robert W. Corrigan, ed. *Tragedy: Vision and Form*. San Francisco: Chandler. 143–47.

Bachelard, Gaston. (1942.) 1983. *Water and Dreams: An Essay on the Imagination of Matter*. Trans. Edith R. Farrell. Dallas: Pegasus Foundation.

Bakhtin, M. M. 1984. *Rabelais and His World*. Trans. Helene Iswalski. Bloomington: University of Indiana Press.

Basinger, Jeanine. 1979. *Anthony Mann*. Boston: Twayne.

Bass, Rick. 1989. "Mexico." In *The Watch: Stories*. New York: Norton. 3–33.

Berger, Harry, Jr. 1997. "Acknowledgments." In *Making Trifles of Terrors: Redistributing Complicities in Shakespeare*. Stanford, CA: Stanford University Press. ix–xxiv.

Bliss, Michael. 1993. *Justified Lives: Morality and Narrative in the Films of Sam Peckinpah*. Carbondale: Southern Illinois University Press.

_____. 1994. "Introduction." In Michael Bliss, ed. *Doing It Right: The Best Criticism on Sam Peckinpah's* The Wild Bunch. Carbondale: Southern Illinois University Press. xv–xxiii.

Bogdanovich, Peter. 1978. *John Ford*. Berkeley: University of California Press.

Booth, Stephen. 1983. King Lear, Macbeth, *Indefinition, and Tragedy*. New Haven: Yale University Press.

Booth, Wayne. 1992. "The *Poetics* for a Practical Critic." In Amelie Oksenberg Rorty, ed. *Essays on Aristotle's* Poetics. Princeton NJ: Princeton University Press. 387–408.

Bowers, Fredson. 1940. *Elizabethan Revenge Tragedy: 1587–1642*. Princeton NJ: Princeton University Press.

Bradley, A. C. (1904.) 1955. *Shakespearean Tragedy*. Cleveland: Meridian.

Braudy, Leo. 1986. "The Sacraments of Genre: Coppola, DePalma, Scorsese." *Film Quarterly* 39 (Spring): 17–28.

Bryson, John. 2008. "The Wild Bunch in New York." In Kevin J. Hayes, ed. *Sam Peckinpah Interviews*. Jackson: University Press of Mississippi. 137–44.

Bushnell, Rebecca. 2008. *Tragedy: A Short Introduction*. Oxford: Blackwell.

Butler, Terence. 1979. *Crucified Heroes: The Films of Sam Peckinpah*. London: Gordon Fraser.

Cagin, Seth, and Philip Dray. 1974. *Hollywood Films of the Seventies*. New York: Harper & Row.

Callenbach, Ernest. 1980. "Review of Paul Seydor's *Peckinpah: The Western Films*." *Film Quarterly* 33 (Summer): 21.

_____. 2008. "A Conversation with Sam Peckinpah." In Kevin J. Hayes, ed. *Sam Peckinpah Interviews*. Jackson: University Press of Mississippi. 3–15.

Campbell, Joseph. 1972. *The Hero with a Thousand Faces*. 2nd ed. Princeton NJ: Princeton University Press.

Camus, Albert. 1969. "On the Future of Tragedy." In Philip Thody, ed. *Lyrical and Critical Essays*. Trans. Ellen Conroy Kennedy. New York: Alfred A. Knopf. 295–310.

Cavell, Stanley. 1969. *Must We Mean What We Say? Modern Philosophical Essays in Morality, Religion, Drama, Music and Criticism*. New York: Charles Scribner's Sons.

Cawelti, John G. 1976. "The Western: A Look at the Evolution of a Formula." In *Adventure, Mystery and Romance: Formula Stories as Art and Popular Culture*. Chicago: University of Chicago Press. 192–259.

_____. 1984. *The Six-Gun Mystique*. 2nd ed. Bowling Green, Ohio: Bowling Green State University Popular Press.

Chan, Wing-Tsit. 1963. *A Source Book in Chinese*

Philosophy. Princeton NJ: Princeton University Press.

Cirlot, J. E. 1971. *A Dictionary of Symbols*. 2nd ed. Trans. Jack Sage. New York: Philosophical Library.

Combs, Richard. 2005. "Shall We Gather." *Film Comment* 41 (May–June): 20–21.

Cook, David A. 1983. "*The Wild Bunch*, Fifteen Years After." *North Dakota Quarterly* 51 (Summer): 123–30.

Countryman, Edward, and Evonne von-Heussen Countryman. 1999. *Shane*. London: British Film Institute.

Cross, Gustav. 1977. "Introduction." In Gustav Cross, ed. *Titus Andronicus*. New York: Penguin. 14–23.

Culp, Robert. 1994. "Sam Peckinpah, the Storyteller and *The Wild Bunch*: An Appreciation." In Michael Bliss, ed. *Doing It Right: The Best Criticism on Sam Peckinpah's* The Wild Bunch. Carbondale: Southern Illinois University Press. 3–13.

Cutts, John. 1969. "Shoot! Sam Peckinpah Talks to John Cutts." *Films and Filmmaking* 16 (October): 4–9.

Dallenbach, Lucien. (1977.) 1989. *The Mirror in the Text*. Trans. Jeremy Whiteley with Emma Hughes. Chicago: University of Chicago Press.

Davidson, John. 2005. *The Gospel of Jesus: In Search of His Original Teachings*. Shaftesbury UK: Element.

Dawson, Gordon, and Sam Peckinpah. 1972. *Bring Me the Head of Alfredo Garcia*. Hollywood CA: Script City.

De la Croix, Horst, and Richard G. Tansey. 1986. *Gardner's Art through the Ages*. Vol. II. 8th ed. San Diego: Harcourt Brace Jovanovich.

Dick, Bernard F. 1990. *Anatomy of Film*. 2nd ed. New York: St. Martin's.

Dickinson, Emily. *The Complete Poems of Emily Dickinson*. Thomas H. Johnson, ed. Boston: Little, Brown, 1960.

Dienstag, Joshua Foa. 2006. *Pessimism: Philosophy, Ethic, Spirit*. Princeton NJ: Princeton University Press.

Dimock, George. 1961. "The Name of Odysseus." In Charles H. Taylor, Jr., ed. *Essays on the "Odyssey": Selected Modern Criticism*. Bloomington: University of Indiana Press. 54–72.

Drummond, Phillip. 1997. *High Noon*. London: British Film Institute.

Dukore, Bernard F. 1999. *Sam Peckinpah's Feature Films*. Urbana: University of Illinois Press.

Dyer, Geoff. (2005.) 2007. *The Ongoing Moment*; New York: Vintage.

Dyson, A. E. 1972. *Between Two Worlds*. London: Macmillan.

Eagleton, Terry. 2003. *Sacred Violence: The Idea of the Tragic*. Malden MA: Blackwell.

Ebert, Roger. 2001. "*Bring Me the Head of Alfredo Garcia*." http://rogerebert.suntimes.com/apps/pbcs.dll/article?AID=/20011028/REVIEWS08/110280301/1023. October 28. 1–3.

Eliade, Mircea. 1978. *A History of Religious Ideas*. Vol. I. Chicago: University of Chicago Press.

Else, Gerald F. 1957. *Aristotle's* Poetics*: The Argument*. Cambridge MA: Harvard University Press.

_____, ed. and trans. 1967. *Aristotle:* Poetics. Ann Arbor: University of Michigan Press.

Engel, Leonard, ed. 2003. *Sam Peckinpah's West: New Perspectives*. Salt Lake City: University of Utah Press.

_____. 2003. "'Who Are You?' 'That's a Good Question': Shifting Identities in Sam Peckinpah's *Pat Garrett and Billy the Kid*." In Leonard Engel, ed. *Sam Peckinpah's West: New Perspectives*. Salt Lake City: University of Utah Press. 199–210.

Farber, Stephen. 1994. "Peckinpah's Return." In Michael Bliss, ed. *Doing It Right: The Best Criticism on Sam Peckinpah's* The Wild Bunch. Carbondale: Southern Illinois University Press. 31–45.

Fine, Marshall. 1995. *Bloody Sam: The Life and Films of Sam Peckinpah*. New York: Hyperion.

Fish, Stanley. 1999. "Prologue: Taking Sides." In *The Trouble with Principle*. Cambridge MA: Harvard University Press. 1–15.

Fitzgerald, F. Scott. 1925. *The Great Gatsby*. New York: Charles Scribner's Sons.

_____. 1945. *The Crack-up*. Edmund Wilson, ed. New York: New Directions.

Foakes, R. A. "Introduction." In R. A. Foakes, ed. *The Revenger's Tragedy*. Cambridge MA: Harvard University Press, 1996. xix–lxix.

Frye, Northrop. 1957. *Anatomy of Criticism: Four Essays*. Princeton NJ: Princeton University Press.

_____. 1963. "The Archetypes of Literature." In *Fables of Identity: Studies in Poetic Mythology*. San Diego: Harcourt Brace Jovanovich. 7–20.

Fulwood, Neil. 2002. *The Films of Sam Peckinpah*. London: BT Botsford.

Gallagher, Tag. 1986. *John Ford: The Man and His Films*. Berkeley: University of California Press.

Garfield, Brian. 1982. *Western Films: A Complete Guide*. New York: Rawson Associates.

Gentner, Richard, and Diane Birdsall. 1981. "Sam Peckinpah: Cutter." *Film Comment* 17 (January–February): 35–37.

Giannetti, Louis. 1981. *Masters of the American Cinema*. Englewood Cliffs NJ: Prentice-Hall.

Girard, René. 1972. *Violence and the Sacred*. Baltimore: Johns Hopkins University Press.

Groff, Edward. 1977. "'Noon Wine': A Texas Tragedy." *Descant* 22: 39–47.

Guerin, Wilfred L., Earl G. Labor, Lee Morgan, and John R. Willingham. 1979. *A Handbook of Critical Approaches to Literature*. 2nd ed. New York: Harper & Row.

Hall, James. 2008. *The Sinister Side: How Left-Handed Symbolism Shaped Western Art.* New York: Oxford University Press.

Halliwell, Stephen. 1986. *Aristotle's* Poetics. Chapel Hill: University of North Carolina Press.

Harbage, Alfred. 1971. "Introduction." In Alfred Harbage, ed. *The Tragedy of Macbeth.* Baltimore: Penguin. 14–20.

Hardin, Richard F. 1983. "'Ritual' in Recent Criticism: The Elusive Sense of Community." *PMLA* 98 (October): 846–62.

Harmetz, Aljean. 1994. "Man Was a Killer Long Before He Served a God." In Michael Bliss, ed. *Doing it Right: The Best Criticism on Sam Peckinpah's* The Wild Bunch. Carbondale: Southern Illinois University Press. 169–74.

Heilman, Robert B. 1965. "Tragedy and Melodrama: Speculations on Generic Form." In Robert W. Corrigan, ed. *Tragedy: Vision and Form.* San Francisco: Chandler. 245–57.

Hemingway, Ernest. *A Farewell to Arms.* 1929. New York: Charles Scribner's Sons.

Honigmann, E. A. J. 2002. "*Macbeth*: The Murderer as Victim." In *Shakespeare's Seven Tragedies Revisited: The Dramatist's Manipulation of Response.* New York: Palgrave. 126–49.

Hough, Sheridan. 1997. *Nietzsche's Noontide Friend: The Self as Metaphoric Double.* University Park: Penn State University Press.

Huberman, Brian, and Jerry Holt. 1983. "Straight Shootin' Sam." *Southwest Media Review* 3 (Spring): 14–19.

Iyer, Pico. 1991. "Is It Really That Whacky?" *Time* 138 (November 18): 109.

Jenson, Lee. 2008. "Sam and Stella." In Kevin J. Hayes, ed. *Sam Peckinpah Interviews.* Jackson: University Press of Mississippi. 62–81.

Kael, Pauline. 1976. "The Nihilistic Poetry of Sam Peckinpah." *The New Yorker,* January 12. 70–73.

Kauffmann, Stanley. 1971. *Figures of Light: Film Criticism and Comment.* New York: Harper & Row.

Keneally, Thomas. 1982. *Schindler's List.* New York: Simon & Schuster.

Kermode, Frank. 1968. *The Sense of an Ending: Studies in the Theory of Fiction.* New York: Oxford University Press.

_____. 1979. *The Genesis of Secrecy: On the Interpretation of Narrative.* Cambridge MA: Harvard University Press.

Kerrigan, John. 1996. *Revenge Tragedy: Aeschylus to Armageddon.* Oxford: Clarendon.

Kerstein, Benjamin. 2006. "The Last Man: An Epitaph for Sam Peckinpah." http://archive.sensesofcinema.com/contents/06/40/sam-peckinpah.html. 1–12.

Keyishian, Harry. 1995. *The Shape of Revenge: Victimization, Vengeance, and Vindictiveness in Shakespeare.* Atlantic Highlands NJ: Humanities.

Kitses, Jim. 1969. *Horizons West—Anthony Mann, Budd Boetticher, Sam Peckinpah: Studies of Authorship within the Western.* Bloomington: Indiana University Press.

_____. 2004. *Horizons West: Directing the Western from John Ford to Clint Eastwood.* London: British Film Institute.

Koelb, Clayton. 1974. "'Tragedy' as an Evaluative Term." *Comparative Literature Studies* 11: 69–84.

Le Cain, Maximilian. 2001. "Drifting out of the Territory: Sam Peckinpah's *Pat Garrett and Billy the Kid.*" *Senses of Cinema.* http://archive.sensesofcinema.com/contents/01/13/garrett.html. 1–7.

LeMay, Alan. 1954. *The Searchers.* New York: Harper & Row.

Lewis, Richard Warren. 1971. "*Playboy* Interview: John Wayne." *Playboy* 18 (May): 75–92.

Liebler, Naomi Conn. 1995. *Shakespeare's Festive Tragedy: The Ritual Foundations of a Genre.* New York: Routledge.

Livingstone, James C. 1989. *The Anatomy of the Sacred: An Introduction to Religion.* New York: Macmillan.

MacIntyre, Alaisdair. 1981. *After Virtue.* South Bend, IN: Notre Dame University Press.

Macklin, F. Anthony. 2008. "Mort Sahl Called Me a 1939 American." In Kevin J. Hayes, ed. *Sam Peckinpah Interviews.* Jackson: University Press of Mississippi. 145–57.

Male, Roy R. 1961. "The Story of the Mysterious Stranger in American Fiction." *Criticism* 3 (Fall): 281–94.

Marx, Leo. 1967. *The Machine in the Garden.* New York: Oxford University Press.

Mast, Gerald. 1977. *Film/Cinema/Movie: A Theory of Experience.* New York: Harper & Row.

_____. 1982. "The Genre Epic: *Red River.*" In *Howard Hawks, Storyteller.* New York: Oxford University Press. 297–346.

Maus, Katharine Eisaman, ed. 1995. *Four Revenge Tragedies.* Oxford: Clarendon.

_____. 1995. "Introduction." In Katharine Eisaman Maus, ed. *Four Revenge Tragedies.* Oxford: Clarendon. ix–xxxi.

May, Herbert G., and Bruce Metzger. 1973. *The New Oxford Annotated Bible with the Apocrypha.* New York: Oxford University Press.

Mays, James L., general editor. 1988. *Harper's Bible Commentary.* San Francisco: Harper & Row.

McAlindon, Tom. 2002. "What Is a Shakespearean Tragedy?" In Claire McEachern, ed. *The Cambridge Companion to Shakespearean Tragedy.* Cambridge: Cambridge University Press. 1–22.

McBride, Joseph. 2001. *Searching for John Ford: A Life.* New York: St. Martin's.

McGee, Patrick. 2007. *From* Shane *to* Kill Bill: *Rethinking the Western.* Oxford: Blackwell.

McKinney, Doug. 1969. *Sam Peckinpah*. Boston: Twayne.

Mellen, Joan. 1977. *Big Bad Wolves: Masculinity in American Film*. New York: Pantheon.

Merrill, Robert. 1974. "Tragic Form in *A Farewell to Arms*." *American Literature* 45 (January): 571–79.

Mesce, Bill, Jr. 2001. *Peckinpah's Women: A Reappraisal of the Portrayal of Women in the Period Westerns of Sam Peckinpah*. Lanham MD: Scarecrow.

Metz, Leon C. 1973. *Pat Garrett: The Story of a Western Lawman*. Norman: University of Oklahoma Press.

Miller, Arthur. 1965. "Tragedy and the Common Man." In Robert W. Corrigan, ed. *Tragedy: Vision and Form*. San Francisco: Chandler. 148–51.

Miller, Mark Crispin. 1975. "In Defense of Sam Peckinpah." *Film Quarterly* 28 (Spring): 1–17.

Miller, Perry. 1959. "The Garden of Eden and the Deacon's Meadow." In *A Sense of History: The Best Writing from the Pages of American History*. Boston: Houghton Mifflin. 113–19.

Mitchell, Lee Clark. 1996. *Westerns: Making the Man in Fiction and Film*. Chicago: University of Chicago Press.

Muir, Kenneth. 1972. *Shakespeare's Tragic Sequence*. London: Methuen.

Murphy, Kathleen. 1985. "Orbits—Sam Peckinpah: No Bleeding Heart." *Film Comment* 21 (March/April): 74–75.

_____. 1999. "*Bring Me the Head of Alfredo Garcia*." http://www.austinchronicle.com/issues/dispatch/1999-10-22/screens_feature7.btml. 1–3.

Murphy, Kathleen, and Richard T. Jameson. 1981. "*Bring Me the Head of Alfredo Garcia*." *Film Comment* 17 (January /February): 44–48.

Murray, Gabrielle. 2004. *This Wounded Cinema, This Wounded Life: Violence and Utopia in the Films of Sam Peckinpah*. Westport CT: Praeger.

Murray, William. 1972. "*Playboy* Interview: Sam Peckinpah." *Playboy* 19 (August): 64–74, 192.

Neale, Steve. 1983. "Masculinity as Spectacle: Reflections on Men and Mainstream Cinema." *Screen 26* 4: 9–23.

Neider, Charles. 1956. *The Authentic Death of Hendry Jones*. New York: Harper & Brothers.

Neill, Michael. 1997. *Issues of Death: Mortality and Identity in English Renaissance Tragedy*. Oxford: Clarendon.

_____. 2005. "English Revenge Tragedy." In Rebecca Bushnell, ed. *A Companion to Tragedy*. Oxford: Blackwell. 328–50.

Oates, Joyce Carol. 1972. *The Edge of Impossibility: Tragic Forms in Literature*. Greenwich CT: Fawcett.

Ornstein, Robert. 1965. *The Moral Vision of Jacobean Tragedy*. Madison: University of Wisconsin Press.

Padel, Ruth. 1980. "Making Spaces Speak." In John T. Winkler and Froma I. Zeitlin, eds. *Nothing to Do with Dionysus? Athenian Drama in Its Social Context*. Princeton NJ: Princeton University Press. 336–65.

Peckinpah, David S. 1954. *An Analysis of the Method Used in Producing and Directing a One-Act Play for the Stage and for a Closed Circuit Television Broadcast*. M.A. Thesis. University of Southern California.

Perez, Gilberto. 1998. "American Tragedy." In *The Material Ghost: Films and Their Medium*. Baltimore: Johns Hopkins University Press. 233–59.

Phillips, Gene D. 1998. *Exiles in Hollywood: Major European Film Directors in America*. Bethlehem PA: Lehigh University Press.

Pippin, Robert. 2010. *Hollywood Westerns and American Myth: The Importance of Howard Hawks and John Ford for Political Philosophy*. New Haven: Yale University Press.

Poole, Adrian. 1987. *Tragedy: Shakespeare and the Greek Example*. Oxford: Basil Blackwell.

_____. 2005. *Tragedy: A Very Short Introduction*. Oxford: Oxford University Press.

Porter, Katherine Anne. 1965. "Noon Wine." In *The Collected Stories of Katherine Anne Porter*. Orlando FL: Harcourt. 222–68.

_____. 1970. *The Collected Essays, and Occasional Writings of Katherine Anne Porter*. New York: Delacorte.

_____. 1990. *Letters of Katherine Anne Porter*. Ed. Isabel Bayley. New York: Atlantic Monthly.

Prats, Armando José. 2003. "Auguries of Redemption: Peckinpah's Mythological Critique of American History." In Leonard Engel, ed. *Sam Peckinpah's West: New Perspectives*. Salt Lake City: University of Utah Press. 19–53.

Prince, Stephen. 1998. *Savage Cinema: Sam Peckinpah and the Rise of Ultraviolent Movies*. Austin: University of Texas Press.

_____. 1999. "Introduction: Sam Peckinpah, Savage Poet of American Cinema." In Stephen Prince, ed. *Sam Peckinpah's* The Wild Bunch. Cambridge: Cambridge University Press. 1–36.

Pye, Douglas. 1996. "Genre and History: *Fort Apache* and *The Man Who Shot Liberty Valance*." In Ian Cameron and Douglas Pye, eds. *The Book of Westerns*. New York: Continuum. 111–22.

Raphael, D. D. 1960. *The Paradox of Tragedy*. Bloomington: University of Indiana Press.

Reardon, Patrick. 2005. "Chronos and Kairos." *Orthodoxy Today*. October 14. http://www.orthodoxytoday.org. 1–2.

Reed, Joseph W. 1984. *Three American Originals: John Ford, William Faulkner, & Charles Ives*. Middletown CT: Wesleyan University Press.

Reisner, Joel, and Bruce Kane. "Sam Peckinpah." 1970. *Action: Directors Guild of America* 5 (May–June): 24–27.

Roberts, Richard Emery. 1947. *The Gilded Rooster*. New York: Putnam.

Rorty, Amelie Oksenberg. 1992. "The Psychology of Aristotelian Tragedy." In Amelie Oksenberg Rorty, ed. *Essays on Aristotle's* Poetics. Princeton NJ: Princeton University Press. 1–22.

Rosen, Michael. 2008. "Down in the Caves." *Times Literary Supplement*. October 17. 8–9.

Sacks, Sheldon. 1964. *Fiction and the Shape of Belief*. Berkeley: University of California Press.

Sam Peckinpah's West: Legacy of a Hollywood Renegade. 2004. A documentary film for the Westerns Channel directed by Tom Thurman, narrated by Kris Kristofferson.

Sarchett, Barry W. 1992. "The Outlaw as Figure, the Figure as Outlaw: Narrativity and Interpretation in Sam Peckinpah's *Pat Garrett and Billy the Kid*." *New Orleans Review* 19 (Fall–Winter): 174–81.

Sarris, Andrew. 1967. "Sticking to His Guns (review of Howard Hawks' *El Dorado*)." In Richard Schickel and John Simon, eds. *Film 67/68*. New York: New American Library. 167–75.

Schorer, Mark. 1967. "Afterword." In Katherine Anne Porter. Pale Horse, Pale Rider*: Three Short Novels*. New York: New American Library. 167–75.

Schrader, Paul. 1994. "Sam Peckinpah Going to Mexico." In Michael Bliss, ed. *Doing It Right: The Best Criticism of Sam Peckinpah's* The Wild Bunch. Carbondale: Southern Illinois University Press. 17–30.

Scofield, C. I., ed. 1909. *The Scofield Reference Bible*. New York: Oxford University Press.

Scott, Nathan, Jr. 1957. "Foreword." In Nathan Scott, Jr., ed. *The Tragic Vision and Christian Faith*. New York: Haddam House. ix–xix.

Sewall, Richard B. 1990. *The Vision of Tragedy*. 3rd ed. New York: Paragon House.

Seydor, Paul. 1980. *Peckinpah: The Western Films*. Urbana: University of Illinois Press.

_____. 1997. *Peckinpah: The Western Films — A Reconsideration*. Urbana: University of Illinois Press.

_____. 1999. "*The Wild Bunch*: The Screenplay." In Stephen Prince, ed. *Sam Peckinpah's* The Wild Bunch. Cambridge: Cambridge University Press. 37–78.

Simmons, Garner. 1998. *Peckinpah: A Portrait in Montage*. 2nd ed. New York: Limelight Edition.

Simons, John L. 2003. "The Double Vision of Tragedy in Sam Peckinpah's *Ride the High Country*." In Leonard Engel, ed. *Sam Peckinpah's West — New Perspectives*. Salt Lake City: University of Utah Press. 63–86.

Skerry, Philip J. 1990. "The Western Film: A Sense of an Ending." *New Orleans Review* 17 (Fall): 13–17.

Slotkin, Richard. 1992. *Gunfighter Nation: The Myth of the Frontier in Twentieth-Century America*. New York: Atheneum.

Spinoza, Baruch. 1982. *The Ethics and Selected Letters*. Seymour Feldman, ed. Trans. Samuel Shirley. Indianapolis: Hackett.

Spittles, Brian. 2002. *John Ford*. Harlow, England: Pearson Education.

Sragow, Michael. 1994. "Sam Peckinpah, 1925–1984." In Michael Bliss, ed. *Doing It Right: The Best Criticism of Sam Peckinpah's* The Wild Bunch. Carbondale: Southern Illinois University Press. 177–88.

Stevens, Brad. 1996. "*Pat Garrett and Billy the Kid*." In Ian Cameron and Douglas Pye, eds. *The Book of Westerns*. New York: Continuum. 269–76.

Storm, William. 1998. *After Dionysus: A Theory of the Tragic*. Ithaca NY: Cornell University Press.

Tatum, Stephen. 1997. *Inventing Billy the Kid: Visions of the Outlaw in America, 1881–1981*. 2nd ed. Tucson: University of Arizona Press.

Thompson, Barbara. 1969. "Katherine Anne Porter: An Interview." In Lodwick Hartley and George Core, eds. *Katherine Anne Porter: A Critical Symposium*. Athens: University of Georgia Press. 3–23.

Thomson, David. 2002. *The New Biographical Dictionary of Film*. New York: Alfred A. Knopf.

_____. 2009. "Dead Man Walking." *Sight and Sound* 19 (February 1): 32–36.

Tompkins, Jane. 1992. *West of Everything: The Inner Life of Westerns*. New York: Oxford University Press.

Turner, Victor. 1974. *Dramas, Fields, and Metaphors: Symbolic Action in Human Society*. Ithaca NY: Cornell University Press.

Utley, Robert M. 1989. *Billy the Kid: A Short and Violent Life*. Lincoln: University of Nebraska Press.

Walsh, Thomas F. 1975. "Deep Similarities in 'Noon Wine.'" *Mosaic* 9: 83–91.

Wanat, Matt. 2003. "'Fall In Behind the Major': Cultural Border Crossing and Hero Building in *Major Dundee*." In Leonard Engel, ed. *Sam Peckinpah's West: New Perspectives*. Salt Lake City: University of Utah Press. 87–113.

Warshow, Robert. (1962.) 2001. *The Immediate Experience*. Cambridge MA: Harvard University Press.

Webster, John. 1996. The Duchess of Malfi *and Other Plays*. René Weis, ed. Oxford: Oxford University Press.

Weddle, David. 1994. "*If They Move, Kill 'Em!*" *The Life and Times of Sam Peckinpah*. New York: Grove.

_____. 1994. "The Making of *The Wild Bunch*." *Film Comment* 30 (May–June): 44–57.

_____. 1997. "Foreword." In Paul Seydor, *Peckinpah: The Western Films — A Reconsideration*. Urbana: University of Illinois Press. xiii–xvii.

Welty, Eudora. 1980. *The Collected Stories of Eudora Welty*. New York: Harcourt Brace Jovanovich.

Westbrook, Max. 1990. "The Night John Wayne Danced with Shirley Temple." *Western American Literature* 25 (August): 157–69.

Westcott, Glenway. 1969. "Katherine Anne Porter Personally." In Lodwick Harley and George Core, eds. *Katherine Anne Porter: A Critical Symposium*. Athens: University of Georgia Press. 24–48.

Whitehall, Richard. 1969. "Talking with Peckinpah." *Sight and Sound* 38 (Autumn): 172–75.

Williams, Bernard. *Shame and Necessity*. 1993. Berkeley: University of California Press.

Williams, Raymond. *Modern Tragedy*. 1966. Stanford CA: Stanford University Press.

Wilson, Emily R. 2004. *Mocked with Death: Tragic Overliving from Sophocles to Milton*. Baltimore: Johns Hopkins University Press.

Winkler, Martin W. 1991. "Tragic Features in John Ford's *The Searchers*." In Martin W. Winkler, ed. *Classics and Cinema*. London: Bucknell University Press. 185–208.

Wurlitzer, Rudolph. 1972. *Pat Garrett and Billy the Kid*. Hollywood CA: Script City.

_____. 1973. *Pat Garrett and Billy the Kid*. New York: New American Library.

Yergin, Dan. 2008. "Peckinpah's Progress: From Blood and Killing in the Old West to Siege and Rape in Rural Cornwall." In Kevin J. Hayes, ed. *Sam Peckinpah Interviews*. Jackson: University Press of Mississippi. 82–91.

Zweig, Paul. 1974. *The Adventurer*. New York: Basic Books.

We have cited throughout from scripts, letters, and other materials housed in the Peckinpah Collection at the Margaret Herrick Library, the Academy of Motion Picture Arts and Sciences, Beverly Hills, California.

We have cited the commentary from five recently released DVD versions of Peckinpah's films, all with the same commentators (Nick Redman, Paul Seydor, Garner Simmons, David Weddle):

Ride the High Country. Metro Goldwyn Mayer (1962). 2006.

Major Dundee. Columbia Pictures (1965). 2005.

The Getaway. Warner Bros. (1972). 2005.

Pat Garrett and Billy the Kid. Metro Goldwyn Mayer (1973). 2005.

Bring Me the Head of Alfredo Garcia. Metro Goldwyn Mayer (1974). 2005.

Index